G000149938

The Political Economy of
South-East Asia

Conflicts, Crises, and Change

The Political Economy of
South-East Asia

Conflicts, Crises, and Change

SECOND EDITION

Edited by Garry Rodan, Kevin Hewison, and Richard Robison

OXFORD
UNIVERSITY PRESS

OXFORD

UNIVERSITY PRESS

253 Normanby Road, South Melbourne, Victoria 3205, Australia

Oxford University Press is a department of the University of Oxford.
It furthers the University's objective of excellence in research, scholarship,
and education by publishing worldwide in

Oxford New York

Auckland Bangkok Buenos Aires Cape Town Chennai
Dar es Salaam Delhi Hong Kong Istanbul Karachi Kolkata
Kuala Lumpur Madrid Melbourne Mexico City Mumbai Nairobi
São Paulo Shanghai Taipei Tokyo Toronto

OXFORD is a registered trade mark of Oxford University Press
in the UK and in certain other countries

National Library of Australia

Cataloguing-in-Publication data:

The political economy of southeast Asia: conflict, crises, and change.

2nd ed.
Bibliography.
Includes index.
ISBN 0 19 551349 5 (pbk.).

1. Political science—Asia, Southeastern. 2. Asia, Southeastern—Economic
conditions. 3. Asia, Southeastern—Economic policy.
4. Asia, Southeastern—Politics and government. 5. Asia, Southeastern—
Foreign economic relations. I. Rodan, Garry, 1955- . II. Robison,
Richard, 1943- . III. Hewison, Kevin.

330.959053

Typeset by Solo Typesetting, Adelaide
Printed through Bookpac Production Services, Singapore

Contents

List of Figures

List of Tables

Contributors

Mark Beeson is a senior lecturer in the School of Asian and International Politics at Griffith University.

Melanie Beresford is a senior lecturer in the Department of Economics at Macquarie University.

Frederic C. Deyo has a joint appointment as professor of sociology at the State University of New York, Binghamton, and research fellow at the NZ Asian Institute at the University of Auckland.

Kevin Hewison is a professor in the Department of Applied Social Studies at the City University of Hong Kong and director of its Southeast Asia Research Centre.

Jane Hutchison is a lecturer in the School of Politics and International Studies at Murdoch University.

Kanishka Jayasuriya is a senior research fellow in the Southeast Asia Research Centre at the City University of Hong Kong.

Khoo Boo Teik is an associate professor in the School of Social Sciences at Universiti Sains Malaysia.

Richard Robison is a professor in the School of Politics and International Studies at Murdoch University.

Garry Rodan is an associate professor in the School of Politics and International Studies at Murdoch University.

Andrew Rosser is a lecturer in the Department of Government at The University of Sydney.

Preface

The social, political, and economic landscape of South-East Asia is ever-changing. In 1996, as we completed *The Political Economy of South-East Asia: An Introduction*, many of the countries of the region were undergoing remarkable transformations, spurred by a decade-long economic boom. Enthusiasm for an 'Asian' development approach was at its peak, and the region was hailed as a model for other developing countries.

How rapidly things change. In 2001 the region is beset with political troubles as it attempts to shake off the economic crisis. Recent events say much about South-East Asia's political economy.

The overthrow of President Soeharto and his New Order regime after more than three decades coincided with the economic crisis. Soeharto had forged a framework of economic and corporate power that was bound in institutional structures and relationships dominated by the oligarchies around the president, his family, and his cronies. Authoritarianism had been harnessed to the needs of burgeoning corporate conglomerates. With the collapse of this edifice, competing forces now struggle to establish new economic and political regimes.

The breakdown means that the Indonesian state can no longer guarantee the systems of social control or centralised organisation of corruption that previously sustained it. Many more organisations, interests, and coalitions are competing with the state and among themselves to establish new sets of institutions. None has yet been able to establish its ascendancy. At times the competition is violent. In part this is because the repression of the past has been released. It is also because the establishment of political and economic dominance is a struggle of immense significance.

The 2001 election in Thailand, based on the reformist 1997 constitution, saw one of Thailand's richest men lead the aptly named Thai Rak Thai (Thais Love Thais) party to a landslide victory. Labelled nationalist and populist, Thaksin Shinawatra built his electoral triumph on promises to the rural poor, the disaffected middle class, and domestic capitalists: the first electoral victory by a 'modern' businessman appealing to a broad base. His recently formed party represents an attempt by domestic business to regain control of the political agenda from a Democrat Party-led coalition government that was resented for having 'humiliated' Thailand.

Domestic capitalists resented the 'sell-off' of Thai businesses and resources to foreign interests. Many felt the government had 'sold out'. They felt humiliated at Thailand's bowing before the International Monetary Fund (IMF) and Western interests. The government's neo-liberal policies were unable to reflate the economy or 'save' local businesses. Thaksin was supported as the saviour of the poor and of the remains of the domestic business class. Thaksin's electoral strategy was forged in struggle. The costs and impact of the economic crisis and recovery meant enhanced competition over Thailand's economic policies and institutions. Thaksin's victory is thus a part of wider struggles over political and economic power.

In the Philippines, which came through the Asian crisis in reasonable shape, we see another popular uprising against a ruler many came to see as corrupt. Joseph Estrada was not a political dictator in the manner of Ferdinand Marcos, but was seen to be engaged in 'creeping authoritarianism'. He was accused of engaging in collusion and corruption that was re-establishing money politics. Business, the middle class, and non-governmental organisations and intellectuals grew weary of this. They also reacted strongly against the way Estrada's cronyism limited opportunities. When the military and police abandoned the president, his fate was sealed, even if the poor, working class, and peasants remained ambivalent. The struggle against Estrada also embodied a restructuring of political and economic alliances and coalitions to ensure a transition. Whereas Soeharto was a dictator spurned, Estrada was an elected president scorned. Apparently, the post-Marcos rules and institutions were unable to control Estrada, and nor did they permit an easy exit.

In these events, seemingly critical to the future of the region, we see nationalism, money politics, and constitutions playing roles. So do international organisations, big business, foreign investors, small farmers, workers, and a range of intellectuals and non-governmental organisations. The vocabularies of openness, rules, good governance, and transparency compete with the language of money, influence, collusion, corruption, and nepotism. These discourses reflect wider political and economic competition. Perhaps some things don't change as fast as we think. Even so, the crisis has caused a reassessment of the nature of these struggles.

The Political Economy of South-East Asia was published in 1997, reflecting on remarkable development and change, and the struggles these entailed. That volume was concerned with explaining development in the region. Many of the chapters focused on the successes of the capitalist economies of the region. The processes associated with industrial development had resulted in fundamental social and political change, and it seemed that the institutions of liberal capitalism were being reproduced in the region. Although some of the chapters in the earlier volume pointed to 'dark clouds' and raised questions regarding the assumed convergence among South-East Asian capitalisms and liberal 'models', the focus was on capitalist successes.

Few accurately predicted a crisis as deep and as sustained as that which afflicted the region from mid 1997. The crisis and its continuing impact necessarily directed the attention of many analysts to a reconsideration of approaches to South-East Asian development. The editors of *The Political Economy of South-East Asia* saw the need for a new volume to address the crisis and the way in which political economists have interpreted boom, crisis, and recovery.

Some of these questions and issues were considered in the earlier volume. Important among these is the nature of the convergence posited in some approaches; the idea that Asian capitalisms will inevitably come to resemble Anglo-American capitalisms. The contrary view was that a distinctively Asian variety of capitalism was emerging. The crisis challenged analysts to re-examine this issue. Likewise, and related, the nature of institutions needed to be re-evaluated as many South-East Asian institutions proved incapable of coping with the crisis.

Analysts were required to consider how a number of issues and reforms might 'fit' South-East Asia. The push for increased neo-liberal reform, transparency, and good governance became especially strong during the crisis, as did resistance to them by vested interests. Calls for democracy and the development of civil society became stronger as the crisis led to political instability. But such calls also coincided with neo-liberal strategies for reform and development. This saw a revival of neo-dependency approaches, often related to populist and nationalist political strategies. Domestic political coalitions were shaken by the crisis and, in many arenas, new domestic forces arose as there was a weakening of old elements. Internationally, the criticisms of the IMF's approach to reform saw calls for a new international financial architecture that extended beyond South-East Asia. The response of the international financial institutions and Anglo-American capitalisms saw the development of a 'Post Washington Consensus', bolstering the alliance of the bastions of capitalism in the West. The political implications of many of these issues have been especially noticeable in Indonesia and Thailand, but have not been insignificant in the other countries of the region.

The importance of these issues and the reassessment they have caused mean that the present collection has undergone such extensive revisions as to be essentially new. Chapters that appeared in the previous volume have been rewritten. The introductory chapter (chapter 1) is predominantly new, and a number of chapters have been added. In the course of addressing the various issues raised above, this collection emphasises a distinctive theoretical approach which is outlined in chapter 1 and systematically pursued thereafter.

Garry Rodan
Richard Robison
Kevin Hewison
January 2001

Acknowledgments

The editors are most grateful to the contributors for their involvement in this volume, including the many constructive direct and indirect engagements with the editors on substantive theoretical issues. Debate within the Asia Research Centre at Murdoch University, where several of the contributors have recently spent terms as fellows, has also been extremely valuable. Thanks further to Janet Payne for her expertise in the production of the manuscript, and the research assistance of Robert Roche and David Savat. The support of the Department of Applied Social Studies, City University of Hong Kong, is also gratefully acknowledged.

Abbreviations

ADB	Asian Development Bank
AEM	Asian economic model
AFTA	ASEAN Free Trade Agreement
APEC	Asia–Pacific Economic Cooperation
ASB	Amanah Saham Bumiputera
ASEAN	Association of South-East Asian Nations
ASN	Amanah Saham Nasional
BI	Bank Indonesia (see also BLBI)
BLBI	Bantuan Likwiditi Bank Indonesia (see also BI)
BN	Barisan Nasional
BNM	Bank Negara Malaysia
BOI	Board of Investment
BPK	Supreme Audit Agency
BPKP	state comptroller of Finance and Development
BPPC	Badan Penyangga dan Pemasaran Cengkeh
BS	Barisan Sosialis
CAR	capital adequacy ratio
CBU	completely built up
CDRAC	Corporate Debt Restructuring Advisory Committee
CDRC	Corporate Debt Restructuring Committee
CEO	chief executive officer
COLT	Commercial Offshore Loan Team
CPF	Central Provident Fund
CPP	Communist Party of the Philippines
DAP	Democratic Action Party
DBS	Development Bank of Singapore
DFI	direct foreign investment
DRV	Democratic Republic of Vietnam

EAEC	East Asian Economic Caucus
EDAS	Economic Development Assistance Scheme
EDB	Economic Development Board
EOI	export-oriented industrialisation
EPZ	export processing zone
FDI	foreign direct investment
FYP	five-year plan(s)
GDP	gross domestic product
GIC	Government of Singapore Investment Corporation
GLC	government-linked company
GNP	gross national product
GSP	generalised system of preferences
HDB	Housing Development Board
HICOM	Heavy Industries Corporation of Malaysia
IAC	International Advisory Council
IAS	International Accountancy Standards
IBRA	Indonesian Banking Restructuring Agency
IBRD	International Bank for Reconstruction and Development
ICA	*Industrial Coordination Act*
IDA	Information Development Authority
ILO	International Labour Organization (or Office)
IMF	International Monetary Fund
INTECH	Initiative for New Technology
IPE	international political economy
IPTN	Industri Pesawat Terbang Nusantara
ISI	import-substitution industrialisation
IT	information technology
JTC	Jurong Town Corporation
'K-Economy'	'Knowledge-based Economy'
KLSE	Kuala Lumpur Stock Exchange
LLL	legal lending limits
MARA	Majelis Amanah Rakyat
MAS	Monetary Authority of Singapore

MCA	Malayan Chinese Association
MDAS	Manpower Development Assistance Scheme
MIC	Malayan Indian Congress
MICCI	Malaysian International Chamber of Commerce and Industry
MIT	Massachusetts Institute of Technology
MITI	Ministry of International Trade and Industry
MNC	multinational corporation
MoF	Ministry of Finance
MSAA	Master Settlement and Acquisition Agreements
NDP	National Development Plan
NEAC	National Economic Action Council
NEP	New Economic Policy
NESDB	National Economic and Social Development Board
NGO	non-government organisation
NIC	newly industrialised (or industrialising) country
NLF	National Front for the Liberation of Southern Vietnam
NOC	National Operations Council
NOL	Neptune Orient Lines
NPA	New People's Army
NPLs	non-performing loans
NSTB	National Science and Technology Board
NTUC	National Trades Union Congress
NWC	National Wages Council
OCBC	Overseas Chinese Banking Corporation
ODA	official development assistance (or overseas development aid)
OHQ	operational headquarters
PAP	People's Action Party
PAS	Parti Islam SeMalaysia
PERNAS	Perbadanan Nasional
Petronas	Petroliam Nasional
PIEU	Pioneer Industries Employees' Union
PKI	Partai Komunis Indonesia
PLN	Perusahaan Listrik Negara
PMIP	Pan-Malaysian Islamic Party
PNB	Permodalan Nasional Berhad
PO	people's organisation

PSA	Port of Singapore Authority
PSB	Productivity and Standards Board
R&D	research and development
RBF	Regional Business Forum
RIDA	Rural and Industrial Development Authority
RVN	Republic of Vietnam
QFB	qualifying full banking
SDP	Singapore Democratic Party
SEDC	state economic development corporation
SET	Stock Exchange of Thailand
SILO	Singapore Industrial Labour Organisation
SingTel	Singapore Telecommunications
SME	small and medium enterprises
SOBSI	Sentral Organisasi Buruh Seluruh Indonesia
SOE	state-owned enterprise
SPSI	Serikat Pekerja Seluruh Indonesia
SPH	Singapore Press Holding
STC	Singapore Technologies Corporation
TFP	total factor productivity
TNC	transnational corporation
UDA	Urban Development Authority
UMNO	United Malays National Organization
WTO	World Trade Organization

Figure A1 A political map of South-East Asia and region

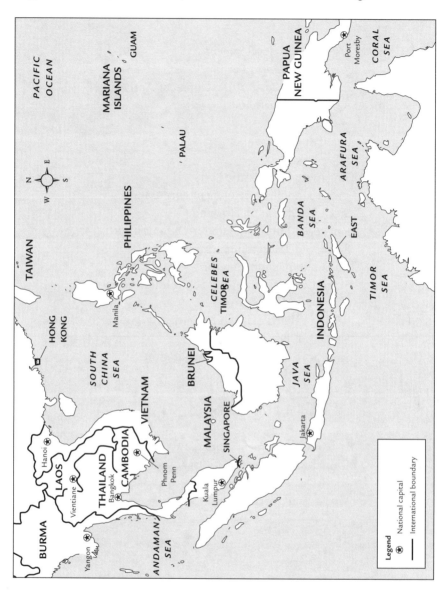

Source: adapted from East Asia Analytical Unit (EAAU) (1995) *Growth Triangles of South East Asia,* Parkes, ACT: Department of Foreign Affairs and Trade, Commonwealth of Australia, p. viii

1

Theorising South-East Asia's Boom, Bust, and Recovery

Garry Rodan, Kevin Hewison, and Richard Robison[1]

Introduction

Explanations of South-East Asia's recent development vary widely. This is especially the case for accounts of boom, bust, and recovery since the mid 1980s. In this chapter we outline the ways in which different varieties of political economy explain South-East Asia's development. As we show, these approaches acknowledge some sort of relationship between the political and the economic; they all posit a relationship between politics and development. However, assumptions vary considerably about the nature and significance of politics, as well as the underlying dynamics of society, and how this shapes the organisation of economic activity. This has profound implications for analysis and leads to dramatic contrasts in their respective assessments and policy prescriptions.

These approaches are, broadly, neo-classical political economy, historical institutional theory, and social conflict theory. Although they are unequally represented in the literature on South-East Asia, each is influential in similar debates on East Asia, Latin America, or Europe. We have been selective in developing these approaches for discussion. The point of this exercise, however, is to show how political economy can be brought to bear on the study of South-East Asian development. In the process of this survey, we will argue that social conflict theory is the most illuminating. In the substantive accounts of development in South-East Asia provided in the subsequent chapters, readers will also observe that social conflict theory is a central theoretical influence.

After clarifying their essential features, we will systematically examine how these approaches explain the formative periods of development in South-East Asia, the subsequent economic booms in the region and, ultimately, the 1997–98 Asian crises and their aftermath. The relative influence in academic and policy circles of each of these different approaches has waxed and waned over time. This can be explained partly by the way in which the course of development appeared to validate or challenge

1

prevailing theory. The degree to which these approaches have resonated or clashed with other powerful ideas and interests is no less important in explaining their impact. These approaches, however, have not always dominated. Modernisation theory and, in turn, dependency theory, were at different times ascendant in the literature on South-East Asia before the mid 1970s. They have resurfaced periodically, plugging into the very debates of concern to political economists. We introduce them below when the economic boom is discussed and thereafter integrate them, where relevant, into the systematic survey of the different ways of accounting for South-East Asian development.

Finally, it should be appreciated that these approaches represent ideal type categories that are convenient and indicative for setting out important theoretical fault lines in political economy debates. Some writers will draw on aspects across these different approaches—not always in a coherent fashion. The value of these categories, however, is in setting out the essential choices for students adopting a political economy approach to the study of the region.

Outlining the approaches

Neo-classical political economy

In neo-classical economic theory the principal preoccupation is with the functioning of 'markets'. The concept of the 'market' is an abstracted notion that is not concerned with the social relationships that it embodies. The assumption is that markets are naturally and universally efficient mechanisms, driven by their own internal laws and the rational choices of individuals who seek to maximise their gains. This results in the most efficient allocation of resources and, in the long run, the greatest wealth for society as a whole. Good public policy is therefore that which gives full expression to the free operation of markets. Where this happens, development occurs; where it is obstructed, notably by state intervention, development suffers. It has been on this basis that international organisations such as the World Bank and International Monetary Fund (IMF) emphasised development strategies based on economic deregulation, privatisation, and fiscal austerity—the so-called 'Washington consensus' that operated until the crisis (Williamson 1994).

When market principles are extended as policy prescriptions for the general conduct of social life, neo-classical theory translates into neo-liberal ideology. Quite often advocacy for free-market reforms consistent with neo-classical economic theory is driven by this general ideological disposition. At such points, the debate goes beyond functional or technical considerations. Neo-liberal ideologues have a normative preference for market relations, which means that they think that these relations *should* be the basis of social activity. This is a statement about a preferred set of power relations and institutional forms.

Many neo-classical theorists are perplexed by the refusal of governments to choose the 'right' market-enhancing policies. To the extent that they have an explanation for this, it rests on a particular notion of 'politics'. Politics in this view is seen as a set of external factors hampering the natural functioning of markets. In particular, groups seeking to gain special advantages through the state, so-called 'rent-seekers', represent a political threat to efficient markets. Good public policy can therefore take one of two forms. First, this involves eliminating the interventions of the state in economic life, or minimising these interventions to a regulatory role. Second, and this is a recent concession made by such theorists in the face of apparent market failure, it means enhancing the capacity of the state to manage markets to insulate rent-seekers and distributional coalitions from a position of influence. In either case, the task of reform is to sweep away politics and entrench a state that provides sufficient regulation to allow the efficient operation of the market. Ironically, then, this approach recognises that a political process, however much otherwise eschewed, is required to remove obstacles to market efficiency. The assumption here is that effecting change is a matter of technical and policy choice. This view has profound implications. In effect, it suggests that democratic or representative politics can be an impediment to good policy development—a position that has, on occasions, been quite explicit from adherents to the neo-classical position, as we will see below.

Two important influences within the neo-classical camp are new institutional economics and public choice theory. New institutional economists argue that individuals create institutions to overcome transaction costs. Development, they maintain, requires solutions to collective problems through general systems of rules and regulation; that is, institutions (North 1981; 1994; 1995). However, expectations that this would take place as rational individuals spontaneously aggregated to solve collective-action dilemmas were not to be realised. Instead, individuals generally preferred to seek their interests in rents. Public choice theorists understood this. They saw the roots of the problem lying in the state. In public choice theory, the political sphere was conceptualised as a marketplace of transactions among individual politicians, officials, and contending interest lobbies. Its product was the appropriation and sale of public policy and public goods in return for political support. The predatory interests of political leaders were seen to lock them frequently into a pattern of rule aimed at keeping contending interests satisfied, ruining the economy in the process (see Bates 1981).[2] At another level, the state itself was seen to have interests in accumulating ever-increasing revenues (Lal 1983; Krueger 1974; Buchanan and Tullock 1962). Such perspectives reinforced the neo-classical theme that there was a struggle between economics and politics.[3] But it also identified the solution as one of constraining the state if predatory behaviour was to be restricted.

However, the weakness of the public choice argument was demonstrated by what followed the collapse of the state in Russia in the late 1980s: chaos, collusion, gangsterism, and widespread market failure. From this point new institutionalist economists began to look increasingly to the state to enforce rules and regulations to safeguard the operations of the market.

What all neo-classical theorists share, however, is an abstract notion of markets and a belief that they are inherently efficient. Differences centre around the precise way this is best realised. Importantly, there is general agreement that marginalising politics from the policy process will help liberate markets. In that sense, all neo-classical theorists understand development as a technical question of how best to unleash the positive forces of markets. As we will see below, historical institutionalist and social conflict theorists in particular have, in their different ways, challenged this understanding of markets and politics.

Historical institutionalism

New institutionalism emerged as a reaction against both behaviouralist and pluralist approaches. In turn, historical institutionalism is distinguished from rational choice economic institutionalism by its interpretations of rationality and preferences which produce different approaches to markets and politics. Whereas rational choice theorists see constraints on rational political actors and values individual agency, historical institutionalists prefer to see actors' choices, interests, and preferences shaped by collective organisations and institutions that carry their own histories and rules, laws, norms, and ideas. Rather than viewing actors as rational, historical institutionalists tend to see them as self-reflective. Much of their theoretical heritage is in the works of Max Weber (Immergut 1998; Thelen and Steinmo 1992).

For the purposes of this chapter, two broad trends in historical institutionalism—an application that is state-centred and one that is more society-centred—can be identified.[4] Rapid growth in East Asia prompted statist historical institutionalists to emphasise the significance of state capacity for development—public institutions with an organisational form that enabled the making and implementation of effective policy. As we have seen, the importance of institutions was also taken up within the neo-classical camp, but historical institutionalists emphasised that institutional forms derived from historically evolved pathways.[5] The form of the state resulting from such contrasting histories could generate varied forms of capitalism. In other words, the state-centred historical institutionalists' view is that capitalism can advance within *various* institutional frameworks, of which liberal capitalism is but one. This contrasts with the neo-classical prescriptions for institution-building, cautioning against both the desirability and feasibility of attempts to impose liberal arrangements against the historical grain.

These theorists emphasise that the state (and its institutions) played a pivotal role among late-industrialising countries. This perspective is based on an appreciation of a common structural predicament facing late-industrialising economies, namely the need to amass large concentrations of investment capital and to make strategic inroads into established global markets (Zysman 1994; Johnson 1982; Amsden 1989). Such experiences have involved state officials in crucial, positive roles as developmental elites. In this account, markets are not abstract entities but are largely constructed by developmental elites. They make their calculations, however, within specific historical pathways defined by previous layers of institutions embedded in structures of social power and culture (Zysman 1994; Johnson, Tyson and Zysman 1989).

After earlier emphasis on insulation from vested interests as necessary for development, state-centred historical institutionalists argued that developmental elites needed to forge coalitions with dominant forces in business (Evans 1995; 1992). This was an implicit endorsement of politics. However, they shared the neo-classical theorists' concern about influences that could subvert the institutional rationality of the state. Such influences are best excluded through an 'embedding' of institutional autonomy. Development thus requires that the state adopt a distinctive organisational logic, one that contrasts with the logic of the unfettered market. In this way, national—rather than private, market-oriented—developmental goals can be pursued. So, although markets might be seen as constructions of politics, there are very definitely preferred state forms. This often sees the introduction of Weberian notions regarding the potential for elites to transform society and economy, together with a view of the policy processes of 'developmental' states in terms of rational action rather than as reflective of broader and deeper political processes.

Society-centred historical institutionalists agreed, but argued that a focus on the role of one or two institutions in development—state and market—drew attention away from an ensemble of non-state and non-market institutions that played important roles in economic success. These included banks, commercial networks, and business associations (Doner and Ramsey 1997). According to Doner and Hawes (1995:168–9), in South-East Asian economies dynamic private sectors were more significant than states. The state was still important but, whereas East Asia displayed relatively strong developmental states, in South-East Asia private institutions have been strong, with states having been relatively weaker. The more constructivist approach taken by historical institutionalists has been useful. The notion of 'historical pathways' and the abiding interests of the state appear helpful n providing explanations for continuity. By focusing on institutions, historical institutionalists identify a concept that allows for a powerful examination of an intersection where structure and agency meet past and present (Katznelson 1998:196). It is also noticeable that society-centred historical institutionalists have, in attempting to address change, given considerable attention to the political and conflictual construction of interests (Immergut 1998:20–2). State-centred analysts tended to miss or down play the complexity of interests involved in state-led development strategies, and of the relations between and within state and society that sustain state-led strategies. Society-centred analysts recognise that these are significant, and tend to define institutions as sites that mediate system-level structures (Thelen and Steinmo 1992:10–12).

Despite these advances, historical institutionalism exhibits a number of shortcomings. First, its concentration on intermediate 'variables' means that system-level structures are left unexplained (Katznelson 1998:196). For all of the competition, complexity, and historical contingency involved in the development and progress of institutions, it must be recognised that the interplay of social relations, power, and politics necessarily goes beyond institutions and the positions held in them by particular actors (Immergut 1998:28). Second, historical institutionalism, in focusing on constraints on institutional change ('stickiness'), emphasises order rather than change (see Peters 1999:68–71).[6] When change is examined, these analysts are concerned principally with addressing change within and as a result of institutions. Third, and related, these analysts tend to engage in institutional determinism (Thelen and Steinmo 1992:16). This is clearest in statist approaches, where developmental states are presented as being insulated from interests and political conflict. Further, for all of their emphasis on interests, historical institutionalists seldom address the 'interests' at work in the development of capitalism.

Social conflict theory

According to social conflict theorists, markets and the institutions that define them are forged within wider and system-level processes of social and political conflict (Hewison, Robison and Rodan 1993; Chaudhry 1994; Chaudhry 1997). This approach is thus concerned to delineate the patterns of power that produce particular institutional, political, and social outcomes. It rejects abstract notions of markets, which are seen to mask the power relations that define the economic and political regimes within which they operate, and the social conflicts associated with their establishment and reproduction. Institutions, then, are not just about efficiency. Markets cannot be understood apart from the power relationships and institutions in which they are located. They are not natural. This applies to liberal markets, no less than to state-led or any other market systems.

The point of the analytical exercise, therefore, is not to uncover the magic responsible for market growth. Instead, it is to explain the particular structure of power and the politics accounting for the form and extent of Asian development. So social conflict theorists focus analytical attention on the different *but competing* interests that structure the development, spread, and enforcement of capitalist markets (see Panitch and Leys 1999). This assists in understanding how policy and institutional transformation take place within broader patterns of social and political power. These analysts thus look to system-level conflict when explaining how it is that particular institutions are arranged, maintained, and changed.

Existing regimes therefore cannot be dismantled at will because they embody a specific arrangement of economic, social, and political power. Institutions that might appear 'dysfunctional' for growth and investment often persist because elites are prepared to sacrifice efficiency where their social and political ascendancy is threatened (see Badhan 1989). Equally, however, these dominant forces might embrace 'reforms' that further their control or weaken their opponents in broad struggles over social, political, and economic ascendancy. The point is that these responses relate to wider struggles and alliances. This contrasts with the historical institutional approach in that it seeks to explain change (and resistance to it) and the configuration of power at the system level.

In this approach, institutions might persist, not because of any simple historical momentum, but because they are integral to a specific set of power relations. Elites struggle to preserve existing institutional frameworks even in the face of what neo-classical theorists would regard as increasingly out-moded and inefficient systems or where the economy is collapsing around them. For example, in Malaysia and Indonesia there has been resistance to the idea that institutions need to be reformed in the face of economic crisis. This is precisely because of the implications this has for the existing mechanisms for allocating power and dispensing patronage. In other words, the question of power must be placed at the centre of analysis. The more normative, functional, and technical approaches of neo-classical theory and historical institutionalism evaluate institutions in terms of their efficiency in promoting development. Social conflict theorists, in contrast, direct their attention to the forces that structure society and its ensemble of institutions.

Change is therefore not driven by rational individuals, neutralising obstacles to a naturally efficient market. Nor is it forged in global conflicts among contending models of economic organisation. Rather, structural changes such as new technologies, dynamic systems of production, the globalisation of markets, urbanisation, and environmental degradation—all products of an evolving capitalist epoch—represent the focal points of conflict. Struggles and competition over production and economic power, as well as over land, property rights, and civil rights, involve various coalitions of class and state interest across and within national borders.

It is not surprising that South-East Asia's official development strategies have supported markets. Market-friendly policies were adopted not necessarily because politicians, bureaucrats, and technocrats were listening to capitalists or including them in policy-making—sometimes they did—but because structural imperatives required that the state support private enterprise. Policy outcomes are not a measure of the abilities of institutions (state or private) or of the relative insulation of decision-makers. Rather, policy results from competition and conflict over production, profits, wealth, and power. These conflicts are intimately bound to the trajectory of various classes and class fractions. This has seen competition within domestic capital, and between domestic and international capital. The crisis highlights that these struggles or conflicts are sharpest when competitive capitalist interests are restructuring. Only by understanding the nature of globalised corporate battles can policy outcomes be adequately understood.

As we will see in more detail below, this idea of conflict also differs from that within dependency theory which focuses on core-periphery, or North–South, divisions in the global system. Dependency approaches treat conflict associated with capitalism as a problem of national dependency rather than of domestic and international power relations. For social conflict theorists, exploitation and questions and issues related to the nature of economic power and control (see Brenner 1977; Kay 1975), the character and power of the state and its relationship to society, must instead be understood as both a domestic *and* external matter (see Miliband 1989).

Before the boom

The approaches mentioned above did not become prominent until the 1970s when many of the East and South-East Asian economies entered a period of rapid growth. Before this, the main theoretical concern was to explain why these economies were seemingly caught in poverty traps. Nevertheless, the antecedents of these contemporary theories can be traced to earlier traditions of intellectual thought. New institutional economics, for example, has affinities with the structural functionalism of Talcott Parsons (1951) and the political order theory of Samuel Huntington (1968). Similarly, many current notions of the global clash between a neo-liberal model of Western capitalism and a more interventionist East Asian model owe something to dependency approaches that emerged in the late 1960s.

Modernisation theory

The first major attempt to explain development in South-East Asia drew heavily on an approach labelled 'modernisation theory'. Theorists asserted that the former colonies could replicate the 'original transition' of Western Europe (see Roxborough 1979:chs 1–2). A variety of modernisation approaches emerged from the different emphases placed on sociological, psychological, and economic factors in the transition (see Larrain 1989:87–98; Hoogvelt 1982:chs 3–4). Modernisation approaches begin by establishing a dichotomy between tradition and modernity, and see an evolutionary movement from the former to the latter. Traditional societies were seen as 'pre-state, pre-rational and pre-industrial' (Higgott et al. 1985:17–18). To modernise, traditional societies needed to adopt the same organisational structures and social and political values of the West. Significantly, this included the adoption of liberal-democratic political arrangements, seen as a natural accompaniment to economic development.

However, the optimism inherent in modernisation theory soon waned as growth languished. It became clear that many of the assumptions about the conditions required for development were not emerging, and young democracies were not maturing but being replaced by authoritarianism. It was Huntington (1968) who made the strongest case that modernisation was threatened by political instability. For him, it was not democracy that mattered, but order. While middle classes remained weak, strong government and political order were required if development was to proceed; democracy could come later, when the middle class assumed centre stage.

For many South-East Asian governments, struggling against political instability, Huntington's ideas provided a handy rationale for the suppression of opposition. This was complemented by policies for economic development, fostered by international agencies, that emphasised the need to maximise growth so that its benefits would eventually 'trickle down' to all levels of society. Growth was to be enhanced through policies attractive to foreign investment, thereby alleviating any shortage of domestic capital (Higgott et al. 1985:24–7). One of the legacies of Huntington's approach was the recognition of institutions and the state as central actors in transforming dysfunctional systems. These elements were revived in the late 1990s as theorists attempted to explain economic crisis.

Dependency theory

At the time that modernisation theory was being revised to account for the apparent failure of development, dependency theory emerged to challenge it in fundamental ways. Dependency approaches had their origins in Latin America, where economists contested the notion that modernisation could be diffused to poor countries (see Larrain 1989:102–10; Frank 1967; 1969). André Gunder Frank radically shifted the focus of analysis to various global factors that conditioned development and the nature of political and economic regimes in developing countries. Frank turned modernisation theory on its head, arguing that the development of the already developed countries depended on the *under*development of poor countries. He contended that poor countries, caught in a web of international political and economic relationships, stayed poor because of the exploitative relationship established between them and the already developed countries.

In explaining this, Frank argued that the economic surplus of poor countries was lost precisely because the structures considered important by modernisation theorists—foreign investment through transnational corporations, foreign aid, international loans, and international trade regimes—were the structures responsible for sucking the surplus from underdeveloped countries. Local capitalists and the state act as compradors, providing the links between the developed and underdeveloped economies necessary for surplus extraction. Although Frank's position was refined by a range of theorists (Amin 1974; 1976; Cardoso and Faletto 1979; Evans 1979; Gereffi 1982; Bennett and Sharpe 1985), his primary proposition remained—stunted or incomplete development resulted from decisions taken at corporate headquarters in the advanced capitalist centres.

When it became obvious that many of the economies of South-East Asia were experiencing sustained growth, both the dependency and modernisation approaches were challenged. The facts that authoritarian regimes tended to oversee this growth, and that controlled rather than free markets were involved, were inconsistent with early modernisation theory. But Huntington was not vindicated. Rapid development under authoritarian rule took place with a vibrant middle class. Indeed, as growth consolidated, some Asian leaders even asserted the functional superiority of these arrangements over Western liberalism—a claim that was eventually accompanied by notions of 'Asian values' underpinning such a model. The emergence of countries such as South Korea, Taiwan, Hong Kong, and Singapore as important industrial exporters in the late 1970s delivered a mortal blow to dependency theory. Rather than being consigned to perpetual underdevelopment in a global system of exploitation dominated by the advanced industrial centres, these 'peripheral economies' increasingly appeared to be clawing their way back to prosperity via substantial export manufacturing. Dependency theorists dismissed this progress unconvincingly as 'dependent' or 'semi-peripheral' development, on the grounds that it lacked the same integrity as earlier industrialisation processes. However, the fact that growth among the 'Asian Tigers'[7] saw significant gains in material life, health, and welfare was a further defiance of dependency predictions.

As the old approaches faded, the three categories of analysis outlined at the beginning of this chapter began to exert increased influence.

Explaining the boom

Neo-classical accounts

Although dependency theorists could not explain the development of East and South-East Asian capitalism, theorists and policy-makers influenced by neo-classical economics were quick to fill the breach and claim superiority. The success of the Asian Tigers, they argued, reflected the adoption of policies that embraced global market forces. Export orientation was seen as crucial in rapid industrialisation—being regarded as a force for greater competitive discipline and a more efficient manufacturing sector. This was contrasted with production primarily for domestic markets, which was often heavily protected and seen as inefficient (see Krueger 1981). Importantly, the basis of export success was considered to be the exploitation of 'comparative advantage'—concentrating production in areas of relative endowment abundance in land, labour, or capital. Initially, in those economies that were labour-rich and capital-scarce, this meant low-cost, labour-intensive production (Little 1981).

Seen in this way, policy-makers in the Asian Tiger economies had simply chosen technically correct economic policies and the lesson was there for others to emulate. This perspective exerted considerable influence on the World Bank, which exhorted developing countries to follow, for example, the South Korean model. Subsequently, loans—especially for structural adjustment—were often conditional on recipient countries accepting an export-oriented industrialisation (EOI) strategy.

Although neo-classical economists urged the withdrawal of the state from economic activity in Asia to consolidate economic gains (Little, Scitovsky and Scott 1970; Bauer 1970; Balassa 1971; Krueger 1974), it became difficult to ignore the fact that Asian industrialisation had often been accompanied by state intervention. Neo-classical economists were initially to deny the importance of the state's role, but later redefined it as a 'market-facilitating' role—assisting decisions that would have been made by the market in any case. However, recognition of the importance of the state in economic development did extract concessions from the influential *The East Asian Miracle* study (World Bank 1993). Significantly, the serious consideration given to the role of the state had followed Japanese pressure regarding the Bank's free-market prescriptions for all developing countries (Awanohara 1993:79).

The Bank's concessions on the importance of the state were extended in the *World Development Report 1997: The State in a Changing World*. This report made a general case for acknowledging and supporting the role of the state in facilitating globalisation. As the report observed, 'Globalization is a threat to weak or capriciously governed states. But it also opens the way for effective, disciplined states to foster development and economic well-being, and it sharpens the need for efficient international cooperation in pursuit of global collective action' (World Bank 1997:11). It seemed that within the Bank it was realised that a deeper internationalisation of capital was reliant upon the effective regulatory and coordinating capacities of states.

Important as this critical World Bank reflection on its theoretical approach was, we should not exaggerate its significance. It conceded the importance of the state in keeping inflation low, maintaining political and macroeconomic stability, establishing the rule of law, encouraging education, keeping taxes low, promoting trade, and encouraging foreign and local investment. The policy lesson was that governments should ensure that they had policies and institutions in place to support the growth of private investment.

Furthermore, states were acknowledged only to the extent that they were able to rise above politics. Politics remained a dirty word. For example, the Thailand study associated with the *Miracles* report explains that the military coup did 'perform an important function'. The military junta 'assumes broad legislative powers, and . . . break[s] the legislative logjam developed in previous elected parliaments' (Christensen et al. 1993:19–20). The former legislature was seen as relatively unproductive 'in making laws, especially when members of parliament are elected'. Almost as an afterthought it is also noted that bureaucrats are not immune to extra-bureaucratic demands.

The *Miracles* report drew attention to the fact that the state in South-East Asia had been less cohesive in its control and marshalling of economic organisation and strategy than in South Korea, Taiwan, or Japan. Protective trade and investment policies and state ownership were not usually tied into strategic, disciplined national programs for building export competitiveness. They were often devices for allocating preferential access or bolstering the interests of the state and its officials. Unlike the developmental states of North-East Asia, they were, in the language of neo-classical political economy, more likely to be predatory states with rent-seeking bureaucrats, rather than the far-sighted bureaucrats. Consequently, the neo-classical debate over South-East Asia has tended to be concerned with the transition from predatory and statist economic systems to 'markets'.[8] As we will show, this concern was to be substantially extended with the advent of the Asian crisis.

Apart from opening up competing interpretations over the roles of states and markets, the Asian economic boom witnessed a remarkable comeback by modernisation theory. The argument that economic development set in train dynamics exerting pressures for democratisation was aggressively reasserted. This time the literature was more sophisticated, with greater attention to the factors mediating the influence of economic development on politics—including culture and leadership. Two influential books, by Huntington (1991) and Fukuyama (1992), did much to reignite the idea that the triumph of capitalism paved the way for democracy (see Diamond, Linz and Lipset 1989; Diamond 1993). According to this argument, authoritarian leaders might resist democratisation, but complex social changes accompanying capitalist development render such efforts problematic. The social pluralism resulting from capitalist transformations was exerting mounting and, in many cases, irresistible pressures for political pluralism.

The burgeoning middle classes were viewed as the strategic agents of political change. The downfall of authoritarian regimes in South Korea and Taiwan gave rise to a confidence that similar changes could be anticipated in South-East Asia.

Historical institutionalist accounts

There was increased interest in historical institutionalist approaches during the boom, especially as the South-East Asian economic performance was compared with that of East Asia. According to state-centred historical institutionalists, the remarkable feature of Asian industrialisation was the role of the state in orchestrating public and private capital to achieve strategic national economic goals—not, as neo-classical economists conceded, in facilitating markets. Within a framework of complex trade and industry regimes, export strategies and systems of state–business cooperation states could organise corporate juggernauts able to successfully assault global markets (Wade 1990; Amsden 1989; Weiss and Hobson 1995; Matthews and Ravenhill 1996; Johnson 1982; Johnson 1987). But this was dependent on 'state capacity' (Weiss 1998). Predictions of an impending 'Asian Century' were accepted within this camp of theorists who depicted these highly organised systems of East Asia as functionally well suited to export-oriented industrialisation.[9]

The idea that authoritarian states could play a positive development role became attractive within the West at a time when growth rates lagged behind some Asian rates. But this was not because of any perception that state-led industry policies were more efficient means of organising resources and global strategies. Within Western business circles many looked approvingly at the state's role in sweeping aside 'distributional coalitions' (labour, welfare, and environmental groups) and instituting low tax regimes. These were the aspects of the Asian experience they believed provided broader economic lessons (see FEER 1994a; FEER 1994b).

State-centred explanations often assumed that the developmental state was the backbone of economic dynamism in Asia. The problem was that, in South-East Asia, it was only Singapore that seriously fitted this model (Haggard 2000a:136). Despite this, rapid industrialisation certainly did occur in Thailand, Indonesia, Malaysia, and, to a lesser extent, the Philippines. As noted above, society-centred historical institutionalists argued that the focus on state and market neglected non-state and non-market institutions. They argued that it was these institutions that had determined much economic success. Focusing on private sector institutions, these analysts argue that such organisations were required to play critical directing roles within the economy (Doner and Ramsey 1997:273). The relationship between business and state was far more problematic in much of South-East Asia under the impact of patronage and cronyism, but business developed its own dynamic institutional arrangements to drive industrialisation. In examining the boom, then, these analysts devoted considerable attention to the development of collective private sector institutions (Hutchcroft 1991; Doner 1992; Anek 1992). The implication was that states and their institutions were important, but that the private sector and its institutions could compensate for relatively weak states.

Social conflict accounts

Within the social conflict perspective, rapid industrialisation was not to be understood in terms of the triumph of 'good' policy or of competent technocrats, developmental elites over self-interested rent-seekers, or necessarily in the ability of business to develop its own institutions. Instead, institutions, elites, and technocrats are seen to operate within a broader power structure where the influence of vested economic and political interests is definitive. Growth in South-East Asia occurred across a range of countries, each with different resource endowments and exhibiting a variety of political regimes. But what was common was a compatibility between political regimes and associated interests on the one hand and the prevailing structures of capital accumulation on the other.

In particular, the boom decade from the mid 1980s was facilitated by the emergence of regimes that altered the nature of their engagement with global markets. From exporters of primary commodities, the major South-East Asian economies became export manufacturers. This different engagement with global markets did not necessarily reflect a neo-liberal political or policy ascendancy. At one level the boom was made possible by structural shifts in the global economy and the attendant mobility of international capital. For example, the 1985 Plaza Accord released a flood of manufacturing investment to the region as Japanese companies sought a new base for low-wage manufacturing. At another level, the engagement was mediated by changes taking place within these countries. In each case, the old hierarchies of power that had been constructed to further commodity trade were reconstituted in the transition to manufacturing and market development.

Hence, a range of social, political and institutional outcomes accompanied the shift from commodity trade to import-substitution industrialisation (ISI) and, in turn, to EOI, and the progressive deregulation of economic life across the region in the 1980s. For example, in Thailand,

EOI and deregulation went hand in hand with the transformation of class power as conglomerates in banking and industry were consolidated while the old trading business groups declined. State officials played a significant role in facilitating this process (Hewison 1989). Importantly, however, these transformations were accompanied by political reform that saw the power of state officials harnessed increasingly to private interests. By contrast, deregulation and EOI in Indonesia in the 1980s, partly enforced by the collapse in oil prices, took place in an economy dominated by coalitions of state and private corporate oligarchies. What transpired was a transfer of public monopoly into the hands of private interest. Unlike Thailand, economic deregulation was not accompanied by political reform. The system of authoritarian state capitalism was simply harnessed to the needs of burgeoning corporate conglomerates. Short-term international bank credit replaced oil as the driving force in the economy (Robison 1986:387–8). New oligarchies and coalitions were liberated from centralised systems of state capitalism and given free reign to borrow short-term to set up enterprises and banks, without regulatory scrutiny.[10]

Of course, these alignments of power and interest in the region were 'doomed'. In a post-Cold War world, Western governments and international financial institutions were less constrained by strategic political considerations to prop up conservative and anti-communist forces with aid and loans. At the same time, increased international competition and the need for financial liberalisation to drive further industrialisation required reconstitution of economic and political power for continued expansion of these economies. Relationships that enabled massive state favours to private projects and huge private debt were likely to be challenged from both domestic and international sources. However, the nature of that challenge was necessarily different in each of the countries of South-East Asia. The economic crisis has been a significant element in this challenge.

Miracles go 'bust'

The optimism regarding South-East Asian development evaporated when the region's economies stalled in 1997. With the exception of Singapore, those economies that had opened their financial sectors to global markets—specifically, Thailand, Malaysia, Indonesia, and, to a lesser extent, the Philippines—experienced significant financial and economic collapse. These downturns resulted in social and political pressure. This chapter is not the place to recount the events of the crisis, especially as there are numerous accounts of the onset, contagion, and economic collapse that followed

Thailand's devaluation in July 1997 (see Robison, et al. 2000; Roubini, Corsetti and Pesenti 1998; Arndt and Hill 1999). Furthermore, much of this will be taken up for each country in the subsequent chapters of the present volume. Our concern will be with the debate about the nature and causes of the crisis. However, there are some points we wish to highlight as background.

The initial impact of the crisis was evidenced in the financial sector, where the collapse of currencies caused havoc as borrowers found they had over-extended. Investment dried up and insolvency mushroomed. Some of this translated into social unrest as unemployment rose and inflation soared. Not surprisingly, these economic and social problems soon had their effects in the political sphere. To different degrees, fiscal crisis and growing opposition besieged governments. Their inability to stem the tide of economic decay undermined what had been a central pillar of their political legitimacy.

Intra-elite friction was precipitated or intensified by these economic pressures. In Thailand, Prime Minister Chavalit Yongchaiyudh was forced to resign in the face of his government's failure to come to grips with the economy's downward spiral and its inability to deal with the IMF.[11] In Malaysia, the economic crisis brought leadership questions to a head, as Deputy Prime Minister Anwar Ibrahim's policy prescriptions contrasted with those of Prime Minister Mahathir. More than differences over the extent of state intervention in the economy, the rhetoric of Anwar and his allies declaring the need to unravel 'crony capitalism' was an attack on Mahathir's power base. Anwar's sacking and arrest ensured that the economic crisis became a full-scale political crisis. Most stunning of all developments, however, was that the crisis precipitated the fall of President Soeharto who had reigned supreme in Indonesia for over three decades.

Turning now to debates regarding the crisis, there are two questions in these debates that will be pursued. First, why did a crisis occur? How was it that such apparently buoyant and vigorous economies as Malaysia, Thailand, and Indonesia suddenly unravelled and, in the latter two cases, found themselves in the hands of the IMF? Second, has the crisis been a fundamental historical watershed, making liberal market systems the model for all economies and, in any case, what is going to determine the future directions of these economies?

Neo-classical accounts

Mainstream neo-classical theorists, particularly those within the IMF, seized on the crisis as validation of their primary arguments concerning the perils of obstructing free markets and the need for governments to embrace markets if development was to be sustained. For IMF head Michel Camdessus (quoted in *AWSJ* 1997) the crisis was a 'blessing in disguise'. The influence and power of international organisations such as the IMF, Asian Development Bank, and World Bank ensured that these views prevailed in policy circles (see Jayasuriya 2000). For beleaguered governments in countries such as Thailand and Indonesia these institutions represented the only viable source of funds to mitigate the crisis. This gave the institutions unprecedented leverage in domestic policy agenda.

With the crisis, collusive state–business relations became the objects of intense critical attention. Whereas the *Miracles* report grudgingly acknowledged that the state had played a significant development role, the crisis allowed neo-classical analysts to reassert aggressively that state involvement distorted markets. They argued that cosy political arrangements, and the absence of 'adequate' accounting standards and transparency, distorted 'price signals', and led to a misallocation of resources. This created 'moral hazard' in which borrowers and lenders of money (especially borrowers) operated in the expectation of government rescue should things go awry (Roubini, Corsetti and Pesenti 1998; Frankel 1998; Arndt and Hill 1999; Wolfe 1998). Market discipline, they argued, was simply not strong enough in these economies, and the task of recovery had to centre on establishing this discipline.[12]

Yet the crisis also led to several challenges to the 'Washington Consensus' that had dominated neo-classical policy strategies for well over two decades—not least from within the neo-classical school itself. It had become clear that where market deregulation was embraced there were often negative consequences. This forced neo-classical theorists to become more interested in the political dimensions of markets, and they focused on questions associated with the rise of rent-seekers and how to dispose of them. Successful deregulation required particular sorts of institutions.

The Asian crisis necessarily reinforced the need for far more attention to be given to state capacity—if for no other reason than the need to enforce deregulation and break the power of cronies (see Camdessus 1998). But institution-building is conceived here in elitist terms, for the ideal remains that a band of rational technocrats are able to operate above the constraints of vested interests (Schamis 1999:236). Interestingly, however, differences surfaced between the IMF and the World Bank over the question of regulation and the role of the state. In particular, the Bank's then senior vice-president and chief economist, Joseph Stiglitz (1998; 1999), advocated a role for the state that went beyond refining the capacity to implement deregulation and insulating policy-makers from vested interests. In effect,

Stiglitz asked, on behalf of the Bank, why institutions could be successfully transplanted in some instances but not others—an issue of concern to new institutional economists in the 1990s, but which had not been convincingly accounted for.[13]

The World Bank had recognised the importance of social and political processes even before the crisis,[14] motivated by development failures and setbacks in Africa and Eastern Europe. Thus the Bank began a somewhat vague advocacy of 'good governance', acknowledging the social under-pinnings of corrupt or weak institutional frameworks (World Bank 1991:6–7). Now, however, Stiglitz and the Bank became more expansive about what this entailed and the reform agenda attached to it. The language of participation, civil society, social capital, and community organisation became prominent as the social basis of sustainable markets was empha-sised (see World Bank 1998). It was asserted that the state needed to work in concert with a range of social organisations to cement the social struc-tures, values, and norms supportive of markets.[15] According to Stiglitz (1998:12): 'The hard part of capacity building is the development of organizational/social capital, including the institutions that enable society to function well'. On these grounds, the Bank distinguished itself from the IMF on the question of fiscal austerity. It began to emphasise social safety nets for those who fell through the cracks in liberalising market systems.[16] Of course, this also reflected a concern about the kinds of destabilising events seen in Indonesia and criticisms that Bank and IMF policies were deepening the crisis there and in Thailand. There was a related worry that such resentment threatened the hegemony of neo-liberal ideas.

The direction taken within the Bank situated it squarely within the so-called 'Post-Washington Consensus'. This embraces the idea of institution-building and sees it as a primary objective in the development of sustainable market systems in South-East Asia. The above theoretical refinements notwithstanding, this position still has some fundamental prob-lems. First, it retains a functional understanding of social institutions, with the emphasis on the way in which social structures and processes can be harnessed to support market systems by producing social cohesion and a sense of community. Implicit in this is a view that the inherently unequal and conflictual power relations and material outcomes of the market require management. The market is thus not analysed as an expression or outcome of competing interests and differential power, but rather as a system with functional requirements essential to its effective operation— and that includes the containment of conflict. This perpetuates the conception of the market in abstract and apolitical terms, and suggests sani-tised notions of civil society. State-sponsored consultation processes in authoritarian states, such as Singapore for example, could be seen as part of the institutions and social capital that enhance the market.

Second, the building of institutions remains one that is conceived in voluntarist terms. Who builds institutions, states, and social capital? How are values and norms institutionalised throughout society? It is one thing to recognise the importance of these things; quite another to theorise how they come into being. Because markets continue to be understood by neo-classical analysts as abstract entities defined in terms of functional efficiency, the assumption of a universally applicable and technically correct set of arrangements still pervaded their thinking. There is no recognition, therefore, of how power structures and social interests might complicate or facilitate the introduction of the requisite structures and values to which they now refer. It is as if these things can simply be supplied and will there-after take root and generate the desired outcome.

In short, for all their emphasis on institutions, the idea of politics and con-flict as something dysfunctional and threatening to markets survives. At the level of political analysis, this approach remains naive.

Crisis as global conflict: historical institutionalists

Whereas neo-classical analysts concentrated on domestic weakness in explaining the crisis, historical institutionalists have, not unexpectedly, directed their attention to institutional problems.

State-centred historical institutionalists have seen the crisis as a conflict between competing models of capitalism. Indeed, the neo-classical account is seen as an apologia for the liberal, Anglo-American variant of capitalism and an unjustified dismissal of the East Asian developmental state model. Far from conceding that the crisis invalidated arguments about state capa-city, statists attributed Asia's economic problems to compromised state capacity due to liberalisation. Furthermore, the question of the functional superiority of the respective models is far from settled, despite the trium-phant mood prevalent in the neo-classical camp.

The work of Robert Wade, extrapolating from the South Korea case, has been central to this argument (Wade 1998a; Wade 1998b; Wade and Veneroso 1998). He characterised Asian industrial capitalism as a 'high debt model', in which domestic banks were able to mobilise high levels of domestic savings that supported productive investments by private firms. This process was often reinforced and harnessed through government incentives. Although this led to high debt-to-equity ratios, it worked to 'propel the region's fast economic development over several decades' (Wade 1998a:362). However, liberalisation altered the logic of the system. Banks and private companies found that they could borrow cheaply from abroad and, often, then on-lend profitably. Foreign banks and finance companies also entered local markets in search of higher returns. Consequently, 'narrow and short-term interests of shifting coalitions' replaced the government–bank–firm productive investment nexus (Wade 1998a:364). Opening the capital account is also seen to have been instrumental in exposing domestic financial structures to new forces and pressures that were not always so productively oriented—especially given the under-developed nature of corporate supervision and governance in the region. According to Wade (1998a:373), fuller integration into international finance markets and the superimposition of a regulatory regime based on Anglo-American prudential norms would exacerbate the problem. From this perspective, recovery necessitated rebuilding institutions consistent with the historical pathways that have accompanied these hitherto successful state-led systems.

Linda Weiss, who locates the cause of the crisis in the vulnerability associated with limited or weakened state capacity, develops a similar theme. The worst-hit crisis economies, she argues, were those where 'the common denominator is weak or decomposing institutional capacities' (Weiss 1999:319). For Thailand and Indonesia this was reflected in their institutional inability to direct investment into productive sectors and to accelerate the pace of skills and technology upgrading. In South Korea, it was reflected in a decline in both institutional capacity and a reduced ideological consistency for state direction. The result in these countries was declining exports, rising current account deficits, excess productive capacity, increased private foreign indebtedness, and a field day for speculators (Weiss 1999:321–3, 326; Weiss and Hobson 2000).

The vulnerability of economies with limited or diminished regulatory capacity contrasted with the strength of US international state power, referred to by state-centred institutionalists as the 'US Treasury–Wall Street–IMF complex'. According to Weiss (1999:332), the USA has used the crisis to open markets further, and has played a role in making an 'ordinary crisis' into a 'deep crisis'. The problem is not just that there are external interests involved, but that the prescriptions coming from these quarters are grounded in assumptions about the universal applicability of a liberal market model.

Far from the crisis signalling 'the death throes of Asian state capitalism', Wade and other statists believe the jury is still out (Wade 1998b:1536). They point out that liberal capitalism in the advanced capitalist countries has its own unresolved and potential critical problems, not the least being the rising social inequalities that accompany neo-liberal globalisation. Its long-term political sustainability remains problematic. Moreover, the structural power of international capital notwithstanding, the crisis has engendered an apprehension and reaction on the part of some Asian leaders about the neo-liberal model. Wade (1998b:1551) predicts that the Asian model has considerable staying power and might still be influential 'in setting norms for international economic and financial regimes'. Weiss's (1999) conclusion is that the crisis shows that strong states are essential to globalisation—not antithetical to it.

Others are less sanguine. Chung-In Moon and Sang-young Rhyu (2000:98) conclude that: 'Convergence to western capitalism is likely to be the fate of the Asian economy. In a sense, Asian capitalism could have been a temporal detour in the longer historical evolution.' From this perspective, the developmental state has been irrevocably damaged. New distributional coalitions have impaired its effective functioning, and the insulation of the state has been breached (Moon and Rhyu 2000:97).

These state-centred historical institutionalists argue that attempts to establish liberal economic institutional change in the region have failed to generate positive results because of their mismatch with historical pathways. In effect, liberal institutions do not fit established 'Asian' institutional pathways. Although this appears to account for post-crisis resistance to change, it does not allow for a disaggregation of the elements of resistance or change. Nor does it direct attention to the forces structuring these elements and sculpting their responses. Change taking place is not a choice between 'models'—whether Asian developmentalist or Anglo-American neo-liberal. Rather, change involves complex questions of power, including the structure and capacities of domestic business, its various linkages with the state and other interests and classes, and the relationships between these structures and the changing international economy.

Those historical institutionalists with a greater focus on society make more of the decline of institutional arrangements. For example, Hutchcroft (1999:474) argues that, in Thailand, the boom saw business gradually establish its collective interests over the state. Market liberalisation, with little attention to building appropriate institutions, together with an increasing tendency for politicians to enhance patronage through access to state coffers and policy, set the stage for crisis.

This theme is taken up by Doner and Ramsey (1999) and Haggard (2000a). Interestingly, their argument is similar to that of the statists, faulting the region's institutions. However, they extend their critique beyond state capacity to include weak political structures or systems, policy mistakes, lack of transparency, and moral hazard. The basic argument is that the institutional arrangements that created the boom were inappropriate for these economies as they internationalised and opened. Indeed, the crisis has revealed previously hidden weaknesses in these arrangements. Whereas Thailand's commercial banks were once at the forefront of private sector dynamism, resolving collective action problems, they are now identified as too powerful (Doner and Ramsey 1999:175, 183). Haggard (2000a:137) argues that it was through government inaction that these same banks became collusive.

These institutionalists favour technocratic solutions to such problems. Clearly they see that institutional failures must be put right. Hutchcroft (1999:488) argues that reform in Thailand requires the political ascendancy of conservative urban elites who must capture the state and parliament from unsophisticated and patrimonial 'country bumpkins' (elected politicians). Haggard (2000a:131–2) also identifies Thailand's party system as encouraging patrimonialism, further noting the instability of multi-party coalitions.[17] This patrimonial and non-transparent pattern was also seen in Indonesia and Malaysia. It is noticeable that this society-focused approach tends to emphasise order. For example, reform is often seen to involve establishing order, stability, and accountability (Hutchcroft 1999:486–8). Similarly, when discussing private-sector actors there is a tendency to down play the competition and conflict among them. Where conflict is discussed, it tends to be in the context of the state and its officials versus the private sector.[18] Among others things, the crisis laid bare the contradictory relationships among the various fractions of capital, and indicated that, although the state was responsible for the interests of capital in general, state actors were also cognisant of the relative power and significance of domestic and international capital, and within domestic capital.

Crisis as global conflict: neo-dependency

In spite of the theoretical attacks discussed above, some versions of dependency theory had remained influential—especially with non-government organisations (NGOs)—and the Asian crisis prompted its re-emergence. The elements of dependency theory that attracted NGO interest, and which were incorporated into explanations of the crisis, included: (i) strong, sometimes moral, critiques of the negative impacts of development; (ii) the power of rich countries (or the North) to exploit, impoverish, and dominate poor countries (the South); and (iii) the need for a radical economic program that emphasises national development (Bello and Rosenfeld 1990; Hart-Landsberg 1991). Some continued to argue that the wealth of the rich countries was extracted from poor countries, with financial domination being a new colonialism (Lummis n.d.; Khor 2000). When the crisis struck, it seemed to vindicate longstanding criticisms of the dependent nature of South-East Asian development (see Bello, Cunningham and Li 1998).

For these analysts, the crisis was a demonstration of the power of rich countries and the weakness of the South-East Asian nations. The IMF was condemned for deepening the crisis through its blind push for neo-liberal reforms. These radicals joined with others in attacking the IMF and the USA for taking advantage of the crisis to reassert their influence in the region through reforms demanding a more thorough-going liberalisation (see Bello 1998a:15; Bullard, Bello and Malhotra 1998:124). Like historical institutionalists, they made much of the so-called 'Washington conspiracy'. This collusion was to enforce policies that reduced damage to developed country banks and gave firms from the North significant advantages in doing business in the region. These advantages were to be derived from neo-liberal reform reproducing institutions and markets that were in 'the image of the US economy' (Bello 1998a:16; Bello 1998b). The triumphalism of various US commentators when the crisis struck apparently confirmed the conspiracy (Bello 2000a).

IMF 'reforms' were thus seen as enhancing policies that were identified as having caused the crisis in the first place. In response, some radicals argued for a more nationalist approach to development, including reorientating production to domestic markets (Bello, Cunningham and Li 1998:249). This was considered the only way to avoid domination by the North (see Raghaven n.d). They also asserted that there must be capital controls to prevent the damage caused by the free flow of finance. Such positions were supported by a number of South-East Asian NGOs (see, for an example, Hewison 2000a). Malaysia's adoption of capital controls and Mahathir's attacks on globalisation as a Western conspiracy and a new form of colonialism were eagerly taken up by radical analysts and NGOs (Chossudovsky 1998; see also Nesadurai 2000). Vietnam, yet to engage in the same levels of financial liberalisation, was also used to illustrate that an economy that was not so open did better when the crisis struck (Bello and Mittal 2000).

This approach necessarily directed attention to national responses to the perceived negative impacts of globalisation, and saw curious political alliances emerge as radicals and NGOs lined up with NGO-unfriendly governments such as Malaysia and a range of US conservatives in opposing free trade agenda. For example, Bello (2000b) endorsed Mahathir as an 'eloquent ... critic of the [West's] development paradigm'. However, Mahathir (1999) was, in fact, extending the idea that economic liberalism— no less than political liberalism—was antithetical to the 'Asian way'.[19] Bello

(2000c) also supported attacks by US conservatives on the IMF and World Bank.

There is a certain resonance between neo-dependency and historical institutionalist accounts, particularly in the way that they both laid much of the blame for the crisis at the door of externally promoted deregulation. However, the former did not conceptualise the clash as one between competing models of capitalism, nor was it in adulation of the developmental states championed by historical institutionalists. Rather, they saw South-East Asian economies as having long been in the adverse grip of a system of global capitalism. The crisis was a manifestation of a new phase of that process. Like those that preceded it, this sacrificed the interests of integrated national economies in South-East Asia on the altar of global capitalist exploitation.

Crisis as social conflict

For many social conflict theorists, the Asian crisis represented a specific manifestation of the normal boom–bust nature of capitalism (Hewison 2000b). On this particular occasion, over-capacity in a number of industrial sectors led to a rapid erosion of rates of return; after all, markets for products embodying low-cost labour were not inexhaustible (Gill 1999; McNally 1999; Bernard 1999). The crisis represented an impasse in export-oriented capitalism, necessitating a restructuring of power and state–society relations throughout the region as new accumulation strategies are developed (Bernard 1999:184–90).[20] Competition among capitalists, and competition between labour and capital, were part of this process, reflected in the impacts of financial liberalisation and globalisation on the region (Tabb 1999:1; see also Tabb 1998). The deregulation of the finance sector, for instance, was seen to serve the interests of various fractions of local and transnational capital in different ways (Bernard 1999:191).

From this perspective, the crisis also exposed the suspect political grounds on which some historical institutionalists have been attracted to the so-called East Asian model—the challenge to free-market forces that it represents (Bernard 1999:201). The class-biased nature of developmental state regimes overlooked during the boom years by enthusiasts for the model were harder to ignore once discriminatory measures to stem the crisis were introduced by these states.[21]

One of the puzzles of the economic crisis has been the widely diverging nature of its consequences for the region's political and economic regimes. Despite the trauma and magnitude of IMF-enforced reforms, many of the institutions regarded by neo-classical analysts as sources of the crisis have been resilient.[22] The crisis, then, is critical precisely to the extent that it makes it possible for entrenched elites to be weakened as a result of the threat to the existing institutional arrangements that previously benefitted those elites. It is also important to the extent that it creates opportunities for reformist coalitions to exert greater influence.

In this context, then, crises might well be decisive events, not because of the lessons they bring in terms of the economic costs of intervention, or because of the benefits of reform, but for focusing attention on contestation within society. At one level this might be between, on the one hand, entrenched regimes attempting to hold together a political and economic fabric that sustains their interests and, on the other hand, those who would alter these arrangements. A crisis might also demonstrate the contradictions of capitalism and the cyclical nature of its production. Crises are one way in which these contradictions are 'worked out', and will require economic, political, and institutional restructuring. But even where an economic crisis delivers fatal wounds to existing authoritarian or predatory regimes, their collapse does not guarantee a shift to liberal markets or democratic politics. It might, but it also opens the door to a fresh round of struggles that could lead elsewhere too.

The social conflicts that are shaping institutional change cannot be understood as efforts to improve functional efficiency in governance, or as the strengthening of civil society. They are about how power is distributed in the processes of production, work, and the accumulation of capital and wealth. These are not simply conflicts between enlightened technocrats and rent-seekers, or between a progressive bourgeoisie and reactionary predators. Instead, fluid alliances are constructed around a vast array of issues that arise as capitalism spreads and is transformed—over property rights, land title, labour rights, corporate law, environmental protection, and trade and financial regulation. In these conflicts, the bourgeoisie is not a necessary force for political liberalism and democracy within these coalitions; indeed, elements of it might well be profoundly illiberal and anti-democractic if this serves their interests.

The importance of the crisis is that it has shifted the structural balance of social, state, and transnational power within which these conflicts operate. In Indonesia, for example, the state is no longer able to enforce the highly efficient systems of social control that previously sustained it. Nor can it guarantee the centralised organisation of corruption. There has been a flowering of competing organisations, interests, and coalitions. But in the ensuing power deflation, none has yet been able to establish its ascendancy.

Corruption and human rights abuses, for example, can no longer be hidden but neither can they be stopped (Robison and Rosser 2000).

If social conflict drives institutional change, how do we explain the way in which social interest is translated into political power, policy agenda, and institutional change? As we have seen, the relationship between the state and social interest has been a constant problem for both neo-classical and historical institutional theorists. It is no less a problem for theorists who emphasise the importance of social conflict as the primary driver of institutional change.

It is true, as historical institutionalists recognise, that social interest exerts an influence in the form of structural constraints on the choices of state managers. For example, even the most authoritarian regimes must ensure that food prices remain under control, not for reasons of social justice but for concerns about stability. Nevertheless, one of the defining features of the political economy of South-East Asia, with the exception of Singapore, is the highly instrumental nature of capitalist control of state power. The money politics of Thailand and the politics of capitalist oligarchy in the Philippines provide mechanisms by which powerful corporate interests directly capture and appropriate state power. In Malaysia, the distinction between the state and the interests of a tight oligarchy is difficult to draw in a situation where the latter is constructed upon state contracts, credit, and economic concessions (Gomez and Jomo 1999). Perhaps this instrumentalism has been most dramatically illustrated in Indonesia. Despite claims from neo-classical supporters of Indonesia's economic technocrats that the Indonesian government was insulated from vested interests (Bhattacharya and Pangestu 1992; Liddle 1991), this autonomy did not extend much beyond macro-economic policy. Nowhere was the crude exercise of state power for private interest more blatant than in the construction of patronage networks and corporate interests for the family of President Soeharto. As Soeharto's children plundered the state it was difficult to distinguish the public and private interest, or to understand the state except in terms of the possession of powerful private oligarchies.

As capitalists renegotiate their competitive arrangements among themselves, locally and internationally, and with labour and other classes, this has necessarily involved the state and its officials. It is both a domestic conflict and a competition between international and national capitals. Hence, the 'international state'—in the form of the international financial institutions—has also been heavily involved, at times mediating and at other times mentoring. This brings together some strange bedfellows. For example, the IMF seeks to impose a common institutional regime that will remove exclusive arrangements favouring local investors. Middle-class reformers often support these moves because they breakdown local concentrations of power. Local investors, on the other hand, often attempt to link with nationalists to 'save the nation' from foreign predators, and are joined in this call by leftist NGOs. The fundamental point is, however, that the crisis is about reshaping class relations, and social conflict theorists seek to understand this.

Arguments of the book

In the subsequent chapters of this volume, we begin with a series of country studies to examine processes of development in detail. This is followed by more thematic and comparative studies examining such issues as economic liberalisation in the wake of the Asian crisis, labour–state relations, and the role of Japan in South-East Asia. Careful readers will detect that the contributions to this book evidence a degree of theoretical heterodoxy. Although all reject the orthodox economic approach, it is notable that they all take seriously the insights of the historical institutionalists. However, there is also a generalised critique of this approach, along lines set out above. Each of the contributors looks to place considerable emphasis on the social, political, and economic forces at work in explaining boom, bust, and recovery.

Jane Hutchison argues in chapter 2 that it is not the recent Asian crisis, but the mid 1980s crisis that has been most significant for the Philippines' contemporary political economy. An end to authoritarian rule, the reintroduction of electoral democracy, a move towards economic liberalisation, and the emergence of new social forces, all followed the earlier economic collapse. Yet institutional reforms lacked depth so that the political system remained open to patronage, enabling powerful oligarchs and their interests to survive change. Indeed, if anything, the 1997–98 crisis has been accompanied by an intensification of cronyism attempting to shore up the power of the oligarchs. Hutchison's analysis thus acknowledges the point of historical institutionalists about the importance of state capacity. However, her explanation for the durability of oligarchic power is sought in the way that these interests intersect with neo-liberal capitalist restructuring agenda and is sustained by class relations beyond state institutions.

In chapter 3 Kevin Hewison also underlines the periodic nature of crisis. He argues that Thailand's capitalist development has been punctuated by crises that herald the emergence of new accumulation regimes. The crisis of 1997–98 has been another cause for accelerated competition among different fractions of capital. In this recent process, foreign capital exerts a greater influence, particularly in the finance sector, than it has previously. Power within the domestic capitalist class is also being transferred increasingly towards export-oriented and internationalised capital. In conjunction with these changes, there is, however, significant institutional development as more rules-based systems are introduced into business and political life. Yet the dynamics behind these policy developments reside in the conflicts among competing capitalists' interests, and the associated struggles involving those affected by these conflicts—which is the story, in effect, of the entire period of Thailand's capitalist development.

Richard Robison's analysis of Indonesia also draws attention to the particular nature of contemporary conflict associated with capitalism. Although precipitated by panic and speculation in global capital markets, the dramatic unravelling of Indonesia's economic and political regimes after 1997, he argues, is rooted in a specific pathology of power and interest. The very predatory arrangements that made possible rapid economic growth, and constituted the cement of a seemingly invulnerable power structure, were also the seeds of its destruction, producing huge private-sector debt and over-investment. The crisis is a watershed because it has fractured the alliances underpinning the regime. In the struggle to carve out new economic regimes, a cohesive coalition is yet to take shape that will drive a coherent reform agenda. In the meantime, old politico–business alliances are attempting to reorganise their ascendancy within new institutional frameworks and in the context of wider social alliances.

Against the background of rising expectations of a reduced economic role for the state in Singapore, in chapter 5 Garry Rodan submits a different view. He emphasises the continuing centrality of the state in Singapore's economic development, but argues that the precise form of this role is very definitely in transition. This is tied to a new phase in capital accumulation that entails a fuller official embrace of internationalisation and promotion of the so-called 'knowledge economy'—a direction that has gathered momentum since the Asian crisis struck. In the process, the state is instituting corporate governance reforms, opening up more of the domestic economy to foreign competition, and selectively promoting the domestic bourgeoisie. Attempts are also being made to forge new alliances between state-owned companies and international capital. Crucially, Rodan locates the economic and political interests of the People's Action Party (PAP) as integral to this direction. He also draws out the various conflicts arising from the economic restructuring process—most notably, rising inequalities—and their political implications.

Khoo Boo Teik's analysis of Malaysia in chapter 6 demonstrates how extensive state economic intervention has been intricately related to 'a political agenda of social engineering', and one that has given expression at various times to open conflict. Khoo rejects the popular portrayal of conflict as fundamentally ethnic and argues, instead, that such tensions 'encompass class conflicts, the emergence of Malay capital, rise and decline of bureaucratic interests, politicisation of business, aggrandisement of powerful conglomerates, and promotion of economic nationalism'. Yet if the contemporary Malaysian political economy is essentially characterised by a continuing power structure divided among the interests of the state, foreign capital, and domestic capital, Khoo nevertheless discerns important changes afoot. The freedom of manoeuvre by the state is being curtailed to some extent as the importance of foreign direct investment declines relative to that of mobile global finance and speculative capital. Bumiputera commercial and industrial conglomerates have also emerged alongside the traditional ethnic-Chinese capital. The dynamic relations among these three centres of power will chart Malaysia's future.

In chapter 7, Melanie Beresford's focus is on Vietnam—a case of transition from a planned to a market economy, which formally began with *Doi Moi* (Renovation) in 1986. This is a transition born out of coalitions between the political leaders and interests standing to benefit from the reforms. However, the trajectory of the Vietnamese political economy is unlikely to see a wholesale shift towards a conventional capitalist economy. Rather, state business interests will remain a powerful brake on the establishment of an economy that is founded primarily on private property. Concern within the party and bureaucracy about the potential for private capital interests to develop a power base for opposition parties acts as another moderating influence.

Kanishka Jayasuriya and Andrew Rosser begin the set of comparative and thematic chapters with a look at the differential progress towards economic liberalisation after the Asian crisis in Malaysia, Singapore, Thailand, and Indonesia. In chapter 8, they argue that these variances are a function of contrasting domestic political and social variables, institutional capacities, and the extent to which the crisis has shifted the balance of power among coalitions of interest. The strong resonances across these countries' development strategies during the boom years, characterised by interventionist states, are diminishing after the crisis. Whereas economic liberalisation reform is under way in Thailand, little is to be found in Indonesia. Meanwhile, an official nationalist backlash is evident in Malaysia and a policy of 'offensive adjustment', rather than wholesale winding-back of state intervention, is occurring in Singapore. Similarly, the crisis appears to have delivered a severe blow to oligarchic and crony capitalism centring around the Soeharto family in Indonesia, but has had much less such impact in neighbouring Malaysia.

In chapter 9, Frederic Deyo investigates the implications for labour of sustained industrialisation in South-East Asia. He identifies the growing global influence of neo-liberal ideas and the adoption of more flexible post-Fordist production systems as crucial dynamics. The net effect of these has been to limit the capacity of enlarged working classes to significantly enhance their political and organisational strength. Instead, elite strategies of industrial management are being consolidated—a pattern not fundamentally altered by the effects of the Asian economic crisis. Deyo argues that it is precisely the continued exclusion of the popular sector from politics that fosters a measure of tolerance by elites for parliamentary institutions. The price of this is, however, potential political instability in the long term, which might even include hostility from within the masses towards democratic institutions that are perceived as mechanisms of exclusion by the elites.

Mark Beeson's description of Japan as a 'quasi-hegemon' in South-East Asia arises out of an analysis of that country's considerable influence in the region, which is ultimately constrained from realising its full potential by a comparatively timid foreign policy. In chapter 10, he argues that economic influence is not matched by political influence, resulting in a neo-mercantilist character to Japan's relations with the region. Huge investments and trading significance, as well as the historical role as exemplar of the developmental state, have been accompanied by a reluctance to adopt an independent and comprehensive foreign policy. This is, in part, due to dependence on the United States for security, argues Beeson. Most recently, however, domestic conflicts of interest over the restructuring of the Japanese economy serve to impair the capacity and inclination of a Japanese leadership role in the region.

Notes

1 We gratefully acknowledge the invaluable constructive criticisms on an earlier draft from Mark Beeson, Jane Hutchison, and Kanishka Jayasuriya.

2 Mancur Olson (1982) saw economic growth in democratic political systems strangled by vested interests seeking to share the spoils of growth (distributional coalitions), preventing good policy in the public interest, and diverting scarce resources from productive investment.

3 Approaches influenced by this version of political economy, juxtaposing rational economic technocrats seeking market reforms with self-seeking officials and politicians dealing in rents, corruption, and grandiose schemes, were applied widely to government in South-East Asia (Liddle 1992; Soesastro 1989; Christensen and Ammar 1993).

4 Thelen and Steinmo (1992:10–11) argue that historical institutionalism is important precisely because it bridges the divide between state-centred and society-centred theories. We contend that these theoretical proclivities, associated with 'systems-level' theories are, in fact, reproduced in 'intermediate-level' historical institutionalist literature.

5 The concept of 'historical pathway' is explained by Zysman (1994:243) thus: 'The particular historical course of each nation's development creates a political economy with a distinctive institutional structure for governing the markets of labour, land, capital and goods. The institutional structure induces particular kinds of corporate and government behaviour by constraining and by laying out a logic to the market and policy-making process that is particular to that political economy.'

6 Immergut (1998:26) contends that historical institutionalists account for change by arguing that institutions are never in equilibrium. However, the literature suggests that there is more attention to explaining persistence rather than change. In any case, pointing to constant change does not amount to an explanation of that change. It is noteworthy that the Asian crisis was a surprise to analysts (Haggard 2000a:130) who focused on institutional stability rather than change. They also failed to assess the changed global and regional context in which institutions operated.

7 A term coined to designate the rapidly growing and industrialising economies of East and South-East Asia.

8 Of course, markets had long existed. In this context, neo-classical theorists were concerned with the development of 'free markets'.

9 Some South-East Asian leaders portrayed 'culture' as an ingredient of the 'Asian model' and pronounced it a political asset. They argued the need for preserving authoritarian political arrangements because, as parts of 'Asian culture', they were essential for economic success (see Robison 1996; Rodan 1996).

10 For social conflict accounts of Malaysia see Jomo (1988); and for Singapore see Rodan (1989).

11 Initial IMF interventions drove these economies into deeper recession.

12 Indeed, the *Economist* (1998), ever the champion of the orthodox neo-classical model, was critical of the IMF's rescue packages—because they protected foreign lenders from the full force of the Asian crisis.

13 In explaining why some countries proved better at constructing efficient institutions, Douglass North (1994:366–7) relied heavily on culture as the factor driving both resistance and innovation, arguing that it was the 'mental models of the actors that will shape choices'.

14 In one report, the World Bank (1991:6–7) insists that: 'While donors and outsiders can contribute resources and ideas to improve governance, for change to be effective, it must be rooted firmly in the societies concerned, and cannot be imposed from outside'.

15 Here the World Bank drew on the earlier academic research of Putnam (1993) who had argued the importance of civil society—through the trust and networks of support and reciprocity that characterise it—to development.

16 World Bank Vice-President Mark Malloch Brown (1999) thus asserted that: 'it is impossible to sustain economic growth, commerce, and trade without investing in the poor. If the world's economic leaders design a new international financial architecture that does not provide for the poor, they will be building on sand.' It is worth noting that the bank was a latecomer to social safety nets, via the criticism of agencies such as Unicef and UNDP, and bitter experiences in Eastern Europe (see Deacon et al. 1997).

17 He does not, however, explain how it is that these same conditions existed for most of the period of the boom after 1985. This example indicates a tendency in historical institutionalist analysis to identify the same institutions with both successes and failures in economic policy and implementation.

18 In this vein, Haggard (2000b:220) contends: 'Reducing East Asia's vulnerability is therefore not simply a question of changing policies, but of reconsidering the privileged position domestic business has enjoyed during the high growth period, and subjecting business to greater regulatory restraint and accountability'.

19 The idea that democracy posed a threat to the East Asian model of development, long expressed by authoritarian leaders in the region, had academic subscribers (see Wu 1996).

20 Gill (1999) maintains that the problems of over-production were compounded by the unprecedented availability of credit associated with the market liberalisations of the 1990s. High-risk investments in construction and real estate made possible by overseas borrowings added to the vulnerability of these economies.

21 Bernard was taking particular exception to the work of Weiss (1997).

22 Malaysia provided a dramatic model in defying the IMF by imposing capital controls and priming its banks with state funds. Despite the corporate and banking meltdown in Indonesia and the rapid unravelling of the seemingly indestructible Soeharto regime, old interests and power have also proven resilient. Corporate restructuring and bank recapitalisation is bitterly contested. Even in Thailand, where the IMF and further liberalisation were initially welcomed, the vigour of opposition has been surprising.

References

Amin, Samir (1974) *Accumulation on a World Scale*, New York: Monthly Review Press.

Amin, Samir (1976) *Unequal Development*, New York: Monthly Review Press.

Amsden, Alice (1989) *Asia's Next Giant: South Korea and Late Industrialization*, New York: Oxford University Press.

Anek Laothamatas (1992) *Business Associations and the New Political Economy of Thailand: From Bureaucratic Polity to Liberal Corporatism*, Boulder: Westview Press.

Arndt, H.W. and Hal Hill (eds) (1999) *Southeast Asia's Economic Crisis: Origins, Lessons, and the Way Forward*, St Leonards, NSW: Allen and Unwin.

Asian Wall Street Journal (AWSJ) (1997), 13 November 1997, p. 1.

Awanohara, Susumu (1993) 'The magnificent eight', *Far Eastern Economic Review*, 22 July:79–80.

AWSJ, see *Asian Wall Street Journal (AWSJ)*.

Badhan, Pranab (1989) 'The New Institutional Economics and Development Theory: A Brief Critical Assessment', *World Development*, 17(9):1389–95.

Balassa, Bela (1971) 'Trade policies in developing countries', *American Economic Review; Papers and Proceedings*, 61:168–87.

Bates, Robert (1981) *Markets and States in Tropical Africa*, Berkeley: University of California Press.

Bauer, Peter T. (1970) *Dissent on Development*, London: Weidenfeld and Nicholson.

Bello, Walden (1998a) 'The Rise and Fall of South-East Asia's Economy', *The Ecologist*, 28(1):9–17.

Bello, Walden (1998b) 'Testimony of Walden Bello before Banking Oversight Subcommittee, Banking and Financial Services Committee', US House of Representatives, 21 April, <www.igc.org/dgap/walden.html>.

Bello, Walden (2000a) 'Davos 2000: Global Conspiracy or Capitalist Circus?', *Focus on Trade*, 45 (February).

Bello, Walden (2000b) 'UNCTAD X: An Opportunity Lost?', *Focus on Trade*, 46 (February).

Bello, Walden (2000c) 'Meltzer Report on Bretton Woods Twins Builds a Case for Abolition But Hesitates', *Focus on Trade*, 48 (April).

Bello, Walden and Anuradha Mittal (2000) 'Dangerous Liaisons: Progressives, the Right, and the Anti-China Trade Campaign', *Focus on Trade*, 50 (May).

Bello, Walden and Stephanie Rosenfeld (1990) *Dragons in Distress: Asia's Miracle Economies in Crisis*, San Francisco: Institute for Food and Development Policy.

Bello, Walden, Shea Cunningham and Li Kheng Poh (1998) *A Siamese Tragedy: Development and Disintegration in Modern Thailand*, London: Zed Books.

Bennett, Douglas C. and Kenneth E. Sharp (1985) 'The Worldwide Automobile Industry and its Implications', in Richard S. Newfarmer (ed.) *Profits, Progress and Poverty: Case Studies of International Industries in Latin America*, Notre Dame: Notre Dame University Press, pp 193–226.

Bernard, Mitchell (1999) 'East Asia's Tumbling Dominoes: Financial Crises and the Myth of the Regional Model', in Leo Panitch and Colin Leys (eds) *The Socialist*

Register 1999: Global Capitalism Versus Democracy, Woodbridge, Suffolk: The Merlin Press, pp 178–208.

Bhattacharya, Amar and Mari Pangestu (1992) 'Indonesian Development Transformation Since 1965 and the Role of Public Policy', World Bank Workshop on the Role of Government and East Asian Success, East–West Center, Hawaii, 19–21 November.

Brenner, Robert (1977) 'The origins of capitalist development: a critique of neo-Smithian Marxism', *New Left Review*, 104:25–93.

Buchanan, James M. and Tullock, Gordon (1962) *The Calculus of Consent*, Anne Arbor: University of Michigan Press.

Bullard, Nicola, Walden Bello and Kamal Malhotra (1998) 'Taming the Tigers: The IMF and the Asian Crisis', in K.S. Jomo (ed.) *Tigers in Trouble. Financial Governance, Liberalisation and Crises in East Asia*, London: Zed Books, pp 85–136.

Camdessus, Michel (1998) 'The IMF and Good Governance', Address at Transparency International, Paris, 21 January, <www.imf.org/external/np/speeches/1998/012198.htm>.

Cardoso, Fernando Henrique and Enzo Faletto (1979) *Dependency and Development in Latin America*, Berkeley: University of California Press.

Chaudhry, Kiren Aziz (1994) 'Economic liberalization and the lineages of the rentier state', *Comparative Politics*, 27(1):1–25.

Chaudhry, Kirin Azizi (1997) *The Price of Wealth: Economic Institutions in the Middle East*, Thaca and London: Cornell University Press.

Chossudovsky, Michel (1998) 'Financial Warfare Triggers Global Economic Crisis', Third World Network, <www.twnside.org.sg/title/trig-cn.htm>.

Christensen, Scott and Ammar Siamwalla (1993) 'Beyond Patronage: Tasks for the Thai State', Paper presented at Thailand Development Research Institue 1993 Year-End Conference, 10–11 December, Jomtien.

Christensen, Scott, David Dollar, Ammar Siamwalla and Pakorn Vichyanond (1993) *The Lessons of East Asia, Thailand: The Institutional and Political Underpinnings of Growth*, Washington, D.C.: World Bank.

Deacon, Bob, Michelle Hulse and Paul Stubbs (1997) *Global Social Policy. International Organisations and the Future of Welfare*, London: Sage Publications.

Diamond, Larry (ed.) (1993) *Political Culture and Democracy in Developing Countries*, Boulder: Lynne Rienner Publishers.

Diamond, Larry, Juan J. Linz and Seymour Martin Lipset (eds) (1989) *Democracy in Developing Countries, Volume Three, Asia*, Boulder: Lynne Rienner Publishers.

Doner, Richard (1992) 'Limits of state strength: toward an institutional view of economic development', *World Politics*, 44(3):398–431.

Doner, Richard F. and Ansil Ramsey (1997) 'Competitive Clientelism and Economic Governance: The Case of Thailand', in Sylvia Maxfield and Ben Ross Schneider (eds) *Business and the State in Developing Countries*, Ithaca: Cornell University Press, pp 237–76.

Doner, Richard F. and Ansil Ramsey (1999) 'Thailand: From Economic Miracle to Economic Crisis', in Karl D. Jackson (ed.) *Asian Contagion. The Causes and Consequences of a Financial Crisis*, Boulder: Westview Press, pp 171–207.

Doner, Richard F. and Gary Hawes (1995) 'The Political Economy of Growth in Southeast and Northeast Asia', in Manochehr Dorraj (ed.) *The Changing Political Economy of the Third World*, Boulder: Lynne Rienner Publishers, pp 145–85.

Economist (1998) 'Risk in penance-free rescue', 10 January, p. 13.

Evans, Peter (1979) *Dependent Development: The Alliance of Multinational, State, and Local Capital in* Brazil, Princeton: Princeton University Press.

Evans, Peter (1992) 'The state as problem and solution: predation, embedded autonomy and structural change', in Stephan R. Haggard and Robert Kaufman (eds) *The Politics of Economic Adjustment*, Princeton: Princeton University Press, pp 139–81.

Evans, Peter (1995) *Embedded Autonomy: States and Industrial Transformation*, Princeton, NJ: Princeton University Press.

Far Eastern Economic Review (FEER) (1994a), 18 August 1994, p. 5.

Far Eastern Economic Review (FEER) (1994b), 24 November 1994, pp 43–9.

FEER, see *Far Eastern Economic Review (FEER)*.

Frank, André Gunder (1967) *Capitalism and Underdevelopment in Latin America*, New York: Monthly Review Press.

Frank, André Gunder (1969) *Latin America: Underdevelopment or Revolution*, New York: Monthly Review Press.

Frankel, J.A. (1998) 'The Asian Model, The Miracle, The Crisis and the Fund', Paper delivered at U.S. International Trade Commission, April, <www.stern.nyu.edu/~nroubini/asia/AsiaHomepage.html>.

Fukuyama, Francis (1992) *The End of History and the Last Man*, New York: Avon Books.

Gereffi, Gary (1982) *The Pharmaceutical Industry and Dependency in the Third World*, Princeton: Princeton University Press.

Gill, Stephen (1999) 'The Geopolitics of the Asian Crisis', *Monthly Review*, 50(10):1–9.

Gomez, James and K. S. Jomo (1999) *Malaysia's Political Economy: Politics, Patronage and Profits*, Cambridge: Cambridge University Press.

Haggard, Stephan (2000a) 'The Politics of the Asian Financial Crisis', *Journal of Democracy*, 11(2):130–44.

Haggard, Stephan (2000b) *The Political Economy of the Asian Financial Crisis*, Washington, D.C.: Institute for International Economics.

Hart-Landsberg, Martin (1991) 'Dragons in Distress: Asia's Miracle Economies in Crisis' (review article), *Monthly Review*, 43(4):57–63.

Hewison, Kevin (1989*) Bankers and Bureaucrats: Capital and the Role of the State in Thailand*, New Haven: Yale University Southeast Asia Monographs Series.

Hewison, Kevin (2000a) 'Resisting Globalization: A Study of Localism in Thailand', *Pacific Review*, 13(2):279–96.

Hewison, Kevin (2000b) 'Thailand's Capitalism Before and After the Economic Crisis', in Richard Robison et al. (eds) *Politics and Markets in the Wake of the Asian Crisis*, London: Routledge, pp 192–211.

Hewison, Kevin, Richard Robison and Garry Rodan (eds) (1993) *Southeast Asia in the 1990s: Authoritarianism, Democracy and Capitalism*, St Leonards, NSW: Allen and Unwin.

Higgott, Richard et al. (1985) 'Theories of development and underdevelopment: implications for the study of Southeast Asia', in Richard Higgott and Richard Robison (eds) *Southeast Asia: Essays in the Political Economy of Structural Change*, London: Routledge and Kegan Paul, pp 16–61.

Hoogvelt, Ankie M.M. (1982) *The Third World in Global Development*, London: Macmillan.

Huntington, Samuel P. (1968) *Political Order in Changing Societies*, New Haven: Yale University Press.

Huntington, Samuel (1991) *The Third Wave: Democratization in the Late Twentieth Century*, Norman: University of Oklahoma Press.

Hutchcroft, Paul D. (1991) 'Oligarchs and cronies in the Philippine state: the politics of patrimonial plunder', *World Politics*, 43:414–50.

Hutchcroft, Paul (1999) 'After the Fall: Prospects for Political and Institutional Reform in Post-Crisis Thailand and the Philippines', *Government and Opposition*, 33(4):473–97.

Immergut, Ellen M. (1998) 'The Theoretical Core of the New Institutionalism', *Politics & Society*, 26(1):5–34.

Jayasuriya, Kanishka (2000) 'See Through a Glass, Darkly: Models of the Asian Currency Crisis of 1997–98', in Holger Henke and Ian Boxill (eds) *The End of the 'Asian Model'?*, Amsterdam/Philadelphia: Hohn Benjamins, pp 141–61.

Johnson, Chalmers (1982) *MITI and the Japanese Miracle: The Growth of Industrial Policy, 1925–1975*, Stanford CA: Stanford University Press.

Johnson, Chalmers (1987) 'Political Institutions and Economic Performance: A Comparative Analysis of the Government-Business Relationship in Japan, South Korea and Taiwan', in Frederic C. Deyo (ed.) *The Political Economy of the New Asian Industrialism*, Ithaca, NY: Cornell University Press, pp 136–64.

Johnson, Chalmers, Laura Tyson and John Zysman (eds) (1989) *Politics and Productivity: The Real Story of Why Japan Works*, Cambridge: Ballinger.

Jomo, K.S. (1988) *A Question of Class: Capital, the State, and Uneven Development in Malaya*, New York: Monthly Review Press.

Katznelson, Ira (1998) 'The Doleful Dance of Politics and Policy: Can Historical Institutionalism Make a Difference?', *American Political Science Review*, 92(1):191–7.

Kay, Geoffrey (1975) *Development of Underdevelopment: A Marxist Analysis*, New York: St Martin's.

Khor, Martin (2000) 'Speech', Opening Session of the Millennium Forum, UN General Assembly Hall, New York, 22 May, <www.twnside.org.sg/title/mk7.htm>.

Krueger, Anne O. (1974) 'The political economy of the rent-seeking society', *American Economic Review; Papers and Proceedings*, 64:291–303.

Krueger, Anne O. (1981) 'Export-led industrial growth reconsidered', in W. Hong and L.B. Krause (eds) *Trade and Growth of the Advanced Developed Countries in the Pacific Basin*, Seoul: Korea Development Institute, pp 3–27.

Lal, Deepak (1983) *The Poverty of 'Development Economics'*, London: Institute of Economic Affairs.

Larrain, Jorge (1989) *Theories of Development: Capitalism, Colonialism and Dependency*, Cambridge: Polity Press.

Liddle, William R. (1991) 'The Relative Autonomy of the Third World Politician: Suharto and Indonesia's Economic Development in Comparative Perspective', *International Studies Quarterly*, 35:403–25.

Liddle, William R. (1992) 'The politics of development policy', *World Development*, 20(6):793–807.

Little, Ian, Tibor Scitovsky and Maurice Scott (1970) *Industry and Trade in Some Developing Countries: A Comparative Study*, London: Oxford University Press.

Little, Ian (1981) 'The experience and causes of rapid labour-intensive development in Korea, Taiwan Province, Hong Kong and Singapore; and the possibilities of emulation', in Eddy Lee (ed.) *Export-Led Industrialisation and Development*, Geneva: International Labour Organisation, pp 23–46.

Lummis, C. D. (n.d.) 'The Myth of Catch-Up', Third World Network, <www.twnside.org.sg/title/myth.htm>.

Mahathir Mohamad (1999) *A New Deal for Asia*, Kelana Jaya: Pelanduk Publications.

Matthews, Trevor and John Ravenhill, (1996) 'The neo-classical ascendancy: the Australian economic policy community and Northeast Asian economic growth', in Richard Robison (ed.) *Pathways to Asia: the Politics of Engagement*, St Leonards, NSW: Allen and Unwin, pp 131–70.

McNally, David (1999) 'Globalization on Trial: Crisis and Class Struggle in East Asia', *Monthly Review*, 50(4):1–14.

Miliband, Ralph (1989) 'Marx and the state', in Graeme Duncan (ed.) *Democracy and the Capitalist State*, Cambridge: Cambridge University Press.

Moon, Chung In and Sang-young Rhyu (2000) 'The state, structural rigidity, and the end of Asian capitalism: a comparative study of Japan and South Korea', in Richard Robison et al. (eds) *Politics and Markets in the Wake of the Asian Crisis*, London: Routledge, pp 77–98.

Nesadurai, Helen E.S. (2000) 'In Defence of National Autonomy? Malaysia's Response to the Financial Crisis', *Pacific Review*, 13(1):73–113.

North, Douglass C. (1981) *Structure and Change in Economic History*, New York: Norton.

North, Douglass C. (1994) 'Economic Performance Through Time', *American Economic Review*, 84(3):359–68.

North, Douglass C. (1995) 'The New Institutional Economics and Third World Development', in John Harris, Jane Hunter and Colin M. Lewis (eds) *The New Institutional Economics and Third World Development*, London: Routledge, 17–26.

Olson, Mancur (1982) *The Rise and Decline of Nations: Economic Growth, Stagflation and Social Rigidities*, New Haven: Yale University Press.

Panitch, Leo and Colin Leys (eds) (1999) *The Socialist Register 1999: Global Capitalism Versus Democracy*, Woodbridge, Suffolk: The Merlin Press.

Parsons, Talcott (1951) *The Social System*, New York: Free Press.

Peters, B. Guy (1999) *Institutional Theory in Political Science. The 'New Institutionalism'*, London: Pinter.

Putnam, R. (1993) *Making Democracy Work: Civic Traditions in Modern Italy*, Princeton, NJ: Princeton University Press.

Raghaven, Chakravarthi (n.d.) 'The Perils of Excessive Financial Liberalisation', Third World Network, <www.twnside.org.sg/peril-cn.htm>.

Robison, Richard (1986) *Indonesia: The Rise of Capital*, St Leonards, NSW: Allen and Unwin.

Robison, Richard (1996) 'The Politics of "Asian Values"', *Pacific Review*, 9(3):309–27.

Robison, Richard and Andrew Rosser (2000) 'Surviving the Meltdown: Liberal Reform and Political Oligarchy in Indonesia', in Richard Robison et al. (eds) *Politics and Markets in the Wake of the Asian Crisis*, London: Routledge, pp 171–91.

Robison, Richard, Mark Beeson, Kanishka Jayasuriya and Hyuk-Rae Kim (eds) (2000) *Politics and Markets in the Wake of the Asian Crisis*, London: Routledge.

Rodan, Garry (1989) *The Political Economy of Singapore's Industrialization: National State and International Capital*, Basingstoke: Macmillan.

Rodan, Garry (1996) 'The internationalization of ideological conflict: Asia's new significance', *Pacific Review*, 9(3):328–51.

Roubini, N., G. Corsetti and P. Pesenti (1998) 'What Caused the Asian Currency and Financial Crisis?', unpublished paper, <www.stern.nyu.edu/~nroubini/asia/AsiaHomepage.html>.

Roxborough, Ian (1979) *Theories of Underdevelopment*, London: Macmillan.

Schamis, Hector E. (1999) 'Distributional Coalitions and the Politics of Economic Reform in Latin America', *World Politics*, 51 (January):236–68.

Soesastro, Hadi M. (1989) 'The political economy of deregulation in Indonesia', *Asia Survey*, 29(9):853–69.

Stiglitz, Joseph (1998) 'Towards a New Paradigm for Development: Strategies, Policies, and Processes', Prebisch Lecture at UNCTAD, Geneva, 19 October, <www.worldbank.org/html/extdr/extme/jssp101998.htm>.

Stiglitz, Joseph (1999) 'Participation and Development: Perspectives from the Comprehensive Development Paradigm', Paper at International Conference on Democracy, Market Economy and Development', Seoul, 27 February, <www.worldbank.org/html/extdr/extme/js-022799/index.htm>.

Tabb, William K. (1998) 'The East Asian Financial Crisis', *Monthly Review*, 50(2):24–39.

Tabb, William K. (1999) 'Labor and the Imperialism of Finance', *Monthly Review*, 51(5):1–13.

Thelen, Kathleen and Sven Steinmo (1992) 'Historical Institutionalism in Comparative Politics', in Sven Steinmo, Kathleen Thelen and Frank Longstreth (eds) *Structuring Politics. Historical Institutionalism in Comparative Analysis*, New York: Cambridge University Press, pp 1–32.

Wade, Robert (1990) *Governing the Market: Economic Theory and the Role of Government in East Asian Industrialization*, Princeton: Princeton University Press.

Wade, Robert (1998a) 'The Asian Crisis and the Global Economy: Causes, Consequences, and Cure', *Current History*, November:361–73.

Wade, Robert (1998b) 'The Asian Debt-and-Development Crisis of 1997–?: Causes and Consequences', *World Development*, 26(8):1535–53.

Wade, Robert and Frank Veneroso (1998) 'The Asian Crisis: The High Debt Model Versus the Wall Street–Treasury–IMF Complex', *New Left Review*, 228:3–23.

Weiss, Linda (1997) 'Globalization and the Myth of the Powerless State', *New Left Review*, 225, September–October:3–27.

Weiss, Linda (1998) *The Myth of the Powerless State*, Cambridge: Polity Press.

Weiss, Linda (1999) 'State Power and the Asian Crisis', *New Political Economy*, 4(3):317–42.

Weiss, Linda and John M. Hobson (1995) *States and Economic Development: A Comparative Historical Analysis*, Cambridge: Polity Press.

Weiss, Linda and John M. Hobson (2000) 'State power and economic strength revisited: what's so special about the Asian crisis?', in Richard Robison et al. (eds) *Politics and Markets in the Wake of the Asian Crisis*, London: Routledge, pp 53–74.

Williamson, J. (1994) 'In Search of a Manual for Technopols', in J. Williamson (ed.) *The Political Economy of Policy Reform*, Washington, D.C.: Institute for International Economics, pp 11–28.

Wolfe, Charles Jnr (1998) 'Blame Government for the Asian Meltdown', *Asian Wall Street Journal*, 5 February:14.

World Bank (1991) *Managing Development: The Governance Dimension. A Discussion Paper*, Washington, D.C.: World Bank.

World Bank (1993) *The East Asian Miracle: Economic Growth and Public Policy*, New York: Oxford University Press.

World Bank (1997) *World Development Report 1997*, New York: Oxford University Press.

World Bank (1998) *East Asia: The Road to Recovery*, Washington, D.C.: World Bank.

Wu Yu-Shan (1996) 'Away from Socialism: the Asian Way', *Pacific Review*, 9(3):410–41.

Zysman, John (1994) 'How Institutions Create Historically Rooted Trajectories of Growth', *Industrial and Corporate Change*, 3(1):243–83.

2

Crisis and Change in the Philippines

Jane Hutchison[1]

Introduction

If crisis marks a turning point in the political and economic affairs of a nation, the Philippines had its most significant crisis of recent times in the mid 1980s rather than in the late 1990s. In the earlier period, economic collapse set in train the end of authoritarian rule through civil protest, the reintroduction of electoral democracy, and a significant policy shift to greater economic openness. The Asian financial crisis cut short a spell of economic growth, but its impact on the Philippines was not as dramatic as elsewhere. Certainly, there was no immediate political disruption, and economic policy was not reoriented as a result. Most specifically, expectations of a furthering of market 'reforms' have not been realised, especially when there has been a resurgence, rather than a reversal, of cronyism in government circles since the crisis began (Wurfel 1999:29; de Dios 1999).

Regional meltdown in itself did not precipitate change in the Philippines because the events of 1997 were only one of a *series* of economic crises to have beset the country before, and since (de Dios 1998). Given that economic collapse is not an unfamiliar national experience, regime arrangements in the Philippines are not as closely tied to developmental success as in some other parts of the region. After decades as the laggard economy of South-East Asia (see table 2.1, page 43), the country's standing was *improved* by its relatively strong showing in the initial stages of the crisis—whereas the economic reputations of other South-East Asian countries were tarnished, some severely, as in the case of Indonesia.

For those in praise of markets, the Philippines' initial resilience was a demonstration of the essential 'correctness' of earlier efforts to liberalise the economy (Noland 2000). To appreciate why cronyism has, if anything, intensified, it is necessary to explain some of the longer-term political features of capitalist development in the Philippines. In this regard, state-centred historical institutionalists offer valuable insights into the 'weak' character of the polity and policy-making (Hutchcroft 1999). However, when 'state capacity' is viewed in terms of particular forms of rational action, important class dimensions of 'crony capitalism' in the Philippines are missed. This chapter indicates some of these.

The chapter begins by comparing different political economy perspectives on Philippines' development. Thereafter, the discussion falls into four sections. The first and second cover significant periods of economic restructuring and the competing social forces that have resulted. The third section deals with the 'weak' nature of the Philippine state and the main factors behind political and policy reforms *vis-à-vis* democratisation, market liberalisation, and state capacity in the post-Marcos era. The fourth section covers the impact of the Asian financial crisis.

Table 2.1 GDP growth for the Philippines and other ASEAN countries (%)

	Philippines	Indonesia	Malaysia	Thailand
Real GDP growth (av. 1969–98)	2.3	3.4	3.8	3.4
Real GDP growth (av. 1993–98)	3.0	1.5	3.6	1.9
Per capita real GDP growth (av. 1969–98)	0.8	2.6	2.9	2.6
Per capita real GDP growth (av 1993–98)	1.3	0.2	1.9	1.1

Source: Kongsamut and Vamvakidis (1999:10)

Political economy perspectives

Neo-classical economists attribute the generally poor economic record of the Philippines to a policy mix that 'misallocates' resources to areas of inappropriate and inefficient economic activity (Ranis 1974; Shepherd and Alburo 1991; Kongsamut and Vamvakidis 1999). They argue that for most of the postwar era protectionist trade and macroeconomic policies encouraged inefficient manufacturing for the domestic market, while also encouraging a form of business behaviour known as 'rent-seeking'. Rents are defined in the economic literature in a number of ways; however, in this context, they are understood as additional returns from government interventions in the market. Rent-*seeking* is therefore the effort applied to competition in the political arena over sources of rent—particularly quotas, tariffs, and public monopolies (Krueger 1974; Buchanan 1980). The neo-classical criticism is that 'by substituting political for economic criteria in many allocative decisions', rent-seeking is antithetical to the operation of market forces and, hence, to the development of an internationally competitive economy (Shepherd and Alburo 1991:155–6). Neo-classical economists argue that the Philippine economy grew in the mid 1990s, and was then able to avoid the worst of the regional financial crisis, in large part because political and policy changes since the late 1980s have generated a more market-oriented and competitive environment for business (Kongsamut and Vamvakidis 1999; Noland 2000).

The role of rent-seeking in the political economy of the Philippines has also been highlighted by state-centred historical institutionalists. However, these writers are less concerned with its distorting effects on the market than they are with its consequences for 'state capacity'. Drawing on the example of 'developmental states' in East Asia, they maintain that the Philippines' poor economic record is the direct result of a 'weak' or 'patrimonial' state (Hutchcroft 1994; Hutchcroft 1999; Rivera 1994a; Evans 1994). Particularly indebted to Weber (1968) on bureaucracy and rational action, they argue that the Philippine polity is unable to steer the course of national economic development because it is constantly subject to the *particularistic* demands of a wealthy elite or oligarchy. This high level of political patronage (or cronyism) compares with the strong 'institutional autonomy' of developmental states 'which is derived from the differentiation of state institutions from the private interests of individuals within society' (Weiss and Hobson 2000:54).[2] The focus of this perspective is thus on the national economic consequences of effective and ineffective states in relation to business governance.

Historical institutionalists direct attention to the organisational form of the state. In this regard, the Philippine state's low capacity for 'legal-rational' action is mostly explained by the persistent encroachment of the personal and family-based interests of the oligarchy on government processes (see Hutchcroft 1991; McCoy 1993). But this account of the particularism or personalism of socioeconomic relations can beg the question of the oligarchy's *class*-based interests and actions in politics and business (Pinches 1992:400). In addition to the institutional aspects of crony capitalism in the Philippines, it is necessary to consider the class capacities of those involved. Class capacities can be defined as 'the capacities of a given class to act in relation to others and the forms of organisation and practice they thereby develop' (Therborn 1983:38). State-centred historical institutionalists miss the class processes in capitalist profit-making when they imply that the wealth and power of the oligarchy is almost entirely bound up with political patronage.

Whereas the historical institutionalists focus on the quality of state–business relations, other approaches direct attention to the organising capacities of alternative social forces. In this volume for example, Deyo (chapter 9) reviews factors behind the industrial and political marginalisation of labour in South-East Asia. But in the Philippines, since the fall of Marcos, there has been considerable scholarly interest in the political mobilisation of various popular forces through non-governmental organisations (NGOs)[3] (Magno 1993; Clarke 1998; Silliman and Noble 1998; Magadia 1999). Interest in this area has been specifically sparked by the role that NGOs might play in deepening democracy and achieving a more equitable distribution of social and economic resources. The focus is thus on how the political space for collective interests other than those of the oligarchy might be enlarged as capitalist development proceeds.

The socioeconomic inequalities arising from capitalist development have been also the particular concern of dependency theorists. But more than the social conflict approach being proposed in this chapter, they are concerned with injustices that arise from the condition of national dependency, considered to be an outcome of trade and investment flows and the part played by the United States, the World Bank, and International Monetary Fund (IMF) in promoting market liberalisation (Bello et al. 1982; Scipes 1999; Bello 2000). From this perspective, the Asian financial crisis was the inevitable outcome of 'a liberal, free market economy that was greatly dependent on foreign capital inflows and foreign markets' (Bello 2000:239–40). Dependency perspectives are important in the Philippine context in that they still influence the thinking of many development NGOs against the prescriptions of neo-classical economists by providing a structural critique of market-based exploitation.

The next section of the chapter covers major turning points in the development of the Philippine economy: the rise of commerical and export agriculture; import-substitution industrialisation (ISI); and the subsequent expansion of export manufacturing. As well, changes in international lending and investment are considered—as they have affected levels of public and private debt. This discussion ends by noting that, in the lead-up to the 1997 crisis, the Philippine economy was less exposed to international capital flows than others in the region.

Economic transformations

Export agriculture

The commercialisation of Philippine agriculture began in the late eighteenth century, under Spanish rule. When, in the first half of the next century, the country's ports were opened to international shipping, the growing of crops such as sugar, abaca, and tobacco for an overseas market was stimulated (Cushner 1971). As manufactures were imported from the United Kingdom and the United States, a 'colonial' pattern of trade soon emerged. This persisted into the early part of the twentieth century when, as a colony of the United States, the Philippines was granted preferential access to that country's large and lucrative market for agricultural commodities. Notably, in the 1930s, the sugar industry expanded to contribute 30 per cent of national income, 43 per cent of government revenue (directly or indirectly), and 65 per cent of the value of total exports (Brown 1989:204).

Import-substitution industrialisation

During the Pacific War the Philippines was occupied by the Japanese and its economy virtually destroyed. Despite gaining formal independence in 1946, the political economy of development continued to be influenced by ongoing ties with the United States. Notwithstanding a renewed free trade agreement with that country, export agriculture was slow to recover at a time when imports of manufactures were fuelled by inflows of war rehabilitation funds. In only three years, a resultant imbalance in trade threatened to bankrupt the nation by draining its reserves of foreign currency. In response, the government introduced import and currency exchange controls in 1949.

The impact of these controls was dramatic. The country entered an era of rapid industrialisation as manufacturing expanded from 8 per cent of GDP in 1950 to 20 per cent in 1960—agriculture falling from 42 to 26 per cent over the same period (Jayasuriya 1987:85) (see table 2.2, page 47). In the region at the time, this level of structural change and economic growth was unprecedented and the Philippines was touted as Asia's second newly industrialising nation after Japan. However, this form of protectionism altered the composition of imports, rather than reducing their actual levels (Ranis 1974:4). As restrictions were mainly placed on 'non-essential' consumer items, imports of raw materials and capital goods continued to grow. At the end of the 1950s the Philippines thus continued to experience balance-of-payments difficulties. Meanwhile, manufacturing growth slowed once the limits of the domestic market were reached as income levels for the bulk of the population failed to rise.

In the early 1960s, controls on foreign exchange were lifted and the peso was devalued by almost half against the US dollar. These changes had a 'serious but not devastating effect' on the manufacturing sector (Snow 1983:26). Profits fell, leading to the closure of some firms, but there seems to have been no major sectoral or intra-firm restructuring as a result. Import-substitution manufacturing thus 'stagnated rather than declined' into the late 1960s, largely because tariffs were introduced which reproduced the structure of protection in favour of consumer items over

Table 2.2 Structure of GDP of the Philippines (%)

	Agriculture	Industry (manufacture in brackets)	Services
1950	42	14 (8)	44
1960	26	28 (20)	46
1970	28	30 (23)	42
1980	23	37 (25)	40
1990	22	35 (25)	43
1998	17	32 (22)	51

Sources: Jayasuriya (1987:85); World Bank (1999b)

intermediate and capital goods (Shepherd and Alburo 1991:206). Although the lifting of controls and devaluation favoured exports of primary products, they coincided with a fall in the world price of these commodities. As a result, the value of imports continued to rise against the value of exports (Boyce 1993:253).

Export restructuring

During the 1970s, various transformations in the world economy converged to influence the later course of economic development in the Philippines. Amid ongoing falls in international prices for agricultural commodities, in 1974 the United States government did not extend the allowable quota on sugar imports from the Philippines. When the world price for sugar fell from 67 cents per pound in 1974 to a low of 7 cents in 1978, the industry was hit very hard. Billig (1994:666) reports that the people of the southern island of Negros 'recall these years as the time when [unsold] sugar was stored in swimming pools, on basketball courts, and even in schools and churches'. World sugar prices rose again in the early 1980s but, by that time, President Marcos had installed one of his 'cronies' as head of the government sugar-marketing authority. Price increases were not passed on to the growers, production was halved, and sugar workers squeezed to the point of starvation (Billig 1994:666–7).

To a small extent, the decline in the value of traditional exports such as sugar and coconuts has been compensated by the expansion of exports of plantation crops (particularly pineapples), fish, and livestock. However, of far greater significance has been the restructuring that has resulted from the growth in exports of 'non-traditional' manufactures, especially garments and electronics. Between 1970 and 1985, the contribution of 'non-traditional' manufactures to the value of total exports increased from 7 per cent to 60 per cent, at the same time as the value of traditional exports fell from 92 per cent to 28 per cent (Montes 1989:71). By 1998, the contribution of 'non-traditional' exports had lifted further to 88 per cent (see table 2.3, below). A feature of this restructuring in the 1990s was the growth in exports of electronics which the World Bank (1999a:47) describes as marking 'a clear long-term tendency' for the composition of exports from the Philippines to 'shift from technologically simple to complex products'. Indeed, the Philippines is now ahead of its neighbours in this regard (see table 2.4, below). In contrast, the garments industry is losing international competitiveness at both the price-sensitive and quality ends of the market, as are other labour-intensive manufactures (ADB 2000:21).

Table 2.3 Structure of Philippines exports (by value) (%)

	1970	1990	1994	1998
Fuels	23	18	13	6
Other primary commodities	70	11	7	3
Manufacturing	7	70	79	88
Electronics	–	24	37	59
Other	–	1	1	3

Sources: Montes (1989:69); World Bank (1999a:85)

Table 2.4 Technological structure of manufactured exports (%)

	Resource-based	Low-tech	Medium-tech	High-tech
Philippines	6	19	7	68
Indonesia	35	42	8	15
Thailand	14	36	14	36
Malaysia	18	13	9	60
Singapore	13	8	14	65

Source: World Bank (1999a:49)

Finally, in the 1970s, labour itself also become a major Philippines' export. The oil boom generated demand for construction and domestic workers in the Middle East. However, more recently, workers from the Philippines have been also employed on contract in large numbers in other countries in the Asian region. Approximately 55 per cent of these workers are now women, mainly in domestic and personal services such as entertainment.[4] With 5 million workers overseas (or just more than 15 per cent of the labour force), the Philippines is the largest exporter of labour in Asia (World Bank 1999a:16, 88; Tigno 1997). The remittances of these workers have helped to lift and maintain consumer spending in the domestic economy, despite the recurrence of economic crises.

Foreign debt crisis

In the 1970s, growth in the Philippine economy was largely financed by international loans to government (Montes 1989:75–9). Public overseas borrowing began in the mid 1960s, but greatly expanded in the following decade as commercial bank lending increased and the Marcos regime sought to provide credit for a range of development programs. Consistent with the cronyism of the regime, many of the loans were dispensed for entirely political ends, and inadequate controls meant that a large proportion simply went offshore as capital flight (Boyce 1993). By the end of the 1970s, sources of cheap commercial loans were disappearing and the government found it more difficult to cover existing debt with new borrowings. Consequently, it became increasingly dependent on the IMF and the World Bank and so more vulnerable to pressures for structural reform. A crucial juncture in the debt crisis was reached in 1983 when the government was forced to place a 90-day hold on its debt repayments. Over the next two years the economy went into recession. GDP fell by 6 per cent in 1984, and by 4.3 per cent in 1985, with industry faring worst with falls of 10.2 per cent in both years (World Bank 1989:3). President Marcos was finally driven from office in early 1986, but foreign debt contributed greatly to the fiscal difficulties of the next administration. President Aquino made debt repayment a high priority—often reducing public sending in areas such as infrastructure development—to retain access to multilateral and Japanese bilateral funds (Jayasuriya 1992:57).

Debt repayment was made more manageable by a restructuring agreement in the early 1990s. But the prolonged economic and political crisis saw the Philippines mostly miss out on the considerable wave of Japanese investment that entered South-East Asia from the mid 1980s (Bello 2000:241–2). Keen not to have this scenario repeated, in the early 1990s the Ramos administration sought to attract new international flows of private capital. As a result, net foreign direct investment (FDI) grew 1.6 times in three years, while net portfolio investment increased almost 17 times over the same period—to levels 2.3 times above that for FDI (de Dios 1998:66). In addition, borrowing by the corporate sector rose more than 100 per cent as a share of GDP between 1990 and 1997 (Noland 2000:403). The point to make here is that, with financial deregulation, international borrowing is centred on the private sector, and not on government, as it was some decades earlier.

Table 2.5 Philippines investment and trade as % of GDP, 1985–95

	Investment	Exports	Imports
1985	14.35	24.02	21.89
1995	23.29	43.50	53.12

Source: de Dios (1998:84)

As a late-boomer, the Philippines' exposure to speculative investment and private debt accumulation before the crisis was significantly below that of its neighbours. This is one reason for the country being less affected by the dramatic drop in investor confidence that was the Asian meltdown (World Bank 1999a:16; Noland 2000). As well, in regional terms, the Philippines' financial system was comparatively robust after earlier reforms, particularly in relation to levels of capitalisation, the percentage of non-performing loans, and exposure to the property market (Noland 2000:405–7). In short, the Philippines did better in the initial stages of the 1997 crisis because it had emerged only relatively recently from its own national economic and institutional crisis under Marcos.

Something of the depth of the Philippines' development malaise over many decades is revealed by the observation that, between 1950 and 1996, national per capita income *fell* from one-seventh to one-tenth of that of the United States, whereas for the same period 'all of its neighbours improved, some spectacularly' (Kongsamut and Vamvakidid 1999:10). Of course, the effects of this fall have been unequally distributed internally. Even before the financial crisis, more than a third of Filipinos (37.5 per cent) were living below the official poverty line, compared with about 11 per cent for the populations of Indonesia and Thailand (World Bank 2000:116). Capitalist development in the Philippines has thus been associated with disparities (in the ownership and control of productive assets, and in personal wealth) that are more commonly found in Latin America. An explanation for this lies in the uneven class capacities of different social forces and interests in Philippines' society. The next part of the chapter discusses power relations beyond the state which neo-classical and neo-Weberian historical institutionalists overlook, albeit for different reasons.

Social structure and development

Land and labour

Long a dominant force in the political economy of Philippine development, the class power of the oligarchy has its origins in the private ownership of land for commercial agriculture. In the period up to the Pacific War, there was a level of domestic capital accumulation in the Philippines, centred on land and its produce, which was unparalleled in South-East Asia at that time (Rivera 1994a:26). From the start, the forms of labour control exerted by the landowners varied according to region, crop type, farm size, and so on. In Central Luzon, for example, work in rice-growing was originally organised largely on a *kasamá* or share-cropping (share-harvest) tenancy basis. As the lot of tenants worsened over time, relations with landlords also became more overtly conflictual and even violent (Kerkvliet 1979; Wolters 1984). In the 1930s, a peasant resistance movement emerged in Central Luzon which, just after World War II, waged a seven-year armed rebellion against landowners, until eventually crushed by government forces (Kerkvliet 1979). In an attempt to ameliorate such unrest, some land reforms were subsequently introduced, but these did little to alter the basic balance of power in the region. From the 1950s, a number of landlords introduced more machinery-intensive forms of rice-growing, largely to circumvent their labour-control problems. These changes set in place an accelerating trend towards greater wage labour and landlessness in agriculture (Kerkvliet 1991:34–58).

In the 1970s, international funds were deployed for a 'green revolution' in Philippine agriculture through the introduction of high-yield varieties of rice. As these new rice strains required more inputs of water, chemical fertilisers, herbicides, and pesticides they transformed the social relations of production—generating new sources of surplus extraction that have tended to decentre the landlord–tenant relationship (Wolters 1984:207–10; Lim 1990:123–6). In particular, although the main lines of credit and indebtedness for the direct producer still involve landowners, they now also include rural banks and commercial traders in agricultural inputs and outputs. Greater economic differentiation has also occurred among the direct producers themselves. Some peasants have prospered from improved yields and have been able to take up more conducive lease arrangements, or have consolidated their own small holdings. Others, in contrast, have lost their land and/or become low-paid contract workers to supplement their income from cropping.

This more complex pattern of class relations in rice agriculture has generated new alliances and conflicts which make it difficult to coalesce direct producers around the issue of land reform. From the late 1960s, violent opposition to socioeconomic privilege resumed in Central Luzon with the formation of the Maoist Communist Party of the Philippines (CPP) and its New People's Army (NPA). In the late 1970s Willem Wolters (1984:214–5) observed the latter organisation attempting to resolve the disparate interests of the landless and small landholders through 'a broad appeal for struggle against the state apparatus in general and . . . President [Marcos] in particular'. After the fall of the dictator, these organising difficulties remain, at a time when the radical Left has become more politically marginalised (Rocamora 1994).

The social relations of production in other sectors of agriculture will not be discussed in as much detail. However, it is worth noting that the important sugar industry in the southern Visayas region has also been historically characterised by a highly concentrated pattern of land (and mill) owner-ship, albeit that wage labour in sugar has always been more widespread than in rice-growing (McCoy 1982). Given the relative abundance of cheap labour, the industry remained labour-intensive—by overseas standards—for a long period. In the 1960s, cheap loans from state and international sources were thus made available to lift industry productivity through mechanisation. The employment and income consequences for workers were severe, and subsequently worsened with falling prices on the world market (Boyce 1993:195–8). In the other important export industry—coconuts—the pattern of land ownership has been less concentrated, and small-scale farming is more common. The use of wage labour is also grow-ing, but the level of political organising in this sector is less than in the sugar industry (Boyce 1993:189–92). Finally, many of the newest sectors in agri-culture—bananas and other fruits, fish-farming, and poultry and livestock production—have high levels of corporate involvement and contract farm-ing, often through vertically integrated, transnational agribusinesses (Boyce 1993:199–203).

Import-substitution industrialisation

Import-substitution industrialisation (ISI) in the 1950s largely reproduced the oligarchic socioeconomic structure that had built up in agriculture (Doronila 1986:42). Given the importance of access to import licences and foreign exchange through the state, between a third and a half of the new industrialists were members of the well-connected landed oligarchy—the other major group having an existing foot in commerce or manufacturing (Carroll 1965; Rivera 1994b:159–64). Industrialisation in the 1950s and 1960s therefore did not unseat the oligarchy—rather it brought new oppor-tunities for investment and rent-seeking in the finance, real estate and other services sector, in construction, and in manufacturing. Nevertheless, the homogeneity and relative cohesion of the dominant economic class was dis-rupted by the entry into manufacturing of individuals with different social and economic backgrounds and interests.

The shift to ISI caused some divisions of interest between protected manu-facturers and members of the oligarchy in export agriculture over economic policy in relation to import and currency-exchange controls. This conflict has been framed in economic nationalism terms: protectionism being justi-fied, not simply as a boon to particular industries, but as a defence against the dependency of the national economy as a whole. These views were widely shared by the radical Left, and within the growing middle class (Pinches 1996:108). But nationalisms are not without class differences. In that the nationalism of the elite lacked a concomitant call for the domestic redistribution of wealth, it did not develop a broad base in the populace (Doronila 1986:44–5). Notwithstanding their avowed economic nationalism, a good number of the protected industrialists in fact 'ran their enterprises as joint ventures' with US companies (Pinches 1996:109). Moreover, consistent with the patronage politics, conflicts over government policy often concealed more particularistic competition within the elite over the spoils of public office and political favours (Hawes 1992:153; Doronila 1992:125).

Before the Pacific War, industry had been a site of social conflict as independent (and often radical) trade unions formed in the sectors where workers were congregated in their hundreds and even thousands—that is, in large-scale agricultural processing (especially the sugar mills), cigar and cigarette factories, and in land transport and stevedoring (Kunihara 1945:72). During the 1920s, the number of unions and their reported membership increased rapidly (Wurfel 1959:584). Cuts to wages and rising unemployment in the 1930s resulted in unprecedented levels of industrial action. Significantly, during this era, there was an almost four-fold increase in the ratio of organised to spontaneous strikes (Kunihara 1945:65). By 1940, an estimated 5 per cent of the workforce was organised—although, less than 2 per cent was in registered unions (Kunihara 1945:72). Just after the war, the labour movement was briefly reconstituted under radical leadership until, in the early 1950s, at the height of state action against the peasant rebellion in Central Luzon, the peak organisation was declared illegal and its affiliated unions deregistered (Infante 1980:110).

With import-substitution industrialisation, the proportion of the labour force in manufacturing grew, peaking at almost 12 per cent (see table 2.6, page 54). This stimulated an increase in the number of unions, although many were company controlled, ineffective, or simply inactive (Snyder and Nowak 1982:48–53). The 1950s saw some pickup in real wages in industry but, in the subsequent decade, they fell by more than a half, signalling a redistribution of income away from the working class. By the mid 1980s, real wages were a quarter of their value twenty years earlier (Doronila 1986:42; Shepherd and Alburo 1991:150; Boyce 1993:27). These trends demonstrate the relative class capacities of capital and labour that underpin the intensification of income inequalities in the postwar era. They are also a consequence of disparities among industrial workers in terms of wages, working conditions, and levels of unionisation. In a postwar legislative environment where industrial disputation has been principally enterprise-based, there is a strong correlation between positive scores for such indicators and enterprise size (as defined by the number of employees in a particular workplace). Given that 82 per cent of the nonagricultural work-force, and 90 per cent in manufacturing, are currently outside the formal sector (Balisacan 1994:127; Buenaventura-Culili 1995:274), it is clear that the vast majority of workers is in little position to exert pressures for socio-economic reform through industrial conflict, particularly as population growth continues to swell the available labour force.

Table 2.6 Structure of employment in the Philippines (%)

	Agriculture	Industry (manufacture in brackets)	Services
1970	54	16 (11.9)	29
1980	51	16 (10.9)	33
1990	45	15 (9.7)	40
1994	44	16 (10.0)	40
1998	40	16 (9.5)	44

Source: ILO *Yearbook*, various years

The rise of export manufacturing in the 1970s has not been reflected in an expansion of manufacturing employment (see table 2.6). Nevertheless, production for an overseas market has been associated with a deepening of capitalist relations of production in industries such as garments (Abad 1975; Hutchison 1992). Although, in the policy literature on the subject, labour-intensive industries are often associated with small-scale enterprises, Tecson et al. (1990) argue that the expansion of the garments industry contributed to the general increase in the number of large-scale enterprises in manufacturing in the 1980s. Such changes can have an important impact on levels of union organisation in manufacturing, but they are often counter-posed by political controls and ideological divisions within the labour movement, divisions that intensified in the early 1990s with the changed political landscape (Rocamora 1994:207). Consequently, even before the 1997 crisis, labour-organising capacities were down from their zenith in the political turmoil of the previous decade.

Middle class and new forces

In agriculture and industry in the postwar era, the number of medium-sized landholders, salaried workers in the public and private sectors, profes-sionals, and the like, has grown. This heterogeneous stratum is often termed 'middle class' according to level of income, occupation type and status, pattern of consumption, and so on. In a more structural sense, the economic location of the professional middle class is thought to bring it into a 'con-tradictory' ideological and political relationship with capital and labour (Wright 1985; Robison and Goodman 1996:7–11). In the Philippines, capitalist industrialisation has increased the significance of this stratum in socioeconomic and political terms. Pinches (1996:109) argues that sections of the middle class first came to national political prominence over their endorsement of government protectionism in the 1950s and 1960s. Their enhanced class capacities since then are reflected in their heavy involvement in the popular movement to overthrow Marcos in the 1980s, and in NGO organising in the 1990s (Pinches 1996:123). Always largely independent of the traditional elite in structural terms, middle-class disaffection with the oligarchy 'and the means by which it has maintained political and economic power' has grown significantly in the post-Marcos era (Pinches 1996:123).

Under Marcos, the dominant force in key sectors of the economy were the presidential 'cronies'. The 'cronies' were mostly *not* from the ranks of the traditional oligarchy, as Marcos himself was not. Yet, they developed or expanded their business operations through privileged access to government-issued licences, monopolies, and loans—in short, through state patronage (Koike 1989:127–9). The 'cronies' were not conspicuous in labour-intensive export manufacturing, largely because this is an area where local monopolies are hard to establish (Hawes 1992:157). The old oligarchy was nevertheless 'harassed but not destroyed' by the Marcos regime (Doherty 1982:30). In tandem with a few surviving 'cronies', many of the old elite returned to economic prominence in the late 1980s. But, at this time, there also emerged some new business players.

Investors of Chinese descent who were once the target of nationalist policies have benefited from the easing of discriminatory legislation under Marcos to emerge with a significant presence in most sectors of the economy. With some exceptions, this group has not been as closely associated with political cronyism on a major scale. In addition, it is well positioned to promote and gain from ethnic Chinese investment networks in the region (Pinches 1996:120; de Dios 1998:79). Less spectacularly but, in the long term, not less significantly, the middle strata of Philippine society has been a vital source of medium-scale investment in export manufacturing. Through international and local subcontracting arrangements, it has been possible for relatively small investors to set up in manufacturing, sometimes as a means to supplement or substitute professional incomes (Pinches 1996:121). The business affairs of this section of the bourgeoisie are also less reliant upon political patronage than many home-market manufacturers.

In sum, industrialisation and the subsequent decline of traditional export crops have induced a more complex and, at times, more overtly conflictual social landscape in the Philippines. The corporate sector continues to be 'dominated by a relatively small number of large groups, and ultimate control ... rests in the hands of a relatively small number of families'

(World Bank 1999a:25). Yet, capitalist development and restructuring have generated new socioeconomic groupings, a number of which has specific interests in a more open investment climate. What is significant for understanding developments since the crisis is that the interests of the economic elite have also undergone changes through the influx of foreign direct and portfolio investment, most notably in relation to trade and investment controls (de Dios 1998:78). Neo-classical economists tend to assert that rent-seeking is simply the result of government intervention. However, as state-centred historical institutionalists argue, interventions can take many forms, and not all actions of the state cause economic inefficiencies (Evans 1994:10–11). To appreciate the impact of the 1997 crisis on the trajectory of Philippine development it is necessary to elaborate on the 'weak' nature of the state.

A 'weak state'

There are two facets to a 'weak' state (see Migdal 1988). The first centres on the relative distribution of power between state and society or, more particularly, between the state and dominant interests in the private sector of the economy—hence the question of *state autonomy*. As Caporaso and Levine (1992:191) put it, this view assumes that causality can be located either 'inside' or 'outside' the state: a weak state is one that is consistently acted upon by 'external' social forces. The second facet is often expressed as *state capacity* and, as previously discussed, heavily draws on the Weberian distinction between patrimonial and rational-bureaucratic polities. On this basis, a weak state is one in which relatively little distinction is made between the personal interests and official duties of decision-makers in the executive, legislature, and/or bureaucracy and, therefore, is one in which the policy-making process is constantly stymied by particularistic demands. In this interpretation, the origins of the weak state are associated with the 'elite' nature of early democracy in the Philippines.

Elite democracy

Democratic political institutions were introduced in the early part of the twentieth century by the United States colonial administration, but they did not deliver representative government. Without concomitant socio-economic reforms, the landed oligarchy was able to exercise its wealth and influence to dominate the national legislature. In power, members of this elite protected their own class and individual interests, not least by appropriating the resources of the state in particularistic ways. As Paul Hutchcroft (1994:230) explains, economic returns from public office in the Philippines thus largely fell to politicians of private means, rather than to an elite within the bureaucracy:

> In contrast to 'bureaucratic capitalism', where a powerful bureaucratic elite is the major beneficiary of patrimonial largesse and exercises power over a weak business class, the principal direction of rent extraction is [in this case] reversed: a powerful oligarchic business class extracts privilege from a largely incoherent bureaucracy.

For this reason, the Philippines state has not been an effective appropriator of domestic economic surpluses—through the taxation system, for example—and nor has it effectively regulated the relations of production in agriculture and industry that generate such surpluses. Instead, the political economy of rent-seeking in the Philippines has centred on the state's interface with the *international* arena through policies to do with trade and currency exchange, and on its function as a conduit for foreign development assistance and loans (Hutchcroft 1994:222). Given the enormous drain on public resources caused by political patronage, the state has been able to survive only as a consequence of the access it has had to overseas sources of funding: 'while the state is plundered internally, it is repeatedly rescued externally' (Hutchcroft 1994:226). As we will later see, this has implications for any reform agenda.

For most of the twentieth century, opposition to the socioeconomic base of political power was not sectionally represented in the formal processes of national-level government. The party system was notoriously characterised by affiliations centred on the shifting terrain of personality-based loyalties, rather than on 'policies aimed at meeting the interests of particular categories of citizens' (Crouch 1984:43; see also Velasco 1999:176). Pressures for significant reform took, as a consequence, mainly extra-parliamentary—and even extra-legal—forms, as seen with successive peasant rebellions on the island of Luzon.

The political landscape of the Philippines has thus long included a large number and variety of 'cause-oriented' groups in both the rural and urban areas.

Authoritarianism

In the postwar period, the state's brokerage role in the distribution of international funds contributed to the rise and fall of political authoritarianism.

Initially, in the 1960s and 1970s, greater access to such funds helped to create certain centralist tendencies in Philippines' politics (Wolters 1984:194–5; Doronila 1992). As summed up by Gary Hawes (1992:150), the locus of power:

> . . . was shifting in favour of the government; and within the government the balance of power was shifting towards the executive branch. The president had always controlled the release of government funds, but with an increase in the role of economic planners, the new emphasis on technical expertise in the control of the economy, growing economic and military assistance from abroad, and an increased resort to foreign borrowing . . . the power of the executive branch grew, and for the first time began to extend out into the countryside and into local politics.

This structural trend was greatly magnified by the political ambitions of Ferdinand Marcos. After his election to the presidency in 1965, he used public funds to win congressional support, at the same time reorganising the bureaucracy to facilitate more direct links with the rural masses—then 70 per cent of the population (Doronila 1992:127–31). When, in 1972, he faced constitutional barriers to a third term in office, he entrenched himself in office by declaring martial law, in the process shutting down the legislature, limiting press and civil freedoms, expanding the police and the military, and bringing significant sections of the economy under state control.

Importantly, the direct political power of the oligarchy was broken under Marcos although, with the exception of some key families, they remained sufficiently influential to protect their private economic base from land and tariff reforms (Crouch 1984). The key actors in the Marcos era were, instead, his closest political supporters who (as previously pointed out) were not as a rule originally from the oligarchy. In addition to political repression, the interests of this group lay in the rent-seeking opportunities provided by favoured treatment by the state. As competition for such treatment was limited, and the magnitude of rents increased by monopolistic controls and foreign borrowings, the scale at which public resources moved into private hands reached unprecedented levels. Yet, the political economy of the Marcos regime was ultimately tied to the availability of overseas funds—hence the factor that contributed to the concentration of political power eventually played a key role in the overthrow of the dictatorship.

Political reform

Mass civil protest brought an end to the Marcos regime in 1986. His successor, President Aquino, reintroduced democratic elections, restored the legislature, disbanded the agricultural monopolies, and privatised a significant proportion of public enterprises. However, as the oligarchy survived the Marcos years, it was able to move back into political prominence. Aquino established the institutional conditions for 'the restoration of elite democracy' (Bello and Gershman 1990). In the 1987 congressional elections, most of those elected were from families with a prior record of political incumbency; although, in keeping with the postwar trend, the main economic base of these 'dynasties' was no longer in agriculture but in industry, banking, and real estate (Wurfel 1979; Doronila 1992:83–9). More broadly, the Aquino regime did little to enhance the class capacities of social movements seeking more fundamental change. Her administration succumbed to wealthy landowner resistance in not pushing through land reform in agriculture. In industry, disputation and wage-bargaining was returned to the regional and enterprise levels—moves that contributed to the fragmentation of the labour movement. As well, the regime oversaw an escalation in the use of violence against political and community activists in failing to control the proliferation of paramilitary and vigilante organisations.

Yet, towards the end of her term in office, Aquino also introduced the legislative conditions for what some commentators are terming 'a new form of governance' (Magno 1993; see also Brillantes 1994). Under the Local Government Code of 1991, NGO representation in various facets of local government was institutionalised, at the same time as sizeable resources (including up to 40 per cent of internal revenue) and decision-making and regulatory powers were devolved from the national to the local level of the state.

What impact have these institutional changes had on the responsiveness of the state to popular demands? If the political space for participation and protest has expanded in the post-Marcos era, has this had an effect on the nature and course of policy-making at a national level?

Answers to these questions are uneven across different government departments and sectors. However, it is widely believed that democracy in the Philippines has been strengthened through the political activities of NGOs as the state is now 'less completely captive of elite interests than previously' (Silliman and Noble 1998:306; see also Clarke 1998). Yet citing the example of agrarian reform, José Magadia (1999:265–66) argues that, when NGOs are consulted over major policy matters, in many cases their inputs have little or no effect on the final outcomes. In his view, many of the traditional features of political decision-making based on patronage thus still remain (see also Hutchcroft 1999). Despite some obvious longer-term changes towards more sectoral modes of public engagement (Kerkvliet 1996; Pinches 1997), the party system remains riven by personal interests

(Velasco 1999). In the 1998 general elections, a party-list vote was introduced for the first time for 20 per cent of House of Representative seats. Aimed at achieving greater political representation and accountability, initial teething problems saw only a quarter of the available seats actually filled (Montinola 1999:137–8).

Yet, in the wake of authoritarianism under Marcos, democratic institutions have a high degree of popular support in the Philippines. Twice in the 1990s, revisions to the Constitution that would have enabled the president to stay in office more than two terms were defeated by organised street demonstrations (Pinches 1997). Reminiscent of the 'people power' that ended authoritarian rule in 1986, the strength and timing of these street protests indicated that democracy, in and of itself, has great popular legitimacy in the Philippines. The street protests occurred just before and after the 1997 crisis when the country's economy was relatively strong, in historical and regional terms. Most significantly, President Ramos was not able to use his performance as an economic manager to obtain the Constitutional changes necessary for him to be eligible for re-election after six years in office. In part, this is because, as poverty levels show, a sizeable section of the population was yet to receive personally the 'trickle down' from economic growth. They were less enamoured with the policies of the president than were his neo-classical economic advisers. Yet, there is also little appetite for the return of 'strong man' politics. In comparison with other South-East Asian countries, authoritarian rule in the Philippines has not gained popular and middle-class legitimacy through the delivery of material benefits.

Political and economic liberalism are not to be conflated. Nevertheless, the association established in the 1980s between authoritarian rule and economic collapse has also had an important influence on the direction of economic policy after Marcos. The following section outlines some of the intersecting factors behind the move to greater market openness, especially as it occurred under Ramos. For, if democratic consolidation was a feature of Aquino's time in office, economic liberalisation was a central platform of her successor's six years.

Market liberalisation

From his election in 1992, President Ramos instituted a range of measures to reduce government intervention in the economy. These included: the privatisation of a number of major state-owned enterprises; the break-up of monopolies and cartels in sectors such as agricultural marketing, air transport, inter-island shipping, telecommunications, and power gener-ation; the lifting of restrictions on foreign investment and the repatriation of profits; and further tariff reductions in trade. As well, the Central Bank was recapitalised and given more independence from government; foreign banks were let in; build–operate–transfer arrangements were introduced to facilitate private investment in various infrastructure developments; large tracts of government land were sold off; and reforms to the taxation system were achieved.

Contests over government protectionism are 'often depicted as the epi-tome of struggle between political and economic forces in the Philippines' (de Dios 1998:57–8). This is the case for both neo-classical and economic nationalist (dependency) perspectives. Given that a close relationship has existed between business rent-seeking and *dirigisme* in trade and invest-ment, market liberalisation in the Philippines might be assumed to put an end to political patronage on a grand scale. As we have seen, in the minds of state-centred historical institutionalists, this outcome is equivalent to the state aquiring greater institutional coherence and autonomy.

Was this the case under Ramos? Did market reforms proceed because the state increased its authority over oligarchic interests? Or were there other factors at work?

It is argued here that some strengthening of the state did occur *vis-à-vis* protectionist interests under Ramos. However, more than there being a marked reversal of causality between state and society, the policies of the Ramos administration were mostly a reflection of domestic changes that are a legacy of the Marcos years. Of particular note is the fact that dominant interests have also proved to be quite adaptable and opportunistic in their responses to these changing circumstances (de Dios 1998:74).

President Ramos was personally quite skilful in negotiating the politics of policy reform through congress. However, his task was made easier by changes to the socioeconomic composition of the legislature as a result of incumbents having a more diverse set of backgrounds after the 1992 elec-tion (Velasco 1999:187). These changes are consistent with previously discussed social and economic transformations that have created new allegiances and interests in the business community and the professional middle class. In general, the new interests are more oriented towards an open economy—most particularly with regard to recent foreign investment in industry, services, and property (de Dios 1998:78). Although it is a mis-take to assume that such interests are unambiguously aligned with a 'free market', it is also the case that they can no longer simply be encompassed by the general category of 'crony' or 'patrimonial capitalism' (Pinches

1996:124–7). On the other hand, popular forces that are resistant to market liberalisation generally lack the class capacities politically to oppose associated policy changes outright.

Aside from these changes, the 'pull back' of the state has been a direct reaction to the Marcos dictatorship. To quote Pinches (1996:126):

> Not only did the Marcos regime take cronyism to extremes, but it also succeeded in greatly discrediting it as a developmental model in the eyes of the broad population, including the non-crony business community, and also in the eyes of foreign bankers and investors.

At a time when other South-East Asian countries were embarking, or so it seemed, on their own development 'miracles', the Philippines looked to be missing the boat. Market reforms under Ramos were not especially the result of any major socioeconomic upheaval—rather, they gained wide support as a way to break with the perceived roots of past economic failures. What is more, oligarchic interests had the class capacities to adjust to the altered circumstances of a changed role for the state (de Dios 1998:74).

But market liberalisation was not the natural policy alternative to what went on before in the Philippines. That the economic planning bureaucracy was dominated by neo-classical economists is particularly significant (Velasco 1999:189–94; Bello 2000:243–44). Known widely as the 'technocrats', these economists have been actively advocating market reforms for a number of decades. However, their influence in the past has been often tied to their role in negotiations with the IMF and World Bank over official loans to government. Not surprisingly, this influence has been greatest during times of severe fiscal crisis. For example, the technocrats are said to have been a force behind the 1972 declaration of martial law to quash social opposition to a more open, exporting economy (Crowther 1986; Hawes 1987; c.f. Hawes 1992). Yet, it was not until the early 1980s, that Marcos was, in fact, obliged to meet the conditions of a World Bank 'structural adjustment' package by introducing a number of market reforms (Broad 1988; Bautista 1989). Crucially, this was 'an unwanted and forced agenda' that was made necessary by the need to access international funds (Montes 1989:80; see also Jayasuriya 1992:60). In other words, under Marcos, the technocrats gained policy ground through the fiscal dependency of the state on foreign sources of income.

In the early 1990s, similar pressures were at work on the Ramos regime due to debt repayments and the loss of United States financial assistance after the 1992 closure of the military bases (Hutchcroft 1994:234). But, by this time, the technocrats were also less marginalised politically, the support for market liberalisation now being more widespread. In this environment,

Bello (2000:243) admits that it is difficult to persist in characterising neo-liberalism as having been imposed on the Philippines by the IMF and World Bank. This is because, as previously stated, the policy debate after Marcos has, in general, shifted away from models of state-centred development. This is by no means to say that there is no opposition to neo-liberalism (see Bello 2000), simply that the country is at present unlikely to pursue an economic path with authoritarian political tendencies, as in Singapore or Malaysia.

Yet, economic liberalisation is not necessarily the antidote to rent-seeking that neo-classical economists assume it to be. Moves to free the market have not been matched by institutional reforms to strengthen state capacities (Hutchcroft 1999). In his dealings with congress, Ramos himself 'consistently relied on old-style "pork-barrel" and patronage politics in order to promote new-style liberal economics' (Hutchcroft 1999:458; see also Agpalo 1995:268). Associated with this, the party system continues to consist mostly of 'personality-based coalitions of politicians with independent power bases'. Hence, 71 members of the House of Representatives had switched to the party of the winning president within twelve months of the 1992 elections (Riedinger 1994:140). In other words, before the 1997 crisis, government processes in the Philippines were still subject to considerable particularism and patronage because little attention has been paid to the bureaucratic reforms that state-centred historical institutionalists see as necessary.

After the 1997 crisis

The 1990s Asian crisis had less impact on the Philippines than the 1980s recession. One reason was that 1990s crisis was generally less severe. However, more importantly, it did not become a political crisis because its origins were not attributed to the state. Indeed, as the country came through the initial stages of the 1997 crisis better than most of its neighbours, Ramos and his administration were able to claim some credit for what had ensued. Political and economic reforms since the fall of Marcos were given further legitimacy by the fact that the Philippines performed relatively well into the following year. Nevertheless, as previously discussed, Ramos was not able to change the Constitution to extend his eligibility for office on the strength of his economic program. In May 1998 Joseph Estrada was elected to the presidency on a populist platform of seeing to the poor, while also committing himself to more market liberalisation.

Up until moves to impeach him, Estrada's style became synonymous with the 'old-style politics' of cronyism (Wurfel 1999:29). The drive to greater competition was stalled by actions to protect rather than dismantle various monopolies—as for example in the airlines industry (de Dios 1999). But, in addition, the implementation of some market reforms involved the disbursement of favours through government decision-making. As de Dios (1998:80) points out, 'some processes in a liberalizing agenda, especially deregulation and privatization, yield substantial rents'. Further, it is a relatively simple matter for 'dominant groups—including those well-represented in government—to use customary rent-seeking to win such battles'. During the two and a half years that Estrada held office, the transfer of state assets into private hands followed a pattern more consistent with political patronage than the pursuit market forces (Bolongaita 1999:248). Although the president himself was accused of amassing wealth largely through his position in government, it is clear that others had the market advantage or class capacity to expand or diversify their business holdings through privatisation.

Conclusion

Any assessment of the impact of the Asian meltdown on the Philippines must take into account the succession of economic crises that the country has experienced in the past three to four decades (Hutchcroft 1999:482). After the country's most severe economic and political crisis in the 1980s, particular factors have coalesced to produce certain political and policy changes. On the one hand, democracy has been restored and, despite some important continuities with the 'elite' nature of democratic processes and institutions before the 1970s, Philippine civil society is South-East Asia's most vigorous and open. On the other hand, the desire to end authoritarian tendencies has paved the way for a number of far-reaching market reforms. However, as state-centred historical institutionalists point out, there has not generally also been a strengthening of state capacities in relation to political patronage. They argue that such strengthening requires bureaucratic reform (Hutchcroft 1999). But it is also the case that it will need changes outside the state, centred on the greater redistribution of wealth, if non-oligarchic forces are to have the enhanced class capacities to be better represented in the political arena. The 1997 crisis itself did not mark a major turning-point in the political and economic affairs of the Philippines. Events surrounding the end of the Estrada regime suggest that cronyism will remain a site of conflict in the longer term, albeit on a terrain that is changed (and changing) through capitalist development and rejection of authoritarianism under Marcos.

Notes

1 Thanks to Kevin Hewison and Donna Turner for their helpful comments on an earlier version of this chapter.
2 This distinction is often applied to different nation states, but Gomez and Jomo (1999:5) argue that both features coexist in the case of the Malaysian state.
3 In the Philippines, a distinction is often made between NGOs and 'peoples' organisations' (POs) on the grounds that the latter tend to be more profession-alised. In this chapter, NGO is used less precisely—and hence more inclusively—to encompass both types of non-profit organisation in civil society.
4 Statistics on overseas workers are drawn from <http://pinoymigrant.dole.gov.ph>.

References

Abad, Ramon (1975) *The Garment Industry, A Study Prepared for the NEDA–PDCP–UP Special Course in Corporate Management and Industry Evaluation, Manila.*

ADB (2000) see Asia Development Bank (ADB) (2000).

Agpalo, Remigio E. (1995) 'The Philippines: Remarkable Economic Turnaround and Qualified Political Success', *Southeast Asian Affairs 1995*, Singapore: Institute of Southeast Asian Studies, pp 259–72.

Asia Development Bank (ADB) (2000) *Asia Recovery Report 2000: May 2000 Update*, Manila: Regional Economic Monitoring Unit, Asia Development Bank.

Balisacan, Arsenio M. (1994) 'Urban Poverty in the Philippines: Nature, Causes and Policy Measures' *Asian Development Review*, 12(1):117–52.

Bautista, Romeo M. (1989) *Impediments to Trade Liberalization in the Philippines*, Trade Policy Research Centre: London, and Gower: Aldershot.

Bello, Walden (2000) 'The Philippines: The making of a neo-classical tragedy', in Richard Robison, Mark Beeson, Kanishka Jayasuriya and Hyuk-Rae Kim (eds) *Politics and Markets in the Wake of the Asian Crisis*, London and New York: Routledge, pp 238–57.

Bello, Walden and John Gershman, (1990) 'Democratization and Stabilization in the Philippines', *Critical Sociology*, 17(1):35–56.

Bello, Walden, David Kinley and Elaine Elinson (1982) *Development Debacle: the World Bank in the Philippines*, San Francisco: Institute for Food and Development Policy.

Billig, Michael S. (1994) 'The Death and Rebirth of Entrepreneurism on Negros Island, Philippines: A Critique of Cultural Theories of Enterprise', *Journal of Economic Issues*, 28(3):659–78.

Bolongaita, Emil P. (1999) 'The Philippines: Consolidating Democracy in Difficult Times', *Southeast Asian Affairs 1999*, Singapore: Institute of Southeast Asian Studies, pp 237–52.

Boyce, James (1993) *The Philippines: The Political Economy of Growth and Impoverishment in the Marcos Era*, London: Macmillan.

Broad, Robin (1988) *Unequal Alliance: the World Bank, the International Monetary Fund, and the Philippines*, Berkeley: University of California Press.

Brillantes, Alex B. (1994) 'Decentralization: Governance From Below', *Kasarinlan*, 10(1):41–7.

Brown, Ian (1989) 'Some Comments on Industrialisation in the Philippines During the 1930s', in Ian Brown (ed.) *The Economies of Africa and Asia in the Inter-War Depression*, London and New York: Routledge, pp 203–20.

Buchanan, James M. (1980) 'Rent Seeking and Profit Seeking', in James M. Buchanan, Robert D. Tollison and Gordon Tullock (eds) *Towards a Theory of the Rent-Seeking Society*, Texas: Texas A&M University Press, pp 3–15.

Buenaventura-Culili, Venus (1995) 'The Impact of Industrial Restructuring on Filipino Women Workers' in Committee for Asian Women, *Silk and Steel: Asian Women Workers Confront Challenges of Industrial Restructuring*, Hong Kong, pp 268–97.

Caporaso, James A. and David P. Levine (1992) *Theories of Political Economy*, New York: Cambridge University Press.

Carroll, John (1965) *The Filipino Manufacturing Entrepreneur: Agent and Product of Change*, Ithaca: Cornell University Press.

Clarke, Gerard (1998) *The Politics of NGOs in South-East Asia: Participation and Protest in the Philippines*, London and New York: Routledge.

Crouch, Harold (1984) *Domestic Political Structures and Regional Co-operation*, Singapore: ASEAN Economic Research Unit, Institute of Southeast Asian Studies.

Crowther, William (1986) 'Philippine Authoritarianism and the International Economy', *Comparative Politics*, 18(3):339–55.

Cushner, Nicholas (1971) *Spain in the Philippines*, Quezon City: Ateneo de Manila University Press, and Tokyo: Charles E. Tuttle.

de Dios, Emmanuel (1998) 'Philippine Economic Growth: Can It Last?', in David G. Timberman (ed.) *The Philippines: New Directions in Domestic Policy and Foreign Relations*, New York: The Asia Society, pp 49–84.

de Dios, Emmanuel (1999) 'Crisis without consequence: recovery without reform', *Philippine Daily Inquirer*, 25 August 1999, accessed 31 May 2000, <www.inquirer.net/issues/aug99/aug25/business/bus_10.htm>.

Doherty, John F. (1982) 'Who Controls the Philippine Economy: Some Need Not Try as Hard as Others', in Belinda Aquino (ed.) *Cronies and Enemies: The Current Philippine Scene*, Philippine Studies Occasional Paper No. 5, University of Hawaii, pp 7–35.

Doronila, Amando (1986) 'Class Formation and Filipino Nationalism: 1950–70', Kasarinlan, 2(2):39–52.

Doronila, Amando (1992) *The State, Economic Transformation, and Political Change in the Philippines, 1946–72*, Singapore: Oxford University Press.

Evans, Peter (1994) *Embedded Autonomy: States and Industrial Transformation*, Princeton, New Jersey: Princeton University Press.

Gomez, Edmund Terence and K. S. Jomo (1999) *Malaysia's Political Economy: Politics, Patronage and Profits*, 2nd edn, Cambridge, UK: Cambridge University Press.

Hawes, Gary (1987) *The Philippine State and the Marcos Regime: The Politics of Export*, Ithaca: Cornell University Press.

Hawes, Gary (1992) 'Marcos, His Cronies, and the Philippines' Failure to Develop', in Ruth McVey (ed.) *Southeast Asian Capitalists*, New York: Cornell University Press, Southeast Asian Program, pp 145–60.

Hutchcroft, Paul D. (1991) 'Oligarchs and Cronies in the Philippine State: The Politics of Plunder', *World Politics*, 43:414–50.

Hutchcroft, Paul D. (1994) 'Booty Capitalism: Business–Government Relations in the Philippines' in Andrew J. MacIntyre (ed.) *Business and Government in Industrialising Asia*, St Leonards NSW: Allen and Unwin, pp 216–43.

Hutchcroft, Paul (1999) 'After the Fall: Prospects for Political and Institutional Reform in Post-Crisis Thailand and the Philippines', *Government and Opposition*, 33(4):473–97.

Hutchison, Jane (1992) 'Women in the Philippines Garments Export Industry', *Journal of Contemporary Asia*, 22(4):471–89.

ILO, see International Labour Organization (ILO).

Infante, Jaime (1980) *The Political, Economic, and Labor Climate in the Philippines*, Industrial Research Unit, University of Pennsylvania.

International Labour Organization (ILO) *Yearbook*, various years, Geneva: International Labour Organization.

Jayasuriya, Sisira (1987) 'The politics of economic policy in the Philippines during the Marcos era', in Richard Robison, Kevin Hewison and Garry Rodan (eds) *Southeast Asia in the 1980s: The Politics of Economic Crisis*, Sydney: Allen and Unwin, pp 80–112.

Jayasuriya, Sisira (1992) 'Structural Adjustment and Economic Performance in the Philippines', in Andrew J. MacIntyre and Kanishka Jayasuriya (eds) *The Dynamics of Economic Policy Reform in South-East Asia and the South-West Pacific*, Singapore: Oxford University Press, pp 50–73.

Kerkvliet, Benedict J. (1979) *The Huk Rebellion: A Study of Peasant Revolt in the Philippines*, Quezon City: New Day Publishers.

Kerkvliet, Benedict J. Tria (1991) 'Everyday Politics in the Philippines: Class and Status Relations in a Central Luzon Village', Quezon City: New Day Publishers.

Kerkvliet, Benedict J. Tria (1996) 'Contested meanings of elections in the Philippines', in R. H. Taylor (ed.) *The Politics of Elections In Southeast Asia*, New York: Woodrow Wilson Center Press, and Cambridge: Cambridge University Press, pp 136–63.

Koike, Kenji (1989) 'The Reorganization of Zaibatsu Groups under the Marcos and Aquino Regimes', *East Asian Cultural Studies*, 28, March, pp 127–43.

Kongsamut, Piyabha and Athanasios Vamvakidis (1999) 'Economic Growth' in Markus Rodlauer and Prakash Loungani (eds) *Philippines: Selected Issues, IMF Staff Country Report No. 99/92*, Washington, D.C.: International Monetary Fund, pp 10–37.

Krueger, Anne O. (1974) 'The Political Economy of the Rent-Seeking Society', *American Economic Review*, LXIV(3):291–303.

Kunihara, Kenneth K. (1945) *Labor in the Philippine Economy*, Stanford: Stanford University Press.

Lim, Joseph Y. (1990) 'The Agricultural Sector: Stagnation and Change', in Emmanuel S. de Dios and Lorna Villamil (eds) *Plans, Markets and Relations: Studies for a mixed economy*, Manila: Kalikasan Press, pp 118–32.

Magadia, José (1999) 'Contemporary Civil Society in the Philippines', *Southeast Asian Affairs 1999*, Singapore: Institute of Southeast Asian Studies, pp 253–68.

Magno, Alexander R. (1993) 'A Changed Terrain for Popular Struggles', *Kasarinlan*, 8(3):7–21.

McCoy, Alfred (1982) 'Introduction: The Social History of an Archipelago', in Alfred McCoy and Ed. de Jesus (eds) *Philippine Social History: Global Trade and Local Transformations*, Quezon City: Ateneo de Manila University Press, pp 1–18.

McCoy, Alfred (1993) *An Anarchy of Families: State and Family in the Philippines*, Madison: University of Wisconsin.

Migdal, Joel S. (1988) *Strong Societies and Weak States: State–Society Relations and State Capabilities in the Third World*, New Jersey: Princeton University Press.

Montes, Manuel F. (1989) 'Philippine Structural Adjustments, 1970–1987', in Manuel Montes and Hideyoshi Sakai (eds) *Philippine Macroeconomic Perspective: Developments and Policies*, Tokyo: Institute of Developing Economies, pp 45–90.

Montinola, Gabriella R. (1999) 'Parties and Accountability in the Philippines', *Journal of Democracy*, 10(1):126–40.

Noland, Marcus (2000) 'The Philippines in the Asian Financial Crisis', *Asian Survey*, 40(3):401–12.

Pinches, Michael (1992) 'The Philippines: The Regional Exception', *Pacific Review*, 5(4):390–401.

Pinches, Michael (1996) 'The Philippines: new rich: capitalist transformations amidst economic gloom' in Richard Robison and David S. G. Goodman (eds) *The New Rich in Asia: Mobile phones, McDonalds and middle-class revolution*, London and New York: Routledge, pp 105–33.

Pinches, Michael (1997) 'Elite Democracy, Development, and People Power', *Asian Studies Review*, 21(2–3):104–20.

Ranis, Gustav (1974) *Sharing in Development: A Programme of Employment, Equity and Growth for the Philippines*, Geneva: International Labour Organization.

Riedinger, Jeffrey (1994) 'The Philippines in 1993: Halting Steps Toward Liberalization', *Asian Survey*, 34(2):139–46.

Rivera, Temario C. (1994a) *Landlords and Capitalists: Class, Family, and the State in Philippine Manufacturing*, Quezon City: University of the Philippines Press.

Rivera, Temario C. (1994b) 'The State, Civil Society, and Foreign Actors: The Politics of Philippine Industrialization', *Contemporary Southeast Asia*, 16(2):157–77.

Robison, Richard and David S. G. Goodman. (1996) 'The new rich in Asia: Economic development, social status and political consciousness' in Richard Robison and David S. G. Goodman (eds) *The New Rich in Asia: Mobile phones, McDonalds and middle-class revolution*, London and New York: Routledge, pp 1–16.

Rocamora, Joel (1994) *Breaking Through: The Struggle Within the Communist Party of the Philippines*, Manila: Anvil Publishing.

Scipes, Kim (1999) 'Global economic crisis, neoliberal solutions, and the Philippines' *Monthly Review*, 51(7):1–14.

Shepherd, Geoffrey and Florian Alburo (1991) 'The Philippines' in Demetris Papageorgiou, Michael Michaely and Armeane Choski (eds) *Liberalizing Foreign Trade Vol 2*, Cambridge, Mass. and Oxford: Basil Blackwell, pp 133–308.

Silliman, G. Sidney and Lela Ganer Noble (1998) 'Introduction' in G. Sidney Silliman and Lela Garner Noble (eds) *Organizing for Democracy: NGOs, Civil Society, and the Philippine State*, Honolulu: University of Hawai'i Press, pp 1–25.

Snow, Robert T. (1983) 'Export-Oriented Industrialization, the International Division of Labor, and the Rise of the Subcontract Bourgeoisie in the Philippines' in Norman Owen (ed.) *The Philippine Economy and the United States: Studies in Past and Present Interactions*, Michigan Papers on South and Southeast Asia no. 22.

Snyder, Kay and Thomas C. Nowak (1982) 'Philippine Labor Before Martial Law: Threat or Nonthreat?', *Studies in Comparative International Development*, 17(3–4):44–72.

Tecson, Gwendolyn, Lina Valcarcel and Carol Nunez (1990) 'The Role of Small and Medium-Scale Industries in the Industrial Development of the Philippines', in *The Role of Small and Medium-Scale Industries in Industrial Development: The Experience of Selected ASEAN Countries*, Manila: Asian Development Bank, pp 313–422.

Therborn, Göran (1983) 'Why Some Classes Are More Successful Than Others', *New Left Review*, 138.

Tigno, Jorge V. (1997) 'Ties that bind: the past and prospects of Philippine labor out migration', *Pilipinas: A Journal of Philippine Studies*, 29, Fall, pp 1–18.

Velasco, Renato S. (1999) 'The Philippines', in Ian Marsh, Jean Blondel and Takashi Inoguchi (eds) *Democracy, Governance, and Economic Performance: East and Southeast Asia*, Tokyo, New York and Paris: United Nations University Press, pp 167–202.

Weber, Max (1968) *Economy and Society: an outline of interpretive sociology*, edited by Guenther Roth and Claus Wittich, New York: Bedminister Press.

Weiss, Linda and John M. Hobson (2000) 'State power and economic strength revisited: what's so special about the Asian crisis?', in Richard Robison et al. (eds) *Politics and Markets in the Wake of the Asian Crisis*, London: Routledge, pp 53–74.

Wolters, Willem (1984) *Politics, Patronage and Class Conflict in Central Luzon*, Quezon City: New Day Publishers.

World Bank (1989) *Philippines: Towards Sustaining the Economic Recovery*, Country Economic Memorandum, World Bank: Washington, D.C.

World Bank (1999a) *Philippines: The Challenge of Economic Recovery*, Poverty Reduction and Economic Management Sector Unit of The World Bank, East Asia and Pacific Region, Washington, D.C.: World Bank.

World Bank (1999b) 'Philippines at a Glance', available <www.worldbank.org/html/extdr/offrep/eap/ph.htm>.

World Bank (2000) *East Asia: Recovery and Beyond*, Washington, D.C.: World Bank.

Wright, Erik Olin (1985) *Classes*, London: Verso.

Wurfel, David (1959) 'Trade Union Development and Labor Relations Policy in the Philippines', *Industrial and Labor Relations Review*, 12(4):582–608.

Wurfel, David (1979) 'Elites of Wealth and Elites of Power: The Changing Dynamic', *Southeast Asian Affairs 1979*, Singapore: Institute of Southeast Asian Studies, pp 233–45.

Wurfel, David (1999) 'Convergence and Divergence Amidst Democratization and Economic Crisis: Thailand and the Philippines Compared', *Philippine Political Science Journal*, 20(43):1–44.

3

Thailand's Capitalism: Development through Boom and Bust

Kevin Hewison[1]

To suggest that Thailand is undergoing a capitalist revolution is not the debatable proposition it once was. There was once a reluctance to use the term 'capitalism' to describe the forces that dragged the society from its agricultural past and plunged it into its industrial present. This is no longer so, especially as the spectre of state socialism as an alternative has evaporated. Capitalism's ascendancy has incorporated Thailand as a part of a world system, subjecting the economy and society to its many vagaries.

Most writers have tended to use 'capitalism' as a shorthand designation for the process of economic change that has taken place within a relatively free enterprise system. Industrialisation has been an important part of this process. It has transformed a subsistence economy to one where production involves the application of capital in enterprises that produce primarily for profit. Trade and commerce take on an increasingly significant role, while the industrial system sees producers separated from their products as they become waged workers, employed by the owners and managers of enterprises who control those products. Capitalist industry occurs within an environment where individuals or groups of investors own businesses, and competition among businesses is considered the norm.

Conceptualising these elements as a system is important. Capitalism, as well as being a way of organising economic production, also structures society. Capitalist enterprise demands a social system where a working class has at least some of its labour for sale, purchased by a smaller class of business owners and managers. National borders do not necessarily bind this structuration, for globalisation is clearly a phenomenon of capitalist development and domination, as seen during the colonial period.

Thailand's economic performance from 1957 to 1996 was unique. Economists observe that this period saw uninterrupted, often very rapid, growth (Warr and Bhanupong 1996). The decade to 1997 witnessed an unprecedented economic boom. The Asian economic crisis has dramatically demonstrated both capitalism's global nature and Thailand's integration in this system.[2]

It is sometimes argued that Thailand's capitalist transition has not matched the history of Anglo-American development (Pasuk and Baker 1998:ch. 4). This is correct, for Thailand's progress has not followed the same trajectory as the United Kingdom, Japan, or the United States. However, some common basic processes have been at work, and the nature of the transformation has much that is recognisable in capitalist transitions.[3] The force of these processes has dominated the past century or so. This chapter presents a discussion of Thailand's capitalism, preceded by a brief outline of the theoretical debates regarding this development.

A sketch of theoretical approaches

Because chapter 1 to this volume has detailed the general approaches that analysts have taken to boom and bust, this section will elaborate upon these only for Thailand.[4]

Modernisation approaches

The dominant perspective on Thailand's society and politics is influenced by modernisation theory. This characterises Thai society as 'loosely structured', where the mass of the population is apolitical, and politics revolves around the politicised elite. Hierarchy and status were important in binding the masses to the elite through a vast patronage network. Writing in the mid 1960s, Fred Riggs described Thailand as a 'bureaucratic polity', a conception of the relations between business and government that remains strong in the literature. Riggs (1966) saw business as having little political influence. The political elite of civil and military bureaucrats adopted a predatory attitude, making business people their clients. Through its control of politics, the elite was able to dictate policy and establish corrupt patron–client relations that fed on economic development. Bureaucrats, especially those in the military, were able to maintain a degree of control over business that ensured the benefits of development served the interests of the military and bureaucracy first and the masses second.

By the 1980s, however, political economists came to regard 'bureaucratic polity' as an inappropriate description of a Thailand experiencing rapid growth and massive social change. The rise of a powerful and increasingly independent business class and the concomitant decline of the military contradicted the model (for example McVey 1992:20–2). They saw the bureaucratic polity replaced by a system where business has far more autonomy than under the bureaucratic polity. This led to the historical institutionalist approaches discussed below, where business–government relations were more of a partnership (Anek 1992:13–15).

These revised approaches did not address Riggs's *theory*. Implicit in their use of Riggs's term as a *description* of state–society relations for a particular era was a rejection of his complex modernisation model for *contemporary Thailand*. Modernisation perspectives, especially those utilising structural-functional conceptions, appeared to have had their day. Remarkably, however, the 1997 economic crash saw a limited resurgence.

Danny Unger (1998) has taken a broadly modernisation perspective in his application of the notion of social capital to Thailand.[5] He identifies the paradox of rapid growth being achieved where the bureaucracy is weak and policy implementation poor. Unger explains this as resulting from a lack of social capital among Thais. His analysis draws extensively on observations from modernisation theory, reviving 'bureaucratic polity' in explaining cultural differences between ethnic Chinese and Thais. The former are seen as more sociable than the Thai, thus providing drive in the economy, albeit with limited inputs into the political system. Unger (1998:18) suggests that limited sociability among Thais has diminished the capacity of state officials to foster social change and the adoption of market strategies, and has led to factionalism and poor coordination among state agencies. In this approach, the 1997 crisis can be seen to have resulted from shortcomings with deep cultural roots.

Like his modernisation predecessors, Unger operates with models of society, politics, and ethnicity that ignore much of Thailand's diversity, political competition, repression, and struggle. He also gives too little attention to the international dimensions of development. The failure to account for these factors means that revised modernisation approaches are unable to capture the full ramifications of either boom or crisis.

Dependency and neo-dependency approaches

As explained in chapter 1, dependency theorists argued that modernisation approaches were inadequate for placing too much emphasis on elite behaviour and ignoring predatory international capitalism. Dependency analysts regarded Thailand's business and state elites as tools of internationalised corporations, assisting the exploitation of their own country (Suthy 1980).

A major problem emerged for this approach when a significant local capitalist class developed. Dependency approaches were unable to explain this, except as an artefact of foreign investment. For example, Hart-Landsberg and Burkett (1998) characterise such developments as tenuous and subject to the vagaries of business decisions made outside Thailand, meaning that it is 'false development'.[6] But this explained little about Thailand's capitalist revolution.

The crisis, however, saw a resurgence of interest in dependency approaches. The attraction lay in its criticisms of the negative impacts of development and the recommendation of national(ist) economic programs. Dependency analysts argued that high-speed growth, fuelled by foreign capital, had promoted the interests of international investors and 'technocratic and economic elites' in the region, rather than the majority. Thailand's development was considered unsustainable and dependent on decisions made overseas. For these analysts, the crisis demonstrated the power of the West and Thailand's weakness. They condemned the IMF and the USA for taking advantage of the crisis to assert their influence through increased liberalisation that reproduced structures and approaches inspired by the US model (Bello 1998; Bullard, Bello and Malhotra 1998:124). The IMF program was seen as enhancing policies that had caused the crisis in the first place. They argued for a nationalist approach to development, including reorientating production to domestic markets, and controls on international capital flows (Bello, Cunningham and Li 1998:249). This was the way to avoid domination by rich countries.

While this approach directs attention to national responses to the negative impacts of liberalisation and globalisation, it does not indicate an approach that overcomes the theoretical problems noted by earlier critics and discussed in chapter 1. Importantly, the alternatives proffered appear unrealistic (Hewison 2000b; Ungpakorn 2000).

Neo-classical economic approaches

Despite fads and fashions, economic growth has been the central pillar of Thailand's public policy for four decades. This emphasis has been based on the view that growth is best achieved through the operation of the free market. As outlined in chapter 1, although the neo-classical approach has asserted the primacy of market over government, this was modified following the success of the East Asian 'model'. Where government has been considered, interest has revolved around notions of 'getting the basics right'. Indeed, this approach saw international financial institutions praising Thailand for its conservative economic policy and resultant growth (Warr and Bhanupong 1996). The advent of the crisis, however, caused a rethinking.

As noted in chapter 1, the crisis prompted neo-classical analysts to identify 'market distortions' as contributing factors, reasserting their preferred theoretical and ideological position that distortions resulted from state intervention. These analysts and their institutionalist allies identified poor policies, weak governance (state and corporate), inadequate institutions, cronyism (resulting in moral hazard), corruption, and the resource misallocation as factors in the crisis. They argued that patronage and rent-seeking meant that state intervention prevented effective policy-making. It was argued that development would have been more rapid if industrial policy had promoted Thailand's comparative advantage through increased labour intensity and agriculture-related processing (Christensen et al. 1993:1–8).[7]

The crisis also saw neo-classical analysts give more recognition to institutions, and they have strongly supported IMF and World Bank liberalising, market-enhancing restructuring, and reform. The problem is that these reforms suggest only a limited appreciation of the social or political nature of institutions. The theoretical outcome is that 'good' public policy is that developed by governments relatively insulated from political influences. For Thailand this sees suggestions that representative politics might be an impediment to good policy development (see Christensen et al. 1993:19–20).

In reforming the state and its institutions neo-classical analysts are most comfortable with technocratic approaches. When technocrats are insulated from political debate they make better policy. Better policy means privatisation, liberalisation, and the development of institutions that can better handle a rules-based market system. Although an abstract model of the market prevails, and it is assumed that universally applicable and technically correct policies are available, their achievement requires that technocrats be able to select these options, free of 'political' demands. That the market and policies are socially and politically constructed is inadequately considered.

Historical institutionalist approaches

There was increased interest in historical institutionalist approaches as Thailand's economic performance during the boom was compared with that of East Asian economies. Analysts argued that the focus on the roles of only state and market drew too much attention away from an ensemble of non-state and non-market institutions that had determined Thailand's economic success. These included private-sector institutions such as banks, commercial networks, and business associations (Doner and Ramsey 1997).

Specifically rejecting the bureaucratic polity, and differentiating Thailand and other South-East Asian economies from North-East Asian developmentalist states, Doner and Hawes (1995:168–9) argue that these countries have been successful due to their dynamic private sectors. They see a 'relative strength' in private institutions and relatively weak states. For Thailand it is argued that some state elements, especially in fiscal and economic offices, were insulated from patronage, but that the private sector has also played a significant directing role (Doner and Ramsey 1997:273). Thus, in the face of market failures and indifferent or predatory state policies, it has been the private sector driving development.

The crisis brought a re-evaluation. The more state-focused historical institutionalists argued that the extent of the impact of the crisis in Thailand demonstrated the state's incapacity to drive the changes required to improve the 'production regime' and to establish the resources required for this (Weiss 1999:319–22). As noted in chapter 1, these analysts also identified 'external factors' as responsible for deepening the crisis. Weiss (1999:329) adds that there was relatively limited insulation of state agencies from 'particularistic interest politics'. More society-focused institutionalists give attention to this latter aspect. Hutchcroft (1999:474) argues that Thailand has exhibited the characteristics of 'bureaucratic capitalism', where the state was relatively stronger than business interests were, and where the state was 'relatively more patrimonial'.[8] However, the boom saw business establish its collective interest over those of the state. Market liberalisation occurred, with little attention to the building of appropriate institutions. This, together with an increasing tendency for rural politicians to enhance their patronage through access to state coffers and policy, set the framework for economic crisis. These politicians besieged the bureaucracy and expanded patrimonialism beyond the bureaucracy, making Thailand's system much more like the Philippines model of the patrimonial oligarchic state. This reflects a weakening of the state *vis-à-vis* business interests (Hutchcroft 1999:474, 495–7).

Such approaches were attractive for explaining differences between Thailand and developmental states, and for including historical arguments about the development of power. However, they have tended to emphasise trust, cooperation, and order among private-sector actors, while down playing competition and conflict among them (Doner and Hawes 1995:169). Reform is often seen to be about establishing order, stability, and accountability (Hutchcroft 1999:486–8). Where conflict is discussed, it is in the context of the state (and its officials) versus the private sector. Among other things, the crisis laid bare the contradictory relationships among the various fractions of capital, and indicated that the state, although responsible for the interests of capital in general, was also cognisant of the shifting power relationships between domestic and international capital, and within domestic capital.

As noted above, institutionalists and historical institutionalists both favour technocratic solutions to economic and political problems. Hutchcroft (1999:488) argues that Thailand's reforms and appropriate policy require that conservative urban elites capture the state and parliament from unsophisticated 'country bumpkins' (elected rural constituency politicians) who engage in money politics and patrimonialism.

Social conflict approaches

If other approaches lack attention to conflict and attach too much significance to 'good' policy, this is not the case for the conflict perspective. As explained in chapter 1, conflict theorists see markets, states, and institutions as products of interests and conflicts emanating from class relations and inequalities generated within societies and by the forces of global capitalism. In this perspective, the use of terms such as 'capitalism' and 'capitalist state' includes an identification of the nature of domination.

From this perspective, Thailand's growth and development during the past century is a part of a capitalist transformation that has irreversibly altered the patterns of social, economic, and political relations. The period of growth from the late 1950s, culminating in the boom of the 1986–96 period, saw a rapid advance of capitalist relations throughout the country, and the rise and diversification of competing capitalist groups, together with increased attention from internationalised capital.

Marxist political economists, then, see the crisis as a moment in this development process. In explaining the crisis they pointed to issues sometimes down played in other approaches—over-expansion, over-production, declining earnings, and the cyclical and crisis-prone nature of capitalism (see Hewison 2000a). Crises are thus unavoidable elements of the logic and contradictions of capitalist production. They also recognise that a crisis will be associated with a recomposition of capital. The tendency for competition among capitalists to become more intense, and for capitalists to turn on each other in times of crisis, means that they invariably result in bankruptcies, mergers, and acquisitions. The crisis is thus a part of global processes of capital accumulation and cycles of crisis. The boom emerged from the aftermath of an earlier crisis in the mid 1980s, and the country was again consumed by crisis in the late 1990s. Although domestic capitalists did exceptionally well during the boom, they are now restructuring locally, but also face competitive pressure from international capital.

In the remainder of this chapter an interpretation of the development of Thailand's capitalism will be outlined. It relies on the characterisation of an accumulation regime in each of the epochs examined.[9] The analytical task is not so much to identify 'good' and 'bad' policy in each epoch, but to outline the ensemble of class forces and the conflicts that led to the emergence of particular policy responses. This means that emphasis will be on delineating the class relations involved in capitalist development, the changing international context of development, the role of the state, and the way in which policy reflects patterns of domination.

The political economy of capitalist development

Early periods of development

While significant socioeconomic change was already under way, Thailand's nascent capitalism was boosted with the signing of the 1855 Bowring Treaty. From this time Thailand became enmeshed in trading patterns that were on Western terms and involved notions of 'free trade', marking the emergence of modern Thailand (Hong 1984; Nidhi 1982).

At the time the relatively small population was overwhelmingly a peasantry engaged in subsistence production. This production took place within family and community units (Chatthip 1999). The links between these and the royal state weakened as distance from administrative centres increased, with state control manifested in obligations on the population, to be met through slavery, corvée labour, military service, or in the delivery of valuable, often tradeable, commodities. External trade was controlled by royalty and nobles who were also state officials, and included important foreign minorities (Reid 1995). They also dominated the class and political structures, drawing their wealth and power from their control of labour, land, and trade. The monarchy, although often in competition with leading noble families, kept close control of government, and developed a highly personalised state, focused on the person of the monarch.

This picture began to change under a range of pressures. First, international trade patterns altered, driven by the industrial production of Western countries and the sustenance of their colonies. Second, colonial expansion in the region and the need to facilitate trade forced Thailand to reform its administration. Territorial boundaries were more carefully defined and national and provincial administration was reformed (Tej 1977; Thongchai 1994). Third, these changes created opportunities for a rapid expansion of exports, initially of rice, and later in timber, rubber, and tin; these commodities remained Thailand's main exports until the 1960s. By 1900 the monarchy had become particularly strong, supported by an increasingly modern military and bureaucracy. Opposition to the regime was vigorously suppressed, and political decision-making tightly controlled by the court.

Economic and political change was associated with a transformation of class relations. Slavery and the corvée were eventually discarded, resulting in the emergence of a free peasantry. The ruling class of lords and nobility increasingly came to rely on land, taxation, and the control of business for their wealth and that of the state (Hong 1984). The development of business, focused on the export trade, saw the ruling class and state—there being little distinction between state assets and those of the monarch—entering into alliances with foreign and Chinese business. This foreign and Chinese business became an important part of the reforms, as tax farmers and business leaders in the new economic system.[10] Tax-farming allowed the state to convert its revenue system to one based on money rather than on commodities and labour services. In business, Chinese merchants, royals, aristocrats, and Western interests developed a supportive, yet still competitive, business structure (Suehiro 1989). Additionally, myriad Chinese merchants and traders spread throughout Thailand, establishing businesses and shops and enhancing commodity trade.

The Chinese also became wage labourers. Labour was in short supply in Bangkok and the southern mines. This was partly due to the small population, but also because Thais, freed from labour obligations, took advantage of agricultural opportunities. The result was that, from the late 1880s to the 1930s, there was an addition of one million Chinese to the population, and they dominated the working class until the 1960s.

Domestic and international events in the 1920s and 1930s brought dramatic change. Within Thailand, rising pressures for political reform were thwarted by King Vajiravudh, his successor Prajadhipok, and their advisers. Economic reform was also stifled, even as the government faced considerable fiscal problems through royal profligacy under Vajiravudh (Batson 1984; Copeland 1994). When combined with the world economic depression and international political instability, the stage was set for change. In June 1932, a small group of commoners, organised as the People's Party, seized the state in a well-planned coup, establishing constitutional rule.[11]

Among other things, the overthrow of the monarchy established new economic and political ways. Although still not a fully fledged capitalist system, the commercialisation, monetisation, and commodification of the economy were well established by the 1930s. The overthrow of the monarchy's accumulation regime was an important step towards a modern economic system. Although unable to entrench the alternative constitutional form, 1932 was a move against unrepresentative politics (Nakarin 1992). Initially brought together by economic nationalism and their opposition to the monarchy and its state, the People's Party government split over economic policy and political representation. Even though no agreement could be reached on these fundamental issues, the regime was held together through its opposition to royalist anti-government plots.

The period from 1932 to 1957 saw continuing conflict between royalists and the People's Party, while debate over economic policy was dominated by nationalism and concerns over state intervention (to stimulate industry and improve the lot of farmers). Initially bitter, with accusations of 'Bolshevism', the dispute eventually centred on the degree of intervention. The result was poorly developed policies promoting ethnic Thai non-agricultural employment and investment. Where necessary or politically expedient, this meant investments by the state and its enterprises.

World War II saw much destruction of infrastructure and the temporary eclipse of the military. However, after the military seized power in 1947, economic policy and practice became more closely associated with senior political figures. Despite military control, there was no widespread opposition to private enterprise. Rather, a haphazard state-led approach to industrialisation developed. State investments were promoted to reduce foreign imports and as an example for the private sector. Riggs (1966) identified this period as the clearest expression of the bureaucratic polity, with powerful military and bureaucratic figures tapping into state enterprises and the resources of Chinese business for personal gain, and to finance political activity. At the same time, there were benefits for businesses linked to powerful political leaders, giving them competitive advantages.[12]

When the Korean War boom waned in the mid 1950s, business became concerned that this accumulation regime was no longer appropriate. For the capitalist class as a whole—as opposed to favoured individuals and firms linked to powerful leaders—the increasingly personalised arrangements required by the existing accumulation regime meant an uncertain investment climate. Demands that the state's investment role be limited to infrastructure received the support of foreign businesses. US companies, the largest foreign investors, took the lead in pressuring the government to be more receptive to foreign capital, and were supported by the use of official aid to encourage positive attitudes (Hewison 1985:276–7).

The coups of 1957–58 that brought General Sarit Thanarat to power ushered in an era of political, social, and economic change. The new government evidenced a determination to promote private rather than state investment. This enthusiasm developed from the realisation that a number of shaky state enterprises could not be saved, and coincided with a range of reports by international organisations recommending increased support for the private sector, import-substituting industrialisation (ISI), and a state restricted largely to infrastructure development (World Bank 1959).[13] These reports echoed a sentiment regarding development strategy that had emerged among a rising group of young civilian officials who took important positions in Sarit's economic agencies. In politics, Sarit established a system of 'despotic paternalism', where a highly authoritarian government was determined to establish order and stability, and make Thailand progressive and 'civilised' (Thak 1979).

The era of import-substitution industrialisation

A seminal World Bank (1959:94–106) report urged an ISI strategy with generous promotional privileges. Sarit and his advisers accepted these recommendations and moved quickly to expand manufacturing through increased incentives to private investment. The first national development plan (1961–66) reinforced these policies and the government accepted US and World Bank assistance in implementing the plan, revising the *Promotion of Investment Act (1960)* and other pro-business policies, and directing state investment to infrastructure.[14]

The focus on industry did not mean that agriculture was neglected. Indeed, in addition to ISI, the first plan emphasised agricultural development. The government was keen for agricultural exports to grow as this allowed capital to be drained from rural areas and directed to industry. Sarit's policies targeting industry and foreign investment, saw substantial investment in manufacturing. For local business the government's approach meant more room to invest, free of state competition. For budding industrialists, the government granted the tariff protection required to develop domestic manufacturing further. Foreign manufacturers were also keen to establish behind protective barriers. The government's emphasis on foreign investment was explained as an effort to overcome shortages of capital, technology, and entrepreneurial skills (Hewison 1985:280–1).

The government created a number of agencies to support ISI, including the Board of Investment (BOI)—a national planning office, later named the National Economic and Social Development Board (NESDB)—and a revamped Ministry of Industry. ISI was reflected in the first and second development plans (1967–71), with the bulk of capital invested with government promotional privileges going to import-substituting industries.

Agricultural taxation and the extraction of household savings into the commercial banking sector assisted by providing capital for industry (Silcock 1967b; Jansen 1990).

Manufacturing's contribution to GDP rose significantly (see table 3.1, below). Not only did high rates of protection encourage domestic investment, but also they further strengthened local finance and banking. This sector was also protected—no foreign banks could enter branch banking, and could offer only limited services—and policies to encourage saving also increased financial sector profitability. These were the big ISI winners. Large conglomerates resulted, many of them with commercial banks at their apex. Business control was consolidated within the 15–20 families dominating commercial banks (Hewison 1989:ch. 8) As well as investing in the developing industrial sector (for example cement, textiles, and garments), these Sino-Thai families established profitable operations in the finance and export of primary commodities. It was their control of finance, when the stock market was in its infancy and raising capital overseas was tightly controlled, that permitted the building of oligopolies in a range of economic sectors. The families also maintained excellent relations with powerful political figures.

Table 3.1 GDP by industrial origin, selected years, 1960, 1971, 1980 (%)

Sector	1960	1971	1980
Agriculture	39.8	29.8	24.9
Mining and quarrying	1.1	1.5	1.6
Manufacturing	12.5	17.5	20.7
Construction	4.6	5.5	5.7
Electricity and water supply	0.4	1.8	1.9
Transport and communications	7.5	6.7	6.4
Wholesale and retail trade	15.2	17.1	16.5
Banking, insurance, and real estate	1.9	4.2	6.0
Ownership of dwellings	2.8	1.9	1.5
Public administration and defence	4.6	4.3	4.2
Services	9.6	9.7	10.6

Source: Bank of Thailand, *National Income of Thailand*, various issues

ISI saw the development of a larger and more diverse working class, coinciding with the class's ethnic and gender transformation. Following the cessation of large-scale Chinese immigration before World War II, ethnic Thais moved into industrial employment, some temporarily, but increasingly on a permanent basis. Although agricultural activities remained predominant, the industrial labour force expanded substantially. Between 1960 and 1979 the total workforce expanded by more than 20 per cent or almost three million persons. The manufacturing workforce expanded by 45 per cent over this period (Hewison 1989:215). Increasingly, too, women began to move into manufacturing employment.

ISI policies protected the big conglomerates. Funds deposited in the banks grew rapidly, allowing the banking families to expand their economic control. The protection of manufacturing and the banks ensured profitability. Support for ISI also came from some influential foreign investors, especially the Japanese, with investments in textiles and auto assembly and parts manufacture (Pasuk and Baker 1995:130–8). State officials also supported the ISI accumulation regime, and there was little policy commitment to a more export-oriented strategy.

Export-oriented industrialisation: the boom

Change required an external 'shock', threatening profits, if EOI—meant to be based on a nation's advantage in producing commodities for a world market, utilising cheap labour—was to be supported by major business and political interests.

Critics of ISI argued that it was too limited by the relatively small domestic market and created disincentives to export (Hewison 1989:118–21). Calls for the promotion of export manufacturing were made in the late 1960s, but these were mainly from technocrats, and there was no great business pressure for change while growth continued and profits were maintained. In fact, under pressure from domestic capitalist groups, protection for import-substituting manufacturing actually increased through the 1970s and into the early 1980s (Pasuk and Baker 1995:144–5). It was not until the mid 1980s that EOI policy was established. The required shock was an economic downturn in the mid 1980s.

This downturn resulted from of a confluence of events. First, from the late 1970s, the baht, being tied to the dollar, began a steady climb, making Thailand's exports (still mainly primary commodities) less attractive on the world market. Second, agricultural commodity prices began a steady descent from the late 1970s. Third, the nature of international investment was changing, with a major relocation of East Asian firms to cheaper labour sites in South-East Asia. Fourth, the second oil crisis saw the government seeking loan funds, significantly raising public-sector debt. Fifth, military assistance had declined from the mid 1970s. Finally, as counter-insurgency became less of a concern, the military embarked on a spending spree, buying new kinds of arms and expanding public debt, arguing that the potential for regional conflict required different military technologies (Hewison 1987:61–76; Pasuk and Baker 1996:ch. 4).

The downturn had a substantial impact on business. Growth continued, but was the lowest for years. Bankruptcies mushroomed, investment dropped precipitously, unemployment increased, and even the biggest and strongest companies reported flat profits or their first losses for years. The downturn also indicated significant problems for state policy. Budget deficits ballooned, official debt reached unprecedented levels, and trade and current account balances were negative and increasing. Even before commodity prices began their steady decline, agriculture was doing poorly. Reflecting the policy emphasis on industry, government and business were little interested in the agricultural sector, except to promote agro-industry and to continue the exploitation of its output and labour. The downturn meant that farmers faced low prices, and workers wages were eroded by inflation and increased government charges.

As Pasuk and Baker (1996:65–6) point out, technocrats were split on the appropriate response to the downturn, and even entreaties from the powerful banking and textile sectors, and from the World Bank, brought few decisions. It was the belated recognition that agricultural prices were not about to save economic growth that brought a major devaluation and a concerted move to embrace EOI. The devaluation did much to make Thailand's cheap labour manufactures more attractive on the world market.

In terms of both policy emphasis and production, EOI was to remain the dominant strategy until the 1997 crisis. The economic results of this emphasis were spectacular. There was a rapid expansion of exports, from average annual growth rates of 6 per cent in the 1960s to 11 per cent in the 1970s, and rising to over 16 per cent per year in the 1980s. Annual rates in excess of 10 per cent were maintained in the first half of the 1990s. But 1996 saw no increase, a warning of things to come. The wider economic significance of the move to EOI can be seen in the data presented in table 3.2.

Table 3.2 GDP by industrial origin, 1985–98 (%)

Sector	1985	1990	1995	1996	1997	1998
Agriculture	15.8	12.7	11.1	11.0	12.9	14.8
Mining and quarrying	2.5	1.6	1.2	1.4	1.8	1.7
Manufacturing	21.9	27.2	28.2	28.4	26.6	27.4
Construction	5.1	6.2	7.3	7.4	6.0	3.8
Electricity and water supply	2.4	2.2	2.4	2.3	2.6	2.8
Transport and communications	7.4	7.1	7.3	7.3	8.7	8.6
Wholesale and retail trade	18.3	17.6	16.2	15.5	14.0	13.9
Banking, insurance, real estate	3.3	5.5	7.5	7.6	6.6	5.4
Ownership of dwellings	4.2	3.0	2.4	2.4	2.5	2.7
Public administration and defence	4.6	3.5	3.7	3.7	4.2	4.5
Services	14.5	13.3	12.8	13.1	14.1	14.3

Sources: TDRI (1995; 1998); Bank of Thailand (2000)

The change in the relative shares of the manufacturing and agricultural sectors in the economy is remarkable (see figure 3.1, page 85). In 1960 agriculture was the most important economic sector. It accounted for 40 per cent of GDP, and most exports, and employed the bulk of the population. Manufacturing made a relatively small contribution to production and employment. The transition took place in the early 1980s. By the mid 1990s, agriculture produced just 11 per cent of GDP, ranking lower than manufacturing, trade, and services. Rapid industrial growth saw manufactured exports expand from just 1 per cent of total exports in 1960 to a whopping 75 per cent by the early 1990s (TDRI 1992:6). This does not mean that agriculture has shrunk. It too has grown, but far less rapidly than manufacturing.

In 1960, 82 per cent of the economically active population people was in agriculture. By 1996 this had declined to just 48 per cent (Economic Section 1998:9). These figures understate the magnitude of change as many agricultural families now rely on income from off-farm sources. At the same time, employment in non-agricultural activities has grown significantly. EOI saw the further development of the working class. Between 1979 and 1998, the total workforce expanded by more than 50 per cent or almost 11 million persons. The manufacturing workforce almost tripled over the same period (TDRI 1999:14). Women made up half of the manufacturing workforce by 1992 (Yada 1998:126).

Growth in this period was driven by the private sector. Measured as a percentage of GDP, private investment in 1975 was about three times greater than public investment. The boom in private-sector investment following the policy changes of the mid 1980s saw private investment levels almost

Figure 3.1 GDP in agriculture and manufacturing, 1960–98

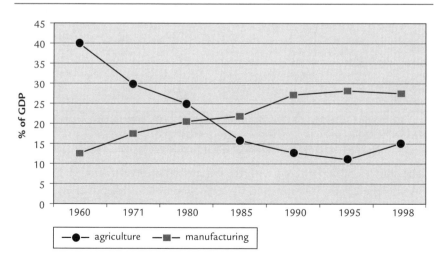

Sources: Bank of Thailand, *National Income of Thailand,* various issues; TDRI (1995; 1998); Bank of Thailand (2000)

five times that of the state. Real gross fixed capital formation grew by an average 20 per cent annually during the boom of 1986–91, and by 10–15 per cent in 1992–96. The value of new business registrations and capital expansions also grew rapidly during these periods, averaging more than 50 per cent in the 1986–91 period. These levels were reduced after 1991, but remained high by international standards until 1996 (Board of Investment 1995; 2000).

Behind these figures was the reality of a powerful domestic capitalist class that expanded rapidly during the 1980s. This expansion saw the class become increasingly diverse. There was also considerable stimulus from foreign investors (Jansen 1997). Domestic investors remained positive towards foreign investment, often preferring joint-ventures when entering new business sectors.[15] Foreign investment was seen as a barometer of business confidence, giving it considerable political significance. As seen in table 3.3 (below), the inflows of foreign capital increased substantially in the late 1980s and remained high until just before the 1997 crash. It is of interest, however, that direct foreign investment (DFI) increased during the early crisis period (discussed below).

Table 3.3 Flows of foreign capital, 1986–98

Year	Net DFI (US$ million)	% Change on previous year	Total capital flows (US$ million)
1986	276.3	55.5	–376
1987	361.7	30.9	896
1988	1 118.5	209.2	2 926
1989	1 827.9	63.4	5 780
1990	2 587.8	41.5	9 910
1991	2 055.6	–20.6	10 726
1992	2 150.6	4.6	9 630
1993	1 674.9	–22.1	10 636
1994	598.1	–64.3	12 229
1995	1 995.5	233.6	21 803
1996	2 298.9	15.2	19 741
1997	3 751.8	63.2	–8 637
1998	5 546.7	47.8	–15 593

Note: For the period 1986–96, US$1 was exchanged at about 25 baht. In 1997, after devaluation, US$1 was averaged at 31.37 baht, whereas, for 1998, the figure was 37.84 baht.

Sources: TDRI (1992; 1995; 1998); Bank of Thailand (2000); Board of Investment (2000)

The sources of DFI altered with the expansion of investment. In 1984 the USA was the largest investor but, by 1986, Japan had this position. Japan's net investments increased nine-fold between 1987 and 1990, and accounted for about 44 per cent of all DFI. Interestingly, Japan, the USA, and Hong Kong remained the largest investors throughout the period.

Although foreign investment was strategically important, local business investments were far greater. For most of the period between 1960 and

1994, although foreign investment increased steadily, its contribution to gross capital formation usually remained in a range of 1–8 per cent (Hewison 1989:112; Pasuk and Baker 1996:35). Even among BOI-promoted firms, between 1960 and 1993, approximately two-thirds of registered capital was identified as domestic (Board of Investment 1995:11). These levels of DFI are relatively low when compared with other ASEAN states. Pasuk and Baker (1996:35) correctly observe that: 'Foreign investment may have sparked the [post-1986] boom . . . [but] Thai investments made it a big boom'.

The boom, driven by ballooning exports, pulled the domestic market along. Bangkok and other urban centres experienced investment booms that saw markets expand and diversify, especially in real estate, construction, and wholesale and retail trade. The outcome was the emergence of an expanded capitalist class (Pasuk and Baker 1995:ch. 5; Pasuk and Baker 1996:chs 3–4). This resulted in a challenge to the financial dominance of the big banks. As noted above, the banks and their controlling families managed the supply of domestic investment funds. From the late 1970s, however, some technocrats sought to reduce the economic power of these families. It was decided that a limit on bank ownership in other business sectors and a widening of bank ownership would enhance growth (Hewison 1989:191). The dilution of family holdings was already under way as the families were unable to keep pace with the capital expansion requirements of their bank. However, it was only the expansion of the boom that was able to loosen banking family control in other business sectors.

Although the banks did well from the boom, and were aggressive in financing exports, a range of factors challenged their dominance.

First, the post-1985 increase in DFI saw foreign investors seeking local partners. The level of demand was such that it went well beyond the boundaries of the bank-dominated cliques.

Second, policy change saw controls on capital flows eased, meaning that domestic borrowers were able to go beyond domestic banks. Another important change was the ability to borrow overseas. At the same time, increased numbers of foreign banks were established in Thailand, and were particularly aggressive in their corporate and business lending. In addition, merchant banking expanded significantly, and several small finance companies were in a position to expand their activities, especially as they were also freed from reliance on the commercial banks.[16]

Third, the banks were challenged by the expansion of the Stock Exchange of Thailand (SET). The SET had existed for years, but had been hampered by a lack of investor confidence, particularly after a finance sector crisis in

1979 (Hewison 1981). However, following the Wall Street crash of October 1987, the SET took off, and capitalisation and turnover expanded markedly (see table 3.4, below). Although still volatile, the SET became attractive to both local and international investors. It mobilised large amounts of capital, loosening the grip of the banks on finance and industry. An important factor in this was the establishment of international securities and brokerage companies in Bangkok (Pasuk and Baker 1996:39).

Table 3.4 Selected statistics on the Stock Exchange of Thailand, 1985–99

Indicator	1985	1990	1996	1997	1998	1999
Annual turnover (US$ billion)	0.6	25.1	52.1	29.6	20.7	42.5
Average daily turnover (US$ million)	2.5	101.6	213.6	120.0	84.7	173.6
SET Index (end of period)	134.9	649.4	910.3	447.2	331.3	395.5
Market dividend yield (%)	8.2	3.6	3.5	6.0	1.3	0.6
Number of quoted companies	97	214	454	431	418	392
Market value capitalisation (US$ billion)	2.0	24.5	102.4	36.1	30.7	58.0

Sources: Board of Investment (1990; 1992; 1995); SET (2000a); Securities and Exchange Commission of Thailand (2000)

For many rising capitalists the expansion of the SET and financial liberalisation were liberating, as they were finally free of the control of the banking families. A range of companies and groups emerged to challenge those who were powerful during the ISI period. Many saw the SET as an unlimited source of funds and an expression of the free-wheeling spirit of capitalism. Manipulation was not unusual, especially as regulation was deliberately loose (Handley 1997).

The result was a larger, more diverse, capitalist class. The dominance of banking and industry was challenged. These areas remained important, but remarkably wealthy capitalist groups were produced by the widened financial sector, and by telecommunications, real estate, tourism, and a range of services (Handley 1997). Some of these upstart business groups even chose to challenge the big families on their own ground, in banking, and there was a number of takeover battles among the smaller banks. Huge profits were made and, although much was reinvested, consumption spending also increased markedly, further expanding the domestic market, but setting the scene for the 1997 bust.

The accumulation regime of the ISI era had seen a small capitalist group dominant, buttressed by its relationships with powerful political figures. Technocrats tended to have control of economic policy-making, but this did not amount to independence. The EOI-driven boom disrupted these relationships. Although many of the links remained, the nature of

Thailand's capitalism meant that technocrats were more concerned to manage an economy that enhanced expanded accumulation, being less particularistic and more concerned with the health of capital in general. This was a better strategy for dealing with a diversified business community. However, the expansion of electoral politics, where success depended on access to enormous quantities of money, saw business and elected politicians establishing relationships not unlike those between officials and business under ISI.

Thailand's consistent economic growth from the late 1950s to 1997 was not unreservedly positive. A range of negative issues was identified (see Medhi 1995). Before examining the crisis, it is appropriate to discuss briefly a central problem of the boom, wealth distribution.

Wealth distribution and the boom

The World Bank (1993) argued that one of the results of East Asian growth was increased equity. For Thailand, however, this was not the experience. As can be seen in figure 3.2 (below), rapid increases in per capita incomes brought significant reductions in absolute poverty. These figures are, however, based on unrealistically low poverty lines.[17] But even if a still very low per-capita figure of US$1 a day is used, whereas 33.6 million were below the poverty line in 1988, this had been reduced to just 9.1 million in 1996 (TDRI 1998:23). People outside the agricultural sector did best.

Significantly, however, income and wealth distribution became increasingly skewed (see figure 3.3, page 90). In urban areas, where workers have

Figure 3.2 Poverty incidence, 1975/76–1996

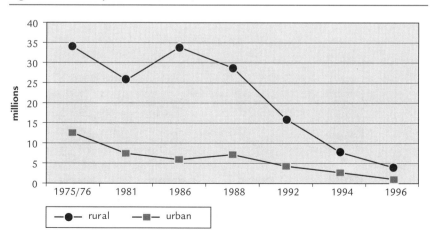

Sources: TDRI (1992; 1995; 1998; 1999)

made significant contributions to economic growth, they have not gained adequate rewards for their labours. Indeed, worker's lives have been characterised by relatively low wages and poor conditions. Such conditions were necessary to establishing comparative advantage in both ISI and EOI strategies. The related phenomenon of widespread exploitation of women and children in small factories and sweatshops is also well known (see Mathana 1995).

Many analysts and policy-makers had expected, and had repeatedly restated their belief, that the benefits of growth would trickle down to all levels of society; few had predicted increased inequality. In the words of one influential economist, '. . . much has been accomplished . . . Measured against what is possible to achieve with . . . five decades of growth, much is wanting' (Ammar 1996:5).

Distribution was most inequitable between rural and urban incomes. The principal reason for this is that smallholder agriculture had become a marginal way of making a living. This is illustrated by comparing population and productivity of the various regions. Bangkok dominates. Most industry is clustered around the capital, meaning that the area is highly productive. Generally, as distance from the centre increases and agricultural activities become more significant, productivity decreases. This is most noticeable for the north-east, the most populous region and heavily reliant on agriculture. The result is that its productivity is low, poverty is high, migrant labour is common, and incomes are the lowest of all regions. Interestingly,

Figure 3.3 Income distribution, 1975/76–1996

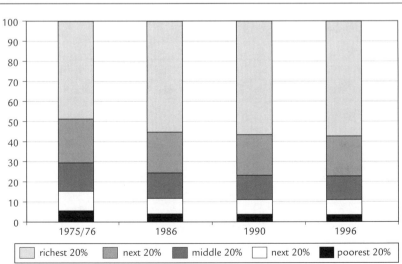

Sources: TDRI (1992; 1995; 1998; 1999)

despite governmental efforts to decentralise development, the gaps have widened.

Some planners and politicians began to view the issue of distributing the benefits of growth as suggesting a potential for conflict (*Nation* 1992). This was a shock as growth had been expected to solve such social problems.[18] Protracted debate led to a recognition that agriculture would stagnate and income disparities could worsen further. The policy answer was to encourage industrial activity in rural areas (NESDB n.d.:99–104). It was considered that this would enhance trickle-down effects in provincial areas, while not compromising growth, and would expand export-oriented industry.

However, this approach did not achieve any short-term impact on distributional issues. There was little consensus in business or government on the need for higher-level skills. The existing accumulation regime produced the boom, and profits seemed to flow easily from both productive and speculative investment. In short, there was no imperative to look beyond existing patterns of investment and exploitation. Continued opposition to any expansion of the limited social welfare system reinforced this. These debates were temporarily abandoned when the 1997 crisis hit.

There were other signs that the economy faced problems. For example, from 1993 the SET began a steady decline. Speculative attacks on the baht began in 1995, and there was a decline in property values, rising vacancy rates for office and condominium space and deteriorating investor confidence before 1997. The 1996 failure of the Bangkok Bank of Commerce and an export collapse confirmed that the economy was in trouble. But booms build confidence, and many simply did not want to believe that the boom was ending.[19]

Thailand: the bust and beyond

There has been a range of explanations for the Asian crisis (see chapter 1, this volume). From these, several important issues emerge for Thailand. Particularly significant were the downturns in investment and exports already noted, partly attributable to the high value of the baht. There was also over-capacity in a range of sectors, including electronics, household appliances, auto construction, textiles and garments, footwear, electricity generation, real estate, and heavy industry (especially cement, petrochemicals, and steel). Despite this, 'hot money' poured into unproductive areas and sectors with over-capacity (US Embassy 1998:1). These factors eventually brought a 'price collapse' and an erosion of 'the rates of return on new capital invested' (Bank for International Settlements 1998:35–6, 117). In addition, as already noted, the troubles of the finance sector in 1996 saw investor confidence begin to weaken.

The 2 July 1997 devaluation marked the beginning of a downward economic spiral. The IMF brokered a US$17 billion support package, demanding substantial reform and restructuring from Thailand's government. The IMF response was based on orthodox economic assessments of the crisis. This was no surprise as the World Bank and IMF had implemented similar programs in Africa, Latin America, and Eastern Europe. What was something of a surprise for these international institutions was that the package deepened the downturn, arguably causing the depression that followed. Devaluation meant the end of many businesses, with hundreds closing in all sectors. The resulting social and economic impacts were substantial (Hewison 2000a). There is no need to detail the events of the crisis here. Rather the focus will be on the class outcomes and the impact on the EOI accumulation regime.[20]

As noted above, crises are elements of the logic and contradictions of capitalist production that include cycles of over-expansion and over-production. Crises also mean a recomposition of capital, as competition becomes intense among capitalists. Invariably there are bankruptcies, mergers, and acquisitions. Such processes are now components of globalised capital accumulation and cycles of crisis. In Thailand, the boom emerged from the mid 1980s crisis. This crisis marked a significant restructuring of domestic capital, responding in part to global economic and competitive change. The crisis of the late 1990s resulted from tendencies generated by the boom. Domestic capital is again faced with the need to restructure under renewed domestic competitive pressure and by aggressive international capital. One result has been a massive reorganisation of ownership and control, including the transfer of assets to other Asian (particularly Japanese), American, and European investors through debt-for-equity swaps, takeovers, investment in devalued local companies, and buy-outs of Thai partners.

The restructuring process has been accepted by significant elements of domestic business, technocrats, and politicians who believe that competitiveness in an era of global capitalism requires open markets and a convergence of regulatory environments (Panitch 1998). Establishing and enhancing these processes was the intent of the IMF, World Bank, and Thailand's government reforms. The centrality of liberalisation and regulatory reform is indicated in the World Bank's program. Although the Bank trumpeted social safety nets, by October 1999 only US$43 million were made available through 'social-sector' activities. For restructuring in business and government reform, the total was more than US$2 billion (Shivakumar et al. 2000:20). The crisis provided an opportunity to promote a raft of changes, sweeping aside national laws and regulations considered restrictive. So there were demands for enhanced transparency, stronger financial systems, further liberalisation, reductions in 'unproductive' government spending, an end to 'cronyism', and more 'cost-effective' spending on health, education, the poor, unemployed, and the environment (Ouattara 1998).

This program, albeit with some rolling-back of the IMF's original monetary extremism, challenged not only the successful boom-period relationships between capital and state, but also that between capitals. It has devastated Thailand's capitalist class. Foreign currency debts and the liquidity squeeze that came with the IMF's program crippled many industrial firms, already reeling from weak exports. Initially, financial, real estate, and construction firms dissolved. Land developers fared particularly badly, with few surviving through 1997 and 1998. The finance sector was in tatters, with only a handful of finance and securities companies remaining after 1997. Industrial investment also collapsed, with up to 400 billion baht in approved investment cancelled or delayed by the end of 1997. This was not helped by a plunge in domestic demand. All manufacturers appeared to be struggling in 1997–98, with over-capacity in many sectors (*BP* 1998d). Survival became the aim as bankruptcies doubled in early 1998, with five thousand companies closing by June 1998 (*Nation* 1998). Even in early 2000, more than 25 per cent of non-performing loans was in the manufacturing sector (*Nation* 2000d). The retail sector was also heavily indebted. Low local demand throughout the 1997–99 period made it difficult for this sector to rebound. The result has been that a very large number of the 1990s high-flyers was wiped out by the crisis, many crushed under the weight of their foreign currency loans.

The crisis has had class impacts that go deeper than the destruction of a swathe of boom-time entrepreneurs. The powerful banking families were also challenged as finance companies and banks failed and capital write-downs reduced family holdings in their core enterprises. The crisis marked a significant moment in the competitive reorganisation of banking capital. As noted above, this process had commenced during the boom. A number of the families found it difficult to recover from the internal conflicts and competitive pressures of the mid 1980s and from state efforts to reduce their power. Banks in this category included the Siam City Bank (Mahadamrongkul family), First Bangkok City Bank (Tejapaibul family), and the Union Bank of Bangkok (Cholvicharn and Penchart families). The Bangkok Bank of Commerce (Jalichandra family) had collapsed in 1996,

despite strong support from political figures. Small family banks, often acting as little more than family treasuries and investment brokers, also came
under pressure during the boom. For example, the Laemthong Bank had
been the subject of takeover battles, and the Nakornthon (Wanglee family)
and the Bank of Asia (Phatraprasit and Euachukiarti families) experienced
periods of weakness. The crisis meant serious difficulties for these troubled
banks. By October 1998 the government had taken over four struggling
banks, and virtually all of the financial sector's companies were gone.

Many of the smaller banks were unable to attract the new capital required
by the Bank of Thailand. When combined with record losses and non-
performing loans averaging about 50 per cent (1.78 trillion baht), the survival of all but the largest banks was in question (*BP* 1998c). Maintaining
family control became a major concern. The Siam Commercial Bank was
able to convince its major Japanese investors to increase their stakes, and
the royal family restructured its vast investments to retain its strong holding. The Bangkok Bank and Thai Farmer's Bank were able to raise new
capital, although this meant moving to 49 per cent foreign ownership,
facilitated by their long-standing international connections, especially with
US investment banks. The shareholdings of the powerful Lamsam (Thai
Farmer's Bank) and Sophonpanich (Bangkok Bank) families had already
been diluted during the 1980s, but these families have been able to maintain management control.[21]

As shown in table 3.5 (page 95), foreign investors have made significant
inroads into the banking sector. This will mean significant changes in the
structure of business and the capitalist class. As already noted, the banking
sector has been the most powerful fraction of domestic capital in the period
since 1957. Formerly protected, family dominance is now seen in only four
banks. Foreign owners and minority shareholders change the patterns of
doing business, suggesting the end of bank-based conglomerates that has
been so central to development since the late 1950s.

Foreign capital has been supportive of the government's reforms and
restructuring, carping only when the pace slows. This is hardly surprising
given the great advances that foreign capital has made. Foreign investors
have made numerous demands of the government, including reform of alien
business laws, revisions to duties, taxes and customs procedures, privatisation, transparency, an end to corruption, and further liberalisation in all
sectors (*BP* 1998b).

Interestingly, the government and big local business have also been
supportive of the reforms. The boom, but especially the crisis, emphasised
the highly competitive nature of international and regional capitalism. As
shown in table 3.5 (page 95), those banks that have survived, avoided state

Table 3.5 Thailand's banks, 1997–99

Bank	Foreign stake (March 1997)	Situation at end of 1999
Bangkok Bank	25.0%	raised capital; 48.78% foreign stake; significant share held by Singapore Investment Corporation
Thai Farmer's Bank	25.0%	raised capital; 48.98% foreign stake; 3% stake held by Singapore Investment Corporation
Siam Commercial Bank	25.0%	raised capital; 49% foreign, mainly Japanese stake
Bank of Ayudhaya	24.9%	40% foreign stake; resisted state recapitalisation; Ratanarak family sold other assets to retain the bank
Thai Dhanu Bank	9.4%	Development Bank of Singapore has 51% stake; now DBS Thai Dhanu Bank
Bank of Asia	6.1%	75% owned by ABN Amro
Nakornthon Bank	5.6%	75% owned by Standard Chartered Bank; now Standard Chartered Nakornthon Bank
Radanasin Bank*	n.a.	75% owned by United Overseas Bank of Singapore
First Bangkok City Bank	n.a.	merged with Krung Thai Bank in late 1998
Siam City Bank	n.a.	taken over by government
Bangkok Bank of Commerce	n.a.	wound down and closed in 1998.
Bangkok Metropolitan Bank	approx. 5%	Tejapaibul family lost control when government took over; for sale to a foreign bank
Thai Military Bank	approx. 12%	military ownership diluted; reluctant to bring in foreigners; recapitalisation long delayed; Thaksin Shinawatra has acquired a substantial stake
Laemthong Bank	n.a.	taken over by government and merged with Radanasin Bank
Krung Thai Bank	approx. 7%	state bank; mired in non-performing loans and corruption scandals
Union Bank of Bangkok	n.a.	taken over by the state and then merged with 13 finance companies (also seized by government) to form BankThai
Asia Trust Bank	n.a.	defunct before the crisis

*Created from Laemthong Bank and several finance and securities companies, all of which had been taken over by the government

n.a. means no data available or not applicable

Sources: Bangkok Post (editorial staff) (1998); BP (1998a; 1999); Nation (2000a; 2000b; 2000c; 2000e); TEM (2000); SET (2000b)

takeover, and maintained majority Thai ownership and control of banks, all had significant levels of foreign investment before the crisis. With the exception of the Bank of Ayudhaya, each also had significant international or regional operations. EOI had required more internationally competitive banking, and internationalisation revealed weaknesses in the structure of the industry. The big banks, although realising the risks of increased competition, were keen that the government push through further reforms. In addition, the fact that the high level of non-performing loans threatened these banks suggested the need for a way to retreat from the business practices established during the boom. To survive and compete, the banks realised that it was in their long-term interest to establish better rules. In the industrial sector it has become clear that the same patterns are emerging, with export-oriented firms appearing to recover quickest.

Although a new accumulation regime is still emerging, it is clear that this will involve a more significant role for foreign capital, a restructured domestic capitalist class (in which export-oriented and internationalised capital will be most powerful), and a state–capital relationship that will be increasingly rules-based. The last will see the government's economic role limited and more attention given to regulatory activities. Further privatisation and liberalisation can be expected. Interestingly, the development of a more rules-based business environment is congruent with reforms in the political sphere, where the 1997 constitution has established numerous rights and responsibilities for citizens and has better defined the roles of politicians and state officials.

Although workers and rural families suffered during the crisis, the focus on regulation and internationalisation might well be in their long-term interest. To be internationally competitive Thai firms must advance beyond low-cost production. This will require better-skilled labour, and investments in improved education and training by the state and capital. This could eventually benefit the poor.

Conclusion

Thailand's economic development can be judged successful in growth terms. The crisis has not altered this judgment, even though it has prompted a reconsideration of the reasons for economic achievement and failure, and the role of the state. Before the crisis, some concluded that Thailand offered little theoretical support for the efficacy of either interventionist or minimalist states. Others argued that Thailand's growth might have been higher had it not been for poor state institutions. The crisis focused attention on institutions capable of facilitating markets through rules-based and predictable systems.

This chapter has attempted to demonstrate that this debate is not always enlightening. In general terms, it is not surprising that Thailand's development strategies and plans have supported the expansion of markets and capitalist accumulation. These policies were adopted not necessarily because politicians, bureaucrats, and technocrats were listening to capitalists or including them in policy-making—sometimes they did—but because structural imperatives demanded that the state support capitalist accumulation.

Beyond the general, the history of Thailand's development has seen the establishment of particular accumulation regimes. These regimes are an amalgam of economic, social and political power, and structure policy development. In other words, policy outcomes are not a measure of the abilities of institutions (state or private) or of the relative insulation of decision-makers. Rather, policy results from competition and conflict over production, profits, wealth, and power. These conflicts are intimately bound to the trajectory of various classes and class fractions. In Thailand, this has been seen in the development, diversification, and competition within domestic capital, and between domestic and international capital. The crisis highlights that these struggles for conflicts are sharpest when capital needs to restructure. Only by understanding the nature of globalised corporate battles can policy outcomes be adequately understood.

Notes

1 Andrew Brown, Garry Rodan, Jane Hutchison, Pasuk Phongpaichit, and Chris Baker provided comments on earlier versions and ideas.

2 These paragraphs are a characterisation. For more detail see Bottomore (1985). Discussions of the development of Thailand's capitalism are in Hewison (1989:16–32) and Pasuk and Baker (1995).

3 For a discussion of the issues involved in the comparative study of capitalist development in Asia and Europe, see Rutten (1994).

4 It should be emphasised that the categorisation used results in a focus on the differences among the various approaches. This is not meant to deny synergies and overlaps between them.

5 The World Bank also has taken up 'social capital' in its post-1997 crisis analysis (Shivakumar et al. 2000), but adopting different definitions from Unger. The Bank assesses the relationship between social capital and the crisis.

6 Writing from a different perspective, Yoshihara (1988), in arguing that South-East Asian capitalism is *ersatz*, develops an analysis that produces conclusions close to those of dependency theorists.

7 Note that this report was strongly influenced by new institutionalism. The connections between the two approaches are set out in Peters (1999).

8 His definition is close to Riggs's bureaucratic polity (Hutchcroft 1999:474–6).

9 The outline is necessarily schematic. It seeks general patterns in periods of rapid change. Such characterisations are meant to convey the essence of

particular accumulation regimes, and tend to give less attention to counter-vailing tendencies.

10 The history of the Chinese in Thailand is analysed by Skinner (1957; 1958). See also Suehiro (1989) and Hewison (1989).

11 The event is usually portrayed as the replacement of one elite by another. It was far more than this. The People's Party, although not cohesive or ideologically coherent, established the fundamentals of the political and economic landscape and discourse. It defined a political opposition (royalists), brought the military to political prominence, and raised economic management, modernisation and progress, constitutionalism, representation, and opposition as important issues.

12 The government's anti-Chinese legislation and support for state enterprises dis-advantaged some Chinese and foreign businesses. At the same time, however, many private enterprises benefited, including commercial banks linked to powerful officials (see Hewison 1989:192–5).

13 Sarit had fewer links to state enterprises than did the leaders of the previous government. His connections were with the private sector (Silcock 1967a:20).

14 The USA had provided substantial aid prior to Sarit, concentrated on military assistance (see Darling 1965). This increased after Sarit came to power.

15 The BOI made no particular distinction between foreign and domestic investors. Promotional privileges to foreign firms have also been available to domestic investors, although a few areas of employment were reserved for Thais. The privileges have been generous. In addition to guarantees against nationalisation, state monopolies, or government competition, BOI promotion offers incentives such as tax holidays and other taxation relief, import bans on competing prod-ucts, tax deductions, repatriation of profits, and substantial and additional benefits for exporters (Board of Investment 1995).

16 Some technocrats and smaller business groups pushed these changes as a further attempt to reduce the business power of the banking families.

17 The poverty line used to calculate these figures in 1996 was annual per capita figure of 5369 baht (US$0.59 per day) for rural areas and 8589 baht (US$0.94 per day) for urban areas.

18 The focus on distribution became politically significant when electoral politics was dominant. One reason for this was that rural areas provided the majority of national MPs.

19 For example, the Bank of Thailand (1997a:5), reporting the first *nine* months of 1997, referred to 'subdued' economic conditions; this when the crisis was under way. Shortly afterwards, the bank's annual report referred to 'severe dif-ficulties' and a 'sharp economic slowdown' (Bank of Thailand 1997b:5–6).

20 The results of the crisis have not been fully played out. Even so, general obser-vations are possible.

21 An important study by Claessens, Djankov and Lang (2000) indicates the strong control that families had maintained in SET-listed companies to 1996.

References

Ammar Siamwalla (1996) 'Two and a Half Cheers for Economic Growth: An Assessment of Long-term Changes in the Thai Economy', *TDRI Quarterly Review*, (11)1:3–5.

Anek Laothamatas (1992) *Business Associations and the New Political Economy of Thailand. From Bureaucratic Polity to Liberal Corporatism*, Singapore: Institute of Southeast Asian Studies.

Bangkok Post (BP) (1998a), 30 May 1998.

Bangkok Post (BP) (1998b), 1 August 1998.

Bangkok Post (BP) (1998c), 23 September 1998.

Bangkok Post (BP) (1998d), 25 September 1998.

Bangkok Post (BP) (1999), 25 June 1999.

Bangkok Post (editorial staff) (1998) *1998 Mid-Year Economic Review*, 30 June, <www.bangkokpost.com/myer98/myer98_01.html>.

Bank for International Settlements (1998) *68th Annual Report*, Basle, 8 June.

Bank of Thailand (1997a) 'Economic Developments in the First 9 Months of 1997', *Bank of Thailand Quarterly Bulletin*, (37)3:5–15.

Bank of Thailand (1997b) 'Economic Performance in 1997 and Outlook for 1998', *Bank of Thailand Quarterly Bulletin*, (37)4:5–20.

Bank of Thailand (2000) 'Bank of Thailand Statistics', <www.bot.or.th>.

Batson, Benjamin A. (1984) *The End of the Absolute Monarchy in Siam*, Singapore: Oxford University Press.

Bello, Walden (1998) 'Testimony of Walden Bello before Banking Oversight Subcommittee, Banking and Financial Services Committee', US House of Representatives, 21 April, <www.igc.org/dgap/walden.html>.

Bello, Walden, Shea Cunningham and Li Kheng Poh (1998) *A Siamese Tragedy; Development and Disintegration in Modern Thailand*, London: Zed Books.

Board of Investment, *Key Investment Indicators in Thailand*, various issues, with the year publication indicated in each reference.

Board of Investment (1995) *A Guide to the Board of Investment*, Bangkok: Office of the Board of Investment.

Board of Investment (2000) *Thailand Information Database*, 19 July, <www.boi.go.th/english/tid/data/BOTMacro_e.htm>.

Bottomore, Tom (1985) *Theories of Modern Capitalism*, London: George Allen and Unwin.

BP, see *Bangkok Post (BP)*.

Bullard, Nicola, Walden Bello and Kamal Malhotra (1998) 'Taming the Tigers: The IMF and the Asian Crisis', in K.S. Jomo (ed.) *Tigers in Trouble. Financial Governance, Liberalisation and Crises in East Asia*, London: Zed Books, pp 85–136.

Chatthip Nartsupha (1999) *The Thai Village Economy in the Past*, Chiangmai: Silkworm Books.

Christensen, Scott, David Dollar, Ammar Siamwalla and Pakorn Vichyanond (1993) *The Lessons of East Asia. Thailand: The Institutional and Political Underpinnings of Growth*, Washington, D.C.: World Bank.

Claessens, Stijn, Simeon Djankov and Larry H.P. Lang (2000) 'The Separation of Ownership and Control in East Asian Corporations', *Journal of Financial Economics*, October, 58, 1–2, pp 81–112.

Copeland, Mathew Phillip (1994) 'Contested Nationalism and the 1932 Overthrow of the Absolute Monarchy in Siam', PhD thesis, Australian National University, Canberra.

Darling, Frank C. (1965) *Thailand and the United States*, Washington, D.C.: Public Affairs Press.

Doner, Richard F. and Ansil Ramsey (1997) 'Competitive Clientelism and Economic Governance: The Case of Thailand', in Sylvia Maxfield and Ben Ross Schneider (eds) *Business and the State in Developing Countries*, Ithaca: Cornell University Press, pp 237–76.

Doner, Richard F. and Gary Hawes (1995) 'The Political Economy of Growth in Southeast and Northeast Asia', in Manochehr Dorraj (ed.) *The Changing Political Economy of the Third World*, Boulder: Lynne Rienner Publishers, pp 145–85.

Economic Section (1998) '1998 Investment Climate Statement for Thailand', Bangkok, Department of State, United States Embassy, <http://usa.or.th/embassy/invcl98.htm>.

Handley, Paul (1997) 'More of the Same?: Politics and Business, 1987–96', in Kevin Hewison (ed.) *Political Change in Thailand. Democracy and Participation* London and New York: Routledge, pp 94–113.

Hart-Landsberg, Martin and Paul Burkett (1998) 'Contradictions of Capitalist Industrialization in East Asia: A Critique of the 'Flying Geese' Theories of Development', *Economic Geography*, 74 (April):87–110.

Hewison, Kevin (1981) 'The Financial Bourgeoisie in Thailand', *Journal of Contemporary Asia*, (11)4:395–412.

Hewison, Kevin (1985) 'The State and Capitalist Development in Thailand', in Richard Higgott and Richard Robison (eds) *Southeast Asia: Essays in the Political Economy of Structural Change* London: Routledge and Kegan Paul, pp 266–94.

Hewison, Kevin (1987) 'National Interests and Economic Downturn: Thailand', in Richard Robison, Kevin Hewison and Richard Higgott (eds) *Southeast Asia in the 1980s: The Politics of Economic Crisis*, Sydney: Allen and Unwin, pp 52–79.

Hewison, Kevin (1989) *Bankers and Bureaucrats: Capital and the Role of the State in Thailand*, New Haven: Yale Center for International and Area Studies, Yale University Southeast Asian Monographs, No. 34.

Hewison, Kevin (2000a) 'Thailand's Capitalism Before and After the Economic Crisis', in Richard Robison, Mark Beeson, Kanishka Jayasuriya and Hyuk-Rae Kim (eds) *Politics and Markets in the Wake of the Asian Crisis*, London: Routledge, pp 192–211.

Hewison, Kevin (2000b) 'Resisting Globalization: A Study of Localism in Thailand', *Pacific Review*, (13)2:279–96.

Hong, Lysa (1984) *Thailand in the Nineteenth Century. Evolution of the Economy and Society*, Singapore: Institute of Southeast Asian Studies.

Hutchcroft, Paul (1999) 'After the Fall: Prospects for Political and Institutional Reform in Post-Crisis Thailand and the Philippines', *Government and Opposition*, (34)4:473–97.

Jansen, Karel (1990) *Finance, Growth and Stability. Financing Economic Development in Thailand, 1960–86*, Avebury: Gower.

Jansen, Karel (1997) *External Finance in Thailand's Development. An Interpretation of Thailand's Growth Boom*, Houndsmill: Macmillan; New York: St Martin's.

Mathana Phananiramai (1995) 'Thailand National Report: Employment Situation, Problems and Policy', *TDRI Quarterly Review*, (10)3:11–15.

McVey, Ruth (1992) 'The Materialization of the Southeast Asian Entrepreneur', in Ruth McVey (ed.) *Southeast Asian Capitalists*, Ithaca, Cornell University Southeast Asia Program, pp 7–33.

Medhi Krongkaew (ed.) (1995) *Thailand's Industrialization and Its Consequences*, Houndmills: Macmillan.

Nakarin Mektrairat (1992) *Kanpatiwat sayam ph.s. 2475* [The Revolution in Siam 1932], Bangkok: Social Sciences and Humanities Project Foundation.

Nation (1992), 14 December 1992.

Nation (1998), 21 July 1998.

Nation (2000a), 10 January 2000.

Nation (2000b), 27 January 2000.

Nation (2000c), 19 February 2000.

Nation (2000d), 21 March 2000.

Nation (2000e), 22 March 2000.

National Economic and Social Development Board (NESDB) (n.d.) *The Seventh Five-Year National Economic and Social Development Plan (1992–1996)*, Bangkok: Office of the Prime Minister.

NESDB, see National Economic and Social Development Board (NESDB).

Nidhi Aeusrivongse (1982) *Wathanatham kradumphi kab wannakam ton rattanakosin*, Bangkok: Thai Khadi Research Institute.

Ouattara, Alassane D. (1998) 'The Asian Crisis: Origins and Lessons', Address at the Royal Academy of Morocco Seminar on 'Why Have the Asian Dragons Caught Fire?', Fez, 4 May, <www.imf.org/external/np/speeches/1998/050498A.HTM>.

Panitch, Leo (1998) '"The State in a Changing World": Social-Democratizing Global Capitalism?', *Monthly Review*, (50)5:11–22.

Pasuk Phongpaichit and Chris Baker (1995) *Thailand. Economy and Politics*, Kuala Lumpur: Oxford University Press.

Pasuk Phongpaichit and Chris Baker (1996) *Thailand's Boom!*, Chiangmai: Silkworm Books.

Pasuk Phongpaichit and Chris Baker (1998) *Thailand's Boom and Bust*, Chiangmai: Silkworm Books.

Peters, B. Guy (1999) *Institutional Theory in Political Science. The 'New Institutionalism'*, London: Pinter.

Reid, Anthony (1995) 'Documenting the Rise and Fall of Ayudhya as a Regional Trade Centre', in Kajit Jittasevi (ed.) *Ayudhya and Asia*, Core University Program between Thammasat University and Kyoto University, 18–20 December, pp 5–14.

Riggs, Fred W. (1966) *Thailand: The Modernization of a Bureaucratic Polity*, Honolulu: East–West Center Press.

Rutten, Mario (1994) *Asian Capitalists in the European Mirror*, Amsterdam: VU University Press.

Securities and Exchange Commission of Thailand (2000) *Capital Market Performance, 1997–1999*, <www.sec.or.th/ann99/app4.html>.

SET, see Stock Exchange of Thailand (SET).

Shivakumar, J., G. Abeysekera, Amara Pongsapich and Bencha Yoddumnern-Attig (2000) 'Social Capital and the Crisis', *Thailand Social Monitor*, Bangkok: World Bank, January.

Silcock, T.H. (1967a) 'Outline of Economic Development 1945–65', in T.H. Silcock (ed.) *Thailand. Social and Economic Studies in Development*, Canberra: Australian National University Press, pp 1–26.

Silcock, T.H. (1967b) 'The Rice Premium and Agricultural Diversification', in T.H. Silcock (ed.) *Thailand. Social and Economic Studies in Development*, Canberra: Australian National University Press, pp 231–57.

Skinner, G. William (1957) *Chinese Society in Thailand: An Analytical History*, Ithaca: Cornell University Press.

Skinner, G. William (1958) *Leadership and Power in the Chinese Community of Thailand*, Ithaca: Cornell University Press.

Stock Exchange of Thailand (SET) (2000a) *Fact Book 2000*, Bangkok: Stock Exchange of Thailand.

Stock Exchange of Thailand (SET) (2000b) *Listed Company Info 1999 (Q3–Q4)*, Bangkok: Stock Exchange of Thailand, CD-ROM.

Suehiro Akira (1989) *Capital Accumulation in Thailand 1855–1985*, Tokyo: The Centre for East Asian Cultural Studies.

Suthy Prasartset (1980) *Thai Business Leaders. Men and Careers in a Developing Economy*, Tokyo: Institute of Developing Economies.

TDRI, see Thailand Development Research Institute (TDRI).

Tej Bunnag (1977) *The Provincial Administration of Siam, 1892–1915*, Kuala Lumpur: Oxford University Press.

TEM, see *Thailand Economic Monitor (TEM)*.

Thailand Development Research Institute (TDRI) (1992; 1995; 1998; 1999) *Thailand Economic Information Kit*, Bangkok: TDRI.

Thailand Economic Monitor (TEM) (2000), February 2000, p. 51.

Thak Chaloematiarana (1979) *Thailand. The Politics of Despotic Paternalism*, Bangkok: Thai Khadi Research Institute.

Thongchai Winichakul (1994) *Siam Mapped. A History of the Geo-Body of a Nation*, Honolulu: University of Hawaii Press.

Unger, Danny (1998) *Building Social Capital in Thailand. Fibers, Finance, and Infrastructure*, Cambridge: Cambridge University Press.

Ungpakorn, Ji Giles (2000) 'Assessing the Rise of Left Nationalism and Community Economics in Thailand', Paper, Asian Studies Association of Australia 2000 Conference, Melbourne, 2–5 July.

United States (US) Embassy (1998) 'Thailand—Economic Trends and Forecast for 1998', Bangkok, <http://usa.or.th/embassy/eco.htm>.

US Embassy, see United States (US) Embassy.

Warr, Peter G. and Bhanupong Nidhiprabha (1996) *Thailand's Macroeconomic Miracle. Stable Adjustment and Sustained Growth*, Kuala Lumpur: Oxford University Press.

Weiss, Linda (1999) 'State Power and the Asian Crisis', *New Political Economy*, 4(3), pp 317–42.

World Bank (1959) *A Public Development Program for Thailand*, Baltimore: The Johns Hopkins Press, for the International Bank for Reconstruction and Development.

World Bank (1993) *The East Asian Miracle. Economic Growth and Public Policy*, New York: Oxford University Press.

Yada Praparpun (1998) 'Small and Medium Enterprises in Thailand: The Effects of Trade Liberalisation on SMEs and Women Workers', in Vivienne Wee (ed.) *Trade Liberalisation: Challenges and Opportunities for Women in Southeast Asia*, Singapore: Unifem and Engender, pp 119–28.

Yoshihara Kunio (1988) *The Rise of Ersatz Capitalism in South-East Asia*, Singapore: Oxford University Press.

4

Indonesia: Crisis, Oligarchy, and Reform

Richard Robison[1]

Of all the Asian economies, Indonesia's experience in the wake of the economic crisis of 1997 was to be the most intense and destructive. The downward spiral of the rupiah created a fiscal crisis for the government while Indonesia's corporate moguls became mired in mountains of debt beyond their capacity to repay. Indonesia's banks were quickly paralysed by a deepening crisis of bad loans. This was to be much more than a financial or economic crisis. What has distinguished Indonesia from other countries in the region is the extent to which the crisis has translated into social unrest, political violence, and the unravelling of state power. Soeharto found himself unable to stem the economic collapse and deal with its deepening social effects, or to maintain intact the institutional underpinning of his political and economic power. The man who created Indonesia's New Order now became its greatest liability and the main obstacle to a resolution of the problem. With Soeharto's fall from power, the crisis had claimed its most important political victim. The last of the Cold War capitalist dictatorships had come to an end.

There is no doubt that economic crisis in Indonesia was precipitated by speculation, panic, and capital flight in highly volatile and mobile global financial markets. But Indonesia was no innocent bystander in the disaster that was to take hold after the currency collapses of 1997. The extensive and destructive path of corporate collapse, financial sector meltdown, social turmoil, and political paralysis that followed derived from contradictions deeply rooted within the economic and political regimes of the Soeharto era. The unconstrained exercise of political power in economic life that generated rapid growth and provided the cement of a seemingly invulnerable architecture of political power also created systemic faults. It was domestic capital, highly vulnerable because of over-investment and over-borrowing, that fled the rupiah when the crisis hit.

It is not a question of whether Indonesian capitalism contained fatal contradictions but why it took so long for them to become manifest. As we shall see, crises in debt, banking, and corporate activities were already endemic in the decade preceding the crisis, propped up only by the political intervention of the government and continuing inflows of short-term loans. As Jeffrey Winters has argued, because global capital was deeply implicated in this growing speculative bubble, its traders and fund managers were unwilling to put a halt to the process (Winters 1997; 2000). The crisis ended the flow of these loans and undermined the capacity of the government to intervene on behalf of floundering companies and state agencies.

It is within this larger pathology of Indonesian capitalism that the dramatic events of the last three years of the twentieth century must be understood. But there is little agreement on the precise nature of this pathology. As we have seen in chapter 1 of this volume, neo-classical economists, particularly within the IMF, saw the crisis in functional terms: interventionist regimes simply collapsed under the weight of their inefficiency and dysfunction. It provided, in the view of such neo-classical economists, a reminder that long-term growth in an era of globalisation required Asian economies and their governments to 'abandon their bad habits' and allow market signals to set prices (*Economist* 1998). In this view of history driven by an abstracted instrumental rationality, the Indonesian pathology was its functional inefficiency.

But the crisis in Indonesia has not ushered in a spontaneous and frictionless transformation to markets and democracy in the liberal model. Indonesia's reformers have faced fierce resistance in their efforts to close insolvent banks and force powerful business groups to hand over assets to cover the costs of recapitalisation. Attempts to bring to court and successfully prosecute any of the major corrupt figures of the old regime have been almost entirely unsuccessful. Although many of the most notorious monopolies underpinning Indonesia's corporate moguls have been dismantled, and although reforms have been forced on strategic gatekeeping institutions, the outcome is contested and uncertain: monopolies, concessions, and off-budget funding persists. The shock of the crisis has been unable either to destroy the old relationships of corporate and political power or to bring to life a dominant neo-liberal coalition.

This is not the first time that crisis and reform have produced outcomes unexpected by neo-classical economists. In 1965, the dismantling of the 'command capitalism' of the Soekarno era and the opening of Indonesia to foreign investment and aid did not lead Indonesia down the path of a liberal market economy. Ironically, such reforms were to prove instrumental in the consolidation of political authoritarianism and state capitalism under Soeharto. Nor did the widespread programs of reform in financial and trade regimes and deeper integration within global financial markets that followed the collapse of oil prices in the 1980s result in the expected transformation to a liberal market economy. They precipitated, instead, a shift from public to private monopoly and the harnessing of state power to the interest of powerful coalitions of private and public oligarchies: an unconstrained form of robber baron capitalism.

Neo-classical analysts face serious dilemmas in explaining these diverging outcomes. If the costs of resisting the market are so high and the benefits of embracing it are so evident, why have successive Indonesian governments consistently resisted reform? More importantly, why have reformist initiatives in opening the economy and deregulating markets often strengthened the interests of predatory officials and 'rent-seeking' business interests? Such trajectories of change cannot be understood within the concept of a history that has no telos except efficiency (Chaudhry 1997:11). What is required is an explanation of the evolution of Indonesian capitalism that embodies a theory of power and an understanding of how politics and social interest shapes change. We require a theory of change that explains why policies of deregulation and the rise of the private interest can lead to diverging outcomes—to liberal markets in some cases and to the money politics of predatory capitalism in others.

A politics of economic change in Indonesia: interpretations

Although it is widely recognised that politics matters in the determination of Indonesia's economic regimes, exactly how it has shaped their emergence and decline is understood quite differently. Modernisation and dependency theory dominated explanations of Indonesian capitalism until the late 1970s. These analyses of conflict and change in Indonesia—of tradition versus modernity, and of centre versus periphery—have been dealt with extensively elsewhere (Robison 1986:105–27). It is the rise of neo-classical theory in the 1980s and its complex amalgamation with elements of structural functional variants of modernisation theory that has constituted the dominant orthodoxy for the past two or three decades. It is the critique of this orthodoxy and the reinterpretation of Indonesia's political economy in as an ongoing process of social conflict that will form the central task of this chapter.

Neo-liberal approaches and the analysis of Indonesia

Neo-classical theory is not just another intellectual tradition. It became the ideology that drove policy agenda within Western governments and within international financial institutions such as the World Bank and the IMF (Toye 1987:45–94). Its practitioners in Indonesia and elsewhere are well aware that imposing neo-classical policy prescriptions is a profoundly political process. But because markets are understood as abstract and universal self-regulating mechanisms driven by their own internal laws, it is the liberation of this natural 'market' from the grip of rent-seeking and predatory coalitions that is the central dynamic in the neo-liberal analysis of change. The only dispute is whether this is achieved by dismantling the very power of the state to intervene in economic life or by constructing a rational regulatory state insulated from politics.

From its very beginnings, close attachments were forged between Indonesia's new economic technocrats and neo-classical economists in the World Bank and various Western universities. Western liberal economists heralded the rise of Soeharto's New Order in 1965 as the victory of rationality over ideology and of economics over politics (Arndt 1967). The 'rational' credentials of Soeharto's New Order were confirmed as it reopened the door to Western investment and appointed Western-trained economic technocrats to the key economic ministries. It was the capacity of Indonesia's economic technocrats to adopt 'pragmatic' policies based on rational technical calculation, transcending the demands of vested interests, that was seen to be the critical factor in three decades of successful development (Hill 1996).

Despite the enthusiasm of neo-classical economists for the way in which Indonesia's technocrats managed fiscal and monetary policy, they nevertheless recognised that they did not have the political muscle to overcome rent-seeking interests. The process of liberal reform was understood as a war of attrition in which economic crises and shocks provided the opportunities for technocrats to convince the government of the need for change and progressively to erode interventionist policies. It was a case of 'good policies in bad times'(Soesastro 1989; Bresnan 1993; Schwarz 1994).

Yet, the view of the New Order as an essentially modern and developmental regime was given its fullest expression in the political analysis of structural functional modernisation theory. Whereas the authoritarianism of the previous (Soekarno) regime had been portrayed as atavistic in nature and defined by traditional culture, the authoritarianism of Soeharto's New Order was to be understood as a modernising force. In the context of the Cold War, a regime that was in its essence anti-communist and opened its doors to Western investment could hardly be regarded as anything else. In terms of the Huntington thesis, the New Order provided the strong institutional cement for a disintegrating society and performed the historical role of the middle class—it was its 'advance guard', its 'spearhead into modern politics' (Huntington 1968:222). In the view of the leading protagonists of this approach in Indonesia, Donald Emmerson and William Liddle, the New Order was the only alternative to chaos and disorder. A return to a parliamentary system offered only anomic and untrusting behaviour, instability, and impotence (Emmerson 1978:104, 105; Emmerson 1976:250; Liddle 1989:23). Not surprisingly, it was a thesis seized upon with alacrity by the theoreticians of the New Order, providing the perfect legitimation for authoritarian rule (Moertopo 1973).

It was Liddle who was to tie this profoundly anti-liberal political ideology with neo-classical economics. Soeharto, he argued, successfully drove economic growth because he was able to rise above the predatory and patrimonial attachments of others within the regime. In his own person he established a relative autonomy from distributional coalitions and escaped the suffocating cultural lenses that forced many Indonesians to resist capitalism. This behaviour, suggested Liddle, is explained in terms of rational calculations about political survival. It is the recognition that his long-term political self-interest lies in the neo-classical agenda, and that its capacity to deliver the economic growth and prosperity will reinforce the legitimacy of the regime and provide a strong revenue base (Liddle 1991:403, 404; Liddle 1992:796–8).

It is not surprising that the crisis came as a shock to many neo-liberals, given the faith they had placed in the New Order and its technocrats and their conviction that the economic fundamentals were good (Hill 1996). Their explanations emphasised shifts in capital flows, panic in global capital markets, and events after the crisis that made things worse—including inappropriate IMF policies and the collapse of political authority (Hill 2000). But there were also reflections on flaws internal to the regime. Ross Garnaut (1998) argued that Indonesian policy-makers made the mistake of pursuing fixed exchange-rate policies at a time of growing capital mobility and business exuberance resulting from the economic boom. For Ross McLeod (1998) the Indonesian economy unravelled as its economic managers tried simultaneously to control more than one of the nominal macroeconomic variables of prices, money supply, nominal exchange rate, and nominal interest rate.

For Liddle, the unexpected turn of events was explained by a sharp shift in the behaviour of Soeharto in the latter years of the regime. Liddle argued that Soeharto's actions had deviated recently from the pragmatic and rational concerns of earlier years, determined increasingly by an indulgence of the rapacious demands of his children as they rampaged through the business world (Liddle 1999). But attempts to protect their earlier assessments of the Soeharto regime by talking about policy errors, global market failure, or aberrations in behaviour, were soon to wear thin. Some neo-classical economists began to give more weight to the view that the dynamics of collapse were indeed embedded within the political arrangements and power relations of the regime itself (McLeod 2000).

If the evolution of Indonesia's economic regimes is more than just a matter of good policy choices prevailing over vested interest, what factors might explain why there has been no inexorable advance to a liberal market economy? Andrew MacIntyre (1999) argued that the lack of institutional constraints on the arbitrary authority of the Soeharto regime prevented an effective policy response and precipitated a downward spiral of investor confidence in the critical weeks following the crisis. The World Bank has recognised for some time that the specific regulatory frameworks are a necessary requirement for the liberal transformation, and institution-building has been an important part of its policy agenda in Indonesia and elsewhere (World Bank 1993:135–64). But how do institutions emerge and change? Why have liberal market institutions failed to take root in Indonesia? Again, neo-classical economists within the World Bank and else-where assume that the supply of institutions is primarily a technical or policy matter—that capacity, transparency, and accountability flow from the introduction of efficient procedures and processes (World Bank 1997:2, 3, 28, 106). In a highly voluntarist approach that does not theorise the political or social dimensions of institutional change, institutions can simply be supplied.

If the crisis demonstrated anything, it was that economic regimes are embedded in structures of power and interest. Institutions are not simply about efficiency; they are about power and its allocation. What is at stake in Indonesia is nothing less than an entrenched social order and an archi-tecture of power relations.

Social conflict

Indonesia's economic regimes have been forged in a series of violent episodes of conflict among and within fluid and shifting coalitions of power and interest. Populism, social radicalism, state and predatory capitalism, as well as liberalism, have threaded their way as the central agenda in the struggles to define Indonesian capitalism. What is significant about the 1997 economic crisis is the damage it has inflicted on the coherence of coalitions that sustained the state-centred predatory systems of the Soeharto era. But the collapse of the old system of highly centralised state authority is only part of the equation; it merely opens the door for a new struggle to reforge coalitions and build regimes. The question in Indonesia is not whether markets and democracy will emerge but what kind of markets and what kind of democracy. Can the dominant interests of the Soeharto era reorganise their ascendancy within new alliances and in the context of different institutions? Can a new reformist coalition establish its authority and subordinate the entrenched oligarchy to legal and democratic constraints? What coalitions can be mobilised behind the neo-liberal agenda?

State capitalism and the incubation of oligarchy

As the old colonial economy decayed around them in the 1950s, Indonesia's new political and economic power-brokers plunged into a struggle to shape the economic regimes of the republic. In a world without large landowning elites or powerful urban bourgeoisie, social radicalism and petty bourgeois populism were to emerge as central threads in the ongoing conflicts that would drive economic change for the coming decades. But populism was focused around a declining rural propertied class and small-town businesses heavily influenced by anti-Chinese xenophobia and resentful of what they perceived to be growing domination by big business and foreign interests. What ideal would carry the capitalist revolution? Liberalism was to be a slender reed in the early decades of Indonesia's postcolonial economic history. In the end, it was to be a complex amalgam of state-centred economic nationalism and predatory oligarchy revolving around the state and its corps of politico-bureaucrats that was to prevail.

The path to 'free fight liberalism' was rejected in favour of the principle that the state has a legitimate economic role in ensuring the national interest and that market forces should be tempered by social objectives. But, although themes of populism and nationalism were to triumph, they did so under the umbrella of a highly centralised state and its corps of officials in the guise of state capitalism and an authoritarian form of organic corporatism. It was the state in the three decades from 1960 to the mid 1980s that embarked on an ambitious program to construct an autonomous industrial base. Nationalism and populism were ideologies sustained by deep-rooted and concrete vested interests. They lay at the heart of the organic notions of power that legitimised de facto possession of the state by its officials and relieved them of problems of accountability and representation. At the same time, an extensive state sector and pervasive industry policy were the perfect mechanisms for entrenching the pervasive authority of the state and its officials in the economic sphere.

Secured by their political victory over the Partai Komunis Indonesia (PKI) and the petty bourgeois populism of Islamic politics, the new rulers of

Indonesia under Soeharto set about entrenching a system of highly central-ised state capitalism. A critical factor in this was the conclusion of agreements with Western powers to provide an inflow of official foreign aid and the introduction of reforms to allow foreign investment into a growing resource and import-substitution manufacturing sector. State capitalism was to reach its peak during the oil boom years of 1973–82 when state coffers were overflowing with petrodollars.[2] As part of a broad drive to expand Indonesia's industrial base (Kartasasmita 1985), the state invested heavily in steel, fertilisers, aluminium, petroleum-refining, cement, and paper. Funding to the state-enterprise sector increased from Rp41 billion in 1973 to Rp592 billion in 1983 (Hill 1996:102–3). According to one esti-mate, the state controlled almost 60 per cent of the equity in all domestic investment and a further 9.2 per cent of the equity in foreign investment projects (*Tempo* 1981).

The shift towards increased state intervention in this period involved a range of highly interventionist policies in foreign investment, trade, and banking. Regulations introduced in the wake of the anti-Japanese riots of 1974, for example, required all foreign investors to adopt local partners, increased the range of sectors closed to foreign investors, and set out requirements for the transfer of joint-venture equity to local investors. In the trade sector, a wide array of restrictions, especially in the form of non-tariff barriers was introduced. Most notable was the establishment in 1982 of the 'approved traders' program, a system of import monopolies that quickly fell into the hands of well-connected private and state companies (Robison and Hadiz 1993). In the banking sector, the government intro-duced credit ceilings and a variety of subsidised lending programs, significantly increasing its control over the allocation of credit (MacIntyre 1994:250–1; Hill 1996:99–116).

At the same time, powerful corporate conglomerates and politico-business families began to emerge under the umbrella of nationalist policies of protection and subsidy, and within monopolistic structures of political favour bestowed by patrons with their hands on the levers of state power. Protected from international competition by restrictive trade, licensing, and investment policies, these conglomerates expanded from forestry, trade, and sole agencies into a variety of industries, including the manufacture of auto components, tyres, batteries, cement, electronics, steel, and the engineering industries that grew around the oil industry. Conglomerates with strong political connections, notably the Soeharto family companies, began to dominate the import and distribution of oil products and to secure the con-tracts for supply and transportation of oil for the state oil corporation, Pertamina (Robison 1986; Shin 1989; Jones and Pura 1986).

By the early 1980s, clear contradictions had begun to emerge within the very structures of authoritarian state capitalism. A new alliance of politico-bureaucrats and corporate moguls with interests that extended beyond those of protecting and preserving state power were now intent on using state power to construct and protect new corporate empires of private interest. Through the State Secretariat (Sekneg), Soeharto and powerful politico-bureaucrats, including Ginandjar Kartasasmita, secured institutional control over allocation of supply and construction contracts for government-funded projects under Presidential Decisions 10 and 14 of 1979 and 1980. Under the flag of economic nationalism it provided off-budget revenue for the regime and was an important channel for distribution of state patronage. Under its patronage an important group of indigenous (*pribumi*) capitalists was nurtured (Pangaribuan 1995:51–67; Winters 1996:123–41).

At this stage, however, the prevailing system of state capitalism was ruptured by the collapse of oil prices in 1981–82, and again in 1986. This led to a decline in the value of Indonesia's gas and oil exports from US$18.4 billion (or 82 per cent of total exports) in 1982 to US$8.3 billion (or 56 per cent of total exports) in 1986. In the same period, government revenues from oil and gas fell from Rp8.6 trillion to Rp6.3 trillion, or from 70 per cent to 39 per cent of total revenues (Robison 1987). The oil price collapse dramatically shifted the options for the players. It signalled the need to mobilise new sources of investment funds from the private sector, to develop new export industries, and to build new revenue bases. Influence over economic policy was to shift from economic nationalists within the government to the economic technocrats.

The triumph of oligarchy

From 1986 onwards, Indonesia's technocrats were able to introduce a raft of important policy reforms. Several important trade monopolies were abolished, including politically sensitive import monopolies in steel and plastics. Extensive reductions in tariffs and import duties were introduced. In the banking sector, restrictions on domestic interest rates were eliminated in 1981 and, in 1988, the door was opened wide to the establishment of private banks. Public-sector monopolies in public utilities, power generation, ports and roads, telecommunications, and television, sectors long regarded as strategically sensitive, were removed (World Bank 1995:40–2).

Such changes were reflected in the changing structure of investment and ownership. Between 1990 and 1995, foreign investment approvals surged from US$9 billion to US$39.9 billion, continuing to climb as the flood of money from North-East Asia into low-wage export manufacturing in South-East Asia followed the Plaza Accord in 1995 (World Bank 1996:12–14). Private domestic banks proliferated. By 1995 they numbered approximately 240, holding 53 per cent of the outstanding bank funds and 47.7 per cent of outstanding bank credit compared with 37 per cent and 41.9 per cent respectively for the state banks (World Bank 1995:17; Econit 1996:4–7). Public fixed investment declined from 69 per cent of the total in 1979/80 to 27 per cent in 1993/94, although public-sector corporations continued to hold book assets of US$140 billion and to produce 15 per cent of GDP in 1995 (World Bank 1995:29, 51). Deregulation created the opportunity for extensive growth in the private sector.

Yet, this was not to be a flowering of business within liberal markets defined by common law and regulation. Instead, deregulation was specific and access to the world of business controlled by layers of political gate-keepers within the state and its banking system. Large sectors of the economy remained controlled by politically sponsored cartels, and public monopolies simply became private monopolies still backed by the authority of an authoritarian state. Such unexpected outcomes were explained by neo-classical economists within the World Bank and elsewhere as the consequence of technical errors in sequencing reforms: deregulating trade and finance regimes before the real sector (Bhattacharya and Pangestu 1992).

But the sequencing of reforms was not a matter of unconstrained technical choice. Indonesia's technocrats deregulated when the political opportunity presented itself. Structural pressures might have forced state planners and gatekeepers to give way in export-competitive sectors, but not in sectors related to domestic markets (Robison 1997:35–6). Financial deregulation, as Jonathan Pincus and Rizal Ramli have pointed out, was often a strategy to outflank state banks and other gatekeeping institutions otherwise immune to regulation and control rather than a technically calculated option (1998:728–32). It is also important to recognise that deregulation now also suited many of the corporate interests incubated within the structures of state capitalism. The heavy hand of the state had become a constraint where it prevented their access to lucrative opportunities in banking, public infrastructure, television, and air transportation. In the final analysis, deregulation was a necessary step for these politico-business conglomerates.

Reform did not pervade all sectors of the economy. Domestic trading cartels continued to exist in cement, paper, plywood, and fertiliser. Apkindo, a compulsory association of plywood producers presided over by Soeharto business partner, Bob Hasan, with the power to set pricing and export quotas price controls (Pura 1995a:1, 4; Pura 1995b:1, 4). Liem Sioe Liong retained his lucrative monopoly in flour-milling (World Bank 1995:43–4; Schwarz 1994:110–12). In 1992, the Ministry of Trade awarded Tommy Soeharto monopoly rights to purchase and sell Indonesia's clove crop. This gift came with US$350 million low-interest loans from Bank Indonesia and a government requirement that cigarette manufacturers purchase exclusively from the new Board (*Prospek* 1992a; *Prospek* 1992b; *Tempo* 1993b; *Tempo* 1993c).

Forestry concessions awarded without transparent tender continued to be a lucrative source of profit for powerful corporate groups and political families. Relatively free of attempts to constrain illegal or damaging logging practices and subject to minimal taxes, forestry companies also attracted large state and foreign loans to finance expansion into plantations and pulp and paper manufacture (World Bank 1993:44–9; Ramli 1992; *Tempo* 1991c). Another refuge was found in the automobile industry where sole appointed agents for major auto producers operated behind tariffs of between 100 and 300 per cent applied to the import of CBU vehicles. Efforts to dismantle these tariffs or require greater levels of local production failed (*Warta Ekonomi* 1996; *Jakarta Jakarta* 1991).

But it was in newly opened sectors and old areas of state monopoly that the conglomerates and the families were provided with new opportunities. Entering the deregulated banking sector, corporate conglomerates and the political families established private cash cows. Operating with little regard for legal lending limits, these banks were to channel the bulk of their loans to other companies within the group (Rosser 1999:81–135; *Infobank* 1995a). The same inadequate regulatory frameworks made the Jakarta Stock Exchange a place where the conglomerates and family groups could raise capital without adequate disclosure (Kwik 1993; *FEER* 1992; *Tempo* 1993a).

As the state sector was stripped of a range of monopolies, well-connected private groups stepped in to the breach, turning public monopoly into state-sponsored private oligopoly. Government authorities such as the Ministry of Public Works and the state electricity authority (Perusahaan Listrik Negara, PLN) now became gatekeeping institutions, allocating contracts and licences, often without tender. The Soeharto family stamped its position as a major corporate player as it secured key contracts and licences in the power-generation industry, in road and port construction, and in refinery construction in the petrochemical industry (Robison 1997:39–41). These new major projects involved large capital outlays and this was made available through the state banks as well as through international banking institutions. Commercial finance capital now replaced oil as the driving force of growth and investment. A private-sector borrowing spree began in the late 1980s as the conglomerates geared up for investment in the projects, prompting warnings from several sources (*Infobank* 1997; *Infobank* 1995b; Nasution 1992).

Serious economic problems began to emerge. Although the economy grew strongly, so did the foreign debt burden and the level of non-performing loans at domestic banks. In the petrochemical industry, for example, foreign investors and banks rushed into arrangements with well-connected licence-holders who were guaranteed protection from foreign imports, provided with subsidised inputs from Pertamina and markets with downstream producers (*AWSJ* 1995; *JP* 1996a; Robison 1997:53–5). Investors and lenders in the power-generation industry were similarly guaranteed subsidised inputs and sales to PLN at above-market prices and in a situation of over-supply (World Bank 1995:71; World Bank 1996:56; Robison 1997:40). These were both classic examples of the moral-hazard problem—the deregulation of the finance sector contributing to a growth in non-performing loans as banks made increasingly risky loans to well-connected individuals, not only in infrastructure projects but also in sectors such as property, consumer finance, and the stock market.

Further cracks were to emerge as Indonesia's economic technocrats proved unable to enforce much needed regulatory reform in the face of opposition from the conglomerates and the politico-business families. A series of scandals in the early 1990s revealed a picture of collusion among officials, borrowers, and powerful political patrons in the allocation of credit by state banks (Kwik 1993; *Tempo* 1991a; *Tempo* 1994a; World Bank 1995:19). Within the private banking sector, poorly enforced prudential regulations allowed banks to concentrate their loans within the group. As a result of this practice, several private banks began to encounter difficulties as they became exposed to a small group of companies, and collapsed when they defaulted on their loan repayments. In several cases, the government stepped in to rescue these banks (Rosser 1999:118–24).

Indonesia's technocrats were well aware of the potential debt problems. Although introducing tighter legal lending limits in 1993 and threatening offenders with legal action, the Central Bank governor found himself without the capacity to enforce these initiatives. Efforts to contain the growth of Indonesia's foreign debt through the establishment of a special team (Team 39 or COLT) to regulate foreign borrowing was ignored by well-connected conglomerates. For instance, attempts to halt massive borrowing for the Chandra Asri petrochemical venture were sidestepped when the government allowed it to proceed as a foreign investment. Protests by the technocrats over this decision were met with the announcement in 1994 that the existing COLT team was to be abolished and replaced by one under Industry Minister Hartato (Robison 1997:54). Subsequently, its function was further reduced to one of regulating state-related foreign borrowing (World Bank 1997:14, 15). In the meantime, the technocrats found themselves with only one weapon to combat growing debt and inflation. In the so-called Sumarlin shocks of 1987 and 1991, monetary policy was used to slow growth, sending interest rates to more than 30 per cent and precipitating a capital flight. Several companies simply took their money offshore (*Tempo* 1991b).

In the post-oil decade of deregulation, private interest not only established its ascendancy over the state and its officials but also achieved a wider political dominance as part of a coalition of power built around the presidential family. This meant that the authority of the state was now increasingly harnessed to the commercial interests of the new politico-business coalitions, rather than to the institutional interests of state officials or to liberal objectives such as the creation of a 'level playing field'. This ascendancy was achieved only by coercive means and opened important political tensions within Indonesian society and politics.

As the new oligarchies seized former public monopolies, high-ranking officials were pushed aside as they attempted to resist demands by Soeharto family members and their associates for allocation of trade monopolies and contracts for supply (Robison 1997:61). Ironically, as we shall see, one dismissed official, Cacuk Sudarijanto of P.T. Telkom, was to return under President Wahid in charge of the Indonesian Banking Restructuring Agency (IBRA) now responsible for requiring the Soehartos and others to hand over assets to cover debt. A struggle for control of state procurement saw various ministries and the military lose this authority to the State Secretariat and to the Board for Research and Technology under B.J. Habibie (Pangaribuan 1995). Tensions erupted into a public squabble among Habibie, Finance Minister Mar'ie Muhammad, and Armed Forces Chief Faisal Tanjung over an attempt by Habibie to purchase old German warships and allocate US$1.1 billion for their repair in his shipyards (*Tempo* 1994b).

Political struggles also began to spill into society. As monopolies were put together with breathtaking speed and daring by the Soeharto family and its associates, other business interests were squeezed. Plywood producers became increasingly agitated at the constraints of Apkindo as prices plummeted and Japan found new suppliers (*Tempo* 1993d:83–4). A bizarre attempt to provide Soeharto grandson, Ari Sigit, with rights to impose tax on beer in Bali propelled him into a collision with brewers and hoteliers that included other siblings (*AWSJ* 1996). As Tommy Soeharto's state-enforced clove monopoly, Badan Penyangga dan Pemasaran Cengkeh (BPPC), began to encounter difficulties, he was plunged into a deepening spiral of dispute with both the clove producers and the cigarette manufac-turers who were the ultimate losers in this adventure (Schwarz 1994:153–7; Robison 1997:44, 45). The decision of the government in 1996 to grant exemptions from import duties and luxury goods taxes to Tommy Soeharto, as part of a plan to produce a national car, led to a new wave of dispute. It brought condemnation from both the US and Japanese govern-ments and reignited the dispute between economic nationalists and liberal reformers within Indonesia. It set the scene also for bitter protest from Indonesia's other car producers, precluded from importing CBU vehicles by 300 per cent taxes (Robison 1997:55–7; JP 1996b; JP 1996c).

Corporate conglomerates now began to attract increasing criticism and resentment in Indonesian society. For liberal critics within Indonesian's growing urban middle class and within the World Bank, conglomeration in Indonesia emerged, not from competition in open markets but as the result of corruption, collusion, and nepotism. It was not only inefficient but also remained concentrated in the protected non-tradeable goods sector, adding nothing to Indonesia's global competitiveness (World Bank 1993:91, 92; World Bank 1995:49, 50; Tempo 1993d:93, 94). Anti-conglomerate feeling spread beyond the urban liberal critics to populist sources in the wider countryside as land and labour disputes began to become entangled with the inexorable spread of big business. Apprehensive that this resentment would mobilise underlying currents of anti-Chinese xenophobia, Soeharto was forced to move. He was publicly to distinguish his policies from those of 'free-fight' liberalism and to point to the strides made over the years in reducing poverty (Soeharto 1990:31, 32; ISEI 1990). In a highly symbolic gesture, he met with 31 of Indonesia's leading business figures at his private ranch in 1990, inviting them to transfer 25 per cent of their company shares to cooperatives, still the symbol of the New Order's commitment to egali-tarian ideals. Predictably, this proposal was to prove a failure in practice (*Editor* 1990).

The destruction of the new order

When the currency speculators attacked the Indonesian rupiah in early July 1997, the fatal flaws of high levels of unhedged debt were soon revealed. Indonesia's debt crisis was driven largely by the private sector. Total private-sector foreign debt, initially thought to be approximately US$54 billion, was revealed to be more than US$81 billion. Much of this was unhedged,

and more than US$34 billion was due in 1998. When the government aban-
doned attempts to defend the rupiah in August 1997 and floated the
currency, it was no surprise, therefore, that the currency attacks set in train
a massive capital flight by Indonesia's domestic investors. Faced with a
rapidly collapsing corporate and banking sector and looming fiscal crisis,
the Indonesian government called in the IMF on 8 October (*FK* 1997a;
AWSJ 1997a). Although Soeharto appeared to be under the impression that
the entry of the IMF would be enough to soothe the waters and end the
crisis, this was not to be the case. The rupiah kept tumbling, reaching more
than 16 000 to the US dollar in January 1998. Nor did it appear that
Soeharto considered seriously the sorts of conditions that the IMF might
impose in return for its US$43 billion bail-out. Yet, from October 1997, the
Indonesian government has signed no less than sixteen Letters of Intent to
the IMF outlining its agreement to fulfil specific terms set out by the IMF
(Government of Indonesia 1997; 1998; 1999; 2000).

Such agreements were to strike at the very heart of the Soeharto regime.
They included a range of fiscal reforms: the postponement or cancellation
of several large industrial projects; the abolition of various state trading
monopolies in flour, sugar, soy beans, and other commodities; and the liquidation of insolvent banks. Also on the IMF list was the abolition of the
clove monopoly, the cancellation of the national car project, and Habibie's
Industri Pesawat Terbang Nusantara (IPTN) jet aircraft project. Later provisions included a requirement for greater independence of the Central
Bank, elimination of cement, paper and plywood cartels, and phased elimination of subsidies for fuel and electricity. Perhaps the central feature of the
IMF plan was the restructuring and recapitalisation of the banking system.
These agreements meant, in effect, that the frameworks of state protection
and privilege that sustained the major corporate conglomerates and
politico-business families were to be eliminated. Officials of the US government and the IMF made it clear that funding would cease if the terms of
agreement were not met (*JP* 1998a; *JP* 1998b).

A period of conflict and negotiation between the Indonesian government
and the IMF therefore commenced, punctuated by periodic halts to funding
disbursement and concessions in agreements. Just days after the October
1997 package was announced, it was revealed that Soeharto had allowed
certain of the large infrastructure projects previously postponed to proceed.
Given that the main beneficiaries of the reversal of the decision were members of the Soeharto family, the IMF was convinced that Soeharto was not
genuinely committed to reform where this interfered with his interests (*JP*
1997d; *AWSJ* 1997b). This impression was reinforced in dramatic fashion

when Soeharto family members reacted angrily to the closure of sixteen insolvent banks by Finance Minister Mar'ie Muhammad, alleging a plot to bring down the Soeharto family. Despite legal action against the government and a disingenuous scheme to reopen a bank owned by Soeharto son, Bambang Trihatmojo, under another name, the banks were closed (*JP* 1997a; *JP* 1997b; *JP* 1997c). Nevertheless, the altercation set the scene for a long struggle over bank recapitalisation.

A further concern for the government was the budget. Under pressure from the IMF to contain spending, such a strategy held real dangers for Soeharto. A contractionary budget would force many Indonesian companies into bankruptcy, including those owned by the family and its close associates. Sharp reductions in food and fuel subsidies brought with it the risk of social unrest and rioting. Yet, immediately after the government's introduction of a mildly expansionary budget in January 1998, the rupiah collapsed to more than 10 000 to the US dollar. This sparked a rush on supermarkets and traditional markets to stock up on food in anticipation of an inevitable inflationary surge (*AWSJ* 1998a; Robison and Rosser 1998:1601, 1602). With no apparent way out of the dilemma, and facing increasing pressure from overseas creditor nations, Soeharto was to turn to the idea of a currency board as the last hope. Lashing out at foreign currency speculators and accusing them of trying to destroy the Indonesian economy, Soeharto announced plans to fix the exchange rate and establish legislation necessary for the introduction of a currency board (*AWSJ* 1998a; *AFR* 1998a; *AFR* 1998b).

For Soeharto, protecting the architecture of power rather than introducing the IMF reforms was clearly the priority concern. This would continue to be done even at the cost of a continuing decline in international confidence in Indonesia and the downward spiral of the rupiah. Institutional change was clearly about power and its distribution, not simply about some abstracted efficiency. The key to the situation was the political regime. For the first time in his long period of power, Soeharto found himself unable to dictate the course of events, to halt the economic collapse, or to protect the political and economic interests surrounding him. As the ruling alliance began to unravel, demonstrations became bolder and criticism grew. In a last desperate gesture, Soeharto appointed a bizarre cabinet made up largely of close cronies, including his daughter, Siti Hardijanti Rukmana (Tutut) and his long-time business associate, Bob Hasan. In the end, however, events were overtaken by the resignation of a besieged Soeharto in May 1998, following a period of violent rioting in Jakarta.

Reorganising the regime

The fall of Soeharto did not open the door to an inexorable march towards a market economy and political democracy. It did, however, shift the balance of power and the terms of conflict. Unable to call upon a powerful centralised state apparatus to secure their interests, the formerly dominant political and business oligarchies were now forced to reinvent their ascendancy within a new system. It was a system in which politics was mediated through parties and parliament, and in which political brokers and fixers—rather than generals and the apparatchiks of the state—were increasingly the conduits of power. The survival of politicians, too, depended upon the construction of new and wider political alliances. In this task they were not badly placed. The system of predatory relations among officials, business, and political entrepreneurs continued to pervade Indonesian politics from Jakarta down to the regions and local towns. Breaking up these old power structures was to be a difficult task. No inflow of foreign investment had poured in to replace the old centres of corporate power. No new domestic bourgeoisie emerged to drive the neo-liberal revolution or to embrace a system of markets governed by transparency and accountability in its rules.

In this task, the old politico-business interests now had to contend with a raft of structural and policy reforms and with revitalised state audit agencies and official audits now required by the IMF. A panoply of private agencies dedicated to the scrutiny of political and business activity emerged, and vigorous and intrusive mass media now scrutinised the activities of public figures and business deals. Several high-profile critics of the former regime and of the conglomerates were to assume strategic ministerial positions. But the reformist alliance that formed under President Wahid proved to be neither politically cohesive nor ideologically coherent. Its authority over the state apparatus was to prove shaky. Although dedicated to the fall of Soeharto and the ending of arbitrary rule and the gross excesses of corruption, there was no broad commitment to liberal market reform within the reformist coalition. Instead, a mix of populist, nationalist, and even social democratic ideals drove the reform movement.

It is within this political context that the reorganisation of Indonesian capitalism was to take place in the period following Soeharto's downfall. There was little prospect of a return to a centralised authoritarian rule. Things had gone too far for that. Instead, it was a contest to decide what sort of markets and what sort of democracy would prevail. Indonesia became absorbed in a struggle over the very institutions and power relations that had sustained the rise of the old politico-business juggernauts. Contending coalitions of power and interest formed around two issues.

First, how to recapitalise Indonesia's moribund banking system and to enforce debt restructuring on its corporate conglomerates. Second, how to deal with the corporate interests that had emerged on the basis of political monopolies and what to do about the strategic gatekeeping institutions that were the very terminals of predatory capitalism.

The struggle to recapitalise banks and restructure debt

As Indonesia's private corporate sector began to founder under a mountain of debt, domestic banks were quickly paralysed by a surge in non-performing loans, estimated by Standard and Poor's to be 85 per cent of total loans at the end of 1999. A banking restructuring agency (the Indonesian Banking Restructuring Agency, IBRA) was established in January 1998 to implement a comprehensive recapitalisation plan that would eventually cost an estimated US$87 billion, or approximately 82 per cent of Indonesia's GDP (*AWSJ* 1999c).[3] By mid 1999, 66 of the 160 private banks that had existed in July 1997 had been closed, and a further twelve had been taken over by the state and recapitalised (World Bank 1999:2.1). Decisions about which banks to close and which to recapitalise were the subject of protracted negotiation and public dispute. Several rescued banks clearly had few prospects for survival and did not meet capital adequacy ratios (CAR) criteria (*AWSJ* 1999a; *AWSJ* 1999b; *JP* 1999a; *JP* 1999f). However, the most difficult aspect of the exercise was not to be the closure and recapitalisation of banks. In the long term, the crucial question was who would pay the bill for recapitalisation and whether it would precipitate a broader restructuring of Indonesia's corporate sector. Would it prove simply to be an exercise in which the Indonesian government carried the cost of the crisis for the old conglomerates?

Despite their efforts to avoid debt-restructuring and retain control of their companies, the conglomerates were hit hard by the crisis. Indonesia's leading tycoons lost control of some of the most important banks and corporations, including such icons as Bank Central Asia, Bank Dagang Negara Indonesia, Astra, Chandra Asri, and Gajah Tunggal in the debt-restructuring exercises that followed the crisis. In the Master Settlement and Acquisition Agreements (MSAA) signed between IBRA and its largest creditors in September 1998, the latter were forced to hand over assets valued at Rp112 trillion to cover their debt to IBRA banks. Yet, by mid 2000, it was clear that the conglomerates not only were able to survive, but also were in a strong position to negotiate the terms of their re-entry into the Indonesian economy. The government found itself carrying much of the cost of recapitalisation.

The conglomerates were rescued initially by the injection of more than Rp146 trillion (US$11 billion) in liquidity funds allocated by Bank Indonesia (BLBI) intended to guarantee deposits and meet interbank loan commitments. According to the Supreme Audit Agency (BPK), Rp80.25 trillion of these funds were allocated to banks that had violated BI's own guidelines on CAR and Legal Lending Limits (LLL) (*JP* 2000b; *FK* 2000). Not only were the troubled banks able to access government largesse virtually without condition, but also they were able to use these funds for new overseas investment, currency speculation, and debt-servicing on other companies. In June 2000, BPK and the state comptroller of Finance and Development (BPKP), reported that Rp62.6 trillion of BLBI funds had been diverted for unauthorised purposes (*Kontan Online* 2000c).

When it came to negotiating the transfer of corporate assets to IBRA to cover the costs of the BLBI and the IBRA bail-out, it proved difficult to penetrate the opaque financial statements of companies to discover the real value of assets. It soon became clear that the government faced a huge shortfall. For example, to cover a debt of Rp47.7 trillion, the Salim group surrendered assets of Rp53 trillion in September 1998, that were subsequently valued at Rp20 trillion, representing an effective loss of Rp30 trillion for the government (*Tempo* 2000b). This was a pattern repeated across the spectrum of IBRA debtors. Yet, at the same time that they were stalling debt negotiations with IBRA and foreign creditors, the conglomerates were able to insulate their highly profitable enterprises in forestry, pulp and paper, agriculture, and agriculture. These provided strong cash flows for more strategic debt repayments and for new investment. For example, the Salim food manufacturer, Indofood, turned a Rp1.2 trillion foreign-exchange loss in 1998 into a Rp209 billion gain in 1999, enabling the group to repay a US$400 million debt without having to spin-off the Bogasari flour mills as earlier planned (*AWSJ* 2000b).

Nor did the domestic debt problems halt the strategic investments of Indonesian conglomerates overseas. The activities of the Salim group are instructive and represent a broader pattern. Cash rich with the US$1.8 billion sale of its Hagermeyer group, Liem was able to buy new foreign assets, including a US$700 million stake in the Philippine Long Distance Phone Company and a 40 per cent stake in Indofood. The latter deal enabled Liem to keep a grip on Indofood, shift the controlling stake overseas, and generate funds to repay overseas creditors (*Warta Ekonomi* 1999; *FK* 1999a; *Tempo* 2000c; *AWSJ* 1999d).

Perhaps the major advantage enjoyed by the conglomerates has been the weakness and corruption of Indonesia's judicial institutions. In a series of startling acquittals in the Bankruptcy Court and the Supreme Court, high-profile business figures walked away from bankruptcy proceedings and criminal charges. It was an arena in which political influence and money were at a premium. Economics Coordinating Minister Kwik Kian Gie, was to complain of '"dark forces" who buy favours' (*Kompas Online* 2000a; *Tempo* 2000a:102, 103). So unsuccessful were both IBRA and foreign creditors in the courts that it was soon recognised that debt had to be resolved through negotiation.

But it was the increasing fiscal pressure brought to bear on a government by the recapitalisation exercise that was to be decisive. To cover the costs of recapitalisation the government had issued bonds to the value of US$54 billion and a further US$28.5 billion to cover BLBI (US Embassy 1 May 2000). Interest on these bonds in 1999/2000 was Rp34 trillion, rising to Rp77 trillion in 2001 (*JP* 2000e). Dispersal of the assets held by IBRA now became a matter of urgency.[4] Of deep concern was the reluctance of foreign investors to buy up Indonesian assets as they had done in Korea and Thailand. The appointment of Cacuk Sudarijanto in January 2000 was seen as a signal that the government intended to increase the pace of seizing and selling assets. In several high-profile cases, property was seized and legal action taken or planned against forty-eight commercial banks for alleged misuse of Rp144.5 trillion of BLBI (US$17 billion). Among those targeted for prosecution were some of Indonesia's most politically prominent business figures.[5]

Tough action against the conglomerates and the Soeharto family was driven not only by the necessity to shore up looming budget shortfalls, but also by widespread popular outrage at the revelations of misuse of the BLBI and avoidance of debt repayment, which led to calls in the press and parliament for cancellation of the MSAA. Former Economic Coordinating Minister Kwik Kian Gie launched a strong attack on the government, accusing it of collusion with unscrupulous tycoons and failing to take legal action against corporate criminals. Under no circumstances, he argued, should they be allowed to buy back their old assets (*JP* 2000i).

However, the government also faced the reality that if investment was to flow back into Indonesia and the banking and corporate sectors put back on track, the conglomerates were the key factors. From this perspective, the government was under pressure to drop its prosecutions, to compromise on debt-restructuring, and to allow conglomerates to buy back their assets. The choice appeared to be one between justice and money. As Hong Goei Siauw of Nomura Securities observed, in the present situation no one wants to outlay US$2.5–3 billion to buy IBRA assets when they know the condition of these assets and Indonesia's circumstances. The re-entry of high-profile conglomerates would act as a magnate to foreign investors (*Tempo* 2000d).

In the end, to speed up the debt-restructuring and assets-sale process, the government began to negotiate discounts to large debtors. Contentious restructuring deals were negotiated with Chandra Asri (effectively bailing-out Marubeni), Texmaco, and other high-profile conglomerates. Liem and other tycoons were reported to be negotiating to buy back into their businesses (*AWSJ* 2000a). President Wahid announced that he had asked prosecutors to delay legal proceedings against Sinivasan, Prajogo, and Nursalim (*JP* 2000m). But the strategy was also a dangerous one politically, raising claims of collusion and fears of a revival of the old predatory relations within the Wahid government.

For the IMF and the World Bank, the situation was contradictory. Although supporting the need for speed in restructuring, they also expressed their concern at the opaque nature of the negotiations between the government and the debtors, and at the generous terms given to companies with poor-quality assets. They warned of future burdens on the public purse (*JP* 2000l). Within parliament, resistance to the perceived bailouts grew. Legislators blocked the planned divestment of IBRA assets in Bank Central Asia and Bank Niaga. Such resistance was driven by the fear that assets were being sold off cheaply. More precisely, it was the prospect that assets would go cheaply to foreign investors or return to the conglomerates at a discount, that propelled nationalist sentiment in the parliament (*JP* 2000k).

Despite the fears and resentments, the return of the conglomerates appeared to be inexorable. Their ultimate strength lay in their economic indispensability. At question only is the institutional and policy frameworks within which they will operate.

Dismantling the predatory arrangements and institutions

Despite the violent economic and political ruptures, the new government inherited a system of politico-business alliances constructed around discretionary allocations of credit, and preferential access to licences, contracts, concessions, and monopolies. These predatory arrangements were concentrated around a vast range of strategic gatekeeping institutions. Perhaps the most pervasive was Pertamina, which presided over the allocation of drilling and exploration leases, contracts for supply and construction, crude oil and fuel distributorships, and insurance arrangements. Following audits by Price Waterhouse Cooper and BPKP, Pertamina management announced a list of 159 companies that had received contracts through dubious means, most of which were associated with the Soeharto family (*JP* 1998h). Huge mark-ups and overpricing imposed substantial costs on Pertamina (*Kompas* 1998; *JP* 1999d).

In the forestry sector, key business interests had seized the lion's share of Indonesia's 61 million hectares of forest concession, allocated without tender by the Ministry of Plantations and Forestry. Prominent among these were companies of the Soeharto family, and close associates Bob Hasan and Prajogo Pangestu. The ministry also controlled a special reforestation fund, established from levies and royalties on producers to develop forests and rejuvenate logged areas. Audits by the Supreme Advisory Agency, Bepeka, and other agencies, revealed the diversion of these funds by presidential decree to the companies of the Soeharto family and their associates. The allocation of Rp400 billion for Habibie's ill-fated aircraft project was only the most notorious instance (*JP* 1998e; *Gamma* 2000).

Within its closed import and distribution monopolies, Bulog provided well-connected interests with lucrative opportunities over three decades. In place since 1967, and still receiving 80 per cent of Bulog orders, Liem Sioe Liong's flour-milling monopoly has been worth an estimated Rp200 billion per annum over this period. Monopolies for the import of sugar, rice, and soy meal also continued to channel millions of dollars into the coffers of Liem and the Soeharto family (*FK* 1999b; *Time* 1999). Not only did predatory business interests benefit from Bulog, but also powerful political figures used it as an important cash cow with a large off-budget facility. Audits by Arthur Anderson and BPKP revealed substantial leakages, and BPKP was tracking more than Rp100 trillion diverted from Bulog accounts since 1992 and allegedly parked in the accounts of officials (*Kontan Online* 2000a). With the deregulation of the power-generation industry, PLN was also to emerge as a strategically important cash cow for well-connected business. In all, twenty-six projects were signed between PLN and various consortia of private energy providers, all of which included forms of the Soeharto and their associates. The director-general of PLN, Djiteng Marsudi, was to claim in 1998 that contracts '. . . were given without tender. I was in one way or another forced to sign the contracts.'(Quoted in *JP* 1998d.)

Because these gatekeeping institutions operated in part as the terminals for predatory raids on public resources, they necessarily involved ongoing costs in foregone efficiencies and imposed huge costs on the government, contributing to the growing losses in this sector. State banks had contributed to this problem. At the end of 1998, accumulated, non-performing loans were estimated at Rp150 trillion or 50–60 per cent of outstanding loans. A Price Waterhouse Cooper audit revealed losses of US$4.69 billion for Pertamina between April 1996 and March 1998, and losses of US$840 million for Bulog in the same period (*AFR* 1999). PLN was forced to buy electricity in US dollars at prices higher than it was permitted to charge public consumers. And this was in circumstances of over-capacity (*FK* 1997b; *JP* 1998c). It faced losses of Rp14.9 trillion in the first half of 1998 and another Rp10 trillion loss for 1999 (*JP* 1998i). In the forestry ministry, accountants Ernst and Young found that US$5.2 billion had been lost in the collection and utilisation of the Forestry Fund in the five years to March 1998 (*JP* 1999g).

Pressure to dismantle these arrangements and the gatekeeping institutions, although part of reformist political agenda, was driven by the government's growing fiscal problems. The state budget faced growing interest payments on Rp624 trillion in government bonds issued to cover the BLBI and to recapitalise banks. These were expected to reach Rp77 trillion in 2001 (31 per cent of total budget) and Rp130 trillion in 2002 (*Bisnis Indonesia* 2000). As the reform agreements with the IMF came into effect, these institutions were subjected to increasing audit from government and private sector auditors. However, the reform of the system was to be hampered by the entrenched nature of the politico-business alliances, by nationalist concerns at the prospect of opening markets, and by the inability of the central government to enforce reforms. Although individual ministers and officials pursued cases with vigour, reformist forces behind the assault lacked cohesion of interest and political organisation.

Action

Reformers were to address these problems with enthusiasm. Within Pertamina, Energy Minister Kuntoro and Director Soegianto began to cancel and renegotiate contracts. The Soeharto family business groups (Cendana group) lost a raft of exclusive monopolies in insurance, the import of fuel and crude oil, the shipping of LNG and crude oil, and the development of gas pipelines and refineries (*JP* 1998f). By the end of 1998, Pertamina had scrapped contract with a total of thirty-two firms, claiming a saving of US$100 million. This was to be a continuing process (*JP* 1998g; *Kompas Online* 2000b).

Within the forestry industry, Minister Muslimin Nasution began a process of reviewing and cancelling the licences of companies with poor forestry management records and those involved in misuse of reforestation funds. In mid 1999, it was announced that thirteen concessions totalling 1.36 million hectares would not be renewed in 2000, and that a further eight concessions owned by the Soeharto family and their associates, totalling 1.17 million hectares, were to be revoked along with oil palm licences (*JP* 1999d). The cancelled concessions would be opened to public tender from cooperatives.

In 1997 and 1998, Bulog's exclusive right to import and distribute soy beans, sugar, cooking oil, and wheat was abolished. Confined to importing and distributing rice and maintaining price stability in competition with private traders, it was required to adopt a system of open tenders (*JP* 1998j). In PLN, Director Djiteng Marsudi took a bold stance, announcing that it would continue to purchase at pre-crisis rates and cancelling several contracts, including that of the president's step-brother, Sudwikatmono. The director threatened to review the contracts of the giant Paiton I and II projects in which Bambang Trihatmojo and Hashim Djojohadikusumo were the central figures (*JP* 1998d).

Problems

Reform was to confront a range of obstacles. Extra-budgetary funds remain attractive sources of discretionary money likely to become only more important if money politics becomes entrenched in Indonesia's fledgling democracy. Ministries and agencies reported the existence of off-budget funds of approximately Rp7.7 trillion (US$860 million) in July 2000 (Government of Indonesia, 31 July 2000:8). A bizarre scandal involving President's Wahid's masseur, Suwondo, and Bulog Deputy Chairman Saupan, in the appropriation of Rp35 billion from Bulog, drew attention to the difficulties involved in eliminating this factor. A BPKP audit reported approximately Rp2 trillion in non-budgetary Bulog funds still in existence with disbursements still going to businesses controlled by the Soeharto family and former Bulog chief, Bustanil Arifin (*JP* 2000c; *JP* 2000g).

As we have seen, reform of BI and IBRA was also subjected to the perceived needs of the government to get investment flowing again. The government's provision of a US$96 million credit facility to Texmaco, and the assumption of Rp19 trillion of its debts by IBRA in March 2000, appeared to be a repeat of the indiscriminate allocation of state funds so disastrously undertaken by BI in 1997 and 1998. Like many of the recipients of BLBI only a year earlier, Texmaco was a company that appeared to be hopelessly bankrupted and without prospects. So puzzling was the rescue that the journal *Tempo* asked whether Tommy Soeharto might not now ask for credit to revive the Timor car project or Prajogo might not seek government assistance to re-enter Chandra Asri (*Tempo* 2000a:98, 99). But although Texmaco raised questions of persisting collusion in politico-business relations, it also illustrates continuing economic nationalist sentiment. As a large export manufacturer, Texmaco was widely perceived as a national company that earned foreign exchange, and one that did not survive on licences and monopolies. Its rescue received a wide degree of support within parliament and the press.

In the forestry sector, attempts to control the industry through progressive resources-rent taxes and cancellation of concessions were to be undermined by the sheer inability of the government to control logging. The World Bank estimates that illegal logging is now a bigger business than legal logging, imposing a US$650 million loss each year on potential royalty and Reforestation Fund payments. These illegal forestry businesses are backed by big money and powerful individuals, including the military, the police and local officials, and parliamentarians (World Bank 2000:40; *JP* 2000h; *JP* 2000j). With the collapse of a powerful central state and the devolution of power, the rise of local and regional predators outside the authority of a central state is likely to be an increasing problem.

It was the experience of PLN that provided an unexpected source of resistance to reform. Foreign financiers and investors had entered into projects riddled with bribery, overpricing, and collusive subcontracting. These were contracts in which the function of PLN was clearly to carry the costs of massive rorting (*AWSJ* 1998b; *AWSJ* 1999e; *JP* 2000a). To extricate itself from the enormous costs it faced, PLN attempted to cancel agreements, suspend purchases, and renegotiate contracts. Foreign governments entered the fray, not least because their import and export banks and insurers had provided more than US$4 billion in financing to big US, Japanese, and German companies involved (*FEER* 1999; *AWSJ* 2000c). As lawsuits were traded, the Indonesian government was forced to abandon its initial strategy for one of negotiation with the suppliers. Companies associated with the Soeharto family which dominated this industry found protection within their corporate relationships. International private corporate interests now collided with reformist attempts to unravel the collusive alliances and restructure arrangements formed as a consequence of these.

Structural reform

The ultimate solution to the problem of predatory capitalism appeared deceptively simple—simply abolish the authority of the state to intervene in the market in specific cases. As we have seen, most of Bulog's control of import and distribution of basic commodities was abolished. A new central banking law was introduced in May 1999 that established BI's independence from government and abolished its authority to channel subsidised liquidity loans to individual borrowers. Its authority to supervise banks was transferred to a new independent institution to be established by the end of 2002 (McLeod 1999:148, 149). Pertamina, too, was to be stripped of its authority to allocate licences for exploration and production and for downstream distribution and marketing. These functions would be transferred to other agencies responsible directly to the minister for Mines and Industry and to the president. Under the terms of legislation proposed by the government, Pertamina would become just another oil company (*Kontan Online* 2000b).

Yet, even these seemingly decisive moves proved inconclusive. In the case of both BI and Pertamina, the transfer of specific authority simply shifted the same potential problem from one government agency to another. As McLeod has noted, the regulatory authority of BI over banks was, in any case, watered-down substantially by the government with the lowering of CAR and LLL requirements. Whoever presided over bank regulation now had reduced powers (McLeod 1999). Nor was there any attempt to reconsider the rules that had allowed banks in Indonesia to be owned directly by larger corporate entities. While this arrangement remained, the structural problems of legal lending limits would continue to be a problem. In the case of Pertamina, an attempt to introduce reform legislation in 1998 was defeated in parliament. It confronted not only powerful vested interests, but also nationalist concerns—that the ending of a national monopoly, however flawed, would only open the door to a foreign-controlled oligopoly of large oil companies (*JP* 1999b; *FEER* 1998).

Nevertheless, the momentum of reform is strong. The Indonesian government's Letters of Intent to the IMF reveal an ongoing process of audit, institutional reform, legal prosecution of uncooperative debtors, privatisation, and deregulation. The question is whether predatory relations of power will be extinguished by these institutional changes. Here, the critical factor is political. Can the reformist coalitions overcome the old interests still entrenched within the state apparatus? Can they contain the new pressures for money politics building outside the state in the new institutions of party and parliament?

Conclusion: a matter of politics

After more than three decades where politics has been frozen and civil society disorganised by an authoritarian regime, the crisis has opened the door to a new political regime based on parliament and parties. Over the next decade two critical questions will be answered. First, will the new

Indonesian democracy be able to assert its authority over a state apparatus and a corps of officials who had evolved under Soeharto into a crude mechanism for allocating power and resources? Second, will the power and influence of politicians, tycoons, and officials be subordinated to a rule of law and the authority of the courts, or will money politics and the authority of political bosses appropriate parliament and government? In the confused and early stages of this conflict, the reform agenda faces two major obstacles: an entrenched judiciary embedded in the old predatory power relations, and an uncertain social base for reform.

Perhaps the litmus test is the struggle to reform the judicial system. The reformist government of President Wahid inherited a corps of judges widely regarded as the instruments of the grand alliance of state power, political oligarchy, and corporate wealth. They operated within a 'black state', outside the rule of law, where the real business of power and politics took place (Lindsey 2000:288). As a *Jakarta Post* editorial noted: '. . . subordination of the judiciary [under Soeharto] paved the way for total control by the state of every aspect of public life in Indonesia' (*JP* 1999e). Wahid also inherited, in the view of Lindsey, a new set of commercial and competition laws designed in haste after the fall of Soeharto to be easily manipulated in favour of entrenched commercial interests in the less-predictable environment of democratic Indonesia (Lindsey 2000:283).

Without an effective judiciary, reformers were to find their agenda seriously undermined. IBRA has met with constant frustration in its attempts to pursue uncooperative debtors through the bankruptcy courts. Of the high-profile business figures, only Bob Hasan has yet been convicted of corruption and jailed. Former President Soeharto has survived protracted attempts by the government to enforce prosecution, and Tommy Soeharto, although convicted, simply refuses to go to prison. With legal actions filed by the attorney-general and IBRA against a range of non-cooperating borrowers and those not complying with MSAA agreements, the viability of the banking restructure is at stake. With the replacement of 70 per cent of the judges sitting in the Jakarta courts in July 2000, including a number of Commercial Court judges, the Wahid government appears to have made a potential breakthrough. New appointments to the Supreme Court are also in train.

The struggle to undermine the power of the old forces is critical. But reform cannot proceed solely on the basis of IMF pressure and the efforts of a few reformist ministers and officials. Embedded reform requires a shift in social power. Yet, constructing a reformist coalition that is politically cohesive and ideologically coherent has proven difficult. This is not, as neo-modernisation theorists have argued, because of the non-existence, or weakness, of a bourgeoisie or a secular rational middle class. Rather, it is because Indonesia's bourgeoisie has been profoundly anti-democratic and uninterested in market reforms. Apprehensive of the latent xenophobia of populism in Indonesia and the prospect of social radicalism, a vulnerable and predominantly Chinese bourgeoisie sheltered under the umbrella of political authoritarianism. Reliant on protection from global competition, and with strategic market position already in their possession, they have flourished under regimes of economic nationalism and predatory capitalism, preferring to build relationships with political gatekeepers rather than fight for market reforms or rule of law.

In the task of mobilising coalitions behind the neo-liberal agenda, it is a system of money politics that will best suit Indonesia's bourgeoisie for whom rules regulation, disclosure, and an effective tax system are more of a threat than the crisis ever was. As in the case of Thailand, a system of parties and parliament animated by money offers real advantages (Anderson 1990).

Notes

1 The themes developed in this chapter are also developed in a larger study of the rise and fall of Soeharto currently being co-authored with Vedi Hadiz.

2 The oil boom consisted of two main phases. Between 1973 and 1974, the international price of oil rose from approximately US$3 per barrel to US$12 per barrel. Between 1979 and 1981 the price rose again, from approximately US$15 per barrel to more than US$40 per barrel. As a result, Indonesia's gas and oil exports leapt from US$1.6 billion (or 50.1% of total exports) in 1973, to US$18.4 billion (or 82.6% of total exports) in 1982. At the same time, government revenues from oil and gas taxes increased from Rp382 billion (or 39.5% of total revenues) in 1973, to Rp8.6 trillion (or more than 70% of total government revenues) in 1981–82 (Republik Indonesia 1994/95; Robison 1987:28–9, 44–6; Winters 1996:120–1).

3 In contrast, the costs of recapitalisation in Thailand, South Korea, and Malaysia are estimated at 35 per cent, 29 per cent, and 22 per cent respectively. Levels of non-performing loans are also lower in these countries, estimated to be 55 per cent in Thailand, 50 per cent in South Korea, and 35 per cent in Malaysia (AWSJ 1998c).

4 IBRA's asset-disposal rate languished at 2.5 per cent in early 2000, compared with rates of 38 per cent in Korea, 40 per cent in Malaysia, and 78 per cent in Thailand (JP 2000d).

5 These included: the head of the textile giant, Texmaco, Marimutu Sinivasan; Soeharto son-in-law and head of the Tirtamas group, Hashim Djojohadiku-sumo; close Soeharto business associate, Bob Hasan; Barito Pacific chairman, Prajogo Pangestu; and Gajah Tunggal chairman, Sjamsul Nursalim (*JP* 2000f; 2000n).

References

AFR, see *Australian Financial Review (AFR)*.

Anderson, Benedict (1990) 'Murder and Progress in Modern Siam' *New Left Review*, (181):33–48.

Arndt, Heinz (1967) 'Economic Disorder and the Task Ahead', in T. K Tan (ed.) *Soekarno's Guided Indonesia*, Brisbane, Jacaranda, pp 129–42.

Asian Wall Street Journal (AWSJ) (1995), 6–7 January 1995, pp 1, 4.

Asian Wall Street Journal (AWSJ) (1996), 27 January 1996, pp 1, 4.

Asian Wall Street Journal (AWSJ) (1997a), 9 October 1997, p. 1.

Asian Wall Street Journal (AWSJ) (1997b), 29 October 1997, p. 1.

Asian Wall Street Journal (AWSJ) (1998a), 9–10 January 1998, p. 1.

Asian Wall Street Journal (AWSJ) (1998b), 9 June 1998, p. 3.

Asian Wall Street Journal (AWSJ) (1998c), 22 October 1998, p. 1.

Asian Wall Street Journal (AWSJ) (1999a), 4 March 1999, p. 1.

Asian Wall Street Journal (AWSJ) (1999b), 15 March 1999, p. 1.

Asian Wall Street Journal (AWSJ) (1999c), 11–12 June 1999, p. 3.

Asian Wall Street Journal (AWSJ) (1999d), 23 June 1999, pp 1, 4.

Asian Wall Street Journal (AWSJ) (1999e), 21 December 1999, p. 1.

Asian Wall Street Journal (AWSJ) (2000a), 13 January 2000, pp 1, 10.

Asian Wall Street Journal (AWSJ) (2000b), 25–26 February 2000, p. 1.

Asian Wall Street Journal (AWSJ) (2000c), 9 March 2000, p. 1.

Australian Financial Review (AFR) (1998a), 16 January 1998, p. 1.

Australian Financial Review (AFR) (1998b), 11 February 1998, p. 11.

Australian Financial Review (AFR) (1999), 12 July 1999, p. 12.

AWSJ, see *Asian Wall Street Journal (AWSJ)*.

Bhattacharya, A. and M. Pangestu (1992) 'Indonesia: Development and Trans-formation Since 1965 and the Role of Public Policy', paper prepared for the World Bank Workshop on the Role of Government and East Asian Success, East–West Centre, November.

Bisnis Indonesia (2000), <www.bisnis.com>, 3 October 2000.

Bresnan, John (1993) *Managing Indonesia: the Modern Political Economy*, New York: Columbia University Press.

Chaudhry, Kiren Aziz (1997) *The Price of Wealth: Economies and Institutions in the Middle East*, Ithaca and London: Cornell University Press.

Econit (1996) *Dampak Kelangkaan Semu Pupuk Urea Terhadap Impor Beras dan Kesejahteraan Petani Tahun*, Jakarta.

Economist (1998), 7 March 1998.

Editor (1990), 31 March 1990, pp 11–23.

Emmerson, Donald K. (1976) *Indonesia's Elite: Political Culture and Cultural Politics*, Ithaca: Cornell University Press.

Emmerson, Donald K. (1978) 'The Bureaucracy in Political Context: Weakness in Strength', in Karl D. Jackson and Lucian W. Pye (eds) *Political Power and Communications in Indonesia*, Berkeley: University of California Press, pp 82–136.

Far Eastern Economic Review (FEER) (1992), 2 April 1992, p. 46.

Far Eastern Economic Review (FEER) (1998), 24 December 1998, pp 42–4.

Far Eastern Economic Review (FEER) (1999), 21 October 1999, pp 63–4.

FEER, see *Far Eastern Economic Review (FEER)*.

FK, see *Forum Keadilan (FK)*.

Forum Keadilan (FK) (1997a), 8 September 1997, pp 24–5.

Forum Keadilan (FK) (1997b), 29 December 1997, pp 12–21.

Forum Keadilan (FK) (1999a), 11 January 1999, p. 61.

Forum Keadilan (FK) (1999b), 22 September 1999, pp 88–9.

Forum Keadilan (FK) (2000), 12 March 2000, p. 12.

Gamma (2000), 1–7 March 2000, pp 22–3.

Garnaut, Ross (1998) 'The Financial Crisis: A Watershed in Economic Thought about East Asia', *Asian Pacific Economic Literature*, May, pp 1–11.

Hill, Hal (1996) *The Indonesian Economy Since 1966: Asia's Emerging Giant*, Cambridge: Cambridge University Press.

Hill, Hal (2000) 'Indonesia: the Strange and Sudden Death of a Tiger Economy', *Oxford Development Studies*, 28(2):117–39.

Government of Indonesia, 'Letters of Intent and Memorandum of Economic and Financial Policies,' 1997, 1998, 1999, 2000, <www.imf.org/external/NP/LOI>.

Huntington, Samuel (1968) *Political Order in Changing Societies*, New Haven: Yale University Press.

Ikatan Sarjana Ekonomi Indonesia (ISEI) 1990 'Penjabaran Demokrasi Ekonomi', Jakarta, 15 August.

Infobank (1995a), 12 October 1995, pp 14–34.

Infobank (1995b), December No. 192 1995, pp 160–1.

Infobank (1997), February No. 206 1997, pp 38–43.

ISEI, see Ikatan Sarjana Ekonomi Indonesia (ISEI).

Jakarta Jakarta (1991), 16–22 March 1991, p. 1.

Jakarta Post (JP) (1996a), 16 February 1996, pp 1, 4.

Jakarta Post (JP) (1996b), 7 March 1996, p. 1.

Jakarta Post (JP) (1996c), 18 March 1996, p. 4.

Jakarta Post (*JP*) (1997a), 2 November 1997, p. 1.

Jakarta Post (*JP*) (1997b), 5 November 1997, p. 12.

Jakarta Post (*JP*) (1997c), 6 November 1997, p. 1.

Jakarta Post (*JP*) (1997d), 8 November 1997, p. 1.

Jakarta Post (*JP*) (1998a), 10 January 1998, p. 1.

Jakarta Post (*JP*) (1998b), 14 January 1998, p. 1.

Jakarta Post (*JP*) (1998c), 19 February 1998, p. 8.

Jakarta Post (*JP*) (1998d), 8 June 1998, p. 1.

Jakarta Post (*JP*) (1998e), 12 June 1998, p. 10.

Jakarta Post (*JP*) (1998f), 23 September 1998, p. 8.

Jakarta Post (*JP*) (1998g), 10 October 1998, p. 8.

Jakarta Post (*JP*) (1998h), 12 October 1998, p. 12.

Jakarta Post (*JP*) (1998i), 28 October 1998, p. 8.

Jakarta Post (*JP*) (1998j), 24 December 1998, p. 8.

Jakarta Post (*JP*) (1999a), 1 March 1999, p. 1.

Jakarta Post (*JP*) (1999b), 1 April 1999, p. 8.

Jakarta Post (*JP*) (1999c), 9 July 1999, p. 1.

Jakarta Post (*JP*) (1999d), 12 October 1999, p. 1.

Jakarta Post (*JP*) (1999e), 22 November 1999, p. 4.

Jakarta Post (*JP*) (1999f), 11 December 1999, p. 1.

Jakarta Post (*JP*) (1999g), 31 December 1999, p. 1.

Jakarta Post (*JP*) (2000a), 7 January 2000, p. 1.

Jakarta Post (*JP*) (2000b), 20 January 2000, p. 1.

Jakarta Post (*JP*) (2000c), 13 June 2000, p. 9.

Jakarta Post (*JP*) (2000d), 21 June 2000, p. 8.

Jakarta Post (*JP*) (2000e), <www.thejakartapost.com>, 1 July 2000.

Jakarta Post (*JP*) (2000f), 5 July 2000, p. 1.

Jakarta Post (*JP*) (2000g), 20 July 2000, p. 4.

Jakarta Post (*JP*) (2000h), 14 August 2000, pp 3, 4.

Jakarta Post (*JP*) (2000i), 16 September 2000, p. 1.

Jakarta Post (*JP*) (2000j), 4 October 2000, p. 10.

Jakarta Post (*JP*) (2000k), 6 October 2000, p. 1.

Jakarta Post (*JP*) (2000l), 7 October 2000, p. 1.

Jakarta Post (*JP*) (2000m), 20 October 2000, p. 1.

Jakarta Post (*JP*) (2000n), 24 October 2000, p. 3.

JP, see *Jakarta Post* (*JP*).

Jones, Steven and Raphael Pura (1986) 'Suharto-Linked Monopolies Hobble Economy,' *AWSJ*, 24 November.

Kartasasmita, Ginandjar (1985) 'Daya Tahan Ekonomi dan Kekuatan Dalam Negeri', *Prisma* 6:42–7.

Kompas (1998), 1 August 1998, pp 1, 11.

Kompas Online (2000a), <www.kompas.com>, 6 March 2000.

Kompas Online (2000b), <www.kompas.com>, 9 May 2000.

Kontan Online (2000a), <www.kontan-online.com>, 28 February 2000.

Kontan Online (2000b), <www.kontan-online.com>, 5 June 2000.

Kontan Online (2000c), <www.kontan-online.com>, 3 July 2000.

Kwik Kian Gie (1993) 'A Tale of a Conglomerate', *Economic and Business Review Indonesia*, 5 June, pp 26–7 and 12 June pp 26–7.

Liddle, R. William (1989) 'Development or Democracy' *Far Eastern Economic Review*, 9 November, pp 22, 23.

Liddle, R. William (1991) 'The Relative autonomy of the Third World Politician: Soeharto and Indonesian Economic Development in Comparative Perspective,' *International Studies Quarterly*, 35:403–27.

Liddle, R. William (1992) 'The Politics of Development Policy', *World Development*, 20 (6):793–807.

Liddle, R. William (1999) 'Indonesia's Unexpected Failure of Leadership', in Adam Schwarz and Jonathan Paris, *The Politics of Post-Suharto Indonesia*, NewYork: Council on Foreign Relations Press, pp 16–39.

Lindsey, Tim (2000) 'Black Letter, Black Market and Bad Faith: Corruption and the Failure of Law Reform', in Chris Manning and Peter van Diermen (eds) *Indonesia in Transition: Social Aspects of Reformasi and Crisis*, Singapore: Institute of Southeast Asian Studies, pp 278–92.

MacIntyre, Andrew (1994) 'Business, Government and Development: Northeast and Southeast Asian Comparisons', in A. MacIntyre (ed.) *Business and Government in Industrialising Asia*, St Leonards: Allen and Unwin.

MacIntyre, Andrew (1999) 'Political Institutions and Economic Crisis in Thailand and Indonesia', in T.J. Pempel (ed.) *Politics of the Asian Economic Crisis*, Ithaca: Cornell University Press, pp 143–62.

McLeod, Ross (1998) 'Indonesia', in R. McLeod and R. Garnaut (eds) *East Asia in Crisis: From Being a Miracle to Needing One?* London: Routledge, pp 333–51.

McLeod, Ross (1999) 'Crisis-Driven Changes to the Banking Laws and Regulations', *Bulletin of Indonesian Economic Studies*, 35(2):147–54.

McLeod, Ross (2000) 'Soeharto's Indonesia: A Better Class of Corruption' *Agenda*, 7(2):99–112.

Moertopo, Ali (1973) *The Acceleration and Modernisation of 25 Years Development*, Jakarta, Centre for Strategic and International Studies:83–8.

Nasution, Anwar (1992) 'The Years of Living Dangerously: The Impacts of Financial Sector Policy Reforms and Increasing Private Sector Indebtedness in Indonesia, 1983–1992,' *The Indonesian Quarterly*, XX/4:405–35.

Pangaribuan, Robinson (1995) *The Indonesian State Secretariat 1945–1993*, Perth: Asia Research Centre, Murdoch University.

Pincus, Jonathan and Rizal Ramli (1998) 'Indonesia: from showcase to basket case' *Cambridge Journal of Economics*, 22(731).

Prospek (1992a), 7 March 1992, pp 70–81.

Prospek (1992b), 10 July 1992, p. 67.

Pura, Raphael (1995a) 'Bob Hassan Builds an Empire in the Forest', *AWSJ*, 20–21 January, pp 1, 4.

Pura, Raphael (1995b) 'Indonesian Plywood Cartel under Fire as Sales Shrink', *AWSJ*, 23 January, pp 1, 4.

Ramli, Rizal (1992) 'Kayu', *Tempo*, 13 June, p. 77.

Republik Indonesia (1994/95) *Nota Keuangan dan Rancangan Anggaran Pendapatan dan belanja Negara Tahun Anggaran 1994/95*.

Robison, Richard (1986) *Indonesia: The Rise of Capital*, Sydney: Allen and Unwin.

Robison, Richard (1987) 'After the Gold Rush: the politics of economic restructuring in Indonesia in the 1980s' in Robison et al. (eds) *Southeast Asia in the 1980s: the Politics of Economic Crisis*, Sydney: Allen and Unwin, pp 16–51.

Robison, Richard (1997) 'Politics and Markets in Indonesia's Post-Oil Era', in Garry Rodan, Kevin Hewison and Richard Robison (eds) *The Political Economy of South-East Asia: An Introduction*, Melbourne: Oxford University Press, pp 29–63.

Robison R. and A. Rosser (1988) 'Contesting Reform: Indonesia's New Order and the IMF' *World Development*, 26(8):1593–1609.

Robison, Richard and Vedi Hadiz (1993) 'Privatisation or the Reorganisation of Dirigism? Indonesian Economic Policy in the 1990s', *Canadian Journal of Development Studies*, Special Issue, December, pp 13–31.

Rosser, Andrew (1999) *Creating Markets: The Politics of Economic Liberalisation in Indonesia Since the Mid-1980s*, unpublished PhD thesis, Murdoch University.

Schwarz, Adam (1994) *A Nation in Waiting*, St Leonards: Allen and Unwin.

Shin, Yoon Hwan (1989) 'Demystifying the Capitalist State: Political Patronage, Bureaucratic Interests and Capitalist in Formation in Soeharto's Indonesia', unpublished PhD dissertation: Yale University.

Soeharto (1990) 'State Address', 16 August.

Soesastro, Hadi (1989) 'The Political Economy of Deregulation' *Asian Survey*, 29(9).

Tempo (1981), 14 March 1981, pp 70–1.

Tempo (1991a), 9 March 1991, pp 86–90.

Tempo (1991b), 17 August 1991, p. 86.

Tempo (1991c), 26 October 1991, pp 26–32.

Tempo (1993a), 10 April 1993, pp 14–16.

Tempo (1993b), 10 July 1993, p. 74.

Tempo (1993c), 25 September 1993, pp 88–9.

Tempo (1993d), 4 December 1993, various pages as cited.

Tempo (1994a), 21 February 1994, pp 26–30.

Tempo (1994b), 11 June 1994, pp 21–7.

Tempo (2000a), 26 March 2000, various pages as cited.

Tempo (2000b), 11 June 2000, p. 130.

Tempo (2000c), 16 July 2000, pp 103, 104.

Tempo (2000d), <www.tempo.co.id>, 27 August 2000.

Time (1999), <www.time.com/time/asia/asia/magazine/1999/990524/cover1.html>, 24 May 1999.

Toye, John (1987) *Dilemmas of Development*, Oxford: Basil Blackwell.

United States Embassy, Jakarta, Indonesia (1 May 2000) 'IMI: Bank Restructuring Update: High Costs; Banks Still in Deep Freeze', <www.usembassyjakarta.org/econ/imibank050100.html>.

Warta Ekonomi (1996), 11 March 1996, p. 19.

Warta Ekonomi (1999), <www.wartaekonomi.com/we10/34lpt2.htm>, 14 January 1999.

Winters, Jeffrey, (1996) *Power in Motion: Capital Mobility and the Indonesian State*, Ithaca: Cornell University Press.

Winters, Jeffrey (1997) 'The Dark Side of the Tigers' *Asian Wall Street Journal*, 12–13 December:10.

Winters, Jeffrey, (2000) 'The Financial Crisis in Southeast Asia', in Richard Robison et al. (eds) *Politics and Markets in the Wake of the Asian Crisis*, London: Routledge, pp 34–52.

World Bank (1993) *Indonesia: Sustaining Development*, Jakarta: Country Department III, East Asia and Pacific Regional Office, May 25.

World Bank (1995) *Indonesia: Improving Efficiency and Equity—Changes in the Public Sector's Role*, Jakarta: Country Department III, East Asia and Pacific Region, June 4.

World Bank (1996) *Indonesia: Dimensions of Growth*, Jakarta: Country Department III, East Asia and Pacific Region, 7 May.

World Bank (1997) *World Development Report, The State in a Changing World*, Washington: OUP.

World Bank (1999) *Indonesia: From Crisis to Opportunity*, Jakarta, 21 July.

World Bank (2000) *Indonesia: Accelerating Recovery in Uncertain Times, East Asia Poverty Reduction Management Unit*, 13 October.

5

Singapore: Globalisation and the Politics of Economic Restructuring

Garry Rodan[1]

Introduction

Important as the impact of the 1997–98 Asian crisis was, the enthusiastic official embrace of globalisation and the so-called 'New Economy' is the most significant feature of Singapore's contemporary political economy. It has given rise to increased economic liberalisation and corporate governance reforms, raising speculation that we are witnessing the beginnings of a major and necessary shift in development strategy. Various commentators argue that the government's current economic objectives require a dismantling of 'Singapore Inc.' and the ushering in of more neutral market conditions and regulations (*STWE* 2000c:14–15; *Australian* 2000; *FT* 2000; *STWE* 2000f; Lian 2000; Tessensohn 2000, *STWE* 2000h:3; Restall 2000).

Invariably, the evaluation of this claim is shaped by the theoretical approach brought to bear on it. So, before identifying the argument of this chapter, let us briefly examine the different ways in which the city-state's development has been understood thus far, with particular reference to the political economy approaches outlined in chapter 1 of this volume. This will not only help situate the above prescription in theoretical terms, but also serve to distinguish the position taken here and the assumptions behind it.

The idea that Singapore's modern economic development has so far been accompanied by a pervasive state is not generally a matter of contest in the literature on Singapore. Debate centres instead on the significance of the state's role. Among neo-classical economists and political economists, the tendency has been to down play this in favour of the impact of market forces, or to interpret the state's role as one of fundamentally facilitating markets. Lim Chong Yah (1983:6) thus contended, for example, that 'Singapore has been able to grow so spectacularly in the economic field throughout the period because it has allowed a free enterprise system to flourish with government support and intervention where necessary'. Similarly, Mohamed Ariff and Hal Hill (1985) argued that state intervention has been non-distortionary by providing incentives and inducements to assist rather than confront the market.

An equally influential neo-classical political economy idea percolating through the literature on Singapore is the notion that politics has been kept in abeyance through the exclusion of rent-seekers and distributional coalitions from the policy process, resulting in sound (and, by definition) pro-market public policy. References to 'correct development policy' (Lim 1983:101) and 'an effective government' (Chen 1983:24) are reflective of such a technical conception of the policy process. This often leads to voluntarism, as in Chen's claim that 'the experience of Singapore's growth strategies provided a useful model for rapid growth for both developing and developed countries', arrived at without any analysis of the social and political basis of economic regimes under the ruling People's Action Party (PAP).

Once we branch out of the orthodox neo-classical camp, the literature doesn't neatly fall into the historical institutionalist and social conflict theory camps. Much of it is descriptive rather than explicitly theoretical, or it reflects conscious or unconscious eclectic theoretical influences. To complicate matters, there are neo-classical political economists who have broken ranks from the above thinking to concede more importance to the role of the state in economic development. Linda Low (1998), for example, recognises the state's historic economic importance but maintains now that a fuller embrace of market forces is required to ensure continued development. Then there is the work of W.G. Huff (1994) which comes essentially out of a classical political economy and Keynesian tradition, but with occasional neo-classical resonance.[2] Thus, although arguing that the Singapore government constantly 'intervened to set the right prices to clear labour markets, which enabled the island's economy to take advantage of opportunities for trade and industrialization' (Huff 1994:368), he also places store in 'good public administration' and what he regards as 'the relative absence of ideology' on the part of the PAP (1994:369).[3]

Remarkably, despite the widely acknowledged parallels among Singapore and the East Asian developmental states of Taiwan and South Korea in the comparative literature, there is little by way of explicit attempts among scholars specialising on Singapore to fit the city-state into an historical institutionalist framework. In 1990 Stephan Haggard (1990) incorporated Singapore into his influential study *Pathways from the Periphery*. But his observation that policy decisions were shaped by the instruments and mechanisms availed by state institutions received little detailed follow-up. One possible exception is the examination of local business groups by Ian Chalmers (1992) which drew, in part, on a society-centred historical institutionalist perspective. More recently, Henry Wai-chung Yeung (2000a) has deployed concepts of institutional capacity and embeddedness into his work, but they are married with a wide range of other theoretical influences.[4] Yeung (2000a:146) nevertheless explicitly aligns himself with leading historical institutionalists Wade and Veneroso (1998) in advancing scepticism about the viability of dismantling institutional capacity in Singapore in the face of the Asian crisis.

What is discernible in the Singapore literature is a broad range of challenges to the orthodox neo-classical account. These challenges have in common an emphasis on the state and how it has contributed to economic development. This might loosely be termed 'statist', although we should be careful not to overlook that there are divergent ways of analysing the state and different purposes for examining it. Some of this work is descriptive of the functional economic role of the state and does not attempt to explain why this role is assumed, nor the politics that sustains it. However, there is also work that delves into the conflict and power relations associated with the state's economic role, such as Frederic Deyo's (1981) study on labour control, Chua Beng-Huat's (1991) analysis of public housing and consumption, and Christopher Tremewan's (1994) general study on social control. The approach here shares with this literature a conception of the state as inseparable from the market which extends to the social, political, and ideological realms. More particularly, and from a social conflict theory perspective, the aim is to explain how power relations and the interests embodied in them have at every turn been crucial to the path of capitalist development in Singapore (Rodan 1989; 1993a), and will continue to be so.

Like the decades of industrialisation behind it, therefore, the current juncture in Singapore's political economy cannot simply be explained in neo-classical economic terms as the irresistible power of free-market processes combining with rational policy choices. Instead, three quite different points must be underlined about the latest phase in the development strategy. First, it represents a refinement in the state's longstanding strategic economic role—not an abandonment of it. Opening up the domestic telecommunications and banking sectors to greater private investment and international competition, for instance, is accompanied by, and in some respects part of, a broader attempt to bolster the relevance of state companies to the global economy. Second, the role of the state in subsidising social and physical infrastructure has not diminished. On the contrary, substantial sums are being channelled into the support and promotion of technological innovation and entrepreneurialism as a complement to traditional infrastructure investments (see Yeung 2000a). Third, various changes to corporate governance regimes are best understood as new forms of regulation of the economy (Jayasuriya 2000), rather than deregulation of the economy, wherein the state continues to exert a crucial role in the social construction of markets. Indeed, Deputy Prime Minister Lee Hsien Loong (quoted in BT Online 2000c) recently acknowledged that neither the 'New Economy' nor the market system associated with it are possible without an activist state: 'It doesn't happen by itself. You can have a free market only if there's a government to manage the rules and enforce them.'

Importantly, the current globalisation push involves new collaboration with select elements of the domestic bourgeoisie—a class from which the ruling People's Action Party (PAP) has traditionally kept its political distance—and an extension of the existing alliance with international capital. These relationships are important to the realisation of the government's ambitious economic objectives. They are tempered, however, by a political imperative to retain a substantial measure of strategic state economic control. State-owned companies and statutory boards are part of a power structure involving the PAP and a public bureaucracy that operates as a virtual arm of the ruling party (see Worthington 2001). State control over economic and social resources is also the basis of a political paternalism that shores up the electoral position of the ruling party. Authorities will thus strive to ensure that the new economic direction does not exert stress on the fundamentals of this structure.

There are other political challenges and social tensions ahead of the government. Industrialisation laid the basis for full employment and major social improvements in areas such as public housing, education, health, and transport. It also generated considerable upward social mobility. However, structural limits to social mobility are now beginning to assert themselves in Singapore as privileged classes and elites consolidate their positions. This is being compounded by globalisation and sharper differentiations in labour market rewards between the skilled and unskilled. The ideological hostility of the PAP to welfare-oriented redistributional policies places it under pressure to devise alternative measures to manage effectively the social and political consequences of economic restructuring.

Indeed, the question of the direction of Singapore's development strategy is inherently a political one. Ideas about neutral market conditions and regulations doing away with politics are illusory. Whatever the rules of economic engagement, they will invariably enhance some interests and damage others. This is no less so in an economy that is wide open to globalisation as it is in one that is structured to partially blunt its impact. Not all fractions of capital are equally capable of participating in the

Singapore government's embrace of globalisation, and uneven rewards will more generally ensue from it. The management of these tensions is becoming an increasingly important issue in the political economy of Singapore.

In what follows, the above arguments will be elaborated and demonstrated via a chronological account of the different phases of capital accumulation in Singapore's development.

Pre-industrial Singapore

Singapore was incorporated under the British colonial umbrella in 1819 and subsequently development as an entrepôt economy. This fundamentally shaped the patterns of capital accumulation by the domestic bourgeoisie. Chinese merchants attracted to the island established an intricate network of domestic commerce and small-scale collection, distribution, and retailing to complement the ascendancy of British and European capital (see Buchanan 1972:33). Over time, this involved a progression from trade and commerce into finance,[5] but no challenge to its comprador role.

It was only after World War II, when Singapore's more stable and rapidly expanding population was accompanied by rising economic nationalism in South-East Asia, that the question of economic diversification began to receive serious consideration by authorities (Turnbull 1982:234). These trends threatened to undercut the rate of economic growth to Singapore's entrepôt economy at precisely the time when employment growth was increasingly required. The first official investigation into the problem resulted in the commissioning of a report by the International Bank for Reconstruction and Development (IBRD) which was presented in 1955. It recommended an import-substitution industrialisation (ISI) strategy to alleviate unemployment. Economic union with Malaya, it was envisaged, would generate a sizeable protected domestic market for manufactured goods, which would attract investors. However, given the preoccupation with the issue of Singapore's self-rule, serious action on industrialisation was shelved.

The domestic bourgeoisie's alignment of interests with colonial capital resulted in a detachment by it from the anti-colonial movement. Thus, when self-government came in 1959, the domestic bourgeoisie found itself politically marginalised. The triumphant People's Action Party (PAP) was predominantly led by a small group of English-educated middle-class nationalists who had formed an alliance of convenience with the closely coordinated leaderships of the labour and student movements dominated by the Chinese-educated. The alliance was to prove a tempestuous and ultimately unsustainable one, but this was, nevertheless, a crucial historical phase shaping Singapore's economic and political direction. In particular, it kept the government insulated from pressures by established business interests in the formation of a manufacturing strategy. There was no political necessity for a domestic, rather than an international, industrial bourgeoisie to prevail in any program to attract private investment. In any case, the legacy of colonial Singapore's class structure meant that the state would necessarily play a critical role in industrialisation in Singapore. If this did not take the form of a heavy direct investment role to compensate for the absence of an industrial bourgeoisie, it was at least to involve the state in extensive measures to attract or nurture private sector investment in industry.

Industrial transformation

The PAP government's first initiative towards industrialisation involved an invitation to the World Bank for advice and consequent visits to Singapore in late 1960 from a United Nations Industrial Survey Mission headed by Dutch economist, Albert Winsemius. What was thus known as the 'Winsemius Report' recommended a program of ISI led by private capital investment, but involving an extensive role for the state in attracting and supporting that investment. This included: control over labour and the holding down of wages; the provision of various industrial estates; upgrading of technical training; tax incentives; and free remittance of profits. In early 1961 the government announced the *Development Plan, 1961–64* (MoF 1961), closely reflecting the recommendations of the Winsemius Report. Central to this was the proposed Economic Development Board (EDB) which was entrusted with a range of responsibilities, including the development of industrial estates, provision of industrial loans, and technical assistance. Some functions were intended to compensate for the lack of industrial expertise of domestic-based capital, others to lower the establishment and operating costs to capital. However, the government's left-wing critics saw a greater role for the state in direct investment to ensure more favourable conditions for workers.

Yet it was the prospect of political merger with the Federation of Malaysia which was to finally precipitate a showdown between the PAP's competing factions. Although the Left had, in principle, supported the idea of political merger with Malaya, when the Federation of Malaysia was proposed in May 1961 by Malayan Prime Minister Tunku Abdul Rahman, this raised the prospect of the Left's persecution by a right-wing federal government. The consequent intensification of internal PAP friction culmin-ated in a permanent split which led, in 1963, to the formation by Prime Minister Lee Kuan Yew's opponents of a new party, the Barisan Sosialis (BS). Support for the newly established BS came not only from the left-wing labour and student movements, but also from elements of the domestic bourgeoisie which shared concerns about the status of Chinese language and culture (see Bloodworth 1986:58–61). This did nothing to endear the PAP leadership to the local business class; instead it engendered further suspicion about it.

The PAP was now not only insulated from political control or significant influence by the domestic bourgeoisie—which incidentally did not entirely exclude some personal links with, and selective co-option of, individual business figures, notably from among the financial bourgeoisie (see Hamilton-Hart 2000)—but it was also largely spared internal pressures by organised labour. Yet this high degree of relative political autonomy also brought the legitimacy of the government into question. The PAP responded by contending that a party that sat above the pressures of particular interest groups or classes was the only one that could represent the national interest. This rationale evolved into a comprehensive ideological case for elitist, technocratic government in the years ahead.[6] Meanwhile, the challenge for the PAP was to hold office after having lost the organisational backbone that mobilised mass electoral support for the party. Although repression of opponents and state-controlled propaganda were core components of the strategy to maintain office, the PAP under-stood that only through real and substantive social and economic improvements for the working class could it survive electorally in the medium-to-long term. This rendered the success of the ISI strategy ever more critical.

Singapore's membership of the Malaysian federation was short-lived. Political differences and mistrust between the governments in Singapore and Kuala Lumpur escalated between 1963 and 1965, culminating in the city-state's abrupt separation from the federation. With this, the vision of industrial expansion through access to a common market seemed an unlikely possibility. Apart from the troubling fact that unemployment was nearly 9 per cent in 1965, the collapse of merger also presented a political opportunity for the PAP's domestic opponents who had opposed merger. To make matters worse, in 1967 the UK government announced its intention to withdraw its military bases from the island. In that year, spending from the bases accounted for 12 per cent of Singapore's total GNP. The spectre of economic crisis loomed large in policy-makers' minds.

In the re-evaluation of strategy, the PAP's relative political autonomy from both capital and labour was to prove especially important. Having remained committed to private sector-led industrialisation, Singapore's policy-makers looked to the experiences of Hong Kong and Taiwan both of which had, by the mid 1960s, successfully embarked on export-oriented industrialisation (EOI) programs. Such a direction would necessitate close attention to labour costs. It would also require the attraction of international capital since the domestic bourgeoisie lacked capital and expertise in sufficient quantities to give serious effect to such a program. Despite some expansion in the 1960s, local industrialists lacked the political or economic clout to frustrate this policy direction.

Similarly, the government set about not only further blunting independent labour, but also marshalling the PAP-affiliated National Trades Union Congress (NTUC) in support of its social and economic policies. Against this background, the *Employment Act 1968* and the *Industrial Relations Act 1969* were introduced, thereby reducing wages and eroding conditions, increasing working hours, and severely curtailing union bargaining powers and the capacity for industrial action. Government intervention in the labour market was further institutionalised with the adoption in 1972 of the National Wages Council (NWC).

Additional measures to promote EOI included a range of specialised institutional initiatives. In this, the EDB assumed a greatly enhanced role in centralising and coordinating the government's investment drive. Among other things, the EDB oversaw a host of generous tax concessions targeting investors in EOI. However, in 1968, the Jurong Town Corporation (JTC) was established to relieve the EDB of responsibility for the rapidly expanding industrial estates that provided centralised infrastructural facilities at low cost. During the same year, the Development Bank of Singapore (DBS) was created to provide below-market-rate finance and engage in equity participation to stimulate industrial ventures. In the following year, the government established Neptune Orient Lines (NOL) to expedite foreign trade and ensure lower freight charges for Singapore-manufactured goods. Through the compulsory government-controlled superannuation scheme, the Central Provident Fund (CPF), and the Post Office Savings Bank, the government also appropriated a considerable portion of domestic savings. Much of this was channelled into physical and social infrastructure. Direct productive investment was also undertaken by the government as a means of boosting manufacturing (Lee 1978:138–9).

In a concerted fashion, then, the government set about trying to generate the social, political, and economic preconditions for industrial investment in export production. This involved it in conscious efforts to influence the costs of the different factors of production. In effect, the government was helping to shape Singapore's comparative advantage in the production of labour-intensive manufactures.

The EOI strategy proved a spectacular success. Foreign investment in manufacturing rose from S$157 million in 1965 to S$995 million in 1970, and to S$3054 million in 1974. In this time, direct manufactured exports from Singapore jumped from a value of S$349 million to S$1523 million, and to S$7812 million by 1974. The contribution of manufacturing to GDP increased from just over 15 per cent in 1965 to 22.6 per cent in 1974. In this economic transformation, assembly work in the electrical and electronics industry was especially important, with international capital adopting Singapore wholeheartedly as an export base for US and European consumer markets. Other low value-added, labour-intensive industries—such as shipbuilding and the textiles, clothing, footwear, and leather group of industries—underwent significant expansion.

Consequently, Singapore's unemployment rate was brought down to below 4 per cent by 1974. Indeed, by the early 1970s, some areas of industry were experiencing labour shortages which soon led to a reliance on imported workers. In this context, consideration was given to an accelerated policy push into middle-level technologies involving higher value-added processes. However, the effects of the global recession hit Singapore hard in 1974–75, resulting in sizeable investment cutbacks and job losses. This quickly returned the policy priority to employment generation and wage control through the NWC. Between 1975 and 1978, however, Singapore's economy staged a spirited recovery under the aegis of international capital. Cumulative foreign investment climbed to S$5242 million by 1978 and industrial exports jumped to a value of S$13 633 million in the same year (see table 5.1, page 147). In fact, labour shortages now posed a more serious problem. For social and political reasons, the government was at the time disinclined to resolve the problem of labour shortages by simply accelerating the importation of guest workers. Instead, it took the view that a rationalisation of the manufacturing sector was in order: scarce labour should not be hoarded by low value-added, labour-intensive industries in which Singapore would be unable to maintain international competitiveness over the longer term.

What transpired was a two-pronged strategy, dubbed the 'Second Industrial Revolution', both to increase technological sophistication and to raise further the contribution of manufacturing to Singapore's economic growth. On the one hand, the strategy involved measures to discourage unskilled, labour-intensive production but, on the other hand, it cushioned

Table 5.1 Selected economic indicators, 1960–84

Year	GDP growth (1985 market prices)	Direct manu-facturing exports* (S$ million)	Manu-facturing value-added per worker* (S$)	Cumulative foreign investment in manufacturing** (S$ million)	Cumulative local investment in manufacturing** (S$ million)	Unemploy-ment rate (%)
1960						
1961	8.5	824	6 100			
1962	7.1	1 158	6 924			
1963	10.5	828	6 900			
1964	–4.3	794	6 845			
1965	6.6	858	7 207	157		8.7
1966	10.6	841	7 732	239		8.7
1967	13.0	912	8 192	303		8.1
1968	14.3	1 014	8 146	454		7.3
1969	13.4	1 971	8 600	600		6.7
1970	13.4	2 044	9 029	995		6.0
1971	12.5	2 362	9 705	1 575		4.8
1972	13.3	2 911	10 388	2 283		4.7
1973	11.3	4 779	12 856	2 659		4.5
1974	6.8	8 520	17 127	3 054		3.9
1975	4.0	7 610	17 763	3 380		4.6
1976	7.2	10 160	19 168	3 739		4.5
1977	7.8	11 412	20 417	4 145		3.9
1978	8.6	13 087	21 179	5 242		3.6
1979	9.3	16 904	23 992	6 349		3.4
1980	9.7	19 875	30 027	7 090	3 471	3.5
1981	9.6	22 894	34 681	8 382	4 060	3.9
1982	6.9	22 227	34 218	9 618	4 910	2.6
1983	8.2	22 922	36 645	10 777	5 646	3.2
1984	8.3	25 058	40 476	12 651	6 798	2.7

*data for 1960–83 include rubber-processing and granite-quarrying
** figure excludes rubber-processing

Sources: Dept Stats, *Yearbook of Statistics Singapore*, various years; EDB, various years; Dept Stats (1983); Huff (1994)

the costs for employers attempting to move towards more skilled, higher value-added production. The chief element of the former was the so-called 'corrective wage policy' of the NWC. By the end of 1981, three years of the policy had resulted in wage-cost increases to employers of more than 50 per cent. Quite intentionally, this hit the most labour-intensive, unskilled operations the hardest. If they were to remain in Singapore, it was expected that technological upgrading would lessen the dependence on labour. Meanwhile, tax incentives, below-market-rate finance, and subsidised training schemes were made available to investors gearing towards higher value-added production. Considerable sums were invested by the government in developing the physical and social infrastructure to support a technological transformation.

The 'Second Industrial Revolution' also witnessed refinements in the role of direct government investment. By 1983 the Singapore government had extensive investments involving fifty-eight companies and S$3 billion paid-up capital (Hon 1983). However, they were now used more strategically to promote higher value-added production. In 1983 Singapore Technologies Corporation (STC) was created with a capital base of S$200 million pooled to promote advanced technologies. The government was also a substantial investor in S$2 billion-worth of joint ventures putting together the first fully integrated petrochemical complex in South-East Asia. A further initiative was the establishment of the Government of Singapore Investment Corporation (GIC) which invested some of Singapore's extensive foreign reserves overseas in leading high-technology multinational corporations (Rodan 1989:153–4).

The state's efforts to foster higher valued-added production extended to the social and political realms. The country's two largest trade unions, the Singapore Industrial Labour Organisation (SILO) and the Pioneer Industries Employees' Union (PIEU), were broken up into nine industry-based unions. Not only was this new structure more functional for the technical aspects of the new industrial program, but also it reduced any potential for organised labour (however constrained by its close relationship with the ruling party) to frustrate the restructuring process.

Beyond export-oriented industrialisation

During the period of the 'Second Industrial Revolution' some significant gains occurred. Foreign investment rose substantially from S$6349 million in 1979 to S$12 651 million in 1984. For the same period, valued-added per worker nearly doubled, from S$23 992 to S$40 476, attesting to the enhanced productivity of the workforce due to capital investment. Industries such as electronics, machinery, chemical, and aerospace underwent major technological upgradings, and Singapore found some significant production niches, becoming a global centre for the computer disk-drive industry, for example (see tables 5.2 and 5.3, pages 149 and 150).

Yet, by the mid 1980s, it became apparent that there were structural limits to the expansion of the manufacturing sector in Singapore. From the start of 1980 to the end of 1984 the rate of manufacturing growth was 6.1 per cent, compared with Singapore's overall economic growth rate of 8.5 per cent (MT&I 1986:26). Consequently, the relative contribution of manufacturing to GDP dropped from 23.7 per cent in 1979 to 20.6 per cent

in 1984 (Dept Stats, *Yearbook of Statistics Singapore* 1984/85:78). The
opportunities for Singapore as an export-manufacturing base were not as
extensive in middle-level technology as they had been in the earlier phase of
low value-added production. The EOI strategy was confronting a paradox:
the further up the technological hierarchy Singapore graduated on the basis
of lower labour costs—albeit in more sophisticated technologies and in
competition with higher-wage countries—the less a proportion labour
became to overall production costs. The global recession compounded this
problem by generally restricting investment and by exposing the vulnerability of Singapore's heavy dependence on the US consumer market,
particularly in the all-important electronics industry. The economy actually
contracted by 2 per cent in 1985, the first experience of negative growth
since independence. Manufacturing declined by 6.9 per cent and 3.4 per
cent during 1985 and 1986 respectively (Dept Stats, *Yearbook of Statistics
Singapore* 1990:3). Even with the repatriation of 60 000 guest workers
(Pang 1994:81), unemployment rose to 6.5 per cent by 1986 (Dept Stats,
Yearbook of Statistics Singapore 1994:16).

Table 5.2 Selected economic indicators, 1985–95

Year	GDP growth (1985 market prices)	Direct manu-facturing exports (S$ million)	Manu-facturing value-added per worker (S$)	Cumulative foreign investment in manufacturing (S$ million)*	Cumulative local investment in manufacturing (S$ million)*	Unemploy-ment rate (%)
1985	−1.6	24 276	42 216	13 160	7 100	4.1
1986	1.9	24 387	48 240	14 120	6 804	6.5
1987	9.4	30 380	52 372	15 830	6 827	4.7
1988	11.3	37 806	55 182	18 131	7 449	3.3
1989	9.4	42 388	58 285	21 524	7 957	2.2
1990	8.8	47 000	61 440	24 133	8 682	2.0
1991	6.7	45 913	65 452	25 831	9 839	1.9
1992	6.0	46 907	69 508	28 565	10 604	2.7
1993	10.1	53 022	79 643			2.7
1994	10.1	62 261	87 743			2.6
1995						2.7

*figure excludes rubber-processing

Sources: Dept Stats, *Yearbook of Statistics Singapore*, various years; EDB, *Annual Report/Yearbook*, various years; Dept of Stats (1983); Huff (1994)

In response to the mid 1980s economic recession there was a major
revision of economic strategy and objectives, enunciated in the report of the
Economic Committee (MT&I 1986) headed by then Acting Trade and
Industry Minister Lee Hsien Loong. The immediate priorities were to resur-
rect Singapore's cost competitiveness in manufacturing *vis-à-vis* other newly
industrialised countries (NICs), and to generate employment. Thus, some of
the pressures on manufacturers introduced under the 'Second Industrial

Revolution', particularly wage costs, were relaxed. However, with the longer term in mind, a shift of emphasis towards the services sector was prescribed.[7] The essence of the new vision was for Singapore to become 'a total business centre'. Accordingly, new tax and other incentives were introduced for companies, extending their commercial and manufacturing roles to include financial, marketing, technical, and other corporate services to their networks of related companies in the region or worldwide—that is, companies making Singapore their operational headquarters (OHQ).

Table 5.3 Sectoral contributions to GDP (%)

Year	1960	1970	1980	1985	1990	1994
Total GDP (S$ million, 1985 market prices)	5 058	12 172	28 832	38 924	57 471	78 765
Commerce	26.0	22.1	18.4	17.8	16.5	16.6
Construction	5.6	9.5	6.9	11.4	5.0	6.7
Financial & business services	14.8	17.0	19.9	20.9	26.1	25.0
Manufacturing	17.6	24.9	28.6	22.2	27.2	26.6
Transport & communications	9.3	7.3	11.6	13.7	13.3	13.7
Other services	26.7	19.2	14.6	14.0	11.9	11.4

Sources: Dept of Stats, *Yearbook of Statistics Singapore*, various years; EDB *Annual Report/Yearbook*, various years; Huff (1994)

Compared with previous policy redirections, the views of the domestic bourgeoisie appeared on this occasion to be given more weight. The Economic Committee not only comprised representatives of the Singapore Manufacturers' Association, the Singapore Federation of Chambers of Commerce and Industry, and leading local entrepreneurs, but also incorporated other local business people through the many subcommittees that were part of the process. The rhetoric in the Economic Committee's report championed entrepreneurship, decried the government's past interventionist economic policies, and recommended a program of privatisation.

Fundamentally, however, the new strategy was informed by a reading of emerging trends in international patterns by transnational corporations (TNCs) in the Asia–Pacific region. This trend included an increasing preparedness by the mid 1980s for TNCs to locate a more comprehensive range of higher value-added processes and services in discrete geographic regions—North America, Europe, and Asia—as opposed to adopting a single, hierarchical global division of labour (Ng and Sudo 1991). Importantly, higher levels of manufacturing investment for regional markets required high value-added services such as accounting, law, training, and management services, and this opened up a potential niche for Singapore. For the domestic bourgeoisie, this meant increased competition and increased opportunity.

Singapore's economic recovery was swift and strong, with GDP growing by an annual average of 9.5 per cent from 1987 to 1990. Although this included the impressive revival of the manufacturing sector, it did not tempt policy-makers to shelve plans for a structural transformation of the economy. The general directions outlined by the Economic Planning Committee (1991) were confirmed and refined in *The Strategic Economic Plan* of 1991. It underlined the importance of continued heavy investment in social and physical infrastructure to position the city-state as a provider of high value-added services for the region.

In response to a new level of organisation and activism on the part of small and medium enterprises (SMEs),[8] in 1989 the government committed itself to a SME Master Plan, with a complementary boost in the number of schemes assisting the development of local entrepreneurs. Private-sector participation in the policy process was still largely at the behest of the state but, during the late 1980s and early 1990s, there was a general increase in the level and institutionalisation of interaction between capital and state in the policy process.[9] To some extent, this was also functionally related to the emergence of a more sophisticated and diversified economy.

From the perspective of the private sector, consultation was also an acknowledgment of state economic power—not least through approximately seventy statutory boards and more than a thousand state-owned companies in manufacturing and commercial enterprises.[10] The coordination and control of economic resources is greatly enhanced by the tight interlocking directorships involving a small coterie of civil servants (see Worthington 2001; Vennewald 1994). This virtual 'class' of public entrepreneurs is closely connected to the ruling political party, the upper echelons of the civil service having been the main recruiting ground for the PAP for some time (see Khong 1993:12).[11] Dependence on the state for contracts and awareness of the political nexus between the civil service and the PAP has promoted co-option rather than forceful and open interest representation to the government.

The government divested its shareholdings in fifty-eight companies in the late 1980s, followed by more significant divestments in the 1990s.[12] But this did not generally involve any surrender of control over the economy. Indeed, Mukul Asher (1994:801) argued that:

> A strong case can be made that in the Singapore context, its privatisation programme will make the role of government even stronger and more extensive. This is because there is an overall budget surplus, so the divestment proceeds are not intended to either reduce taxes or expand expenditure. Instead, these can be invested at home and abroad.[13]

Thus, between 1988 and 1990, 288 new government-linked companies (GLCs) were created and offshore initiatives were to loom large in the operations of state companies.

Regionalisation and Singapore Inc.

One of the Singapore government's most imaginative and symbolic policy initiatives in support of greater integration with regional economies was the 'Growth Triangle'. First outlined by Deputy Prime Minister Goh Chok Tong in 1989, the idea of the Growth Triangle was for the Malaysian state of Johor and the nearby Riau Islands of Indonesia to combine with Singapore as a coherent, trans-state economic zone of complementary specialisations. This involved Singapore government-owned companies in enormous direct investments to establish the necessary industrial infrastructure in Indonesia's Batam and Bintan Islands, as well as in the development of heavy industry and tourist resorts in other parts of the Riau Islands. The central role of Singapore's authorities—especially the EDB—in establishing administrative systems and coordinating projects offshore has been of no less significance (Rodan 1993b; Parsonage 1992; Parsonage 1997).

In early 1993 a report was also handed down by the Committee to Promote Enterprise Overseas, again comprising membership drawn from leading local businesses (see MoF 1993:44–8). The government subsequently introduced various incentives to support a bigger regional investment and trade push. This concerted attempt to integrate Singapore-based enterprises more fully with regional economies was an attempt to transcend the limitations of a city-state economy, and was variously referred to by authorities as the building of an 'external economy', a 'second wing', or 'expanding the economic space of Singapore' (see Mahizhnan 1994; Goh, in Kraar 1996:172). In the development of this 'external economy', the government saw itself playing a pivotal role, freely describing this in terms of a 'Singapore Inc.' (see EDB *Yearbook* 1994:3). Huge investments went into what one author has described as a series of 'mini-Singapores' (Kraar 1996:172), involving integrated projects of factories, roads, and power plants, and established as industrial enclaves within China, India, Indonesia, Burma, and Vietnam (see Yeung 2000a).

The most ambitious of these projects was the S$28 billion Suzhou Township, of 70 square kilometres, involving a 22-member consortium led by the Singapore GLC's Keppel Group in partnership with the Suzhou municipal council. In an unprecedented move, Chinese authorities granted the Singaporeans managerial autonomy in the project (Kwok 1995:294). However, this project turned sour and became a matter of considerable embarrassment for the Singapore government, resulting in projected losses of S$151 million and a decision to hand over majority ownership and management control to China (*STWE* 1999). It fell victim to a combination of competitive market forces and, ironically, the inability of GLCs to operate within an alien set of bureaucratic structures. As Yeung (2000b) points out, the agreement negotiated by the central government of China with its Singapore counterpart was never a reflection of the local Chinese interests—which invariably shaped the project's implementation at the ground level.

The new emphasis on international accumulation strategies has not only included GLCs but also private Singapore-based companies (either as joint-venture partners or independent entities) in the consortia and other projects in which Singapore GLCs have played a leading role (see Rodan 1993b:242). However, for the bulk of Singapore's 80 000-plus SMEs in manufacturing, commerce, and services, overseas investment was either not appropriate or beyond their realistic capacity in the foreseeable future.

Total direct investment abroad rose from S$16.9 billion in 1990 to S$28.2 billion in 1993 and, by the end of 1997, $70.6 billion (Dept Stats 1994:5; Aggarwal 1999).[14] Wholly locally owned or majority locally owned companies accounted for more than half the total of $29.2 billion direct investment abroad in 1993, and accounted for $7.9 billion of the 1997 total of $15.1 billion invested (Dept Stats 1994:44–5; Aggarwal 1999). The stock of total direct equity investment by companies based in Singapore also rose from S$13.6 billion to S$21.2 billion between 1990 and 1993, and increased further to $53.5 billion by the end of 1997 (Dept Stats, *Yearbook of Statistics* 2000:70).[15]

Between 1990 and the end of 1997, approximately half of all direct investment abroad went to Asia, with investment in China surging by a remarkable 73 per cent in 1996 and surpassing Malaysia as the principal destination of offshore investment the following year.[16] Manufacturing and real estate represented the bulk of investment in China but, for the other countries, investments were concentrated in the financial sector. Overall, the vast majority of Singapore's total direct investment abroad continued to be concentrated in financial services, which accounted for 48 per cent compared with 23 per cent for manufacturing (Aggarwal 1999; 2000).[17] When the Asian crisis struck in 1997–98, there was further offshore expansion in response to new opportunities created by the plight of various banks in the region. In Thailand, for example, two GLCs—the Development Bank of Singapore and the Singapore Government Investment Corporation—as well as the United Overseas Bank of Singapore, all made significant investments (see Hewison, chapter 3, this volume).

In addition to these general developments, major TNCs across consumer electronics, construction, transportation, pharmaceuticals, and other industries had begun to make Singapore their Asia–Pacific headquarters from the mid 1980s. This was now being extended to the use of Singapore as a regional broadcasting centre as international television networks and multimedia organisations set up operations to service rising regional demand. All of this suggested that, during the 1990s, there was a significant increase in Singapore's economic integration with the region and that a concomitant diversification of the city-state's economic base was under way.

In spite of this progress, Paul Krugman (1994:70) contended that Singapore's exceptional economic growth owed most to 'an awesome investment in physical capital'. Increased efficiency in the application of capital and labour, referred to as 'total factor productivity' (TFP), still eluded Singapore according to Krugman (see also Young 1995; Cardarelli, Gobat and Lee 2000). The advent of the Asian crisis, however, prompted a new sense of urgency by the Singapore government on the need for a structural economic transformation. It viewed the crisis as, in part, symptomatic of globalisation, and coinciding with the emergence of what is variously referred to as the 'New Economy' or 'Knowledge-based Economy' ('K-Economy'). The government was convinced that the only option for Singapore was to embrace change. As Lee Hsien Loong (2000) explained: 'Our policy is to accelerate, rather than delay, our integration with the global economy, to become more competitive rather than to shelter ourselves from competition'.

Asian crisis, globalisation, and the 'New Economy'

Although Singapore was not as adversely affected as neighbouring countries by the Asian crisis of 1997–98 (see Cotton 2000), it was not unscathed. Economic growth dropped from 8.4 per cent in 1997 to a mere 0.4 per cent in the following year. Non-performing loans amounted to S$35.8 billion (S$31.2 billion involving regional countries) or 14.5 per cent of the total assets of Singapore-incorporated banks in September 1998. Unemployment levels thus rose from 1.7 per cent in 1997 to 3.3 by 1999 (see table 5.4, page 155), peaking in December 1998 at 4.3 per cent. There were a record 29 100 retrenchments in 1998 (*STWE* 2000l). Cost-cutting measures in response to the crisis also significantly reduced the effective incomes of the lowest-paid workers. This included NWC-supported wage cuts in 1998, and a 50 per cent reduction in employers' contributions to the CPF (down from 20 per cent to 10 per cent of the wages bill). Nevertheless, the government seized on the crisis as an opportunity to enhance regional economic supremacy and extend restructuring. George Yeo, the then minister of Information and the Arts, who subsequently became minister for Trade and Industry, declared: 'We intend to be a net winner in the crisis' (quoted in *AWSJ* 1998).

Table 5.4 Selected economic and social indicators, 1996–2000

Indicator	1996	1997	1998	1999	2000
GDP growth (per cent)	7.5	8.4	0.4	5.4	9.9
Unemployment growth (per cent)	2.2	1.7	2.3	3.3	
Net foreign investment manufacturing commitments S$million	5 792	5 964	5 214	6 257	
Direct manufacturing exports S$million	72 964	76 450	75 530	85 395	
Total assets/liabilities of commercial banks (change)	12.5%	14.6%	7.0%	5.3%	
Official reserves S$billion	101.75	119.62	124.58	128.46	

Sources: Dept Stats 2000 *Yearbook of Statistics Singapore*; IMF (2000); Ng (2001)

In particular, plans hatched on the eve of the crisis to elevate the financial sector were boosted thereafter. When Deputy Prime Minister Lee Hsien Loong was appointed chairman of the Monetary Authority of Singapore (MAS) in 1997, he declared his intention to transform Singapore into an international (not just a regional) financial centre. This was to include substantial fund management, foreign exchange, bond, and equity markets, as well as risk-management and world-class banking and insurance industries. It is an extremely ambitious objective, especially with the conspicuous absence, in Singapore, of the free flow of information that is widely regarded as an essential ingredient in the success of centres such as London and New York. Transparency levels, whether in strict commercial terms or broader political terms, are low in Singapore. However, in its attempt to promote the city-state as a financial centre, the government embraced the rhetoric of transparency, and even introduced specific measures raising the extent and quality of certain types of market-relevant information (Committee on Banking Disclosure 1998). Nevertheless, state information control is still extensive and media control is being consolidated rather than weakened (see Rodan 2000).

The promotion of the finance sector again involves complementary state initiatives and market reforms. This includes: the opening-up of some state-controlled superannuation funds to private fund managers; the issuing of bonds by cash-rich statutory boards to promote Singapore as a debt-capital hub; the liberalisation of guidelines on the internationalisation of the

Singapore dollar to facilitate the foreign exchange market; and the exposure of domestic banking to greater, albeit controlled, international competition.[18] As with the earlier corporatist practices in manufacturing, the MAS has tried to involve key executives of major transnational corporations in the reform process, notably through the establishment of the International Advisory Council (IAC).

Although transparency reform might have been limited, various corporate and financial governance reforms have accompanied the plan to make Singapore an international finance centre. These amount to a reregulation, rather than a deregulation (see Jayasuriya 2000), in response to the increasingly integrated nature of financial markets. In particular, an *Omnibus Securities and Futures Act* is being introduced to ensure consistent prudential regulation across industries where there has been considerable convergence and a blurring of institutional and product boundaries (*STI* 2000b). Regulatory frameworks to support the establishment of Internet-only banks are also being developed by MAS (*BT Online* 2000a). In other moves, all local banks have been given three years (as from 2000) to restructure and separate their financial and non-financial activities, such as property holdings, to bring them into line with international practice and limit the risks of contagion to the banks (*STWE* 2000h:17).[19]

It was, however, the manufacturing sector that saw the Singapore economy through the recession. Strong demand for electronics exports, particularly semiconductors, underpinned growth. Nevertheless, targeted areas of the finance sector—such as bonds, fund management, and equity markets—have developed impressively in Singapore.[20] Certainly initial progress contradicted the idea that the absence of transparency would be a serious impediment for investors. They seemed to place greater weight on other governance factors, including the predictability and reliability of institutions, and political stability (Rodan 2000).

However, the Asian crisis precipitated a more general reappraisal of Singapore's economic trajectory by policy-makers that was given detailed expression in Prime Minister Goh's 1999 National Day Rally Speech. 'A powerful force is sweeping across the world: globalisation, because of technology and the Internet,' Goh (1999) asserted, converting the world into a single '. . . global shopping mall'. More specifically, he contended that: 'We have to transform ourselves—from a regional economy to a first-world economy' (Goh 1999). The strategy to achieve this must entail the building of 'world-class Singapore companies', a point Goh (1999) made with approving references to the existing achievements by state-owned entities in the provision of airlines, seaports, and airports.

According to Goh, the regional push over the past decade had also been valuable, even if adversely affected by the Asian crisis. But, Goh (1999) declared: 'We should now go global by forming strategic alliances or mergers with other major players. Indeed, we have no choice—where the industries are consolidating worldwide, we either become major players, or we are nothing.' He pointed out that, although Singapore Telecommunications (SingTel) is the country's largest company in terms of capitalisation, it ranks only twentieth in size among telecommunication companies worldwide. Moreover, leading MNCs have 'organisational strength, technology, access to global markets, and a worldwide network' (Goh 1999).[21]

One of the first steps in line with this statement was the introduction of international managers to executive positions within major state-owned companies and institutions to facilitate internationalisation.[22] Further to the reforms in the banking sector to increase competition, the government's planned liberalisation of the telecommunications sector—in response to World Trade Organization (WTO) and other pressures from and on behalf of international companies—was brought forward by two years to take effect from 1 April 2000. Foreign equity limits on telecommunications companies were also abolished in an attempt to shore-up Singapore's position in the rapidly expanding e-commerce market within Asia. In other reforms, foreign law firms and medical practitioners have also been allowed to enter the local market for the first time.

In the past, liberalisation has often resulted in greater competition among different GLCs—described by Singh (1999) as 'guided competition'—rather than in a major transfer of economic power to the private sector. Certainly this strategy is being applied to the media industry where foreign shareholding in local companies remains restricted to no more than 3 per cent. In June 2000 authorities announced that competition would be increased by the issuing of television and radio licences to the government-owned newspaper monopolist Singapore Press Holding (SPH), and a newspaper licence to the government-owned broadcaster Media Corporation (*BT Online* 2000b). But, in other sectors such as telecommunications, GLCs do face new foreign competition. Interestingly, however, StarHub, the first competitor to SingTel before the announcement of the accelerated liberalisation, has complained about, what it regards as, anti-competitive practices entrenching SingTel's dominance.[23]

The continued dominance of GLCs, which accounted for as much as 60 per cent of Singapore's external economy in 1998 according to Lian and Chung (2001), is also a key assumption behind the strategy announced by

Goh. Indeed, as with regionalisation, the globalisation push is impossible to disentangle from the interests and pressures associated with the capital accumulation of GLCs. For these companies, consolidating and extending their influence in a globalising world does indeed necessitate the strategic alliances referred to by Goh. However, their capacity for this has been brought into question recently following unsuccessful merger attempts in key sectors. Private-sector analysts, fund managers, business executives, academics, and journalists seized on these events to argue for a dismantling of state enterprises. State ownership and control must give way to private entrepreneurship, it is argued, to ensure the creativity and flexibility essential to prosper in the New Economy (*STWE* 2000c:14–15; *Australian* 2000; *FT* 2000; *STWE* 2000f; Lian 2000; Tessensohn 2000; *STWE* 2000h:3; Restall 2000).

This argument surfaced after a series of abortive or failed takeover and acquisition attempts by GLCs between 1999 and 2000. These included: the failure by Singapore Airlines in a bid to procure 50 per cent of the private Australian carrier Ansett Airlines (Air New Zealand being the successful bidder); an unsuccessful merger bid by SingTel with Cable and Wireless (C & W) HKT; the Singapore Airlines' failure to secure a controlling interest in Air New Zealand;[24] and the abandonment by Malaysia's Time Engineering of a proposed alliance with SingTel. A recurring theme in most of these was apprehension about possibly handing over strategic assets to companies under the direct or indirect control of the Singapore government. In the SingTel case, the government owns 78 per cent through its holding company Temasek, and Lee Hsien Yang—the second son of Senior Minister Lee Kuan Yew—heads it. Several non-executive directors of C & W HKT were reported to have demanded that Temasek reduce its shareholding in SingTel for the deal to go through. Similarly, New Zealand Prime Minister Helen Clark commented that it was not acceptable for people to perceive the national carrier as 'effectively controlled by the Singapore Government' (quoted in *Australian* 2000). More generally, the perception of political influence is also informed by the knowledge that many board members and executives of GLCs are civil servants, military officers, or government MPs who are, by definition, part of the PAP establishment.

In recognition of the apparent problem posed by the perception of political influence, Prime Minister Goh has foreshadowed an accelerated divestment of the government's interests in large companies (*Star Online* 2000). But, as pointed out above, regular divestments since the 1980s have not necessarily meant a diminution of control, and it remains to be seen how far the government is prepared to go in surrendering this. With Temasek Holdings Ltd still having 100 per cent ownership of such major companies as PSA Corporation, Media Corporation of Singapore, Singapore MRT, and Singapore Power, there is obviously considerable scope yet for general divestment without sacrificing strategic control across different sectors. Nevertheless, maintaining control abroad is obviously more problematic for those GLCs attempting to forge alliances with partners who are more powerful, more technologically endowed, and better networked.[25]

The need for adjustment was reinforced in Goh's 2000 National Day Rally Speech: 'We must operate like "insurgents" or revolutionaries who challenge the established way of doing things'. Otherwise, 'revolutionary' companies would beat 'incumbent' local firms in their own game, Goh explained (Goh 2000; see also Latiff 2000).[26] The trajectory, however, is more likely one of increasingly complex collaboration between the Singapore state and international capital rather than the wholesale offloading of state assets. Meanwhile, the selective building up of domestic-based private entrepreneurs, via social and physical infrastructure outlays, can be expected to continue.

It is crucial to keep in mind that the question of divestment of GLCs is not simply technical. There are ideological, material, and political interests aligned to the program of economic liberalism advocated for Singapore. This includes various sections of the private sector that could gain directly or indirectly from divestment and privatisation, as well as journalists, academics, and others with a normative preference for a more free-market direction. Opposition parties have also understood that championing such a program resonates with the sentiments of sections of the local business community, and that a dismantling of the GLCs has the potential to diminish the PAP's capacity for political co-option and paternalism (see New Democrat 2000).

Whatever the future of GLCs, the role of the state in infrastructure provision is in no way being diminished by the latest economic direction. Even before Goh's 1999 speech, huge public outlays had been made to put in place one of the most comprehensive information technology (IT) infrastructures anywhere in the world (see Einhorn 1999; James 1999; Arun and Mui 2000). More recently, the Singapore government has set about trying to transform tertiary institutions so they are more internationalised. One dimension of this is the establishment of strategic alliances with major overseas institutions to promote joint teaching and research.[27] Considerable sums have also been poured into government agencies such as the National Science and Technology Board (NSTB), the Infocomm Development Authority, and the EDB to assist both individuals and companies.[28] The emergence of some innovative domestic high-technology companies in niche areas, nurtured through government-funded infrastructure, such as the Kent Ridge Digital Laboratories, has encouraged authorities (*STWE* 2000g). Meanwhile, however, many of Singapore's SMEs are struggling to make the transition to the New Economy and e-commerce.

Political management of social change

Apart from the dynamics described above in state–capital relations, the diversification and restructuring of the economy have brought a more substantial and variegated middle class (see Rodan 1996a, 1996b).[29] In general, this class has benefited considerably from the economic growth over which the PAP has presided. State employment demand has also been heavily skewed towards professionals with the skills most pertinent to the functioning, administration, and accounting of the economy—rather than to social security and related activities (see Ramesh 2000). These professionals and administrators are not only well paid, but also enjoy high levels of social status ensuing from the institutionalised ideology of meritocracy under the PAP. Indeed, these material and ideological conditions foster an intersection of values and interests between the government and a substantial element of the middle class (Rodan 1996a:31–2).

The middle class that has emerged over the past few decades, then, has not been one that has any special need or desire to challenge the ruling party's exercise of power. This does not mean that there are not pressures to influence the policy process, as increased social differentiation generates new, discrete interests. But it does mean that the potential for this to be satisfied through extended forms of political co-option, rather than competitive political process, is real. The government is thus attempting to incorporate into PAP-controlled institutions a range of different interests—including business, professional, ethnic, and women's groups.[30] To date, cases of middle-class activism involving the establishment of genuinely independent organisations outside these mechanisms have been limited (see Rodan 1993b; Rodan 1996b; Brown and Jones 1995).

In April 1999, the Singapore government released a vision statement, *Singapore 21* (Singapore 21 Committee 1999), which seeks to reinforce this direction. Among its recommendations, the most significant is an emphasis on the need for 'active citizenship'. The essence of 'active citizenship' is the idea that civic groups combine in a 'positive and co-operative way' with the private and public sectors to assist in the improvement and implementation of public policy. Around the same time, an initiative by NGOs, artists, and various individuals under the banner of 'The Working Committee' began conducting a series of forums and workshops to explore the question and purpose of civil society. A wide range of interests has been represented in these deliberations, from social activists to apolitical community and cultural organisations. It is apparent that although a minority is seriously interested in opening up genuinely independent political space, most are nervous about this direction.

Another initiative that represents an alternative to the fostering or tolerating of genuine competitive politics based on the actions of independent organisations, is the introduction of a Speakers' Corner in September 2000. This happened in the wake of the prosecution and imprisonment of Chee Soon Juan, secretary-general of the Singapore Democratic Party (SDP), for speaking in a public place without a permit. Chee's jailing was a public relations disaster for a government keen to attract international investment in knowledge-intensive industries. The PAP government subsequently designated Hong Lim Park, on the outskirts of the city centre, as a space for individuals to make public speeches. However, in contrast to London's Hyde Park Corner, on which it was modelled, participants at Speakers' Corner in Singapore not only have to be registered, but also must take into account the extremely litigious political culture within the PAP establishment. The fear of internal security surveillance also engenders apprehension among some Singaporeans about Speakers' Corner (see Koh 2000). Major opposition political figures have decried the experiment, but a small group of middle-class members of the Working Committee has embraced the idea in the hope that it might provide a useful political opening—by accident if not by official design.[31]

Rising inequalities

The major political issue since the early 1990s has been the unequal distribution of material rewards associated with Singapore's economic development, rather than middle-class pressure for a liberal civil society. A more complete embrace of globalisation is likely to intensify an emerging sense of marginalisation among the working class and lower middle class.

The decline in the government's support at the 1991 election from the PAP's traditional social base—the ethnic Chinese working class—was the first manifestation of this sense of marginalisation (Rodan 1993b; Singh 1992). Following the election, the government established the parliamentary Cost Review Committee (MT&I 1993) to address public concerns about rising costs of living and inequalities. However, the official claim that income inequality was declining in Singapore was not consistent with the work of academics. This work either contended that the statistical evidence was too weak to claim a narrowing of the gap between rich and poor (Rao 1990; 1996a; 1996b), or actually argued that the disparities were widening (Islam and Kirkpatrick 1986; Krongkaew 1994). In any case, Prime Minister Goh conceded that significantly rising absolute inequalities, if not relative inequalities, were engendering a sense of deprivation among lower-income earners (*ST* 1996).

At times, the government has shown a distinct political insensitivity to this, as when increases in ministerial salaries, which were already among the highest in the world, precipitated a public outcry in late 1994 and early 1995.[32] There was a considerable public relations effort to justify further ministerial increases in 2000 (*STWE* 2000i; *AWSJ* 2000b; *STWE* 2000j)— under which the prime minister's salary rose to S$1.94 million, more than five-fold that of the US president. Still, negative public reaction was even more intense on this occasion (see Webb 2000).[33]

Amid depictions, by opposition parties, of the government as being mean and lacking compassion for people least benefiting from Singapore's rapid economic development, the PAP ironically began projecting itself as generous in public welfare provisions. The prime minister announced in March 1996 that for the previous year a total of S$1.65 billion of surplus government funds had been disbursed through various schemes.[34] However, the prime minister insisted that these benefits were not to be seen as welfare entitlements, which is why co-payment was usually involved (*STWE* 1996b). Goh has, in the past, argued that 'the disadvantaged do not expect and cannot demand that they be looked after by the State as a matter of right' (*STWE* 1993). The PAP's concern is to preserve a paternalistic political relationship more than to avoid public spending. In this relationship, Singaporeans are effectively 'rewarded' by a benevolent government; they are not citizens with intrinsic rights that the government is obliged to honour.

They can effectively be 'punished' too—as was revealed at the general election in the 1997. The PAP foreshadowed priority in social-development programs, notably major upgrading of public housing estates in electorates that supported the PAP (Ganesan 1998:232). Over 80 per cent of Singaporeans live in properties purchased from the government on the basis of a 99-year lease. Prime Minister Goh warned voters who were contemplating supporting the opposition: 'In 20, 30 years' time, the whole of Singapore will be bustling away, and your estate, through your own choice, will be left behind. They [sic] become slums' (quoted in *Asiaweek* 1997). Heavy dependence on state-provided services renders electors vulnerable to such intimidation. It was thus difficult to separate fear of retribution from outright approval of the government's performance in the resounding PAP victory—when it secured 65 per cent of the vote and all but two parliamentary seats (see da Cunha 1997).

The Asian crisis and the fuller embrace of globalisation have bolstered the trend towards increased inequality. As a result of cuts and restraint in 1998–99, wage costs were reduced by 5.8 per cent. The relative unit labour costs fell a dramatic 19 per cent, taking them back to 1990–91 levels, and the ratio of wage share to GDP also plummeted to 41.4 per cent—the same level as 1988 (*STWE* 2000d:7). In 1999, household income of the top 20 per cent, compared with the bottom 20 per cent, was eighteen times more. This compares with fifteen times in 1998. The gini coefficient, an economist's measure of inequality, thus rose from 0.446 in 1998 to 0.467 in 1999 (*STWE* 2000d:1). More worrying, however, was the broader trend. Between 1990 and 1997, and thus before the crisis, Singapore's bottom 10 per cent of households suffered an average income decline of 1.8 per cent while all other households, to differing degrees, experienced increases (*STWE* 2000e). Even the Department of Statistics' chief statistician, Paul Chueng, finally conceded: 'We are observing the beginning of a trend of increasing income disparity in Singapore and the gap may remain' (quoted in *STWE* 2000d:1).

Instead of trying to prevent the gap widening, Deputy Prime Minister Lee sees the role of government as 'making sure that we look after the people in the lower-income groups, making sure that they continue to have income growth' (quoted in *STWE* 2000f). The government has declared education, training, skills upgrading, job creation, and asset enhancement as the way ahead (*STWE* 2000b).[35] Most challenging of all, the government will have to address the problem of structural unemployment which disproportionately affects older, less-educated workers least equipped to move into the expanding areas of the New Economy requiring high levels of skills.[36] High levels of low-cost guest labour have long suppressed wage levels at this end of the market to exacerbate the plight of such workers.

Drastic changes are also projected that will test the NTUC's capacity to mobilise workers behind the government's reform agenda. Deputy Prime Minister and Minister for Defence Tony Tan observed that: '. . . the country which makes it easiest for companies to lay off workers ends up with the lowest unemployment rate and the highest economic growth. Going over to this new philosophy on labour market flexibility will require fresh thinking and wrenching changes for our manpower policies and trade unions' (Tan 2000). It was the nexus between the PAP and the NTUC that proved so effective in the decisive cost-cutting measures enacted during the crisis. The attempt to cement this relationship occurs amid opposition calls for more autonomy to trade unions, better legislation, and social security to protect workers and minimise inequalities associated with globalisation (*STWE* 2000k).

Conclusion

The economic development of Singapore since the 1960s has involved a considerable guiding hand by the state. As the city-state's policy-makers promote economic restructuring and a fuller embrace of globalisation, the emphases and forms of the state's economic role are undergoing both adjustment and consolidation. The role of the state in the provision of social and physical infrastructure is reinforced and extended as the importance of technology, knowledge, and innovation intensifies in line with the push towards the New Economy. Corporate governance reforms that smooth the way for globalisation are also becoming increasingly important. At the same time, GLCs are finding that they have to form strategic alliances with other international companies to entrench and extend their economic position within and beyond Singapore, and to secure a foothold in the New Economy. For similar reasons, the state is opening up more of the domestic economy to international competition and investment.

These directions suggest that maintaining traditional levels of state economic control will be more difficult, if not impossible. However, for political reasons, the PAP will be reluctant to surrender any more control than is absolutely necessary. The pervasive economic and social role of the state is the foundation of political paternalism that has proven a remarkable success for the PAP. Singaporeans have been highly dependent on the state for a wide range of services and resources which, when delivered, engenders a gratitude that translates into electoral support. This dependence also provides the basis for social control and renders the electorate vulnerable to intimidation (see Chua 1995; Tremewan 1994).

The current restructuring involves modifications to state–capital relations, including ever more specialised mechanisms to foster the cooperation of capital in helping official goals to be realised. In particular, this includes attempts to co-opt international finance capital through policy consultation comparable to that already adopted in the manufacturing sector. Selective elements of the domestic bourgeoisie are also being brought into this process, notably those functional to the offshore investment program and the New Economy. It reflects the increasingly complex nature of the PAP state and the power relationships that reproduce it.

Certainly there are expectations among many commentators that some of these relationships will unravel as the imperatives of globalisation assert themselves. From this perspective, the requisite creativity and innovation for the New Economy will compel a loosening of official controls over social and political life and a dismantling of Singapore Inc.. As to whether this proves to be the case, or simply amounts to liberal optimism, remains to be seen. The most serious political challenge facing the attempt of the authorities to reconcile the social and political order with the charted economic direction might lie elsewhere—in managing the differential impacts of development. Growing disparities among different fractions of domestic-based capital are unfolding as those capable of embarking on, or consolidating, offshore investment and contributing to the technology drive can benefit considerably from state initiatives and resources, and might even be consulted in the policy process. More broadly, disparities of income and wealth across the Singapore population are increasing, and are likely to be compounded by globalisation.

In confronting this challenge, the government is grappling with competing political and ideological impulses. The PAP remains committed to an extreme elitism which it sees as a functional necessity for continued economic success. Yet it is not indifferent to the plight of those least rewarded under this system and wants to ensure they are not left behind. In an economy that is highly integrated with the dynamic global economy, this will become an increasingly difficult task without extensive social policies to redress the social dislocation and inequitable effects of markets. The government is resistant to redistributive welfare measures, for fear of institutionalising the concept of citizenship rights and all that this implies for politics in Singapore. It is hoping that training programs to ameliorate structural unemployment will be sufficient.

Singapore's successful economic development over the past three decades cannot be explained as simply the consequence of sound policies. However those policies are described, they are a reflection of a dynamic set of power relationships and social structures. In that sense, the current phase of economic restructuring that is unfolding is no less political. What is distinctive is the particular complexion and coalition of interests constituting it. But as we have seen, although there are new elements of capital being brought into this coalition, the ascendancy of the politico-economic interests of the PAP state is yet to be challenged.

Notes

1　I am grateful to Kevin Hewison, Richard Robison, Jane Hutchison, and Kanishka Jayasuriya for comments on an earlier version of this chapter.

2　For a discussion of classical political economy and Keynesianism and their contributions to development theory, see Toye (1987).

3　Huff's most distinctive contribution to the literature, however, is the argument that the origins of Singapore's contemporary success in both manufacturing and services lies in historic patterns of economic activity that cumulatively generated suitable preconditions. He traces this process to Singapore's adoption as a staple port, which preceded the city-state's international entrepôt status. In subsequent work, Huff (1999) has drawn more on state-centred historical institutional literature and the concept of the developmental state.

4　In the case of 'embeddedness', Yeung doesn't so much discuss the social coalitions constituting the political basis of institutional practices. Rather, he uses it for more abstract theorisation about the relationship between states and international capital. He argues, for example, that transnational corporations are critically dependent upon the 'action of embedded states because it is in the interests of the latter that the former succeeds in capital accumulation on a global scale' (Yeung 2000a:139).

5　Five domestic banks were set up between 1903 and 1919. The three largest were founded by Hokkien traders and later merged to form the Overseas Chinese Banking Corporation (OCBC), which is today one of the so-called 'Big Four' local banks. Although there were some direct productive investments by local Chinese in the tin and rubber industries, these were also largely circumscribed by European capital (Puthucheary 1960:83).

6　This ideology also, in time, lent itself to the rationalisation of a type of developmental state referred to by James Cotton as a an 'enterprise association' or 'purpose-governed community'. According to Cotton (2000:155): 'Such a community is to be distinguished from a "civil association", which is a body of individuals governed by rules (legal, moral, conventional) that regulate their conduct *but which is not committed to any particular identified purpose*'. [Emphasis is original.]

7　Transport and communications had already increased its share of GDP from 12 per cent in 1980 to 17 per cent in 1984, and financial and business services rose from 20.5 per cent to 24 per cent in the same period (Dept Stats, *Yearbook of Statistics Singapore* 1990:87). Singapore's rapid development as a financial centre since the late 1970s had been aided by a host of provisions and incentives by the Singapore government (see Rumbaugh 1995:39–40).

8 Apart from the instances (cited in the text) of new forms of consultation with the local private sector, in 1986 the Association of Small to Medium Enterprises was established.

9 Thus, in 1994, the EDB appointed an International Advisory Council (IAC) comprised of chairmen and chief executive officers of the world's leading TNCs. The EDB expected this forum to strengthen its capacity to ascertain the thinking of international capital and its plans and aspirations for the region. Similarly, in 1994, the Regional Business Forum (RBF) was established, bringing together leading local private-sector and public-sector figures to coordinate the regionalisation drive.

10 By 1990, for example, through the three holding companies—Temasek, Singapore Technology, and Health Corporation Holdings—the Singapore state was the sole shareholder of fifty companies with interests in a further 566 subsidiaries. The total assets of these enterprises amounted to S$10.6 billion (see *STWOE* 1992; Soon and Tan 1993:23; Vennewald 1994:27–8) An analysis of the top 500 Singapore-based companies in 1988 also depicted government-linked companies responsible for 60.5 per cent of total realised profits (see Vennewald 1994:25–8).

11 This has been complemented lately by the armed services (see Huxley 1993).

12 This included a halving of Temasek's shares in NOL from 62 to 33 per cent and a reduction in its stake in Singapore Airlines from 77 to 56 per cent (*STWE* 2000c:15).

13 Asher points out that the arguments for privatisation in Singapore have been quite different from those elsewhere. The broadening and deepening of the stock market has been an objective, but this has not necessarily meant a diminution of the public sector. Rather, it has opened up opportunities for younger technocrats in the civil service, and has thereby retained talent that might otherwise have been lost to the private sector. Also, instead of promoting private firms outright, the process has more often fostered private-sector–public-sector partnerships (see Asher 1994:800–2).

14 Despite the Asian crisis, this figure grew by a further 9 per cent in 1998 to reach S$173 billion by the end of that year (Aggarwal 2000).

15 Data after 1993 include investment undertaken by financial institutions such as banks, finance companies, and insurance companies.

16 At the end of 1998, China accounted for 16 per cent and Malaysia for 12 per cent of total offshore Singapore investment. Hong Kong and Indonesia ranked next in importance (Aggarwal 2000).

17 The bias towards this sector was especially evident in direct equity investments throughout the 1990s. In 1992, for instance, it accounted for S$9.75 billion (55 per cent) of the total direct equity investment abroad, compared with manufacturing's S$3.76 billion (21.2 per cent) share. By 1997, the finance sector represented S$32.31 billion (60.4 per cent), and manufacturing S$9.96 billion (18.6 per cent) (Dept Stats, *Yearbook of Statistics* 2000:70).

18 Under these changes, the 40 per cent foreign ownership limit on local banks was eliminated, provision was made for up to six foreign banks to be granted newly created qualifying full banking (QFB) licences, and Singapore dollar lending limits for qualifying offshore banks rose from 3000 million to 1 billion. A QFB licence requires that a majority of the members of a bank's board of management be Singaporeans or permanent residents of Singapore.

19 This reform derives from the MAS's *Report on Banking Disclosure* (1998).

20 Between late 1998 and early 1999, for example, Ford and General Electric Capital Corporation made respective bond issues of S$500 million and S$300 million. Similarly, the total assets under fund management by the end of June 1999 stood at S$204.1 billion—having grown by 36 per cent in the first half of that year (*BT Online* 1999).

21 The ideas contained in Goh's speech were subsequently reinforced and amplified by prominent ministers (Lee Kuan Yew 2000; Lee Hsien Loong 2000; *STWE* 2000a; Yeo 2000a; Yeo 2000b). They were also pushed through the local media around the theme of the challenges associated with the New Economy (see, for example, *STI* 2000a). The familiar idea of a vulnerable city-state having to respond to external threats again resurfaced in official rhetoric.

22 This included the appointment of an American, John Olds, as chief executive officer of the Development Bank of Singapore (DBS), and a Dane, Flemming Jacobs, to the same position within Neptune Orient Lines (NOL).

23 StarHub is a consortium that includes GLCs such as companies in the Singapore Technologies group and Singapore Power, as well as British Telecommunications and Japan's Nippon Telegraph & Telephone. In a submission to the Info-communications Development Authority of Singapore (IDA), StarHub observed: 'The sheer weight of cash assets at SingTel's disposal, relative to the size of the market open to competition, is tremendous. Added to that, SingTel's ubiquitous network, large experienced workforce, impressive resources and customer loyalty, entrenched by the fact that every Singaporean is directly or indirectly a stakeholder in SingTel, makes the task of any new entrant very difficult.' (Quoted in *ST* 2000.)

24 Singapore Airlines was prevented from buying a 40 per cent share of Air New Zealand, being limited to 25 per cent.

25 However, it should be borne in mind that the Hong Kong and New Zealand cases cited above, together with the abortive merger between SingTel and Time

Engineering—the parent company of which, Renong, has close connections with the Malaysian government—all involved special sensitivities because of both the size of these economies and regional competitiveness. Parallel with the high-profile merger failures, the GIC in particular, and other GLCs more generally, have also been successfully buying into a wide range of companies within the region and worldwide (see *AWSJ* 2000a; *STWE* 2000h:2).

26 For a discussion of restructuring of GLCs that had begun before the crisis, see Yeung 2000a:148–150.

27 Such arrangements have thus far included such prestigious universities as the Massachusetts Institute of Technology (MIT) and Johns Hopkins University.

28 This includes a US$1 billion Technopreneurship Investment Fund by the NSTB used as seed money to foster relationships with international venture capital firms. In the first six months of operation, $443 million was committed to twenty-one venture capital funds in Asia and the United States. This included a $100 million partnership with Silicon Valley firm Draper Fisher Jurvetson (*Australian* 2000). A *National Science and Technology 2005 Plan* also earmarks S$7 billion in the aim of raising R&D expenditure to between 2 and 3 per cent of GDP, as is the case for most developing countries (see Soh 2000).

29 The combined share of the total workforce accounted for by professionals and technicians, as well as administrators, executives, and managers, rose from 18 per cent in 1980 to 24 per cent in 1990 (Dept Stats 1991:22). Significantly, professional workers constituted a major component of the expansion, especially from within the finance and business service industries where they accounted for 43 per cent of all workers and were among the highest paid of all professionals in Singapore in 1990 (Lewis 1993:26–7).

30 This has been attempted through such mechanisms as parliamentary select committees, a nominated members of parliament scheme, the Feedback Unit established by the Ministry of Community Development to take suggestions from the public and explain government policy, and a public policy thinktank (see Rodan 1992; 1996a:37–9).

31 Members of the small discussion group, The Roundtable, have been most active supporters of the Speakers' Corner.

32 The Singapore prime minister's annual salary of S$1.1 million (US$812 858), for example, was already more than three-fold that of the president of the USA (*STWE* 1996a).

33 By this time, only 2 per cent of the 10 per cent cut in employer contributions to employees' superannuation had been restored.

34 This included: S$800 million for the Share Ownership Top-Up and Central Provident Fund Top-Up schemes; S$770 million for students, for the aged, and for Housing Development Board (HDB) flat-owners, shopkeepers, and

stallholders; and S$80 million for welfare, charitable, and community self-help groups to assist the poor.

35 'Asset enhancement' involves the transfer of funds for tied purposes—such as education, share purchases, and housing—but these subsidies are not means tested.

36 A range of schemes has been devised for this purpose. These include: the Initiative for New Technology (INTECH) program under the Economic Development Assistance Scheme (EDAS) with a budget of S$800 million, a S$200 million Manpower Development Assistance Scheme (MDAS), and the National Skills Recognition System administered by the Productivity and Standards Board (PSB), with a budget of S$166 million for 2000–2005, to help workers with less than Secondary 4 level education.

References

Aggarwal, Narendra (1999) 'Investments abroad surged by end-1997', *Straits Times* (weekly edn), 11 September, p. 24.

Aggarwal, Narendra (2000) 'China top investment spot for Singapore', *Straits Times* (weekly edn), 16 September, p. 17.

Arun, Mahizhnan and Mui Teng Yap (2000) 'Singapore: The development of an intelligent island and social dividends of information technology', *Urban Studies*, 37(10):1749–56.

Asher, Mukul G. (1994) 'Some aspects of role of state in Singapore', *Economic and Political Weekly*, 2 April: pp 795–804.

Asian Wall Street Journal (AWSJ) (1998), 12 November 1998, p. 1.

Asian Wall Street Journal (AWSJ) (2000a), 11 May 2000, p. S4.

Asian Wall Street Journal (AWSJ) (2000b), 2 July 2000, p. 5.

Asiaweek (1997), 17 January 1997, p. 17.

Australian (2000), 2 May 2000, p. 25.

AWSJ, see *Asian Wall Street Journal (AWSJ)*.

Bloodworth, Dennis (1986) *The Tiger and the Trojan Horse*, Singapore: Times Books International.

Brown, David and David Martin Jones (1995) 'Democratization and the myth of the liberalizing middle classes', in Daniel A. Bell, David Brown, Kanishka Jayasuriya and David Martin Jones (eds) *Towards Illiberal Democracy in Pacific Asia*, Oxford: Macmillan and St Martin's Press, pp 78–106.

BT Online, see *Business Times Online (BT Online)*.

Buchanan, Iain (1972) *Singapore in Southeast Asia*, London: G. Bell and Sons.

Business Times Online (BT Online) (1999), <http://business-times.asia1.com.sg>, 3 November 1999.

Business Times Online (BT Online) (2000a), <http://business-times.asia1.com.sg>, 11 April 2000.

Business Times Online (BT Online) (2000b), <http://business-times.asia1.com.sg>, 6 June 2000.

Business Times Online (BT Online) (2000c), <http://business-times.asia1.com.sg>, 22 September 2000.

Cardarelli, R., J. Gobat and J. Lee (2000) *Singapore: Selected Issues*, IMF Staff Country Report No. 00/83, July, Washington, D.C.: International Monetary Fund.

Chalmers, Ian (1992) 'Loosening state control in Singapore: the emergence of local capital', *Southeast Asian Journal of Social Science*, 20(2):57–84.

Chen, Peter S.J. (1983) 'Singapore's Development Strategies: A Model for Rapid Growth', in Peter S.J. Chen (ed.) *Singapore Development Policies and Trends*, Singapore: Oxford University Press, pp 3–26.

Chua Beng Huat (1991) 'Not Depoliticised but Ideologically Successful: the Public Housing Programme in Singapore', *International Journal of Urban and Regional Research*, 15(1):24–41.

Chua Beng Huat (1995) *Communitarian Ideology and Democracy in Singapore*, London: Routledge.

Committee on Banking Disclosure (1998) *Report on Banking Disclosure*, Singapore, Monetary Authority of Singapore, May.

Cotton, James (2000) 'The Asian Crisis and the Perils of Enterprise Association: Explaining the Different Outcomes in Singapore, Taiwan and Korea', in Richard Robison, Mark Beeson, Kanishka Jayasuriya and Hyuk-Rae Kim (eds) *Politics and Markets in the Wake of the Asian Crisis*, London: Routledge, pp 151–68.

da Cunha, Derek (1997) *The Price of Vistory: The 1997 Singapore General Election and Beyond*, Singapore: Institute of Southeast Asian Studies.

Department of Statistics (Dept Stats), *Yearbook of Statistics Singapore*, various years, Singapore.

Department of Statistics (Dept Stats) (1983) *Economic and Social Statistics 1960–1982*, Singapore.

Department of Statistics (Dept Stats) (1991) *Census of Population 1990*, Advance Data Release, Singapore.

Department of Statistics (Dept Stats) (1993) *Direct Investment Abroad of Local Companies, 1991*, Occasional Paper on Financial Statistics, Singapore.

Department of Statistics (Dept Stats) (1994) *Singapore's Investment Abroad 1990–1993*, Singapore.

Department of Statistics (Dept Stats) (1995) *Income Growth and Distribution*, Occasional Paper on Social Statistics, Singapore.

Dept Stats, see Department of Statistics (Dept Stats).

Deyo, Frederic (1981) *Dependent Development and Industrial Order: An Asian Case Study*, New York: Praeger.

Economic Development Board (EDB) *Yearbook*, various years, Singapore.

Economic Planning Committee (1991) *The Strategic Economic Plan: Towards a Developed Nation*, Singapore: Ministry of Trade and Industry.

EDB, see Economic Development Board (EDB).

Einhorn, Bruce (1999) 'So This Is Asia's Net Hub?', *Business Week Online*, 10 January.

Financial Times (FT) (2000), 13 May 2000.

FT, see *Financial Times (FT)*.

Ganesan, N. (1998) 'Entrenching a City-State's Dominant Party System', in Derek da Cuhna and John Funston (eds) *Southeast Asian Affairs*, Singapore: Institute of Southeast Asian Studies, pp 229–43.

Goh Chok Tong (1999) 'First-World Economy, World-Class Home', National Day Rally Speech, Singapore, 22 August, <web3.asia1.com.sg/archive/st/1/one1/one1a.html>.

Goh Chok Tong (2000) 'Prime Minister's National Day Rally Speech', Singapore, 20 August, *Policy Digest*, 36, <www.gov.sg/feedback/archives/policy_digest/pol_digest.html>.

Haggard, Stephan (1990) *Pathways from the Periphery: The Politics of Growth in the Newly Industrializing Countries*, Ithaca and London: Cornell University Press.

Hamilton-Hart, Natasha (2000) 'The Singapore State Revisited', *Pacific Review*, 13(2):195–216.

Hon Sui Sen (1983) 'Statutory bodies and government-owned companies', a response from the Minister for Finance to a question in parliament from Toh Chin Chye, *Parliamentary Debates Singapore*, 43(1), 30 August, columns 12–15 and 89–96.

Huff, W. G. (1994) *The Economic Growth of Singapore: Trade and Development in the Twentieth Century*, Cambridge: Cambridge University Press.

Huff, W.G. (1999) 'Turning the Corner in Singapore's Developmental State?', *Asian Survey*, 39(2):214–42.

Huxley, Tim (1993) 'The Political Role of the Singapore Armed Forces' Officer Corps: Towards a Military-Administrative State?', Strategic and Defence Studies Centre, Working Paper No. 279, Canberra: Australian National University.

IMF, see International Monetary Fund (IMF).

International Bank for Reconstruction and Development (1995) *The Report of the International Bank for Reconstruction and Development on the Economic Development of Malaya*, Baltimore: Johns Hopkins University Press.

International Monetary Fund (IMF) (2000) *Singapore: Selected Issues*, IMF Staff Country Report No. 00/84, July, Washington, D.C.: International Monetary Fund.

Islam, Islam and Colin Kirkpatrick (1986) 'Export-led development, labour-market conditions and the distribution of income: the case of Singapore', *Cambridge Journal of Economics*, (10):113–27.

James, Kenneth (1999) 'Singapore One shifting into higher gear', *BT Online*, 30 August.

Jayasuriya, Kanishka (2000) 'Authoritarian Liberalism, Governance and the Emergence of the Regulatory State in Post-Crisis East Asia', in Richard Robison, Mark Beeson, Kanishka Jayasuriya and Hyuk-Rae Kim (eds) *Politics and Markets in the Wake of the Asian Crisis*, London: Routledge, pp 315–30.

Khong Cho Oon (1993) 'Managing conformity: the political authority and legitimacy of a bureaucratic elite', paper presented at the workshop on Political Legitimacy in South-East Asia, 23–26 February, Changmai, Thailand.

Koh, Leslie (2000) 'Govt not tracking speakers', *Straits Times* (weekly edn), 9 September, p. 6.

Kraar, Louis (1996) 'Need a friend in Asia? Try the Singapore connection', *Fortune*, 4 March:172.

Krongkaew, Medhi (1994) 'Income distribution in East Asian developing countries: an update', *Asian–Pacific Economic Literature*, 8(2):58–73.

Krugman, Paul (1994) 'The myth of Asia's miracle', *Foreign Affairs*, 73(6): 62–78.

Kwok Kian-Woon (1995) 'Singapore: consolidating the new political economy', *South-East Asian Affairs 1995*, Singapore: Institute of Southeast Asian Studies, pp 291–308.

Latiff, Asad (2000) 'Can S'pore become a nation of insurgents?' *Straits Times* (weekly edn), 2 September, p. 14.

Lee Hsien Loong (2000) 'US Role in Asia in the 21st Century: An Asia in Recovery', Speech at the Williamsburg conference, 3 March, <sgdaily@list.sintercom.org>.

Lee Kuan Yew (2000) 'How will Singapore Compete in a Global Economy', Speech at Nanyang Technological University, Singapore, 15 February, <sgdaily@list.sintercom.org>.

Lee Sheng-Yi (1978) *Public Finance and Public Investment in Singapore*, Singapore: Kong Brothers Press for the Institute of Banking and Finance.

Lewis, Philip (1993) 'On the Move: The Changing Structure of Singapore's Labour Market', Asia Research Centre Paper 1, Perth: Asia Research Centre, Murdoch University.

Lian, Daniel (2000) 'Singapore Inc.—New Economy Patron or Old Economy Saint?', Morgan Stanley Dean Witter comment on Singapore's economy, <www.msdw.com/GEFdata/digests/2000605-mon.html#anchor5>.

Lian, Daniel and Anita Chung (2001) 'Singapore: External Economy—Low Return is a Concern', *Global Economic Forum*, <www.morganstanley.com/GEFdata/digests/20000914-thu.html>.

Lim Chong Yah (1983) 'Singapore's Economic Development: Retrospect and Prospect', in Peter S.J. Chen (ed.) *Singapore Development Policies and Trends*, Singapore: Oxford University Press, pp 89–104.

Low, Linda (1998) *Political Economy of a City-State: Government-Made Singapore*, Oxford: Oxford University Press.

Mahizhnan, Arun (1994) 'Developing Singapore's external economy', *Southeast Asian Affairs 1994*, Singapore: Institute of Southeast Asian Studies, pp 285–301.

Ministry of Finance (MoF), Republic of Singapore (1961) *State of Singapore, Development Plan, 1961–1964*, Singapore: Government Printer.

Ministry of Finance (MoF), Republic of Singapore (1993) *Final Report of the Committee to Promote Enterprise Overseas*, Singapore: Singapore National Publishers.

Ministry of Trade and Industry (MT&I), Republic of Singapore (1986) *The Singapore Economy: New Directions*, Report of the Economic Committee, Ministry of Trade and Industry, Singapore.

Ministry of Trade and Industry (MT&I), Republic of Singapore (1993) *Report of the Cost Review Committee*, Singapore: Singapore National Publishers.

MoF, see Ministry of Finance (MoF), Republic of Singapore.

Mohamed Ariff and Hal Hill (1985) *Export-Oriented Industrialization: the ASEAN Experience*, Sydney: Allen and Unwin.

Monetary Authority of Singapore (1998) *Report on Banking Disclosure*, Committee on Banking Disclosure, Monetary Authority of Singapore, Singapore, May.

MT&I, see Ministry of Trade and Industry (MT&I), Republic of Singapore.

New Democrat (2000), Issue 2, 2000.

Ng Chee Yuen and Sudo Sueo (1991) *Development Trends in the Asia–Pacific*, Singapore: Institute of Southeast Asian Studies.

Ng, Irene (2001) 'Slowdown brings home sober message, says PM', *Straits Times Weekly*, 31 March, p. 1.

Pang Eng Fong (1994) 'Foreign Workers in Singapore', in Wilbert Gooneratne, Philip L. Martin and Hidehiko Sazanami (eds) *Regional Development Impacts of Labour Migration in Asia*, UNCRD Report Series No. 2, United Nations Centre for Regional Development, Nagoya, Japan, pp 79–94.

Parsonage, James (1992) 'Southeast Asia's "Growth Triangle": a subregional response to global transformation', *International Journal of Urban and Regional Research*, 16(2):307–17.

Parsonage, James (1997) 'Trans-state Developments in South-East Asia: Subregional Growth Zones', in Garry Rodan, Kevin Hewison and Richard Robison (eds) *The Political Economy of South-East Asia: An Introduction*, Melbourne: Oxford University Press, pp 248–83.

Puthucheary, James J. (1960) *Ownership and Control in the Malayan Economy*, Singapore: Eastern Universities Press.

Ramesh, M. (2000) 'The Politics of Social Security in Singapore', *Pacific Review*, 13(1):243–56.

Rao, V.V.B. (1990) 'Income distribution in Singapore: trends and issues', *The Singapore Economic Review*, XXXV(1):143–60.

Rao, V. V. B. (1996a) 'Singapore household income distribution data from the 1990 census: analysis, results and implications', in B. Kapur et al. (eds) *Development, Trade and Asia–Pacific: Essays in Honour of Professor Lim Chong Yah*, Singapore: Prentice-Hall, pp 92–104.

Rao, V. V. B. (1996b) 'Income inequality in Singapore: facts and policies', in Lim Chong Yah (ed.) *Economic Policy Management in Singapore*, Singapore: Addison-Wesley, pp 383–96.

Restall, Hugo (2000) 'Singapore Contemplates Change: It's time to take the state out of the economy', *Asian Wall Street Journal*, 12 July, p. 10.

Rodan, Garry (1989) *The Political Economy of Singapore's Industrialization*, London: Macmillan.

Rodan, Garry (1992) 'Singapore's leadership transition: erosion or refinement of authoritarian rule?', *Bulletin of Concerned Asian Scholars*, 24(1):3–17.

Rodan, Garry (1993a) 'Preserving the one-party state in contemporary Singapore', in Kevin Hewison, Richard Robison and Garry Rodan (eds) *Southeast Asia in the 1990s: Authoritarianism, Democracy and Capitalism*, Sydney: Allen and Unwin, pp 75–108.

Rodan, Garry (1993b) 'Reconstructing divisions of labour: Singapore's new regional emphasis', in Richard Higgott, Richard Leaver and John Ravenhill (eds) *Pacific Economic Relations in the 1990s: Cooperation or conflict?*, St Leonards NSW: Allen and Unwin, pp 223–49.

Rodan, Garry (1993b) 'The growth of Singapore's middle class and its political significance', in Garry Rodan (ed.) *Singapore Changes Guard: Social, Political and Economic Directions in the 1990s*, New York: St Martins Press, pp 52–71.

Rodan, Garry (1996a) 'Class transformations and political tensions in Singapore's development', in Richard Robison and David S.G. Goodman (eds) *The New Rich in Asia: Mobile Phones, McDonalds and Middle Class Revolution*, London and New York: Routledge, pp 19–45.

Rodan, Garry (1996b) 'State–society relations and political opposition in Singapore', in Garry Rodan (ed.) *Political Oppositions in Industrialising Asia*, London and New York: Routledge, pp 95–127.

Rodan, Garry (2000) 'Asian Crisis, Transparency and the International Media in Singapore', *Pacific Review*, 13(2):217–42.

Rumbaugh, Thomas (1995) 'Singapore's experience as an open economy', in Kenneth Bercuson (ed.) *Singapore: A Case Study in Rapid Development*, Occasional Paper 119, Washington: International Monetary Fund, pp 34–41.

Singapore 21 Committee (1999) *Singapore 21: Together, We Make the Difference*, Chaired by Teo Chee Hean, Minister for Education, Singapore: Singapore National Printers.

Singh, Bilveer (1992) *Whither PAP's Dominance? An Analysis of Singapore's 1991 General Elections*, Petaling Jaya: Pelanduk Publications.

Singh, Kulwant (1999) 'Guided Competition in Singapore's Telecommunications Industry', *Industrial and Corporate Change*, 7(4):585–99.

Soh, Natalie (2000) '$7b thrust for Science and Tech', *Straits Times* (weekly edn), 28 October, p. 1.

Soon Teck-Wong and Tan C. Suan (1993) *The Lessons of East Asia: Singapore, Public Policy and Economic Development*, Washington: World Bank.

ST, see *Straits Times (ST)*.

Star Online (2000), <http://thestar.com.my>, 19 March 2000.

STI, see *Straits Times Interactive (STI)*.

Straits Times (ST) (1996), 2 May 1996, p. 1.

Straits Times (ST) (2000), 6 June 2000, p. 68.

Straits Times Interactive (STI) (2000a), <http://straitstimes.asia1.com.sg>, 4 March 2000.

Straits Times Interactive (STI) (2000b), <http://straitstimes.asia1.com.sg>, 11 April 2000.

Straits Times Weekly Edition (STWE) (1993), 18 September 1993, p. 1.

Straits Times Weekly Edition (STWE) (1996a), 10 February 1996, p. 24.

Straits Times Weekly Edition (STWE) (1996b), 16 March 1996, p. 2.

Straits Times Weekly Edition (STWE) (1999), 25 September 1999, p. 17.

Straits Times Weekly Edition (STWE) (2000a), 11 March 2000, p. 24.

Straits Times Weekly Edition (STWE) (2000b), 15 April 2000, p. 1.

Straits Times Weekly Edition (STWE) (2000c), 6 May 2000, various pages, as cited.

Straits Times Weekly Edition (STWE) (2000d), 3 June 2000, various pages, as cited.

Straits Times Weekly Edition (STWE) (2000e), 10 June 2000, p. 15.

Straits Times Weekly Edition (STWE) (2000f), 17 June 2000, p. 2.

Straits Times Weekly Edition (STWE) (2000g), 21 June 2000, p. 36.

Straits Times Weekly Edition (STWE) (2000h), 24 June 2000, various pages, as cited.

Straits Times Weekly Edition (STWE) (2000i), 1 July 2000, p. 4.

Straits Times Weekly Edition (STWE) (2000j), 15 July 2000, p. 23.

Straits Times Weekly Edition (STWE) (2000k), 26 August 2000, p. 6.

Straits Times Weekly Edition (STWE) (2000l), 11 September 2000, p. 24.

STWE, see *Straits Times Weekly Edition (STWE)*.

STWOE, see *Straits Times Weekly Overseas Edition (STWOE)*; note that *STWOE* has recently been renamed *Straits Times Weekly Edition*.

Straits Times Weekly Overseas Edition (STWOE) (1992), 29 August 1992, p. 20.

Tan, Tony (2000) 'Moving from the Old Economy to the New Economy: Implications for the Formulation of Public Policies', Speech at the Administrative Service Dinner, Shangri-La Hotel, Singapore, 27 March.

Tessensohn, John (2000) 'The Pink Elephant & Merger Interruptus', 15 March, <www.sintercom.org/sef97/john/singtel.html>.

Toye, John (1987) *Dilemmas of Development*, Oxford: Blackwell.

Tremewan, Christopher (1994) *The Political Economy of Social Control in Singapore*, Houndmills, Basingstoke: Macmillan.

Turnbull, C. Mary (1982) *A History of Singapore 1819–1975*, Kuala Lumpur: Oxford University Press.

Vennewald, Werner (1994) 'Technocrats in the State Enterprise System in Singapore', Working Paper No. 32, Asia Research Centre, Perth: Murdoch University.

Wade, Robert and Frank Veneroso (1998) 'The Asian Crisis: The High Debt Model Versus the Wall Street–Treasury–IMF Complex', *New Left Review*, 228:3–23.

Webb, Sara (2000) 'Singaporeans Protest Officials' Pay: Public Gets Vocal About Raises in Rare Demonstration of Anger', *Asian Wall Street Journal*, 10 July, p. 4.

World Bank (1993) *The East Asian Miracle: Economic Growth and Public Policy*, New York: Oxford University Press.

Worthington, Ross (2001) *Governance in Singapore: Myth and Reality*, London: Curzon.

Yeo, George (2000a) 'In the Mind of a Minister', Interview with Irene Ng, *Straits Times*, 5 March, <sgdaily@list.sintercom.org>.

Yeo, George (2000b) 'Sink or Swim in Ocean of Global League', Interview with Irene Ng, *Straits Times*, 6 March, <sgdaily@list.sintercom.org>.

Yeung Wai Chung (2000a) 'State Intervention and Neo-liberalism in the globalizing world economy: lessons from Singapore's regionalization programme', *Pacific Review*, 13(2):133–62.

Yeung Wai Chung (2000b) 'Local Politics and Foreign Ventures in China's Transitional Economy: The Political Economy of Singaporean Investments in China', *Political Geography*, 19.

Young, Alwyn (1995) 'The Tyranny of Numbers: Confronting the Statistical Realities of East Asian Growth Experience', *Quarterly Journal of Economics*, August, pp 641–80.

6

The State and the Market in Malaysian Political Economy

Khoo Boo Teik

For much of the forty-three years since it gained Merdeka (independence) from British colonial rule in 1957, Malaysia was held to be a moderately successful, middle-income, commodity-producing, and net oil-exporting country. A state-supported program of industrialisation, largely based on foreign direct investment in the labour-intensive and export-oriented manufacture of textiles, garments, and electronic products had commenced in the 1970s. This program was followed in the 1980s by a state-sponsored drive towards heavy industrialisation in the automobile, cement, and steel sectors. However, in the span of almost a decade beginning in the late 1980s, high rates of export-oriented and manufacturing-led growth (averaging over 8 per cent annually) turned Malaysia into a second-tier, newly industrialising country (NIC). As the indicators in table 6.1 (page 179) suggest, such a transformation included a major structural shift in the economy typically associated with a transition from an agrarian to an industrial society, with social changes particularly significant to Malaysian society.

Indeed, by early 1991, Malaysia's political leaders and business elite were already confidently envisaging, in strategic planning terms, that the country would attain 'developed country status' by 2020 (Mahathir 1991).

According to certain neo-classical economic arguments, notably those advanced by the World Bank, Malaysia's economic transformation, not unlike that of other Asian NICs, was the outcome of an intricate mix of market-augmenting macroeconomic policies (World Bank 1993). To that extent, the state has been lauded for adopting 'pro-growth', 'pro-investment', and 'pro-market' policies that kept the economy open to domestic private investment, attractive to foreign direct investment, and integrated with international trade. Such an interpretation of economic transformation accords a central role to neutral techniques of planning and management, and rational choices of 'policy menus'. It credits efficiently functioning market processes as the ultimate determinant of economic performance. Leaving aside academic criticisms of this interpretation (see chapter 1, this volume), it is doubtful that the Malaysian political, business,

Table 6.1 Economic and social transformation, 1960–98, selected indicators

Sectoral share of GDP	1960	1998
Agriculture	40.5%	12.3%
Manufacturing	8.2%	34.4%
Share of total export value	1960	1998
Top 5 primary commodities	71.9%	
Manufacturing products		82.9%
Share of total labour force	1960	1998
Agriculture	55.2%	12.8%
Manufacturing	6.4%	27.0%
Poverty	1970	1997
Incidence of poverty (households)	49.3%	6.8%
Share of corporate equity	1969	1997
Malay/bumiputera share of corporate equity	1.5%	19.4%

Sources: Malaysia (1965:23–4, table 2-2; 35, table 2-10); Malaysia (1971:40, table 3-1); Malaysia (1981:33, table 3-1); Malaysia (1999:41, table 2-3; 67, table 3-1; 80–1, table 3-5; 89, table 3.9; 208, table 7.1); Jomo (1990:43, table 3.4; 79, table 4.1)

and bureaucratic elites would agree with it. Successive regimes have prided themselves on being pragmatic and non-ideological in economic matters, meaning that they have been responsive to market needs and demands in their maintenance of a capitalist economy. However, since 1969, they have 'governed the market' through extensive state economic intervention, the many forms and details of which were conditioned by social circumstances and political pressures.

As this chapter demonstrates, political agenda of social engineering underlay the state's economic intervention. The agenda, officially described as constituting a plan to 'restructure Malaysian society', were germane to the state's management of social and political tensions. Yet the pursuit of these agenda, under economic vicissitudes, and against the opposition of specific social classes, ethnic communities, and institutional centres of power and influence, continually led to political conflicts. That the conflicts, for Malaysia, are often exclusively posed in ethnic terms is understandable: interethnic 'economic imbalances', essentially the wealth and income disparities between the Malay and Chinese communities, have long been a source of political contention. But the conflicts that state policies have sought to manage, or have even created, extend beyond ethnic problems. They encompass class conflicts, the emergence of Malay capital, the rise and decline of bureaucratic interests, the politicisation of business, the aggrandisement of powerful conglomerates, and the promotion of economic nationalism.

This chapter approaches these politico-economic developments by tracking state–market relations as they changed over several periods, here distinguished according to the *laissez-faire* of the Alliance (1957–69), state economic intervention of the first New Economic Policy decade (1970–80), early Mahathirism (1981–90), the consolidation of Malaysia Incorporated (1991–97), and the semi-autarchy since July 1997. The chapter also links major changes in state–market relations—characterised by the degrees to which the market was shaped by state regulation, intervention, or liberalisation—to shifts in the balance of power among different alliances and coalitions of state, bureaucratic, party, and capitalist interests. Hence, this chapter argues two principal points of theoretical interest. First, it contends that the main themes of Malaysian political economy cannot be understood by seeing economic transformation as an apolitical expression of rational choices, technocratic options, and market processes. Instead policy choices, technocratic interventions, and market processes must be analysed in political terms because they embody the 'conflictual nature of economic development and the importance of the state as an arena for this' (Robison, Rodan and Hewison 1997:15). Second, it holds that politics and the agency of powerful coalitions have been critical to the construction and reconstruction of the market during various phases in the postcolonial transformation of Malaysian capitalism.

The Alliance and the failure of *laissez-faire* capitalism

On the eve of Merdeka the political economy shaped by colonial capitalism had created certain patterns of uneven development, economic disparities, and social divisions. The locus of advanced economic activity lay in foreign-owned plantations, mines, and agency houses that produced and exported primary commodities (rubber and tin being the most important) to the rest of the world. James Puthucheary's pioneering study of 'ownership and control in the Malayan economy' in the 1950s found that European-owned companies controlled 84 per cent of large rubber estates (of more than 500 acres each), 60 per cent of tin output, 65–75 per cent of exports, and 60 per cent of imports (Puthucheary 1960:xv, 26–7, 85–6). On the whole, 'foreign, especially British, interests, dominated nearly every facet of the colonial economy, including plantations, mining, banking, manufacturing, shipping and public utilities' (Searle 1999:28). Domiciled Chinese capital maintained a sufficiently strong presence in comprador activities, banking, small-scale manufacturing, retailing, and services so that the 'ubiquitous activity of the

Chinese middleman' lent weight to the 'popular misconception that commerce is controlled by the Chinese' (Puthucheary 1960:xv). Political control and the administration of the state apparatus had been mostly turned over to Malay aristocrats who had been trained for civil service by the colonial state. Hence, the social origins of the ruling elite were those of the expatriate representatives of foreign capital, indigenous Malay aristocrats, and domiciled Chinese capitalists and traders.

Malaya's west coast had a developed urban sector that stretched north–south from Penang to Singapore. This sector contained the towns, ports, public works, and major infrastructure that integrated the domestic economy with the global economy. Here lived a broad spectrum of middle and working classes, including lower-level bureaucrats, professionals, teachers and clerks, shopkeepers, petty traders and hawkers, and industrial and service workers. Their numbers had grown with economic diversification and bureaucratic expansion under colonialism. Nearly 60 per cent of the economically active population, however, worked in the rural sector, mostly as peasants cultivating rice on their own or rented land, smallholders growing rubber and other cash crops, wage labourers working in plantations, and squatters illegally raising cash crops on state land.

The economic disparities and social divisions were complicated by an ethnic division of labour not uncommon to the social organisation of labour in other former colonies, such as Burma, Fiji, and the countries of East Africa. Colonial design (Lim Teck Ghee 1984), as well as the peasantry's 'refusal to supply plantation labour' (Alatas 1977:80), left the Malay peasantry chiefly engaged in food production. Migrant Chinese and Indian labour mainly worked the tin mines, and rubber estates and public works projects respectively. As a consequence of this ethnic division of labour, the Malay peasantry escaped the harsh conditions of early colonial capitalism that took a heavy toll on migrant labour. But the rural Malay community was thereby locked into an immiserating close-to-subsistence sector, whereas sections of Chinese and Indian migrants took advantage of an expanding urban sector to gain upward mobility through commerce, education, and the professions.

The first ruling coalition, the Alliance—comprised of the United Malays National Organization (UMNO), Malayan Chinese Association (MCA), and Malayan Indian Congress (MIC)—did not change the fundamental features of the political economy. This was largely because of the character of Malaya's decolonisation. The colonial state had defeated a post-World War II insurrection of communists, left-wing nationalists, former wartime partisans, radical sections of the working class, and squatter-farmers. After that, the colonial state and the Alliance forged a 'Merdeka compromise'.

The compromise protected foreign economic interests (which were not nationalised, as happened, say, in Indonesia under Soekarno), preserved the position of domiciled Chinese capital, and largely ceded the control of the state apparatus to the Malay aristocrats who led UMNO. More broadly, a federal constitution reserved a 'special position' for the Malay community in recognition of its indigenous status, but guaranteed the non-Malays a new-found citizenship and accompanying rights.

The Alliance's compromise expressed a balance of power by which the state played a 'restrained role' in what approximated a *laissez-faire* capitalism (Jesudason 1989:52–67). To be sure, the Alliance regime made some departures from the colonial policy regime of minimal taxation, strict avoidance of budget deficits, and the maintenance of an unprotected market (Jesudason 1989:48). For example, the state expanded its revenue base by raising export duties on rubber and tin, imposing an 'excess profit tax' on tin, and introducing a 'development tax' on company profits (Jesudason 1989:49). Public development expenditure was increased, to the point of incurring small budget deficits (Jesudason 1989:49). The Alliance progressively protected the domestic market as shown by its removal of a Commonwealth preferential tariff rate that had favoured imports of British origin. It also promoted import-substituting industrialisation (ISI) by offering fiscal, tax, and other incentives to firms engaged in pioneer industries.

Beyond these measures, however, the Alliance adopted a conservative stance in economic affairs that continued to favour foreign and domestic capitalist interests. The ISI program attracted some foreign investment to manufacturing for the domestic market. Taking advantage of some degree of the 'Malaysianisation' of the economy, Chinese capital expanded into banking, manufacturing, trade, and construction and property development. The thrust of development was directed at improving urban infrastructure, implementing limited rural development schemes, and providing small-scale assistance to incipient Malay business. The state's own involvement in development was limited by an underlying concern to restrain the levels of domestic borrowing and foreign debt. Few things more clearly showed the regime's commitment to leaving the market 'free' than the regime's reluctance to intervene on behalf of sections of UMNO's Malay base. In a notable instance, the Alliance rejected Minister of Agriculture Aziz Ishak's proposal to adopt a populist scheme of turning the control of privately owned rice mills over to farmer-cooperatives when the scheme was opposed by Chinese business interests (Jesudason 1989:55; von Vorys 1975). The regime used institutions such as Bank Bumiputera, the Majlis Amanah Rakyat (MARA, or the Council of Trust for the Indigenous People), and the Rural and Industrial Development Authority (RIDA) to assist nascent Malay businesses. Yet, despite a growing Malay frustration with the lack of progress in redressing their 'relative economic backwardness', the regime's orientation in this area was supportive rather than aggressive (Jomo 1988:253–4).

Left to itself, the market could not resolve problems of increasing unemployment, declining incomes, and widening inequalities. By the late 1960s, the Alliance was hard pressed to meet social expectations unleashed by decolonisation and mass politics. A marginalised Malay peasantry sought release from poverty, indebtedness, and landlessness, most dramatically by 'opening' state land as when Hamid Tuah led land seizures in Sungei Sireh, Teluk Gong, and Binjal Patah (Husin Ali 1975:157–9). A combination of Malay bureaucrats, intelligentsia, and the middle-class wanted concerted state assistance and economic parity *vis-à-vis* the Chinese community, and Chinese capital in particular. On the other hand, non-Malay middle and working classes refused to accept that their opportunities for employment, education, and upward mobility could be prejudiced by constitutional safeguards of the 'special position' of the Malays. Also during the 1960s, disaffection among organised labour in the plantation and manufacturing sectors resulted in exceptionally high numbers of workdays lost to strikes in 1962, 1964, and 1968 (Todd and Jomo 1994:48–53, tables 2.16–2.19).

These mass economic expectations became ethnically divisive and politically volatile as they coincided with real and imagined fissures in the areas of language, culture, and citizenship during the formative period of a Malaysian nationhood. Despite being ethnically divided, the opposition to the Alliance crystallised into an electoral revolt. In the May 1969 general election, an informal electoral pact helped diverse opposition parties—the Pan-Malaysian Islamic Party (PMIP, now Parti Islam, or PAS), Democratic Action Party (DAP), and the Gerakan Rakyat Malaysia (Gerakan, or Malaysian People's Movement)—erode the Alliance's hold on power. On 13 May, Kuala Lumpur was engulfed in interethnic violence. The Alliance's political framework collapsed, and with it a 'ridiculous' (Mahathir 1970:15) *laissez-faire* formula of 'politics for the Malays' and 'economics for the Chinese'.

New economic policy and state intervention

A National Operations Council (NOC), headed by Deputy Prime Minister Tun Abdul Razak, ruled under a state of emergency from 1969 to 1971. Parliament was suspended while Prime Minister Tunku Abdul Rahman, the personification of Alliance consociationalism, was sidelined (Rahman eventually retiring in 1970). Razak's regime had no more use for the *laissez-faire* capitalism and devised the New Economic Policy (NEP). NEP would remake the political economy to manage the class pressures and ethnic demands that an unregulated market had not satisfied. Malaysian economic planning being carried out via five-year plans, NEP was designed to be implemented over two decades, beginning with the Second Malaysia Plan 1971–75.

NEP's premises were that poverty, the ethnic division of labour, and Malay resentment of interethnic income inequalities lay at the heart of the May 1969 eruption. NEP's two major objectives were 'poverty eradication irrespective of race', and 'restructuring to abolish the identification of race with economic function'. The state's 'Outline Perspective Plan 1971–90' targeted a decline in the incidence of poverty, from 49 per cent of all households in 1970 to 16 per cent in 1990. Restructuring was planned to raise the *bumiputera* (indigenous, but predominantly Malay) share of corporate equity from 2.5 per cent in 1970 to 30 per cent in 1990. To eliminate 'the identification of race with economic function', NEP envisaged affirmative action that favoured the *bumiputera* community. To accomplish these objectives, the state used ethnic quotas and targets to regulate access to state assistance, business opportunities, tertiary education, and civil service recruitment.

NEP's subsequent elaboration and implementation encompassed several major developments. Restructuring was promoted as an exercise to redress interethnic imbalances by redistributing corporate wealth ownership as well as employment. It became a massive social engineering project that altered the class structure of Malaysian society by sponsoring the rise of a combination of Malay capitalist, professional, and middle-classes (later described as a Bumiputera Commercial and Industrial Community). The state no longer confined its activities to 'limited programmes aimed at ameliorating rural discontent and the frustrations of a rising Malay intelligentsia' (Khoo Khay Jin 1992:50). Rather, by becoming a *provider* of opportunities for Malays, the state enlarged the existing corps of Malay entrepreneurs, graduates, and professionals. It gave aspiring Malay entrepreneurs financial assistance, credit facilities, contracts, preferential share allocations, subsidies, and training. It established new public universities and all-Malay residential schools and colleges at home, and sent tens of thousands of Malays, young students, and mid-career officers to universities abroad. The result of this social engineering was a full range of Malay entrepreneurs and capitalists (Searle 1999:81–95), a sizeable Malay middle-class (Abdul Rahman 1995), and a considerable '*bumiputera* participation rate' in the professions (Jomo 1990:82–3, table 4.2; Malaysia 1999:85, table 3-7).

Simultaneously, the state became a determined *regulator* of business, both local and foreign, although the regulation of the former was politically more contentious. The state strengthened its regulatory powers and enforced compliance with NEP's restructuring requirements by using legislative means (*Industrial Coordination Act [ICA] 1975*) and bureaucratic procedures (set by the Foreign Investment Committee). NEP's restructuring requirements set a quota of at least 30 per cent *bumiputera* equity participation and employment in companies covered by *ICA*.[1] In 'expanding government power over firms', *ICA* gave the minister of Trade and Industry wide discretionary power over licensing, ownership structure, ethnic employment targets, product-distribution quotas, local content, and product pricing (Jesudason 1989:135–8). Even at the level of state and local government, non-Malay businesses came under stringent bureaucratic regulation. In a non-manufacturing area such as real estate development, for example, many authorities—including land offices, town and country planning departments, municipal councils, and state economic development corporations—imposed 'NEP requirements' on such seemingly technical matters as land-use conversion or planning guidelines.

Finally, the state became a major *investor*. It expanded public-sector ownership of corporate equity by acquiring assets on behalf of the Malays. Public enterprises proliferated in number from 22 in 1960 to 109 in 1970, to 656 in 1980, and to 1014 in 1985. State agencies, banks, and funds sought, bought, and otherwise held equity 'in trust' for *bumiputeras*. Some of the best known of these state agencies were Bank Bumiputera, Urban Development Authority (UDA), Perbadanan Nasional (PERNAS, or National Corporation), Permodalan Nasional Berhad (PNB, or National Equity Corporation), Amanah Saham Nasional (ASB, or National Unit Trust Scheme), and the state economic development corporations (SEDCs) (Searle 1999:61–6; Gomez and Jomo 1997:29–39).

Rupture between state and capital

The state's economic intervention led to critical shifts in the tripartite balance of power among the state, foreign capital, and domestic capital. The fundamental shift was revealed by the state's 'economic nationalist' attitude towards foreign and Chinese capital. NEP targeted a 30 per cent Malay share of corporate equity by 1990, but also allowed for a rise in non-Malay ownership from about 34.3 per cent in 1970 (with the politically more contentious Chinese share accounting for 22.8 per cent in 1969) (Malaysia 1971:40, table 3.1) to 40 per cent in 1990 (Malaysia 1976:86, table 4-16). Thus, increases in Malay and non-Malay shares were to be attained at the expense of foreign ownership which would decline from 63.3 per cent in 1970 to 30 per cent in 1990 (Malaysia 1976:86, table 4-16).

During NEP's first decade, the state acquired foreign companies or foreign equity. State enterprises, led by PERNAS and PNB, bought foreign companies—such as London Tin, Chartered Consolidated, Sime Darby, and Guthrie—that had long dominated the mines, plantations, and trading houses. Faced with state acquisitions or restructuring, certain foreign companies chose to relinquish ownership or control of their Malaysian subsidiaries (Searle 1999:72–4). One exception to the success of the state's acquisitive trend was the refusal of foreign oil companies to share management control with Petronas (Petroliam Nasional, or National Oil Corporation), as stipulated by the *Petroleum Development Act 1974* (Searle 1999:69–70). In response to this Act 'which smells of nationalization, and . . . cannot be acceptable to any foreign interests . . . foreign investment in Malaysia [came] to a standstill' (Grace 1976, cited in Jomo 1988:281, fn 69). Thus there was an investment strike that ended only after the state had renegotiated with the oil companies and dropped the management conditions.[2]

Chinese capital was not averse to a reduction in foreign ownership. But the danger to Chinese capital was that the state's economic nationalism took the hues of a 'Malay nationalism' which the Chinese business community and political parties were too weak to resist. Under the Alliance, MCA leaders had held the ministries of Finance and Trade, and exerted considerable 'Chinese influence' over economic planning and policy-making. By 1974, however, when Razak replaced the Alliance with an enlarged coalition, Barisan Nasional (BN, or National Front), UMNO leaders had monopolised policy-making, and the balance of power between 'Malay state' and 'Chinese capital' had swung to the former. Chinese capital could not match the state's penetration of key economic sectors. In banking, for example, where Chinese capital had expanded in pre-NEP years, the state enlarged its assets and restructured both foreign-owned and Chinese-owned banks. By 1990, the three biggest banks were the state-owned Malayan Banking Berhad, Bank Bumiputera Berhad, and United Malayan Banking Corporation (Searle 1999:75, table 3.2). Nor could Chinese capital escape stricter regulation, as was demonstrated by the failure of MCA and the Associated Chinese Chinese Chambers of Commerce and Industry of Malaysia, despite repeated attempts, to have the *ICA* repealed (Jesudason 1989:134–42).

Foreign and Chinese capital distrusted state intervention, disliked NEP's nationalism, and baulked at *ICA*'s regulations. Still, the relations between the state and capital were not always antagonisic. Foreign capital was mollified in at least two ways. First, the old foreign capital of the plantation houses, mines, banks, and trading houses was never threatened with out-right nationalisation. 'Malaysianising' the ownership of established companies by restructuring was accomplished by market transactions. NEP's 'backdoor nationalisation', as foreign critics characterised the state acquisitions, was tantamount to only 'relatively gentle . . . encroachments on the terrain of foreign capital' (Jomo 1988:281, fn 68). Second, the new foreign capital of manufacturing multinational corporations (MNCs) was highly favoured as the state initiated a program of export-oriented indus-trialisation (EOI). Here NEP interfaced with a 'new international division of labour'. The state's urgent need to create mass employment matched the MNCs' search for cheap labour in politically stable offshore production sites. The state offered the MNCs the comparative advantages of: lower wages; prohibition of unionisation among a new industrial labour force; subsidised physical and social infrastructure; and fiscal, tax, and other incentives. The state established export processing zones (EPZs), the best known of which was the Bayan Lepas Free Trade Zone on the island of Penang—which became a leading centre for the production of semicon-ductors for the global electronics industry. The MNCs were not subjected to NEP's 'wealth restructuring' requirements, but they met NEP's 'employ-ment restructuring' goal by proletarianising large numbers of rural, young (and often female) Malays within the modern sectors of the economy. In this context, state intervention reshaped markets in labour, land, infra-structure, and services on behalf of foreign capital.

Chinese capital never enjoyed the MNCs' privileged treatment. Portions of Chinese 'old wealth', typically family businesses controlled by indiv-idual tycoons, were unable or unwilling to adjust to the intensifying institutionalisation of NEP practices. These 'pursued easy and safe areas of expansion, investing heavily in property development and finance, and avoiding sectors like manufacturing which entailed larger risks and longer periods to recuperate investment outlays' (Jesudason 1989:163). Other Chinese businesses discovered opportunities that were, arguably, attribut-able to NEP. During NEP's first decade, real GDP growth averaged 7.6 per cent per year (or 7.3 per cent over the Second Malaysia Plan period of 1971–75 and 8.6 per cent in the Third Malaysia Plan period of 1976–80). Under such conditions, business in general prospered, and the non-Malay (predominantly Chinese) share of corporate equity rose between 1970 and 1985. Some, typically big, Chinese businesses adapted to the NEP-altered balance of power at elite levels. Offering varying combinations of capital, networks, and expertise, they courted, were courted by, or otherwise built commercial relationships with aspiring Malay capitalists or influential

Malays situated in the aristocracy, bureaucracy, military, and the dominant Malay political party (Heng 1992:132–4; Sieh 1992:110–11). Soon a distinctive NEP creation—the *'bumiputera–non-bumiputera* joint venture'— emerged as a corporate platform from which adaptable Chinese capital, both 'old wealth' and 'new money', partook in the state-led demand and public enterprise investment enormously boosted by high commodity and oil revenues.

The state and Malay capital: power shifts and emerging conflicts

Away from ethnic considerations, the state-sponsored creation of Malay capital was dependent upon three critical factors. First, UMNO, as the dominant political party in government, supplied the political power to push through NEP's social engineering. Second, the Malay-dominated bureaucracy provided the capacity for implementing NEP programs. Third, the performance of an incipient class of Malay capitalists had to vindicate the state assistance and nurture that they received.

Influential coalitions emerged from among the ranks of party, bureaucracy, and class. But, as resources were controlled by bureaucrats and technocrats, as UMNO entered business on a large scale, and as individual Malay capitalists emerged, these coalitions contended for power, access to resources, and opportunities for accumulation. Over time, their agenda could less and less be amicably subsumed under NEP: all based their claims on restructuring, but each pursued its disparate interests. Many flashpoints of competition were thereby created, which continually strained the integrity of this party–bureaucracy–class axis.

Within only a few years of NEP's beginning, one such flashpoint emerged between the party and the bureaucracy. Razak's regime had rapidly moved to enlarge its corps of bureaucrats and technocrats as Razak insisted that development required more 'administration' than 'politics'. A whole generation of Malay administrators, technocrats, and professionals was trained at state expense and equipped with the resources to take charge of economic development under NEP. But the transition to an NEP state involved a power shift, too—from UMNO's 'old guard' to younger UMNO politicians who were being groomed by Razak. Just as NEP repudiated the Alliance's *laissez-faire*, so the rise of Razak's coterie of 'young Turks' marginalised UMNO's 'old-style politicians' who supposedly lacked the 'vision and technocratic skills to carry through the restructuring of society' (Crouch 1980:17, 32–3). Not coincidentally, Razak's protégées included

Mahathir Mohamad and Musa Hitam (who had attacked Tunku Abdul Rahman's leadership after May 1969) and their associate, Tengku Razaleigh Hamzah. After Razak died in January 1976, a crisis developed in UMNO when the old guard struck at Razak's allies by accusing several of them of being 'communists' (Crouch 1980). However, this bizarre witch-hunt turned out to be the last gasp of an old guard being swept aside by NEP's 'technocratic shift'.

Another source of conflict lay in the bureaucracy as it expanded in terms of funding, resources, and personnel (table 6.2, below). Bureaucratic involvement in economic activities grew—such that by 1983 the state had taken over the 'commanding heights' of the economy. Then public enterprises controlled an estimated 45 per cent of 'modern agriculture', 50 per cent of mining, and between 70 and 80 per cent of banking (Parti Gerakan 1984:187, table 2). But the performance of public enterprises was itself a major problem. For political and other reasons, many public enterprises could not meet market criteria of efficiency and profitablity (Rugayah 1995:75–78; Gomez and Jomo 1997:76–7). Many officers regarded their public enterprises as 'social enterprises' with goals of redressing interethnic imbalances that were not readily measured in pecuniary values. The state tended to accept or overlook the deficits, debts, and losses of the public enterprises as being the price of providing the Malays with experience, employment, and skills. But the scale of deficits and losses was daunting. Total public-sector deficit rose from RM400 million in 1970 to RM15.2 billion in 1982. State governments, statutory bodies, and public enterprises owed the federal government RM8.743 billion in 1982 (Mehmet 1986:133–4), and 'approximately 40–45 per cent of all SOEs [state-owned enterprises] have been unprofitable throughout the 1980s', of which 'almost half (or 25 per cent of all SOEs) had negative shareholder funds' (Adam and Cavendish 1995a:25).

Table 6.2 Expansion of public sector, 1970–85, selected indicators

Public expenditure	
First Malaysia Plan 1966–70	RM4.6 billion
Second Malaysia Plan 1971–75	RM10.3 billion
Third Malaysia Plan 1976–80	RM31.1 billion
Fourth Malaysia Plan 1981–85	RM48.9 billion
Development expenditure as % of GDP	
1971	8.5%
1980	14.4%
Public-sector employment (excluding military and police)	
1970	139 476 employees
1983	521 818 employees

Sources: Jomo (1990:106, table 5.1); Mehmet (1986:9, table 1.3; 133, table 6.1)

A politically more contentious issue was the transfer of public enterprise assets. In principle, public enterprises run by political appointees and state managers held those assets 'in trust' for the Malays. But the more commercially oriented trust agencies, such as PNB, were empowered to acquire profitable companies. Even as powerful a public corporation as PERNAS was required to tranfer eleven of its most profitable companies to PNB in 1981. Commercial imperatives became more urgent after PNB established Amanah Saham Nasional (ASN, or the National Unit Trust Scheme). ASN bought PNB's assets at cost, and individual Malays bought units of ASN shares. The companies remained 'within the community', and individual shareholders received returns on their investment. ASN was a novel solution to the problem of asset transfer. Yet some managers of public enterprises were reportedly burdened by a 'disincentive to profit-making' for fear of PNB's taking over their enterprises (World Bank, cited in Gomez and Jomo 1997:77). Public enterprises also faced pressure from Malay entrepreneurs who wanted the assets to be directly transferred to them, or complained of 'unfair' state competition. Not a few state managers chose to become entrepreneurs, sometimes by acquiring the very enterprises they managed. Contention over the transfer of public assets grew acute as UMNO entered business, and its managers used the party's dominance to compete for state projects, contracts, and assets. Within a few years of starting Fleet Holdings (for the purpose of generating party funds), UMNO had built up an economic empire that penetrated most economic sectors (Gomez 1990; Searle 1999:103–26). Subsequently, notable UMNO 'nominees, trustees or proxies'—people to whom the party assets were entrusted—became big capitalists in their own right (Searle 1999: 135–53).

Early Mahathirism: a new state–capital alliance

The conflicts brewing along the party–bureaucracy–class axis intensified after Mahathir became premier in July 1981. Mahathir's approach to development can be summarised as a composite of bureaucratic reformism, economic nationalism, and privatisation. It was modelled after the East Asian 'developmental state', and was inspired particularly by the economic success of Japan and South Korea.

Mahathir set out to tackle the 'structural problems' arising out of the 'size and extent of the government's involvement in the economy' (Khoo 1995:129). He was ambivalent towards state expansionism. He favoured having an interventionist state implement NEP's social engineering. But he was contemptuous of public-sector inefficiency and was persuaded by the private sector's supposed dynamism. His first administration introduced reforms to improve the performance of the bureaucracy. When commodity prices and state revenues fell in the early 1980s, he reduced the involvement of public enterprises in business. The pace of this curtailment of the bureaucracy's involvement in business was accelerated under Minister of Finance Daim Zainuddin during the recession of 1985. But the curtailment adversely affected the interests of the managers of public enterprises, as well as a range of Malay businesses dependent upon state assistance and political largesse (Khoo Khay Jin 1992). Their ensuing disaffection contributed to UMNO's split from 1987 to 1990.

Mahathir also launched a heavy industrialisation drive based on the production of steel, automobiles, motorcycle engines, and cement. Because domestic capital was reluctant to bear the heavy costs, high risks, and long gestation periods, he chose a combination of state investment via the state-owned Heavy Industries Corporation of Malaysia (HICOM), technology sourced from Japanese and South Korean firms through joint ventures, and indigenous (that is, Malay) management (Machado 1989–90; Machado 1994). HICOM's program began with an import-substituting character: its industries enjoying credit facilities, subsidies, and tariff protection. Its intermediate objectives included technological upgrading and the creation of extensive linkages in the economy. Its eventual goal was export competitiveness.

As with East Asian state-led late-industrialisation elsewhere, HICOM's program had a strong nationalist impetus. Mahathir, too, personified capitalist impulses that went beyond the ethnic fixations of other NEP advocates. For those reasons, Mahathir wanted to heal the rupture between the state and domestic capital. NEP had not quite created an independent class of Malay capitalists, but it had produced Malay entrepreneurs and technocrats with business experience. State regulation had also rendered NEP more acceptable to non-Malay capital. Thus Mahathir encouraged a new state–capital alliance, but one that had a major role for Malay capital. This was revealed by Mahathir's 'Privatization' and 'Malaysia Incorporated' policies (Khoo 1995:129–36). Privatisation was originally justified as the means to reduce expenditure on unprofitable public enterprises and to improve economic performance. But it shifted the burden of investment and growth to the private sector, and served as the mode of transfer of assets 'held in trust' to Malay entrepreneurs. Malaysia Inc. promised cooperation between the state and a national capital that was no longer synonymous with domestic Chinese capital.

The economy contracted by 1.0 per cent in 1985, and grew by only 1.2 per cent in 1986. Three factors were principally responsible—a huge decline in commodity prices,[3] an escalation in public debt,[4] and the reduction in the government's development expenditure at the same time that total private investment declined.[5] The recession's impact was particularly severe on Malay businesses, while austerity measures—including a job-and-wage freeze, and cuts in development expenditure—were forced upon the bureaucracy and public enterprises. In a bold if desperate move to attract private, and especially foreign, investment, Mahathir suspended NEP's restructuring requirements. As the 1987 UMNO party election approached, the ranks of the party, bureaucracy, and Malay capital were polarised. At one end stood a 'pro-growth' camp that supported NEP's suspension to boost investment and growth. At the other was a 'pro-distribution' camp that wanted to continue NEP restructuring. The former, pro-Mahathir, camp was backed by bigger, and more successful, Malay businesses, whereas the latter, Razaleigh Hamzah-led, camp found support among smaller, and less independent, Malay businesses and disgruntled sections of the bureaucracy (Khoo Khay Jin 1992:67–71).

The crisis deepened in April 1987, when Mahathir narrowly survived the combined challenge of Razaleigh Hamzah and Musa Hitam, and again in late October, when deteriorating interethnic relations became the pretext for the regime's general suppression of dissent (Khoo 1995). Still, Daim's austere response to recession and Mahathir's authoritarian reply to opposition gave the regime time to recover. From 1985 to 1987, the state liberalised the investment regime, initially for foreign capital, but later for domestic (Chinese) capital too. Limits on foreign-equity ownership were removed and fresh investment incentives were offered. These measures coincided with moves by Japanese and other East Asian MNCs to relocate part of their production because of the post-Plaza Accord yen appreciation, an anticipated loss of the generalised system of preferences (GSP) privileges, and escalating domestic labour and production costs. Subsequently, a wave of East Asian investment that began to arrive in the late 1980s helped to effect another trend of rapid economic growth that lasted until July 1997.

Conglomerates and the consolidation of Malaysia Inc.

With economic recovery, privatisation was 'entrenched in the policy matrix' and, by 1991, a *Privatization Masterplan* had been completed, the scope of which portended a 'radical shift to the private sector' (Adam and Cavendish 1995b:135). The reliance on a partnership between the private sector and the state—'Malaysia Inc.' in short—was promoted as 'the way forward' in

Mahathir's *Wawasan 2020* (Vision 2020) (Mahathir 1991). Yet accelerating privatisation and the consolidation of Malaysia Inc. had several consequences for the economic structure, power alignments, and 'governance' that laid some of the conditions for another crisis.

The practice of privatisation came to encompass the sale of profitable state monopolies (in energy and telecommunications, for example), the awarding of large infrastructural works (the North–South Highway and the Bakun Dam being the largest), and the opening of new areas (social services such as health care and tertiary education) to domestic capital. To the extent that more and more sectors, companies, and projects passed into private hands, privatisation entailed rolling back the frontiers of the state. But privatisation did not operate under market conditions. Huge privatisation projects were awarded without open competition, and often without any tendering process at all.[6] In this tightly controlled 'market', rent-seeking and money politics were rife as coalitions formed around domestic conglomerates and powerful politicians who competed to become privatisation's chief beneficiaries.

A new category of politically connected Malay, non-Malay, or often interethnic conglomerates arose and evolved into privileged oligopolies.[7] These conglomerates did not manufacture for the world market where success relied on technological innovation, research and development (R&D), and international competitiveness. Some operated in primary commodity production that could trace its competitiveness to colonial times, or in resource-based industries where local sourcing was an obvious strength. Most of the conglomerates congregated in banking, resource exploitation, construction, property and real estate, gaming, tourism, transport, utilities and services, and selected import-substituting industries. These were precisely sectors in which state policies and protection made the difference between success and failure. The conglomerates adopted an almost standard business strategy (although not necessarily in the following order of activity): deal in property and real estate; build up construction capacity; lobby for infrastructural and utility works; secure a banking or finance arm, or a brokerage licence; buy up plantations; diversify into tourism; and enter newly privatised areas such as telecommunications and social services.[8]

Conglomerate after conglomerate followed a predictable mode of expansion: having a 'flagship' in one area, they used takeovers, acquisitions, mergers, or applications to the state to build up a 'fleet' of companies. Their expansion drew financial support from two main sources: external borrowings, and capital raised on the Kuala Lumpur Stock Exchange (KLSE). Since the late 1980s, the financial system had been reformed to liberalise the capital market, support its growth, and introduce some competition (Mohamed Ariff 1996:328–31; *FT* 1995; Zainal et al. 1996:318). The liberalisation made it easier for the conglomerates to raise external loans or internal capital. Between 1988 and 1990, the private sector's medium-term and long-term external debt was less than RM5 billion but, thereafter, grew at an average annual rate of 33.8 per cent, or from RM6.723 billion in 1991 to RM38.650 billion in June 1997 (see table 6.3, below).

From 1992 to 1996, net inflows of portfolio investment funds ranged from RM5.345 billion (1995) to RM24.667 billion (1993) (table 6.4) and helped to boost KLSE's growth (table 6.5).

Semi-autarchy: the state against the market

By 1991, the balance of power had settled upon fairly cordial relations among the state, foreign capital, and the domestic conglomerates. NEP had been replaced with a National Development Plan (NDP) that emphasised 'growth' rather than 'restructuring', although NEP's ethnic considerations were retained in practice. State policies continued to privilege the MNCs and welcomed speculative capital that arrived as part of the international money market's investment in 'emerging markets'. The conglomerates con-stituted a more self-confident national capital and enjoyed the status of the vanguard of Malaysia Inc.. It took the 1997 East Asian financial crisis to threaten the survival of the conglomerates and to upset the state's relations with the market or, more precisely, with the international money market.

Table 6.3 Private sector medium-term and long-term debt, 1987–97

Year	Medium-term and long-term debt (RM billion)
1987	5.559
1988	4.855
1989	4.613
1990	4.943
1991	6.723
1992	10.471
1993	15.498
1994	24.203
1995	28.080
1996	33.474
1997 (June)	38.650
1997 (total)	61.089

Source: Bank Negara (February 1998:103)

Table 6.4 Portfolio investment in shares and corporate securities, 1991–97

Year	Receipts (RM million)	Payments (RM million)	Net inflow (RM million)
1991	13 645	15 524	−1 879
1992	33 324	26 481	6 843
1993	116 743	92 076	24 667
1994	129 953	115 521	14 432
1995	90 987	85 642	5 345
1996	127 590	120 899	6 691
1997 (to June)	69 797	78 279	−8 482
1997 (total)	113 212	138 675	−25 463

Source: Bank Negara (February 1998:117)

Table 6.5 Kuala Lumpur Stock Exchange, selected indicators, 1990–97

Year	Composite Index	Turnover (RM billion)	Number of listed companies	New share issues (RM billion)	Market capitalisation (RM billion)
1990	505.92	29.522	285	8.6496	131.66
1991	556.22	30.097	324	4.3914	161.29
1992	643.96	51.469	369	9.1815	245.82
1993	1 275.32	387.276	413	3.4326	619.64
1994	971.21	328.057	478	8.5479	508.85
1995	995.17	178.859	529	11.4376	565.63
1996	1 237.96	463.265	621	15.9244	806.77
1997	594.44	408.558	708	18.2247	375.80

Source: Bank Negara (February 1998:68–9, 72)

An understanding of the complexities of the origin and spread of the July 1997 crisis lies beyond the scope of this chapter (see Rodan, Hewison, and Robison, chapter 1, this volume; and Jayasuriya and Rosser, chapter 8, this volume). In Malaysia, the crisis depreciated the currency, reduced KLSE's market capitalisation, and sent the economy into recession. The ringgit fell from a peak exchange rate of RM2.493 to US$1 in April 1997 to its lowest rate of RM4.88 on 7 January 1998. KLSE's market capitalisation declined from RM806.77 billion in 1996 to RM375.80 billion in 1997, and to RM182 billion in September 1998. These currency and share-price falls spared few—whether they were businesses dependent on imports, middle-class punters who had channelled savings into KLSE, or students abroad whose state-borne or family-borne expenses were denominated in foreign exchange.

But the conglomerates seemed destined to collapse first and spectacularly. Their dependence on external borrowings and stock-market capitalisation had exposed them to bloated loan repayments, plunging asset values, and imminent insolvency. The financial system was imperilled as the banking sector's non-performing loans (NPLs) rose from 4 per cent in 1997 to 15.8

per cent in August 1998.[9] Worse, the money market and the International Monetary Fund (IMF) insisted that crisis management required the remedies of currency floats, higher interest rates, restrained liquidity, market liberalisation, financial-sector reform, and good governance. Any of these remedies, properly applied, would have been bitter medicine for the conglomerates. Taken together they would have been fatal to Malaysia Inc.: a free market would have governed a non-interventionist state!

Those who led the state were compelled to negotiate a new stance *vis-à-vis* the money market. Their initial attempts backfired. In August 1997 the KLSE banned the short-selling of a hundred index-linked stocks, hoping to arrest the share-price decline (Hiebert and Jayasankaran 1997). In September the regime announced a RM60-billion fund that would selectively buy stocks from Malaysians but not from foreigners (Hiebert and Jayasankaran 1997). Those measures were swiftly reversed or modified after share prices plunged as stocks were dumped by fund managers who feared being locked into a falling market. Then followed attempts by Deputy Prime Minister and Minister of Finance Anwar Ibrahim, and by Daim Zainuddin (appointed executive director of the newly established National Economic Action Council), to placate 'investor confidence'. The 1998 Budget, presented by Anwar in October, showed fiscal restraint, made budget cuts, and adopted some IMF-type structural adjustment measures.[10] In December, Anwar announced stricter austerity measures.[11] A month later, the Foreign Investment Committee changed corporate takeover rules. It permitted United Engineers Malaysia to acquire 32.6 per cent of its parent company, Renong Berhad (UMNO's holding company), without making a general offer to shareholders (Fox 1998; Lim Kit Siang 1998:45–7, 130–35; RAM 1998). Market dismay sent the ringgit and the Kuala Lumpur Composite Index to their lowest levels (Shameen 1998; Tripathi 1998). In March, Petronas took control of Malaysian International Shipping Corporation, and the latter acquired the shipping assets of Konsortium Perkapalan Berhad which was 51 per cent owned by Mahathir's son, Mirzan Mahathir (Subramaniam 1998:2–5). Further plans were announced to rescue debt-ridden banks and companies (Jayansankaran 1998; Shameen 1998). In response, capital flight became a capital strike: the market would not return if the state could not be disciplined.

On 1 September 1998, the state showed a desperate resolve. Bank Negara Malaysia (BNM) instituted 'exchange control mechanisms' that ended the free convertibility of the ringgit (*NST* 1998). The ringgit, trading at RM4.0960 to US$1 on that day, was pegged at RM3.800 to US$1 the next day. Holders of offshore ringgit accounts were given a month to repatriate their funds to Malaysia: beginning 1 October, the ringgit could not be traded overseas. For the money market, the most serious controls were those that prohibited non-resident correspondent banks and stockbroking firms from obtaining domestic credit facilities, and residents from obtaining ringgit credit facilities from non-resident individuals. Non-residents were required to deposit their ringgit securities with authorised depositories, and to hold the proceeds from the sale of such securities in external accounts for at least one year before converting them to foreign currency (*NST* 1998). BNM insisted that the controls would curb currency speculation but not affect the 'general convertibility of current account transactions' and 'free flows of direct foreign investment and repatriation of interest, profits and dividends and capital' (*NST* 1998). But had the state not acted, in the words of the acting governor of BNM, to 'bring the ringgit back into the country' (*NST* 1998), the currency would have collapsed. Instead, the capital controls halted the trend of capital flight, if only by trapping remaining foreign funds for a year, and even reversed it, if only by forcing the return of offshore ringgit funds. The currency peg gave domestic businesses and foreign direct investment a measure of stability by which to plan, contract, and manage.

Mahathir and Daim's political priority was to save strategic economic sectors and the conglomerates by domestic intiative. They had nothing better. Capital outflow for 1998 was RM21.7 billion (Mahani 2000:185). And capital was still on strike. Rating agencies (Moodys, and Standard and Poor's) downgraded Malaysia's credit-worthiness when the regime planned to issue new bonds, and the plan was abandoned. Thus the capital controls presaged a semi-autarchic regime of reflating the economy, relaxing monetary policy, and resuscitating local business.[12]

The state established three institutions to deal with the financial system. First, Danaharta, an 'asset management company', took charge of 'remov(ing) NPLs from the balance sheets of financial institutions', thus 'free[ing] the banks from the burden of debts that had prevented them from providing loans to their customers' (Mahani 2000:186). In 1999, Danaharta purchased RM45.5 billion in NPLs from banks and financial institutions.

Second, Danamodal, a 'Special-Purpose Vehicle', recapitalised the financial sector by giving 'credit injections' totalling RM7.59 billion to leading banks.

Third, the Corporate Debt Restructuring Committee (CDRC) managed sixty-seven debt-restructuring applications involving RM36.3 billion. CDRC's best-known and most controversial applications came from the UMNO-owned Renong, the state-owned Bank Bumiputera, and Sime Bank.

Recapitalisation largely depended on three sources: public funds (notably the Employees Provident Fund and Petronas's reserves), external loans (from Japan and the World Bank), and bonds that were eventually issued. BNM increased liquidity and facilitated bank-lending to the corporate sector. BNM steadily lowered the banks' statutory reserve requirements, from 13.5 per cent to 4 per cent between February and September 1998. From June to October, the base lending rate was reduced from 12.27 per cent to 6.79 per cent. The classification of NPLs was changed back from three months (March 1998) to six months (September 1998). BNM directed a higher target for bank-lending. It made credit more easily available for private consumption (and on more favourable terms than pre-July 1997 terms) to support key sectors, such as the automobile industry and the property market.

Conclusion: a new compromise

The state's recapitalisation, rescue, and reflation scarcely accorded with the reforms that the money market had demanded of Asian crisis-stricken regimes.[13] Yet, by late 1999, trade surpluses had built up the country's reserves and the economy had begun to emerge from recession. Share prices had recovered substantially with the support of domestic institutional funds. The regime claimed to have reversed 'the wrong turns taken during the initial stage of the crisis' (by Anwar, that is, in his last year as minister of Finance) (Malaysia, NEAC 1998). Critics attributed the end of recession to a regional recovery, and a fortuitous growth in exports. They insisted that the controls could not work in the long run, and that they harmed Malaysia's position as a destination of foreign investment.[14] But the capital controls had already been relaxed in Febuary 1999 to permit the repatriation of foreign funds subject to a graduated exit tax. Some investment funds (notably Templeton) were adamant about staying away from Malaysia even after September 1999 when the 'trapped' funds could exit without penalty. Still, the government and Petronas were able to raise bonds of US$1 billion and US$500 million respectively from the money market, albeit with Japanese backing and at punitive premiums. And Morgan Stanley Capital International reincorporated Malaysia in its index in early 2000 which paved the way for fund managers to re-enter KLSE. In short, the money market had reached a rapprochement with the state, despite disagreements in principle. Or, as an *Asian Wall Street Journal* editorial (23 June 1999) cajoled Mahathir, 'Now that the pressure of the Asian crisis has abated, it's time to declare victory and rejoin the global economy' (*AWSJ* 1999).

As with the 1985–86 recession, July 1997 brought a political crisis. Mahathir and Anwar had subtly differed over the waiver of UEM's take-over of Renong, rescue plans for several conglomerates, monetary policy, and the need for reform.[15] Anwar seemed to heed the sentiments of several non-unified constituencies: technocrats, small businesses, and part of the Malay and non-Malay middle-classes.[16] The Mahathir–Anwar differences represented a 'policy gridlock' (Saludo and Shameen 1998:44) that showed the narrowing of options available to the political leadership.[17] Mahathir himself despaired that market demands had changed from the management of economic fundamentals to acceptance of IMF conditionalities, forced closures of financial institutions, opening corporations to foreign owner-ship, and, ultimately, to changes of government (Spaeth 1998). It was over this last point that Anwar fell. At the June 1998 UMNO general assembly, his allies staged a half-hearted criticism of Mahathir that signalled Anwar's readiness to replace Mahathir—which was, at that time, the ill-disguised hope of the money market, international institutions, and media. On 2 September, Mahathir sacked Anwar from the government.[18] After that, Anwar was expelled from UMNO, prosecuted and convicted in two trials, and imprisoned for fifteen years. Rarely have 'technocratic policy choices' so skimpily covered their political substance! An account of the 'Anwar affair', the movement for reform (*reformasi*) that it sparked, and UMNO's unprecedented loss of Malay support in the November 1999 election belongs elsewhere (Khoo 2000). What is relevant here is that Barisan Nasional's electoral victory, however flawed, left policy direction in the hands of Mahathir and Daim, and has left unreformed the conglomerates allied to them.

Political economy, properly speaking, is not about state power and elite behaviour alone. But, given the concerns of this volume, one might argue that Malaysian political economy today rests on a tripartite division of power among the state, foreign capital, and domestic capital—as it has done for more than the past four decades. Not everything has been unchanged, of course. The state, which once governed the market in the mould of an East Asian developmental state, has had its scope of freedom curtailed. Foreign capital is not just the foreign direct investment welcomed by the state, but also a globalising speculative capital which the state regards with an unease that will not disappear before Mahathir departs from power. And domestic capital is not pre-NEP 'Chinese capital', but a conglomerate-dominated national capital the ranks of which have been filled, however imperfectly, by the Bumiputera Commercial and Industrial Community. If the past is a sound guide to the foreseeable future, the changes in relations among these three centres of power will continue to set the parameters of Malaysian political economy.

Notes

1 Originally *ICA* provisions applied to any manufacturing firm having at least RM100 000 in shareholder capital and employing a minimum of twenty-five workers.

2 Tengku Razaleigh Hamzah, who led the passage of the offending legislation, resigned as head of Petronas.

3 Commodity export earnings were RM37.6 billion in 1985, instead of the RM63.1 billion forecast by the economic planners after a three-fold increase in earnings in 1975–80 (Jomo, Khoo and Chang 1996:80).

4 Public debt rose from RM34.16 billion in 1981 to RM87.06 billion in 1986, because of NEP-based deficit spending, the HICOM projects, and the post-1985 Plaza Accord yen appreciation (Jomo, Khoo and Chang 1996:80).

5 Development expenditures were RM6.756 billion in 1985 and RM7.521 billion in 1986 compared with RM11.189 billion for 1982. Total private investment fell from RM13.3 billion in 1984 to RM10.1 billion in 1986, and foreign corporate investment fell from RM3.26 billion in 1982 to RM1.73 billion in 1985, and to RM1.26 billion in 1986 (Jomo, Khoo and Chang 1996:80–1).

6 See Jomo (1995:44–8) for a discussion of the cases of the North–South Highway, Sistem Televisyen (Malaysia) Berhad, Sports Toto, Pan Malaysian Sweeps, Totalisator Board of Malaysia, Jalan Kuching–Jalan Kepong Interchange, Indah Water Konsortium, Bakun Hydroelectric Project, Food Industries of Malaysia, and Peremba Berhad.

7 For excellent profiles and case studies of some of the conglomerates see Gomez (1990; 1994) and Searle (1999).

8 Gomez and Jomo (1997:179–80) observed of the 'contemporary conglomerate style of growth' that it has increasingly involved 'mergers, acquisitions and asset-stripping, with scant regard for relevant experience and expertise' and that it reflected 'the greater attention to financial accumulation rather than the difficult but ultimately necessary development of internationally competitive productive capacities'.

9 The official working definition of an NPL changed changed twice in 1998.

10 These included reducing federal government expenditure by 2 per cent, postponing 'mega projects', reducing the current-account deficit, reducing corporate tax by 2 per cent, limiting credit growth to 15 per cent by the end of 1998, and consolidating the prudential standards and regulations covering non-performing loans and liquidity within the banking system (Malaysia 1998: chapter 1).

11 Significant measures included: a reduction of the current-account deficit to 3 per cent of GNP in 1998, an 18 per cent reduction in federal government expen-

diture in 1998, a lowering of the projected 1998 growth rate to between 4 per cent and 5 per cent, deferment of non-strategic projects, stricter criteria for approvals of 'reverse investment', enhanced corporate information disclosure, and closer regulation of corporate restructuring (Malaysia 1998:chapter 1).

12 The government's policies are set out in the White Paper; see Malaysia, National Economic Council (1998), *Status of the Malaysian Economy*, <www.topspot.com/NEAC>.

13 Jorgen Borhnoft, outgoing president of the Malaysian International Chamber of Commerce and Industry, expressed MICCI's 'concern that there does not seem to be enough strong action against those people who were responsible for that massive spate of irresponsible borrowing, and just as irresponsible lending', mentioned that MICCI supported the capital controls of September 1999 'on the basis that they are clearly seen to be short-term measures', and urged 'serious structural adjustments' to some troubled companies (Dow Jones 1999).

14 See 'Capital controls erode', <www.freemalaysia.com/economic/loss_of_control.htm>, for a neo-liberal criticism of the capital controls.

15 For Anwar's views on issues related to the crisis and how to manage the ailing banking system, see Assif Shameen (1997). On interest rate levels, for example, Anwar defended BNM's 'stance to keep a tight rein on the monetary policy to maintain a stable exchange rate' whereas Mahathir opposed high effective lending rates (Toh 1998).

16 The BNM and Treasury technocrats offered economistic solutions—imposing budget cuts, reducing credit growth, raising interest rates, controlling inflation, and stabilising the ringgit. Small businesses, including small Malay businesses, were not indifferent to arguments for disciplining the conglomerates. Parts of the Malay and non-Malay middle-classes were offended by the 'cronyism, corruption and nepotism' associated with Malaysia Inc. (Spaeth 1998; RAM 1998).

17 From Mahathir: 'What the IMF wants us to do is to increase the interest rates, to reduce credit, to increase taxes. Now all of these things would bankrupt our companies . . . If you cannot top up, our regulations say you will be considered to have a non-performing loan after six months—the IMF says no, it must be three months. But in three months they cannot pay. But if we do not follow the IMF, the result will be a loss of confidence and down goes our currency.' (Quoted in *Time* 1998.)

18 A few days earlier, BNM governor, Ahmad Don, and his deputy, Fong Weng Phak, resigned in disagreement over Mahathir's decision to implement exchange controls (Keenan et al. 1998:11).

References

Abdul Rahman Embong (1995) 'Malaysian Middle Classes: Some Preliminary Observations', *Jurnal Antropologi dan Sosiologi*, 22:31–54.

Adam, Christopher and William Cavendish (1995a) 'Background', in K.S. Jomo (ed.) *Privatizing Malaysia: Rents, Rhetoric, Realities*, Boulder, Colorado: Westview Press, pp 11–41.

Adam, Christopher and William Cavendish (1995b) 'Early Privatizations', in K.S. Jomo (ed.) *Privatizing Malaysia: Rents, Rhetoric, Realities*, Boulder, Colorado: Westview Press, pp 98–137.

Alatas, Syed Hussein (1977) *The Myth of the Lazy Native*, London: Frank Cass.

Asian Wall Street Journal (AWSJ) (1999) 'Malaysia Needs to End Isolation', editorial 23 June.

Assif Shameen (1997) 'A Difference in Style', *Asiaweek*, 19 December 1997, p. 25.

AWSJ, see *Asian Wall Street Journal (AWSJ)*.

Bank Negara (1998) *Monthly Statistical Bulletin*, various issues.

Crouch, Harold (1980) 'The UMNO Crisis: 1975–1977', in Harold Crouch, Lee Kam Hing and Michael Ong (eds) *Malaysian Politics and the 1978 Election*, Kuala Lumpur: Oxford University Press, pp 11–36.

Dow Jones (1999) 'Foreign investors want more reform: MICCI', 15 June 1999, <http://freemalaysia.com/reformasi_investors.htm>.

Financial Times (FT) (1995) *Banking in the Far East 1995*, pp 195–201, London: FT Financial Publishing.

Fox, Justin (1998) 'The Great Emerging Markets Rip-Off', *Fortune*, 11 May 1998, <www.pathfinder.com/fortune/1998/980511/gre.html>.

FT, see *Financial Times (FT)*.

Gomez, Edmund Terence (1990) *UMNO's Corporate Investments*, Kuala Lumpur: Forum.

Gomez, Edmund Terence (1994) *Political Business: Corporate Involvement of Malaysian Political Parties*, Townsville, Queensland, James Cook University of North Queensland, Centre for South-East Asian Studies.

Gomez, Edmund Terence and K. S. Jomo (1997) *Malaysia's Political Economy: Politics, Patronage and Profits*, Cambridge: Cambridge University Press.

Grace, Brewster (1976), 'The Politics of Distribution in Malaysia', *American Universities Field Staff Report*, 24, 9.

Heng Pek Koon (1992) 'The Chinese Business Elite of Malaysia', in Ruth McVey (ed.) *Southeast Asian Capitalists*, Ithaca: Cornell University Southeast Asia Program, pp 127–44.

Hiebert, Murray and S. Jayasankaran (1997) 'What Next?', *Far Eastern Economic Review*, 18 September:62–64.

Husin Ali, Syed (1975) *Malay Peasant Society and Leadership*, Kuala Lumpur: Oxford University Press.

Jayansankaran, S. (1998) 'Art of the Bail', *Far Eastern Economic Review*, 30 April:62–3.

Jesudason, James V. (1989) *Ethnicity and the Economy: The State, Chinese Business, and Multinationals in Malaysia*, Singapore: Oxford University Press.

Jomo K.S. (1988) *A Question of Class: Capital, the State, and Uneven Development in Malaya*, Singapore, Oxford University Press.

Jomo K.S. (1990) *Growth and Structural Change in the Malaysian Economy*, London: Macmillan.

Jomo K.S. (1995) 'Overview', in K.S. Jomo (ed.) *Privatizing Malaysia: Rents, Rhetoric, Realities*, Boulder, Colorado: Westview Press, pp 42–60.

Jomo K.S., Khoo Boo Teik and Chang Yii Tan (1996) 'Vision, Policy, and Governance in Malaysia', in Leila Frischtak and Izak Atiyas *Governance, Leadership, and Communication: Building Constituencies for Economic Reform*, Washington: World Bank, pp 65–89.

Keenan, Faith et al. (1998) 'Desperate Measures', *Far Eastern Economic Review*, 10 September:11–12.

Khoo Boo Teik (1995) *Paradoxes of Mahathirism: An Intellectual Biography of Mahathir Mohamad*, Kuala Lumpur: Oxford University Press.

Khoo Boo Teik (2000) 'Unfinished Crises: Malaysian Politics in 1999', in *Southeast Asian Affairs 2000*, Singapore, Institute of Southeast Asian Studies, pp 165–83.

Khoo Khay Jin (1992) 'The Grand Vision: Mahathir and Modernisation', in Joel S. Kahn and Francis Loh Kok Wah (eds) *Fragmented Vision: Culture And Politics In Contemporary Malaysia*, Sydney: Allen and Unwin, pp 44–76.

Lim Kit Siang (1998) *Economic and Financial Crisis*, Petaling Jaya, Democratic Action Party.

Lim Teck Ghee (1984) 'British Colonial Administration and the "Ethnic Division of Labour" in Malaya', *Kajian Malaysia*, 2, 2 (December):28–66.

Machado, Kit (1989–90) 'Japanese Transnational Corporations in Malaysia's State Sponsored Heavy Industrialization Drive: The HICOM Automobile and Steel Projects', *Pacific Affairs*, 62:504–31.

Machado, Kit (1994) 'Proton and Malaysia's Motor Vehicle Industry: National Industrial Policies and Japanese Regional Production Strategies', in K.S. Jomo (ed.) *Japan and Malaysian Development: In the Shadow of the Rising Sun*, London: Routledge, pp 291–325.

Mahani Zainal Abidin (2000) 'Malaysia's Alternative Approach to Crisis Management', in *Southeast Asian Affairs 2000*, Singapore, Institute of Southeast Asian Studies, pp 184–99.

Mahathir Mohamad (1970) *The Malay Dilemma*, Singapore: Donald Moore.

Mahathir Mohamad (1991) 'Malaysia: The Way Forward', *New Straits Times*, 2 March.

Malaysia (1965) *First Malaysia Plan 1966–1970*, Kuala Lumpur.

Malaysia (1971) *Second Malaysia Plan 1971–1975*, Kuala Lumpur.

Malaysia (1976) *Third Malaysia Plan 1976–1980*, Kuala Lumpur.

Malaysia (1981) *Fourth Malaysia Plan 1981–1985*, Kuala Lumpur.

Malaysia (1998) *National Economic Recovery Plan: Agenda For Action*, Kuala Lumpur.

Malaysia (1999) *Kajian Separuh Penggal Rancangan Malaysia Ketujuh 1996–2000* (Mid-term Review of the Seventh Malaysia Plan 1996–2000), Kuala Lumpur.

Malaysia, National Economic Action Council (NEAC) (1998), *White Paper: Status of the Malaysian Economy*, <www.topspot.com/NEAC/>, Box 1, accessed 2001.

Mehmet, Ozay (1986) *Development in Malaysia: Poverty, Wealth and Trusteeship*, London: Croom Helm.

Mohamed Ariff (1996) 'Effects of Financial Liberalization on Four Southeast Asian Financial Markets, 1973–94', *ASEAN Economic Bulletin*, 12, 3 (March):325–38.

NEAC, see Malaysia, National Economic Action Council (NEAC).

New Straits Times (NST) (1998) 'Moves are intended to insulate Malaysia from further instability', 2 September.

NST, see *New Straits Times (NST)*.

Parti Gerakan Rakyat Malaysia (1984) *The National Economic Policy—1990 and Beyond*, Kuala Lumpur.

Puthucheary, James (1960) *Ownership and Control in the Malayan Economy*, Singapore: Eastern Universities Press.

RAM (1998) 'The NEAC: Accountability Subverted', *Aliran Monthly*, (18)2:2–5.

Robison, Richard, Garry Rodan and Kevin Hewison (1997) 'Introduction', in Garry Rodan, Kevin Hewison and Richard Robison *The Political Economy of South-East Asia: An Introduction*, Melbourne: Oxford University Press, pp 1–28.

Rugayah Mohamed (1995) 'Public Enterprises', in K.S. Jomo (ed.) *Privatizing Malaysia: Rents, Rhetoric, Realities*, Boulder, Colorado: Westview Press, pp 63–80.

Saludo, Richard and Shameen, Assif (1998) 'How Much Longer?', *Asiaweek*, July 17:36–44.

Searle, Peter (1999) *The Riddle of Malaysian Capitalism: Rent-seekers or real capitalists?*, St Leonards NSW: Allen and Unwin.

Shameen, Assif (1998) 'The Bailout Business', *Asiaweek*, 27 March, 30–1.

Sieh Lee Mei Ling (1992) 'The Transformation of Malaysian Business Groups', in Ruth McVey (ed.) *Southeast Asian Capitalists*, Ithaca: Cornell University Southeast Asia Program, pp 103–26.

Spaeth, Andrew (1998) 'Broken Dreams', *Time* , 15 June:24–8.

Subramaniam Pillay (1998) 'Bailout Blues', *Aliran Monthly*, 18, 3:2–5.

Time (1998), 15 June 1998.

Todd, Patricia and K.S. Jomo (1994) *Trade Unions and the State in Peninsular Malaysia*, Kuala Lumpur: Oxford University Press.

Toh, Eddie (1998) 'Cutting rates will put M'sian financial system at risk: Anwar', *Business Times* (Singapore), 2 June 1998.

Tripathi, Salil (1998) 'Savings at Risk', *Far Eastern Economic Review*, 30 April: 60–1.

von Vorys, Karl (1975) *Democracy Without Consensus: Communalism and Political Stability in Malaysia*, Princeton: Princeton University Press.

World Bank (1993) *The East Asian Miracle: Economic Growth and Public Policy*, New York, Oxford University Press.

Zainal Aznam Yusof, Awang Adek Husin, Ismail Alowi, Lim Chee Sing and Sukhdave Singh (1996) 'Financial Reform in Malaysia', in Gerard Caprio et al. (eds) *Financial Reform: Theory and Experience*, Cambridge: Cambridge University Press, pp 276–320.

7

Vietnam: The Transition from Central Planning

Melanie Beresford

Introduction

Vietnam is unique among the countries covered in this book in that it is in the process of transition from central planning to a market economy. To understand the special characteristics of this transition we need first to comprehend the nature of the socialist economy as it developed between 1954 and 1980—the social basis of the state and the way in which interests of different groupings in society were represented within the state apparatus. This is what gave Vietnamese socialism its particular institutions and economic structure. During the 1980s these began to undergo dramatic changes, partly as a result of spontaneous developments at the grassroots level and partly as a result of state efforts to manage the process. The structure and institutions that Vietnam has today can be understood only as the outcome of a protracted struggle among various interests over the shape of the socialist state, a struggle that necessitated constant reform and has ultimately led to the demise of the planned economy. As one Vietnamese intellectual put it to the present author: 'The system was patched and repaired so many times that it was eventually repaired out of existence. It became something quite different.' The relations of power that developed throughout this process of struggle and reform are evident in the existing institutions and structure that give the Vietnamese market economy its peculiar characteristics today. Although the ultimate result of the current market-oriented transformation might be some form of capitalism, Vietnam is still ruled by a communist party, the distinction between public and private property remains blurred, and there is continuing pressure from parts of the state to defend the rights of workers and poor peasants. This means that the path is still unclear and likely to be characterised by considerable social and political tensions in future.

This chapter first gives a brief outline of the division of the country between north and south during 1954–75 and the attempts to construct rival socialist and capitalist economies in the two halves. (More detail can be found in Beresford 1988.) There follows a discussion of the socialist reality in northern Vietnam focusing on the role that economic interest played in creating the north's economic structure and institutions and the forces generating the transition process, particularly after reunification of the country in 1976. The third section looks at developments since the Sixth Communist Party Congress in 1986 at which the historic decision to institute *Doi Moi* (Renovation) was taken. It focuses on the interaction between interests and policy in promoting (or obstructing) change, and discusses the ways in which contending social forces organise and find expression— within the framework of a communist party state. The final section discusses the major issues in contention today.

Historical background

For two decades, from 1954 to 1975, two separate regimes claimed sovereignty over the whole of Vietnam. The Democratic Republic of Vietnam (DRV) was based in the northern half of the country with its capital at Hanoi. It had been established by an indigenous nationalist movement (the Viet Minh), led by the Vietnamese Communist Party, on 2 September 1945 following the surrender of Japan. It had fought and won a nine-year war against France's attempt to retake its former colony, a war that culminated in the humiliating French defeat at Dien Bien Phu in 1954. During this war, the Viet Minh had extended its control over nearly three-quarters of the country, although the French and some anti-communist groups had managed to retain the main cities and some of the rural areas, particularly in the far south. The inability of the communist-led movement to win decisively in the south provided the basis for the formation of an alternative regime, initially led by the Emperor Bao Dai who was favoured by the French to promote their own interests. As the French war effort faltered, however, the USA increasingly took over the role of preserving Western interests in Indochina and, by 1955, had installed in Saigon a political leader, Ngo Dinh Diem, less subservient to the French. From that year the southern regime became known as the Republic of Vietnam (RVN).

During 1954 an international conference at Geneva had temporarily divided the country at the 17th parallel with an agreement to hold reunifying elections in 1956. Knowing that the Viet Minh would have won easily, the Diem regime and its US supporters refused to hold these elections. Between 1956 and 1959 the struggle between the regime and the southern Viet Minh gradually escalated until, in 1960, the DRV officially formed the National Front for the Liberation of Southern Vietnam (NLF) and began a war to reunify the country. US combat troops were introduced in 1964, and systematic bombing of the DRV by the US Air Force began in 1965 and lasted until 1968. By 1969 the USA had more than half-a-million troops in the country and yet it had become clear by then that no end was in sight. For all the expense and effort that the USA had put into defending the RVN, the communists' Tet (Vietnamese New Year) offensive in early 1968 had driven home the lesson that US war strategies were not working. In the USA itself the war became increasingly unacceptable politically and, by 1973, the last US troops were withdrawn. Within two years the RVN collapsed completely and the DRV armed forces entered Saigon on 30 April 1975.

The economic policies pursued in the two halves of Vietnam during 1954–80 reflected the different social bases of the regimes. In the case of the DRV its economic structure was initially developed in response to the needs of the peasantry who constituted more than 80 per cent of the population, although their interests and those of the state were later to diverge in ways that, as we shall see, led to pressure for reform. The RVN, on the other hand, drew its support from a much narrower base: large landowners, the small indigenous capitalist class, and the bureaucrats.

Popular support for the DRV in the northern half of the country was consolidated during the 1950s by agrarian reform policies, beginning with rent-reduction campaigns from 1951 and culminating in land reform during 1954–56 that saw 810 000 hectares redistributed from landlords and rich peasants to poor and middle peasants (White 1983; Moise 1976). However, a push from the poorest farmers and more radical sections of the party spilled over into the collectivisation of agriculture, commencing as a spontaneous movement during 1957–58 and acquiring an element of compulsion during 1959. Collectivisation had advantages for poor peasants because, even after land distribution, plot sizes in the crowded northern river deltas were often too small to provide an adequate subsistence, let alone surpluses. Moreover, poor peasants lacked draught animals and equipment, and access to irrigation water, and therefore faced potential economic insecurity. Collectivisation guaranteed access to these, as well as providing minimum standards of nutrition, health, education, and welfare. From the point of view of the state, collectives were seen as a means of increasing agricultural productivity (through consolidation of fields, rehabilitation and construction of large-scale irrigation works, more equal distribution of equipment and animals, and improvements in social security and living standards). This, in turn, provided agricultural surpluses to finance industrialisation. Support for collectivisation also came from other socialist countries, notably China.

Cooperatives were therefore established in the rural economy in three stages (basically following the Chinese model of the mid 1950s), beginning with the formation of production solidarity groups, then graduating to lower-level cooperatives (in which land and equipment were collectivised and a small rent paid to their former owners) and, finally, to higher-level cooperatives in which all income was distributed according to a system of workpoints (Beresford 1988:130; Gordon 1981). By the mid 1960s virtually the whole rural population had been incorporated into these higher-level cooperatives.

Industrial development in the north was to be carried out through a series of five-year plans (FYPs). Following nationalisation of the remaining French-owned plants, the first FYP was instituted for 1961–65 and resulted in the establishment of much new industrial capacity which, in turn, was brought progressively under the control of Soviet-type planning institutions. Output targets and prices, input supplies, domestic wholesale and retail trade, and imports and exports were determined by central government (usually via the intermediary of provincial and district authorities). The planners intended to establish a vertically integrated economy in which individual production units had no commercial contact with each other, exchanging goods only with higher levels which, in turn, distributed them according to plan. The State Bank of Vietnam was responsible for recording the value of transactions against the accounts of individual units and transferring revenue among these accounts and the state budget, thus eliminating the need for cash.

Renewed warfare against the US-backed southern regime created many difficulties for this newly created socialist economy. However, as we shall see below, the economic system itself was responsible for many of the problems besetting the DRV during the 1960s and 1970s. An overwhelming focus of the authorities on fighting war, their ability to rely on extensive aid from the Soviet Union and China, as well as strong popular support for the objective of national reunification, meant that many of these economic problems were not tackled, or even regarded seriously, until much later. Indeed most in authority genuinely believed that the wartime emergency called for stronger centralisation and planning, rather than less. In the meantime, there occurred numerous (mostly illegal) experiments by individual households and production units aimed at overcoming the day-to-day difficulties imposed by the system. These experiments ultimately were to provide the foundations of the reformed economy.

Meanwhile the southern half of the country continued to develop a capitalist economy. Although the narrow political base of the RVN regime ensured that the demands of the peasantry were largely ignored in areas under its control during the 1960s, land reforms were carried out by the NLF. Land ownership remained a contested issue until 1970–73 when the RVN decided to distribute 'land to the tiller'—effectively legitimising occupancy under NLF reforms and finally resolving a problem that had led the majority of farmers to give their support to the communists. This reform came too late to save the RVN from military defeat, but it did have the effect of boosting agricultural production in the fertile Mekong River delta region as, with the ending of landlord domination, farmers gained control over their surplus output (Beresford 1989:66–7, 101–3; Ngo Vinh Long 1984).

During the war, US economic aid flowed into the RVN, allowing high levels of consumption of imported goods. Under normal circumstances, these might have boosted economic growth. However, speculative investments were encouraged by insecurity and inflation while productive investment suffered. Commerce, services, and bureaucracy expanded while the economy as a whole stagnated. Corruption became a serious problem in both civilian and military life. Refugees flooded into the main cities to escape the devastation of US bombing and chemical warfare, leading to the growth of slums and a large unemployed or semi-employed population. The complete withdrawal of US aid in 1975 thus provided the basis for a serious crisis of the southern economy, although the reformed agricultural sector also implied the possibility of a fairly rapid recovery. This recovery failed to materialise—largely because, after the official reunification in 1976, the DRV attempted to impose its own economic model on the south.

Vietnamese socialist economy and pressure for reform

Tensions over agrarian policy were already evident during the land reform of the 1950s, as many in the party leadership would have preferred a reform less damaging to the interests of rich and upper 'middle-class' peasants whom they regarded as more productive and likely to foster rapid agricultural development. A 'Rectification Campaign' carried out in 1956 went some way to redressing this problem, but tensions between poor and rich peasants, and among party factions, remained. Although subsequent collectivisation appears to have had an impact in reducing tension (Elliott 1974; White 1983), it proceeded throughout the 1960s against some resistance from local forces. During 1960–63 the number of peasant households belonging to cooperatives actually fell, while there was an apparent lack of

interest from upper 'middle' and rich peasants,[1] who provided a high proportion of both party membership and cooperative management boards
(Gordon 1981:30–5). The move towards establishing higher-level cooperatives was renewed in 1964, but Adam Fforde's (1989) detailed study of the
cooperative management system during the 1970s shows that few actually
functioned as the government intended. Instead, a wide variety of arrangements existed, including extension of household plots beyond the 5 per cent
of land officially permitted (often in favour of cadres and their families and
friends) and refusal to issue plan targets by cooperative managers. Like
other socialist economies, Vietnam developed an 'outside' (in the
Vietnamese terminology) or second economy that, as we shall see, both fed
on the socialist structures and tended to undermine them in the long run.

The basic problem with cooperatives, not only in the north but also in the
south after 1976, lay in the lack of incentives for increased output and productivity. At the root of this problem was the official pricing system which
offered low procurement prices to cooperatives to maintain low wages in
the urban sector and to boost industrial profits of state-owned enterprises.
Market prices for both agricultural produce and industrial goods, on the
other hand, tended to be above the official prices from 1960 onwards,
encouraging the diversion of state-supplied goods on to black markets and
leading farmers to devote more time and effort to production on their
household plots, the output from which could be legally sold on the free
market. Estimates of peasant income earned from these plots rose from
approximately 40 per cent in the 1960s to 60–70 per cent by the late 1970s.
Because those with priority access to state-supplied goods were generally
party members and officials, the system created opportunities for capital
accumulation and new class divisions within the countryside. It is important to note here that it was their position within the cooperative structures
that gave cadres such opportunities to profit from outside activities, and
this is one of the key factors leading to widespread perception of the unfairness of the system.

Distribution of income within the cooperatives also created problems for
increasing output and productivity. It was, in a formal sense, highly
egalitarian, because minimum supplies of food and security of land tenure
were guaranteed, and health, education, and other welfare facilities (such as
child care) were also provided to all members. The advantages to poor
peasants and to women were enormous: life expectancy, infant mortality,
literacy levels, and other social indicators were all better than for other
countries at similar per capita income levels (Beresford 1995b). But these
benefits came at a high cost, as cooperative production stagnated in the
long term and egalitarianism became a case of 'shared poverty' rather than

rising overall living standards. Moreover, as demands from the government for procurement to feed urban cadres and industry rose, the residual output available for distribution to cooperative members declined, creating further incentives to reduce labour in cooperative fields and to increase that applied to household plots and to commercial activities outside the plan (Beresford 1989; Fforde 1989).

Conflict of interest was, therefore, very apparent in the actual functioning of the cooperative system in Vietnamese agriculture. The needs of the poorest families for a more equal distribution differed from those of households most able to benefit from outside activities, as did those of cooperative farmers as a whole and those of the government. Pressure on lower-level and middle-level cadres tended to increase as, on one side, farmers' demands to reform the cooperative system increased and, on the other side, the centre's procurement requirements also rose.[2] These contradictions only sharpened after reunification, particularly in the Mekong delta–Ho Chi Minh City region where the market economy was firmly entrenched. The so-called 'middle' peasants, the chief beneficiaries of land reforms in the 1960s and 1970s, stood to lose substantially through the collectivisation campaign of 1977–78. Their passive resistance meant that available surpluses dropped sharply (Beresford 1989:113–15) and that black market activities intensified, despite the massive government clampdown on mainly ethnic Chinese businesses during 1978.

As Vietnam entered the 1980s, the scope of 'outside' economic activity in the rural areas continued to increase, and a powerful coalition of rural interests in favour of system reform began to emerge. Southern provincial politicians, in particular, fearing the loss of their peasant support base, became vocal spokespersons for change within the party and government apparatus. They found allies among the generation who had earlier argued that collectivisation in the north had gone too far.

A similar state of affairs existed within the state-owned industrial enterprise system. This had expanded rapidly following implementation of the First FYP (1961–65), but problems were already emerging (Fforde and Paine 1987) before US wartime operations destroyed much of the capacity created. High investment rates in industrial capacity, particularly in heavy industry projects with long lead times, created demand for resources that could not be met from the existing stream of output (Beresford 1989). Although the resulting shortages were, to some extent, alleviated by foreign aid, they were never eliminated altogether, and the Vietnamese economy, like other socialist economies, became characterised by chronic disequilibrium between supply and demand. Moreover, shortages within the planned sector were aggravated by the difference between official and market prices which diverted resources to the outside economy (Fforde and Paine 1987).

In the debates over reform of the economic system that began in the 1970s, two basic positions can be identified. The first essentially accepted the ability of planners to achieve an equilibrium growth path within the framework of central planning and, in general, opposed high rates of capital construction and insufficient attention to the real financial and resource capacity of the economy. The second located the real problem of the planned economy precisely in the attempt to achieve equilibrium by *administrative* means, and pointed to a built-in tendency to disequilibrium that could not be overcome, due to the existence of real conflicts of interest. Once established, the shortage economy provides incentives to managers and planners that ensure that the tendency to disequilibrium is exacerbated rather than overcome. (See Beresford 1989, and de Vylder and Fforde 1988, for a fuller discussion.)

In reality, large capital construction projects involved vested interests among the ministries, managers, and employees engaged on them, so that simply scrapping them became politically difficult. Although the use of market forces and 'loose' planning norms to allow more local initiative could alleviate the shortages, they threatened the positions of those in the central ministries whose control over resources was reduced and who exerted pressure to recentralise control. Market forces, on the other hand, allowed for the accumulation of capital independently of the centre. Such capital could be private, especially in the farm and retail sectors, but was more likely to take the form of 'corporatisation' (that is, the separation of legal ownership and control) in the state-owned enterprise (SOE) sector (Beresford 1993). The ability of the planning authorities to reimpose centralisation after a period of decentralisation, then, depended crucially on its power *vis-à-vis* such relatively independent *loci* of capital accumulation.[3] In my view, the emergence of such capital accumulation in the periphery in Vietnam introduced not only a systemic *tendency* towards breakdown of the planned economy, but also structural changes that laid the foundations for a relatively successful transition to a market economy.

In the political sphere, the ability and willingness of the state to reimpose centralisation determined whether the planned economy continued to exist in a recognisable form, or whether an irreversible transition was to take place. The planned economy in Vietnam was not a straightforward 'top–down' system, but one in which the plan emerged as the outcome of a process of negotiation among groups with differing, often conflicting, interests. The most important interests that can be identified here are: first, that of central authorities whose power derived from the planning system and whose control was threatened by outside activity; second, that of local authorities and enterprise managers (including cooperative managers) who strove to minimise surplus extraction to higher levels and to accumulate capital within their own sphere; and, third, those who drew little benefit from the planning system due to lack of access to the kinship and/or party networks that held local power.

The process of negotiation among the contending factions and interests led to a balance of power that began to shift in the late 1970s and early 1980s. During 1979–81 a number of key reforms was pushed through, essentially legalising some outside activity by individuals and production units. The earliest reforms, in the second half of 1979, allowed limited autonomy to farmers and enterprises. More important were the introduction in 1981 of output contracts in agriculture that permitted allocation of cooperative land to production groups and sale of surplus product on the free market, and the so-called 'Three Plan System' in industry that, for the first time, sanctioned production for the market by SOEs. In the same year, prices and wages were brought closer to market prices. By early 1982 a recovery was under way and party fears of the re-emergence of capitalism were renewed, causing the party to take measures against further private-sector development, including a renewed attempt to collectivise southern agriculture. However, the structural changes that had taken place after the second half of the 1970s meant that these attempts were only partially successful, if at all. The outside economy continued to expand whereas the difficulties of the planned sector continued, not least because, in reality, the bulk of state investment still flowed into large-scale heavy industry projects. Shortages in the planned sector were exacerbated by the attempted recentralisation, leading to higher inflation in the increasingly monetised outside economy (176 per cent in 1984, according to World Bank 1994:131). Moreover, the necessity to subsidise unprofitable SOEs contributed to high budget deficits, inability to finance the external debt, and renewed stagnation in the agricultural sector.

In face of the new crisis, in September 1985 the government introduced a further round of reforms aimed at price liberalisation, ending the ration system and monetisation of wages for state employees. By that time almost all of the southern and central provinces, plus a number in the north, were refusing to implement plan directives and/or pressuring the government for wider reform. However, the impact of this reform was blunted by several different political pressures on the government at this time. The southern provinces were already at a more advanced stage of commercialisation, with a correspondingly higher cost of living, and demanded big wage increases for government workers that resulted in large budget deficits.

SOE directors, especially those in the older, less-efficient northern sector, demanded retention of the two-price system for industrial inputs.[4] Within three months of the reform's implementation Vietnam had galloping inflation,[5] and the reform was partially reversed. Nevertheless, a further substantial shift towards commercialisation of the economy had been achieved.

Doi Moi (Renovation)

By 1986 the Vietnamese socialist economy had already undergone major structural and institutional changes towards the formation of a market economy. Official statistics on this period do not reflect these changes because they continued to measure only the planned economic sector. However, other evidence indicates strongly that transactions taking place outside the scope of the plan were of increasing importance (de Vylder and Fforde 1988). Not only was a large proportion of agricultural output being marketed, but also there were signs of a rudimentary capital market as SOEs sought ways to utilise capital accumulated through non-plan activities. Under the impact of these developments, and the fact that the rationing system had largely disappeared after the 1985 reform, political pressure increased for further changes to the system.

Not enough research is available for a full understanding of how the Vietnamese political system works and how pressures from interests associated with increased commercialisation of the economy are translated into policy changes at the top.[6] The major reason for this has been the essentially closed character of this system to outsiders, and the concern of party leaders from earliest times to present a unified front to the rest of the world. We therefore have little understanding of how political positions are achieved or, in other words, how the leadership gains its political constituency. What we do know is that several of the top leaders in Vietnam have held different political positions in relation to key issues, and that alliances within the leadership have often been quite fluid (Beresford 1988:88–90). This suggests that, far from being communist ideologues, the Vietnamese leaders have behaved much like politicians elsewhere, and that their power is contingent upon building coalitions of interest that provide support for particular sets of policies. It follows from this that, if the structure of interests changes substantially, the position of political leaders on questions such as reform must change accordingly. Members of key party organisations who continue to reflect the dominant interests of the old system are likely to be replaced by representatives of the new dominant interest groups.

This appears to be what happened at the Sixth Party Congress in December 1986. Membership changed in favour of a younger generation with less experience of revolutionary activity and more versed in the problems of managing the socialist economy, particularly at the local level. There was also increased representation in the highest positions of those with long experience in the south (Beresford 1988:113), a change that seems to reflect recognition of the relative success of the more commercialised southern region in overcoming the constraints of the planning system. Moreover, the emergence of reformers at the top in turn opened the way for many more junior cadres to express their views freely.

Doi Moi in the economic sphere

The 1986 congress was a turning point for the reform process in the sense that it took a conscious decision to build a market economy in Vietnam, although this was (and still is) portrayed by the party leadership as 'a socialist market' or 'a market economy under state guidance'.

By the late 1980s the planned economy had disintegrated to the extent that there was no longer sufficient strength of interest in attempting to make it work. Even within the SOE sector, which had strongly resisted the proposal to implement market prices in 1985, there were differences of interest between those enterprises that continued to depend heavily on price subsidies and those in which the majority of their activities were by now market oriented. The upsurge of inflation during 1986 forced state sector workers, unable to survive on their official wages, to devote more and more time and effort to outside activities. Productivity in the SOEs declined, requiring higher levels of subsidy and generating yet more inflation through rising budget deficits. Although Soviet aid continued to be available in the late 1980s, the rise of Gorbachev to power and the introduction of *perestroika* (restructuring) in the Soviet Union in 1986 meant that aid would no longer be provided on the same generous terms as before (being finally cut in 1991). The Vietnamese state was therefore faced with a looming fiscal crisis that convinced even the highest levels that further reform was their only option. Whereas reform before 1986 was largely spontaneous in character, with the state attempting to manage (sometimes even reverse) the process of change, it is only after 1986 that we can speak of the state playing a role in pushing the pace of change.

The reforms of the late 1980s are widely regarded in the Western literature as the only ones of importance. Indeed a number of authors has described the reform package of 1989, in particular, as constituting a 'Big Bang' or 'shock therapy' type of reform that introduced a market economy for the first time in Vietnam. What we have seen in this chapter, however, is that a market economy had been developing in Vietnam since the late 1970s. To understand the relative success of these reforms in Vietnam (as compared, for example, with the results of 'shock therapy' in some East European countries or in the Soviet Union), it is important to understand that, to all intents and purposes, the Vietnamese economy by the late 1980s was already a market economy. Policies designed for a market economy are more likely to work in a market economy than in a planned economy.

The first major reform of *Doi Moi* was the Foreign Investment Law, passed in December 1987 and implemented in the following year. By South-East Asian standards, this was a very liberal law, allowing for 100 per cent foreign ownership and profit repatriation, significant tax holidays, and concessions for enterprises investing in a number of priority areas (including exports, consumer goods, technology transfer, and processing of local raw materials). The resulting inflow was small at first but, by 1996, it amounted to US$8.5 billion in new project commitments per annum, and constituted approximately a third of Vietnam's total investment effort. The majority was in joint ventures with Vietnamese partners, mostly SOEs. Moreover, in the 1990s, Western aid to Vietnam began to increase rapidly, and this brought with it a stream of foreign contractors. Foreign companies and aid donors now constitute an important interest group applying pressure for further market-oriented reforms and for changes to the legal system to bring it into line with international norms.

In March 1988, Resolution 10 of the politburo effectively led to decollectivisation in the Vietnamese countryside. Although many cooperatives continued to exist, their functions were severely curtailed and, most importantly, they were no longer given a role in production. Instead land was distributed for a period of fifteen years (or fifty years in cases of perennial crops) to households who were put in charge of all decisions relating to production and investment. Government procurement contracts were abolished and all output could be sold at market prices, whether to the government or to the open market. This reform had very positive effects on agricultural output and, in 1989, Vietnam shifted from being a net importer of rice to being the world's third-largest exporter (although, as we shall see below, the immediate increase in supply was also related to the success of anti-inflation measures in that year). However, a number of the more useful functions provided by the cooperatives was adversely affected. In particular, householders were reluctant to make contributions to cooperative health and welfare facilities, and the cooperative maintenance of irrigation schemes also tended to suffer. Responsibility for provision of these, as well as for other local infrastructure, has shifted to the commune (village) and district levels of government—yet these also suffered severe cuts in revenue after 1989. The impact of these changes has inevitably fallen hardest on the poor. However, as overall living standards have risen, the potential for rural class conflict has been blunted at the same time.

During 1989 the government abolished official prices (except for a handful of government monopolies), floated the exchange rate, and introduced positive real interest rates in the banking system. The first two of these mean that all prices, including the exchange rate against foreign currencies, are now basically market prices, although the state bank does control the exchange rate through its market operations. Direct subsidies from the state budget to SOEs were effectively ended. Positive real interest rates,[7] temporarily reversed in 1990–91, were used to encourage savings, halt the 'dollarisation' of the economy,[8] eliminate SOE subsidies via cheap credit provision, halt the growth of the budget deficit, and bring inflation under control.

The impact of this package on the economy was dramatic. Inflation was reduced from 308 per cent per annum in 1988 to only 36 per cent in 1990 (World Bank 1994:131), and the domestic savings ratio improved. With the reduction in inflation, much of the incentive to hoard goods for speculative purposes disappeared and there was an increase in supply (particularly of rice) so that shortages were eliminated. Industrial output has also risen rapidly since the reform. At the same time, many of the least-profitable SOEs closed their doors—the number of enterprises still operating had been halved by 1993—and there was a significant reduction in industrial employment as formerly subsidised SOEs sought to become profitable. Within the state-owned sector, the total number of employees was reduced from 3.86 million in 1985 (approximately 15 per cent of the total labour force) to 2.92 million in 1993 (or 9 per cent). Employment in the cooperative industrial sector declined even more precipitously—from 1.2 million in 1988 to 287 600 in 1992 (GSO 1994)—affecting mainly women workers. Unemployment rose to 13 per cent of the workforce, but many of those laid off were able to find work in the burgeoning household sector or in the informal sector, particularly in farming, trade, and services. There was therefore a substantial shift in the employment structure.

Control over inflation has seen a significant return of confidence in the Vietnamese currency, increased savings ratios, and rapid growth of GDP (at over 8 per cent per annum in 1992–97). These sustained high growth rates in a labour-intensive economy mean that unemployment has begun to diminish although, given the irregular character of much informal-sector employment, underemployment remains a serious problem affecting especially farmers and women.

One of the implications of the above analysis is that the high growth rates of the early 1990s were brought about chiefly through improvements in efficiency. The elimination of hyperinflation reduced speculation and waste of resources, and the abolition of subsidies to SOEs provided incentives for improved productivity and a shift of resources into more profitable areas of production. A major issue in the economic debates has therefore been how to improve rates of investment to sustain growth over the long run. This has a parallel in government concerns to improve revenue-collection—to finance much-needed infrastructure projects, and to restore funding to education and health—without having to resort to inflationary deficit-financing. Reform of the financial sector and taxation system have thus been key priorities (see below).

Social and political impact of *Doi Moi*

The impact of this series of reforms on the politics and culture of Vietnam was just as dramatic as that on the economy. As Vietnam has opened to the world market there have been significant gains in the ability of individuals to become involved in decisions concerning their livelihood and in freedom of speech (although not without setbacks). Debates in the national assembly have become much more lively and, for the first time in 1992, candidates not 'approved' by the party were permitted to run for election. The demise of the cooperative system in the rural areas has also allowed the revival of traditional Vietnamese cultural and religious practices. Kinship networks have become more important in village life. New types of cooperative organisation, such as the numerous credit groups, have also spontaneously arisen to fulfil some of the social functions previously carried out by the cooperatives. Independent trade unions are permitted and some have already emerged in private enterprises, although so far mainly of the 'house union' type. There has been a number of strikes in foreign-invested enterprises where unfamiliar (and, to Vietnamese workers, harsh) labour-management systems have been introduced. The government has so far shown no inclination to interfere in the independent settlement of these disputes.

Vietnam is now a much more open society than at any stage in the so-called socialist period (Thayer 1991:26–33). The party's concern for political stability has ensured that such freedoms have not extended beyond the limits of what it considers acceptable at any given time, but these limits are still expanding. As in the 1980s, when policy tended to attempt to manage change but was unable to control it, the desire of party leaders to preserve legitimacy means that they have been forced to react to shifts in public opinion.

This was evident, for example, in the movement to create a society 'ruled by law' in the first half of the 1990s. 'Rule by law' (often mistranslated in English language sources as 'rule of law') represented the attempt to codify Vietnamese laws and regulations into a coherent and internally consistent system to increase the transparency of bureaucratic processes and to eliminate opportunities for corruption, nepotism, favouritism, and arbitrariness from their implementation. As such, it implied reform of the bureaucracy as well as the rewriting of many laws to make them applicable to a market economy. Unlike the Western concept of 'rule of law', however, law did not represent a higher authority than the party-state. It did attempt to create a level playing field in which the popular perceptions of unfairness in the application of law, which characterised the socialist and earlier transitional society, will be eliminated.

In the latter half of the 1990s the pace of change tended to slow down, due, at least in part, to a perception by party leaders that increased freedom had brought a startling rise in corruption, smuggling, and other crime, as well as higher divorce rates, juvenile delinquency, and other signs of a breakdown in social cohesion. Recognising that those in positions of authority are often the source of these 'social evils', many commentators have interpreted the resulting clampdown simply as a measure to maintain party privileges and control. Such an interpretation was certainly borne out by measures taken in 1999 to restrict media criticism of party and government. However, the leadership has also responded by taking steps to increase accountability by promoting 'grassroots' democracy—in other words, by attempting to defuse conflict by channelling it into lawful avenues and restricting the capacity of individuals openly to flout the law. One reason for such apparently contradictory measures being able to operate side by side is that grassroots challenges to authority rarely take on the character of challenges to the regime, and tend to be soluble within the existing political framework. Intellectuals, on the other hand, are more likely to issue challenges to the political system itself.

Current issues

Sustainable growth

For the party and government, the main question is how to sustain economic growth at a sufficient rate to catch up to its South-East Asian neighbours in ASEAN.[9] This is seen as the surest way to avoid the potential for social conflict inherent in the reform process, and to maintain communist party rule in the medium term.

There have been four main areas of concern in this search for sustainable growth. The first is efficient use of resources.

As mentioned above, high growth rates of GDP in the early 1990s came largely from improvements in the efficiency with which resources were used. Gross investment in the state sector in 1992 was approximately 8 per cent of GDP, which is far too low to sustain rapid economic growth. (This did not, however, include investment in the private sector and in own-capital of SOEs.) Raising the rate of savings and investment has therefore had a high priority. In 1997 the estimate for all investment had risen to approximately 27 per cent of GNP.

Although domestic savings rose in importance as a source of investment finance during the 1990s, foreign direct investment (FDI) also played a key role. Towards the end of the decade, however, FDI fell dramatically and, by 1999, was back to its 1992 level. With hindsight it is apparent that the foreign investment boom formed part of the bubble economy affecting the South-East Asian region as a whole, and did not reflect the true attractiveness of Vietnam. In the early 1990s there was something of a 'last frontier mentality' among investors, yet the realities of red tape, poorly developed infrastructure, and conflicting regulations had led to a slowdown in the rate of new investments by the second half of 1996. Thus the onset of the Asian crisis in mid 1997 served only to accelerate the downturn, and recovery in the rest of Asia seems unlikely to return it to its previous levels. Domestic investment was able partially to offset this decline and Vietnam was otherwise relatively insulated from the impact of the crisis by virtue of its lack of global financial integration, so that growth rates were maintained at approximately 4–5 per cent during 1998/99. However, the loss of foreign investment represented a blow to the government's growth strategy, which had largely depended on FDI to provide technology transfer and boost the efficiency of the SOE sector through joint ventures. Since there were also considerable domestic linkages deriving from FDI—in the form of subcontracting, components supply, and so on—the longer-term effects of the decline might be stronger than initially indicated.

The second main area of concern in the search for sustainable growth in the 1990s was reform of the financial sector. In 1990 the government separated commercial banking from the central bank functions of the State Bank of Vietnam and established four commercial banks which, in principle, were to lend only according to commercial criteria. However, the process of commercialisation of the banking system has been slow. During the period of negative real interest rates, the demand for funds by SOEs remained high, and savings deposits were low with many banks being technically insolvent. When interest rates were raised again to positive levels in 1992, many SOEs were unable to repay their loans and the state bank was forced to provide funds to cover these non-performing debts—which meant that the system of subsidising SOEs continued by an indirect method. More recently the Agricultural Bank, in particular, has been under pressure to shift its lending portfolio away from SOEs towards private farmers, and it has made some progress. But given the lack of adequate accounting practices in all Vietnamese enterprises, banks have little genuine ability to assess commercial risk and therefore continue to prefer SOEs because of the greater certainty that they will be bailed-out by the government. Private ventures have had to rely on informal borrowing which is both more risky and limits the capital available. This is one of the factors restricting the growth of large-scale private capitalists in Vietnam—a situation with which many in the party might be content if they see an emerging bourgeoisie as a threat to party rule.

A third area of concern in relation to sustained economic growth has been the fiscal system. As explained above, the main sources of finance for state-led industrialisation were the profits of industrial enterprises and foreign aid. However, by the 1980s the majority of SOEs were clearly unprofitable and, of more than 12 000 then existing, the government was forced to rely on only a few hundred to provide the bulk of revenue. The flow of aid from the West remained slow, and Soviet aid was withdrawn in 1991. Expenditure needs, on the other hand, continued to grow, and the resulting large budget deficits could be financed only in an inflationary way. The need to stabilise the economy by reducing the budget deficit provided a strong impetus to reform of the fiscal system, both to increase revenue collection and to widen the tax base to include the private sector.

Revenues increased substantially, from a low of 11 per cent of GDP in 1988 to 26 per cent in 1994, and the deficit was greatly reduced. Since 1986 some of the revenue burden has shifted from SOEs to taxes on foreign trade and oil production. However, attempts to increase the private sector's tax share have been less successful. Personal income tax provides only 1 per cent of revenue (World Bank 1994:127; IMF 1994:58), and other taxes have not been increased. For this reason, the government introduced a value-added tax in 1999. One of the main factors leading to popular resistance to tax payments is that, in recent times, the severe compression of local budgets during the fiscal crisis led local authorities to extract 'contributions' from the population. This practice has, rightly or wrongly, often been tarred with the brush of corruption. Moreover, contributions tend to be highly regressive, impinging on the poor more heavily than on the rich. People now question why they should pay twice, to the central government and to the localities.

A fourth issue of concern to the sustainability of growth is the environment. The socialist system was certainly not free of environmental problems (Beresford and Fraser 1992) but, given the priorities of the regime and the lack of countervailing power, these did not become an important issue. The emergence in the government's agenda of environmental issues in the 1990s is testimony both to its greater openness and to the increasing ability of the people to organise themselves. As the growth rate has accelerated, the socialist economy's legacy of poorly developed infrastructure and dirty industrial plants has proven highly inadequate. In rapidly expanding urban centres such as Hanoi and Ho Chi Minh City, the drainage system of the colonial-period can no longer cope with the volume of effluent. Old factories, new construction sites, and growing numbers of motorbikes pour dust and chemical pollution into the atmosphere. Public transport systems are run down, and traffic clogs the multitude of narrow streets. In the country as a whole, only 17 per cent of households has access to a reticulated water supply or deep-drilled wells with a pump, and the rest rely on hand-dug wells, rivers, lakes, natural springs, ponds, or rain water (SPC–GSO 1994). The latter group is most vulnerable to pollution and is concentrated in the Mekong River delta.

Institutional frameworks for dealing with environmental problems remain weakly developed and, when conflicts of interest arise, solutions can be the result of an ad hoc public protest—as in the case of the successful campaign against construction of a coal-washing plant in a residential area (Beresford 1995a). The government has also acted firmly in cases where public safety is threatened. However, it seems more likely to act in favour of those with market power; that is, when pollution and congestion become evident as bottlenecks to growth. For the time being, environmental guidelines are often flouted.

Social equity

The distributional impacts of growth are very much on the agenda. Since *Doi Moi* there has been a significant widening of income differentials, most notably in the growing gap between urban and rural areas. In popular perception, increased inequality is also linked to corruption and lack of transparency at all levels of the state apparatus. These issues are seen as central to maintenance of the regime's legitimacy and its credentials as a leader of the transition to socialism. During the crisis period of the late 1970s and 1980s the party suffered a loss of legitimacy and its attempt to rebuild is largely based on the simultaneous attempt to sustain economic freedoms and promote growth while providing a social safety-net for the poor. However, the party and government contain a diversity of views on the relationship of growth and equity, leading to a continuing struggle over relative priorities.

Some of these concerns are reflected, for example, in the labour and land laws passed in 1993 and 1994. The Labour Law contained many provisions aimed at protecting the rights of workers, but it is by no means clear that these will be fully implemented if, as is also the intention, foreign direct investment and private domestic investment are also to be encouraged. The Land Law also prominently addressed the security needs of farmers and consequently contained a number of provisions inimical to the development of markets in land and to the development of capitalism in agriculture. This also might turn out to be impossible to implement in many areas.

The future of the health and education sectors are also key equity issues. The legacy of the socialist system in this area was relatively high levels of literacy and public health indicators (Beresford 1995b) as well as high popular expectations, particularly in relation to education. In the fiscal crisis of the late 1980s and early 1990s, however, public spending in both these areas dropped significantly. Teachers and health workers found it impossible to live on their state salaries and most took up second occupations or left the system completely. Schools began to demand contributions from parents to maintain classes but, with staff frequently demoralised by their poor wages and conditions, standards fell and well-off parents found it necessary to pay for private tuition outside school hours. The rise of the household economy has also led to higher school drop-out rates, particularly in the rural areas, and the gap between boys' and girls' education levels has increased markedly. In health care, there has been a shift away from the use of clinics and private practitioners towards self-prescribed drugs that are freely available in the new market environment. As state revenues have begun to recover, there are signs of some improvement in health-sector funding, especially at the local level, and foreign non-governmental organisations are also now active. Education remains more problematic because it not only requires more funds (private sector education can take a small portion of the burden for this), but also requires extensive restructuring of the curriculum to adapt to the needs of a market economy.

Centre–local relations

Centre–local relations have been one of the most difficult areas of reform within the state apparatus. From the point of view of the centre, its capacity to manage the economy is affected by the distribution of power existing at the outset of the reform process, by uneven regional development, and by the degree of integration of local levels into the national administrative apparatus. Problems can emerge, in particular, from:

(a) regional autarchy arising from the operation of the socialist system with incomplete market reform giving rise to a situation in which regions are able to defy central policy directions (this also refers to the rise of local networks using family, party, and business connections to build quasi-independent control over a protected local economy);

(b) the emergence of wide regional disparities between provinces and regions together with essentially contrived attempts to equalise income differentials which can lead to resentment (by wealthier regions at having to subsidise the poorer ones, and by the poor regions at perceived privileges meted out to the more prosperous).

Under the impact of market-oriented reforms, competition between centre and localities over budget resources became a major issue. Under the traditional socialist system, local budgets of the poorer regions or those with a large number of 'political' production units were heavily subsidised by the centre. After reform, these subventions were reduced as chronic fiscal deficits could no longer be tolerated because they fuelled inflationary tendencies. The problem was exacerbated by the low revenue-raising ability of the centre. However, increased buoyancy of revenues since 1993, and corresponding deficit reduction, reduced the pressure on the localities. Nevertheless, a majority of provinces continue to require subsidies—which leads to tensions between these and the wealthier provinces.

The purpose of reforms that decentralised economic decision-making (as initiated in 1979) was to unleash productive energies of individual units, and the new policies did not at first contain any well-articulated regional dimension. However, the emergence of a de facto regional 'policy' can be seen in Vietnam where the autarchic policies of the 1970s have been replaced by a more market-oriented system that promotes trade and investment links with the international economy. In the 1990s regional differences in growth rates began to emerge more strongly, with the southern region around Ho Chi Minh City significantly outstripping other areas in both growth rate and per capita income. The northern industrial centres around Hanoi and Haiphong have more recently experienced similar rapid rates of growth, whereas some rural provinces, especially in the highlands, the central coast, and the Mekong delta, have lagged behind. The two industrial regions have not received differential treatment in fiscal relations (as such regions did in China), but the relative independence of the southern region has nevertheless been bolstered by its greater wealth, corresponding lower dependence on central subventions, and higher levels of rents.

The normal expectation is that, as the level of market influence extends throughout Vietnam, there will be a gradual erosion of the strength of regional political autonomy and of the ability of local authorities to allocate resources independently of (or in contradiction to) the direction of central policy. Higher levels of regional integration will ensure that it is in the interests of localities to contribute to central budgets for maintenance of inter-locality infrastructure and for macroeconomic stabilisation and growth policies. However, this will not occur if localities are at the same time denied resources needed to sustain local growth and social welfare systems. The answers will have implications for the distribution of accumulation and growth, the efficiency of resource allocation, and the longer-term ability of the centre to manage the economy. These questions are also closely related to the equity issues discussed above. At the present time, capital construction expenditures (including those financed by aid) by the central authorities are tending to be spent on large infrastructure projects that will have benefits primarily for the high-growth regions, and for the centrally managed SOEs and foreign investments concentrated in those regions.

State enterprise reform

Financial autonomy of SOEs has been progressively increased since 1981, allowing the process of capital accumulation and cross shareholdings. Since 1989 direct budget subsidies have ended and cheap credit has been progressively eliminated, with the result that enterprises must restructure and become profitable, or close down. Although many assets of these enterprises are still owned by the state and a capital 'fee' is charged, the growth of relatively autonomous capital accumulation has implied an increase in the proportion of 'own-capital' which is regarded by the enterprises themselves (although not by the bureaucracy) as their collective property. Workers are entitled to a share in the enterprise profits in the form of bonus and welfare funds which grow in size as productivity rises and serve to reinforce the ethos of collective ownership. In at least a few SOEs bonus funds have been distributed in the form of shares (although these might not yet be legally recognised). Labour recruitment practices also reflect this ethos, especially in the north, where many enterprises try to provide employment security and to recruit new workers from among family members of the existing workforce. The question of ownership of the SOEs is therefore very unclear. Increased autonomy from government control suggests a process of 'corporatisation' of public enterprises (Beresford 1993), and there also appears to be developing a corporatist, rather than a confrontational, model of labour relations.

Corporatisation of the state-owned sector does not necessarily represent the formation of a private sector. Administrative interference in the operation of enterprises still exists, both directly via the line ministries and indirectly via the banking system. Soft budget constraints on enterprises, although considerably reduced since the beginning of the reform, are also still in existence. The political difficulties associated with imposing genuine bankruptcy on unprofitable SOEs mean that, in common with other reforming planned economies, Vietnam has been subjected to a stop–go cycle in relation to financial discipline. There still exists a lot of confusion between the macroeconomic management role of the *government* in a market economy (as the reformers see it) and the productive function of the *state* ministries and enterprises. Moreover, there is now considerable anecdotal evidence pointing to the formation of a state 'business interest' (Fforde 1993:310). This does not yet imply the privatisation of assets, because control over enterprises remains dependent on directors' positions within the state apparatus. In fact, attempts to use state positions to accumulate *private* capital have been clearly identified as corrupt and, where possible, severely punished. The state 'business interest' forms a powerful sectional interest within the state preventing the establishment of a capitalist economy based on private property, most clearly by creating barriers to entry for new capital. Moreover, given the power of the 'state business interest', the continuing low rate of investment by this sector must throw some doubt on sustainability of growth.

State enterprise reform remained one of the most sensitive areas in the mid 1990s. As market discipline on enterprises became greater, pressure on workers seemed likely to increase, both for increased productivity and to end the sharing of profits between worker funds and investment funds. Moreover, foreign investors and international competition are likely to generate pressure to halt the real wage increases that state sector workers have experienced in recent years. Development of a stronger labour market and the movement of new, inexperienced workers into the waged labour force is also likely to see dilution of the culture of social or collective-enterprise ownership. Although the government currently favours worker participation in privatisation or equitisation schemes for SOEs, little has been achieved.

Equitisation of enterprises is presently considered a more appropriate model of ownership reform than privatisation, and implies that the state will retain a considerable share in enterprise ownership, along with managers, workers, other SOEs, and private capitalists. Some pilot projects had been carried out in small enterprises by the late 1990s, but large-scale equitisation has yet to happen. Steps had also been taken to increase corporatisation through measures to remove the control of line ministries over production-related decisions, and some of these ministries had been amalgamated or abolished. In several industries, enterprises were incorporated into large vertically integrated corporations in an effort to rationalise production capacity, finance, and lines of management authority. To date, however, the reorganisation has shown few results.

Conclusion

The planned economy in Vietnam by no means corresponded to the 'command economy' model favoured by Western commentators on 'actually existing socialism'. Rather it was a system in which the demands of conflicting interest groups within society were negotiated through the mediation of the state apparatus. These interests included: sections of the state apparatus itself that derived power from their control over the planned allocation of resources; local authorities, enterprise and cooperative managers, and their dependants who strove to minimise surplus extraction to higher levels and accumulate capital within their own sphere; and, last, those who lacked access to the networks holding local power. The fundamental legitimacy of the regime, due to its nationalist credentials and reliance on popular mobilisation during wartime, not only blunted any social conflict inherent in the system, but also created a tradition in which negotiated solutions were possible. After unification of the country in 1976, the shift in the balance of interests in favour of relatively independent capital accumulation led to an increasing erosion of the power of interests associated with the planning system as inflation tended to aggravate shortages generated within the plan. Serious economic crises in 1978–80 and in the mid 1980s progressively destroyed the remaining legitimacy of the planning system within the central apparatus itself, and led to the political consensus around *Doi Moi*. Moreover, by the end of the decade, structural and institutional change had proceeded far enough to ensure that abolition of the remaining vestiges of planning produced little serious dislocation of the economy.

State-led marketisation of the economy under *Doi Moi* has very much reflected the interests of those groups that rose to dominance during the early part of the transition: SOE managers (often in alliance with the new group of foreign investors), as well as local and provincial kinship, and political networks linked to relatively autonomous capital-accumulation processes. However, within the increasingly plural Vietnamese society, new groups are emerging that are not necessarily linked to the above networks. These include private domestic capitalists and can also include wealthy farmers. Until now, their potential for expansion has been limited by discrimination in policy implementation and lack of capital, and they are unlikely to become a dominant class in the foreseeable future. Those SOE workers who remain in employment after the shakeout of the early 1990s have also benefited through their ability to share in the profits of enterprises that most still regard as collectively owned. However, as market discipline on enterprises increases over time, and as a labour market becomes more established, these benefits are likely to diminish.

At the bottom end of the scale are those who have not participated in capital accumulation and who are largely excluded from state power: poor peasants, the unemployed, and underemployed. Women are in the majority in all of these categories. For many, their livelihood has become increasingly precarious, although there is so far no evidence that this is true for the great majority. Nevertheless, the crisis in health and education, increasing regional differentiation, and increasing income differentials mean that there is potential for social conflict. Therefore, not only the sustainability of growth, but also equitable distribution of the benefits, are likely to remain important issues for some time to come. Within the party–state apparatus the perceived need to maintain the legitimacy of communist party rule is also likely to ensure, however, that the interests of the poor are not completely ignored. Although what might be called the 'state–business bloc' remains powerful, there are many in the party and bureaucracy who see a continuing need for compromise with the interests of the poor to block the rise of opposition parties based on interests associated with private capital.

Notes

1 The category of 'middle' peasants, defined as those producing 'on average' sufficient for household subsistence and not requiring hired labour, is problematical as it includes many above-average farms that produced a marketable surplus. In the southern region in the 1970s, it was the 'middle' peasants, accounting for 72 per cent of the rural population, who produced the bulk of the south's large marketed grain surplus (Beresford 1988:149).

2 In the late 1970s, for example, there were reports that procurement officials were sometimes arrested by cooperative members and their own bicycles were appropriated because the centre was unable to supply the contracted amounts of industrial goods in exchange for procurement quotas.

3 The term 'relatively independent' is used here because capital accumulation in the periphery remained, in many cases, contingent upon access to resources, supplied at low official prices within the plan, that could then be diverted on to parallel markets.

4 The system of subsidised input prices continued at approximately 60–70 per cent of the market price, while the government's wages bill rose by 220 per cent. The budget deficit rose from 24 per cent of expenditure in 1984 to 31 per cent in 1986 and 39 per cent in 1988 (Spoor 1988:125; World Bank 1994:126).

5 Inflation during 1986 was 487 per cent per annum (World Bank 1994:131).

6 Some insights are provided by Dang Phong and Beresford (1998).

7 Meaning that the rate was pegged a few points above the inflation rate.

8 One of the characteristics of high inflation in all the former socialist countries has been increasing use by the population of the US dollar as the preferred currency for domestic transactions because it holds its value better than the local currency.

9 Party Secretary Do Muoi, in delivering the political report to the Mid Term National Conference of the party held in January 1994, enumerated four basic challenges facing the country today: 'The challenges lie in: the danger of our economy falling further behind those of other countries in the region and the world due to our low starting point, our still low and unstable growth rate and the fact that we have to develop in an environment of tough competition; the possibility of our going astray from the socialist orientation if we fail to correct deviations from the path laid down for its implementation; corruption and other social evils; "peaceful evolution" schemes and activities undertaken by hostile forces' (CPV 1994:24).

References

Beresford, M. (1988) *Vietnam: Politics, Economics and Society*, London: Pinter.

Beresford, M. (1989) *National Unification and Economic Development in Vietnam*, London: Macmillan.

Beresford, M. (1993) 'The political economy of dismantling the "bureaucratic centralism and subsidy system" in Vietnam', in K. Hewison, R. Robison and G. Rodan (eds) *Southeast Asia in the 1990s*, Sydney: Allen and Unwin, pp 213–36.

Beresford, M. (1995a) 'Economy and environment', in Ben Kerkvliet (ed.) *Dilemmas of Development: Vietnam Update 1994*, Political and Social Change Monograph 22, Canberra: Department of Political and Social Change, RSPAS, Australian National University, pp 69–88.

Beresford, M. (1995b) 'Political economy of primary health care in Vietnam', in Paul Cohen and John Purcal (eds) *Health and Development in Southeast Asia*, Australian Development Studies Network pp 104–19.

Beresford, M. and L. Fraser (1992) 'Political economy of the environment in Vietnam', *Journal of Contemporary Asia*, 22(1):3–19.

Communist Party of Vietnam (CPV) (1994), 'Political Report of the Central Committee (7th Tenure) Mid Term National Conference', Hanoi: The Gioi Publishers.

CPV, see Communist Party of Vietnam (CPV).

Dang Phong and M. Beresford (1998) *Authority Relations and Economic Decision-Making in Vietnam*, Copenhagen: Nordic Institute for Asian Studies.

de Vylder, S. and A. Fforde (1988) *Vietnam: An Economy in Transition*, Stockholm: SIDA.

Elliott, D. (1974) 'Revolutionary reintegration', PhD thesis, University of Michigan: Ann Arbor.

Fforde, Adam (1989) *The Agrarian Question in North Vietnam 1974–78*, New York: M.E. Sharpe.

Fforde, A. (1993) 'The political economy of reform in Vietnam—some reflections', in Borje Ljunggren (ed.) *The Challenge of Reform in Indochina*, Cambridge MA: Harvard University Press, pp 293–326.

Fforde, A. and S.H. Paine (1987) *The Limits to National Liberation*, London: Croom Helm.

General Statistical Office (GSO) (1994) *Nien Giam Thong Ke 1993*, Hanoi.

Gordon, Alec (1981) 'North Vietnam's collectivisation campaigns: class struggle, production and the "middle peasant" problem', *Journal of Contemporary Asia*, 11(1):19–43.

GSO, see General Statistical Office (GSO).

IMF, see International Monetary Fund (IMF).

International Monetary Fund (IMF) (1994) *Vietnam: Recent Economic Developments*, Washington, June.

Moise, E.E. (1976) 'Land reform and land reform errors in North Vietnam', *Pacific Affairs*, 49.

Ngo Vinh Long (1984) 'Agrarian differentiation in the southern region of Vietnam', *Journal of Contemporary Asia*, 14(3):283–305.

SPC–GSO, see State Planning Committee and General Statistical Office (SPC–GSO).

Spoor, Max (1987) 'Finance in a socialist transition: the case of the Democratic Republic of Vietnam (1955–64)', *Journal of Contemporary Asia*, 17(3):339–65.

Spoor, Max (1988) 'State finance in the Socialist Republic of Vietnam', in David G. Marr and Christine P. White (eds) *Postwar Vietnam: Dilemmas in Socialist Development*, Ithaca: Cornell University, Southeast Asia Program, pp 111–32.

State Planning Committee and General Statistical Office (SPC–GSO) (1994) *Vietnam Living Standards Survey*, Hanoi, September.

Thayer, Carlyle (1991) 'Renovation and Vietnamese society: the changing role of government and administration', in D.K. Forbes, T.H. Hull, D.G. Marr and

B. Brogan (eds) *Doi Moi: Vietnam's Renovation Policy and Performance*, Political and Social Change Monograph no. 14, Canberra: Australian National University, pp 21–33.

White, Christine P. (1983) 'Mass mobilisation and ideological transformation in the Vietnamese land reform campaign', *Journal of Contemporary Asia*, 13(1):74–90.

World Bank (1994) 'Vietnam: Public Sector Management and Private Sector Incentives Economic Report', 20 September.

8

Economic Crisis and the Political Economy of Economic Liberalisation in South-East Asia

Kanishka Jayasuriya and Andrew Rosser

In the wake of the Asian economic crisis, scholars have been quick to declare the end of the Asian economic model (AEM), in both its developmental and oligarchic/crony capitalist forms. Neo-liberal economists, for instance, have argued that the crisis has exposed the inherent weakness of the AEM and, as such, provided 'a historic opportunity' for the region to shift towards more market-based systems of economic organisation (Frankel 1998:11; see also Cathie 1997; Fukuyama 1999; and comments by Michel Camdessus in *AWSJ* 1997). Theorists have also suggested that the crisis has strengthened the position of the 'Wall Street–IMF–Treasury complex' and thus made it politically impossible for regional governments to continue with *dirigiste* policies (Jomo 1998; Winters 1999). Indeed, some have even speculated that the crisis will produce a growing convergence between regional economic systems and the Western neo-liberal model (Beeson 1998).

We argue that predictions of the end of the AEM and the victory of liberal markets are premature. By increasing the need of countries within East and South-East Asia to attract internationally mobile capital, the Asian crisis has clearly generated strong structural pressures for liberal market reform within the region. Yet, we argue that this has not made such reform inevitable. The reason for this is that these structural pressures have been refracted through domestic political and social systems that have varied in terms of the extent to which they have been conducive to reform and hence in the extent to which they have been vulnerable to these pressures. The result, we suggest, has been an uneven pattern of reform: economic liberalisation has gone further in those countries where domestic political and social systems have been relatively conducive to reform than it has in those countries where domestic political systems have not been so conducive to reform. This argument clearly fits in with the social conflict theory outlined in chapter 1 of this volume.

To illustrate these points, we examine the dynamics of economic liberalisation in four South-East Asian countries—Singapore, Malaysia, Thailand, and Indonesia—since the onset of the Asian economic crisis. In essence, our argument is that the extent of economic liberalisation in these countries has been a function of three domestic political and social variables: (i) the extent to which liberal market ideas are accepted within society; (ii) the extent to which the institutional environment is capable of supporting liberal markets; and (iii) the extent to which the crisis has shifted the balance of power within society away from coalitions that are opposed to reform and towards those that support it. In each case we have chosen to focus on these variables—rather than many alternative variables— because there are strong intuitive and theoretical reasons for believing that they are related to reform outcomes.

Understanding reform outcomes

In explaining reform outcomes in developing countries, neo-classical political economists have emphasised the political nature of the reform process (Krueger 1993; Williamson 1994). Economic policy-making, they have argued, is not simply a technical matter involving rational deliberations over the merits of alternative policy positions but a political process in which there are winners and losers. However, they have also tended to emphasise the economic rationality of political elites who advocate economic reform and construe the role of politics in negative terms. That is, they have tended to view struggles over economic reform as essentially struggles between, on the one hand, economic rationality, as represented by liberal technocrats and, on the other hand, vested political and social interests (Schamis 1999; Rosser 1999a). As such, they have presented a highly voluntarist account of the dynamics of economic reform: in their view, reform outcomes depend, not on the extent to which material interests get behind reformist strategies but, rather, on the extent to which economic policy-makers are able to rise above behaviour that serves vested political and social interests (see chapter 1, this volume).

Examples of this approach abound. John Williamson (1994:13–15), for instance, has argued that reform in developing countries needs to be understood in terms of the role of 'technopols' or 'policy-maker[s] who [are] motivated to pursue the objectives postulated by traditional normative economic analysis'. Similarly, James Buchanan (1980:360, 367) has argued that reform is 'particularly difficult to accomplish in a rent-seeking environment' and that reform outcomes thus depend to a large degree 'on the ability of political and intellectual leaders to think in terms of, and be persuasive about, general constitutional changes in the whole structure of social and economic institutions'. And Arnold Harberger (1993:343) has suggested that a crucial feature of successful reform initiatives in Latin America has been the existence of 'a handful of heroes' who exhibited, at least in one case, the 'conviction, courage, and determination' to carry out reform despite strong political resistance.

In contrast to this approach, we argue that reform outcomes are best understood in terms of three variables.

The first of these is ideas. As a number of scholars has pointed out, responses to economic crises are shaped at least in part 'by the intellectual lenses through which economic advisors and political leaders perceive the crisis and the available options' (Nelson 1990:29; see also Haggard and Kaufman 1992:13–14). As such, extensive reform is most likely where orthodox ideas have gained widespread acceptance among a country's policy elite. Reform is much less likely to occur, by contrast, in societies where nationalist and radical populist economic agenda are dominant and liberal economic ideas have become tainted by an association with colonial rule, neo-colonial domination, or past economic crises. In these societies, as Chaudhry (1994) among others has pointed out, the ideological resources needed for governments to create more liberal economies simply do not exist. In this chapter we bring ideas into the analysis by distinguishing between 'internationalist' ideological influences within the technocracy and 'nationalist influences'. It needs to be pointed out that, although these ideas will reflect broadly the material interests of various political coalitions, ideological influences are located within institutional structures (such as the technocracy) that have their own specific history.

The second variable that plays a role in shaping reform outcomes is institutional capacity. As the World Bank (1997:1) has argued, markets cannot exist unless they are supported by effective states: 'An effective state is vital for the provision of the goods and services—and the rules and institutions— that allow markets to flourish and people to lead healthier, happier lives' (see also Evans 1992; Polanyi 1944). A key characteristic of an 'effective state' is that it is coherent and coordinated in organisational terms—that is, that it has a high degree of administrative capacity (MacIntyre 1994:4). The importance of this is *not* that it makes a country more likely to introduce economic reforms. As Haggard and Kaufman (1992:11–12) have pointed out, the evidence in this area is mixed. Rather, it is important because it affects a country's ability to implement reforms properly and to ensure that regulatory functions are adequately performed. In other words, it affects a country's ability to consolidate programs of reform once they have been initiated. In this chapter, we bring institutional factors into the analysis by distinguishing between states with high and low levels of capacity.

It is important to point out that our approach here is different from that of those political economists who have emphasised the importance of state autonomy in promoting economic reform. Although we agree with their view that coherence and coordination are important determinants of whether reforms are successfully implemented, we are sceptical of the claim that state autonomy is a necessary prerequisite for economic reform. The point is that markets are not natural phenomena that exist independently of their political and social context. Like any other sorts of economic systems, they embody the interests of specific elements within society and require the continued support of these elements to survive (Chaudhry 1993; Robison and Rosser 1999; Evans 1995). Market creation thus requires, not an autonomous state, but one that is closely aligned with political and social coalitions that support market-oriented reform (see chapter 1, this volume).

This leads to our third variable. Reform outcomes are also a function of the extent to which economic crises shift power and influence away from anti-reform coalitions of interest and towards pro-reform coalitions of interest. In neo-classical and rational-choice institutionalist accounts of economic reform, economic crises are important because they 'have the effect of shocking countries out of traditional policy patterns, disorganizing the interest groups that typically veto policy reform, and generating pressure for politicians to change policies that can be seen to have failed' (Williamson and Haggard 1994:562–4; see also World Bank 1997). That is, they are important because they weaken the position of anti-reform coalitions and make apparent the inherent economic rationality of market-oriented policies. However, this view obscures the way in which political and social interests are embedded in market-oriented policies, and hence the way in which these interests underpin the process of reform. The point here is that economic crises not only weaken anti-reform coalitions but also strengthen pro-reform coalitions. It is thus more reasonable to argue that reform outcomes depend not on the extent to which economic crises weaken anti-reform coalitions and cause policy elites to realise the mistakes of the past, but—as noted above—on the extent to which they shift power away from anti-reform coalitions and towards pro-reform ones (Rosser 1999a). In this chapter, we bring these factors into the analysis by distinguishing among: (i) those cases where economic crises have weakened anti-reform coalitions and strengthened pro-reform coalitions; (ii) where they have had little or no impact on the coalitional structure of society, effectively leaving dominant anti-reform coalitions in a position of continued dominance; and (iii) where they have weakened dominant anti-reform coalitions but where pro-reform coalitions have been too weak to assume power.

Our analysis thus far is similar to that of Pempel (1998). In an insightful analysis of the political changes wrought by economic restructuring, he has suggested that political outcomes need to be understood within the context of a specific 'regime'—which he defines as a set of dominant socioeconomic coalitions, a set of institutional arrangements, and a stable set of policy strategies. Yet our analysis is different in two important respects.

First, our dependent variable—that which we seek to explain—is the extent of economic liberalisation rather than the nature of regimes. As such, we are interested in the extent to which there has been a fundamental shift in the nature of regimes rather than resistance or reconstitution within existing regimes.

Second, the role of political and social coalitions is more central to our analysis than it is to Pempel's. Pempel likens the relationship among the three elements on which he focuses to the relationship among the legs of tripod: each reinforces the other, and when one is removed the whole edifice collapses. Our framework, by contrast, is best characterised as being similar to a 'pyramid' with coalitions at the base, institutions in the centre, and ideas at the apex. The reason for this difference is that in our view, although appropriate ideas, institutions, and coalitional structures are all essential for the emergence of markets, it is the coalitional structure of society that exercises the greatest influence on reform outcomes. This is because, above all else, markets are allocative mechanisms for determining who gets what, why, and how. As such, they can exist only if some sort of compromise, forced or otherwise, is reached among competing interests about how society's resources are to be allocated.

This framework yields a total of six broad reform trajectories (and twelve overall reform outcomes) depending on the particular configuration of the three variables. These are summarised in table 8.1 (page 238).

In summary, the analysis presented here suggests that it is problematic to analyse a set of economic reform strategies as a rational set of economic policies that arise in response to the imperatives of market forces. Rather, economic reform is an intrinsically political process because any given set of economic strategies needs to be underpinned by a coherent dominant coalition of interests, a set of institutional structures, and a set of dominant ideas. We discuss these elements in more detail below in relation to South-East Asia, but the point that needs to be underlined here is that economic

Table 8.1 Expected reform outcomes

No.	Impact of the crisis on coalitional structure	Ideological character of society	Broad reform trajectory	Institu-tional capacity	Expected reform outcome
1	Dominant anti-reform coalition remains strong	Nationalist	Very little reform	(a) Low	1(a) Very little reform and poor implementation
				(b) High	1(b) Very little reform with good implementation
2	Dominant anti-reform coalition remains strong	Internationalist	Limited reform	(a) Low	2(a) Limited reform with poor implementation
				(b) High	2(b) Limited reform with good implementation
3	Dominant anti-reform coalition weakened but pro-reform coalition too weak to assume power	Nationalist	Partial reform	(a) Low	3(a) Partial reform reform with poor implementation
				(b) High	3(b) Partial reform with good implementation
4	Dominant anti-reform coalition weakened but pro-reform coalition too weak to assume power	Internationalist	Substantial reform	(a) Low	4(a) Substantial reform with poor implementation
				(b) High	4(b) Substantial reform with good implementation
5	Anti-reform coalition weakened and pro-reform coalition strengthened	Nationalist	Widespread reform	(a) Low	5(a) Widespread reform with poor implementation
				(b) High	5(b) Widespread reform with good implementation
6	Anti-reform coalition weakened and pro-reform coalition strengthened	Internationalist	Thorough-going reform	(a) Low	6(a) Thoroughgoing reform with poor implementation
				(b) High	6(b) Thoroughgoing reform with good implementation

reform implies a dramatic change in the previously dominant or influential configuration of interests, institutions, and ideas and that, for this reason, any shift in economic strategies will bring forth serious resistance from political and social interests.

The political economy of economic liberalisation in post-crisis South-East Asia: four cases

Thailand

Thailand fits the profile of model 6(a) in table 8.1 (page 238). Nationalist and more specifically populist economic ideas were very influential during the two and a half decades following the overthrow of the Thai monarchy in 1932. At this time, figures within the populist People's Party and, later, the military government under Field Marshal Phibun, argued that the Thai state needed to intervene in the economy to reduce foreign control over the economy (which had increased with the opening of the country to foreign trade in the mid nineteenth century) and to promote the employment and investment of ethnic Thais, particularly in non-agricultural sectors (Hewison 1997:100–1). Since that time, however, these ideas have been much less influential than internationalist ones. Although the country adopted an import-substitution industrial strategy during the 1960s, this was not done in the name of autonomous economic development but, rather, reviving the Thai economy with the help of foreign aid and investment. Furthermore, the country has not produced any influential champions of inward-looking high-tech industrial projects along the lines of Indonesia's Habibie or Malaysia's Mahathir. Nor has there been a strong concern to restrain the economic role of ethnic Chinese and to promote that of indigenous people as there has been elsewhere in the region, largely because ethnic Chinese have been much better integrated into Thai society than they have been into some other societies.

Also in accordance with model 6(a) (table 8.1, page 238), the state has had a relatively low degree of institutional capacity. In contrast to its counterparts in the East Asian newly industrialised countries (NICs) (that is, South Korea, Singapore, Hong Kong, and Taiwan), the Thai government has been characterised by high levels of inefficiency and corruption. Personal connections have been a far stronger determinant of business and political success than has genuine ability, and there has not been a clear separation between bureaucratic incumbents and their offices (Riggs 1966; Girling 1981). At the same time, as MacIntyre (1999) has pointed out, the fractured multi-party character of the country's parliamentary system has made economic decision-making extremely difficult. With so many parties in parliament and parliamentary coalitions so unstable, gridlock in relation to important economic issues has been common. Finally, the Thai judiciary has been inefficient and corrupt, meaning that a proper enforcement mechanism for economic rules has not been in place (Pasuk and Baker 1998:302).

The impact of the Asian economic crisis on Thailand's coalitional structure has also been consistent with model 6(a) (table 8.1, page 238). The crisis dramatically strengthened the structural leverage of mobile capitalists and, in particular, their supporters at the IMF, which was called in by the Thai government during 1997 to bail the economy out. With the country desperately needing the IMF's aid, the Thai government had little option but to agree to a series of IMF-sponsored reform agreements. The crisis also led to a shift in the balance of power and influence within Thailand itself, away from well-connected provincial business groups and bureaucratic mandarins and towards metropolitan capitalists. The crisis made it apparent that the system of patronage and corruption in which the interests of provincial business groups and mandarins were embedded was no longer functional for capitalist development. This contradiction was clearest in the financial sector where senior members of Chart Pattana, a political party with strong connections to provincial business groups, had substantial interests in ailing finance companies. Despite the fact that these companies were haemorrhaging severely, Chart Pattana figures were able to arrange for the central bank to provide them with generous financial support, in turn contributing to a substantial blowout in the money supply and an increase in inflation (MacIntyre 1999:146–7). In this context, the position of metropolitan capitalists—who, as Pasuk and Baker (1997:25) have pointed out, have in recent years developed an interest in technocratic economic management and efficient business development—was to strengthen considerably. This shift in coalitional structure was to be consolidated by the fall of the Chavalit government, which had been based on a parliamentary coalition dominated by parties with strong connections to provincial business groups and the military, and the formation of a new government under Chuan Leekpai. In contrast to these parties, Chuan's Democrat Party, which constituted the dominant element in the new governing parliamentary coalition, was considered to be relatively free of corruption and to have a strong commitment to deregulation, privatisation, and regulatory reform.

In accordance with our framework, Thailand appears to be undergoing a thoroughgoing program of neo-liberal reform in the wake of the crisis, but experiencing serious implementation problems with this program. This can clearly be seen, for instance, in the area of insolvency law.

Before the Asian economic crisis, Thailand's regulatory and institutional framework for dealing with corporate insolvency was extremely weak by international standards. The country's bankruptcy law, which was originally enacted in 1940, had not been amended since 1983 and was becoming increasingly out of date. Most importantly, it did not allow for the establishment of a special court to deal with insolvency-related matters, nor provide a mechanism by which corporate debt could be rescheduled and corporate debtors reorganised (*AB* 1997; *EAER* 1997; Gibbons 1996). The receivership process also was widely considered to be cumbersome, expensive, and time-consuming. According to one source, for instance, it usually took three to five years for creditors to claim the assets of bad debtors, and could take as long ten years (*AB* 1997). The result, as one commentator pointed out, was that 'the entire bankruptcy process in Thailand [was] very rarely used and inadequate to address the type of complex, multinational, cross-border insolvency situations that are becoming increasingly common in this day and age' (Gibbons 1996).

When the Thai baht collapsed in mid 1997, the Thai government came under increasing pressure to revamp its insolvency framework. The collapse of the baht left most of the corporate sector insolvent and led to the closure of a large number of finance companies. With further lending to Thai companies to some extent contingent upon successful debt-rescheduling and the reorganisation or liquidation of insolvent local companies, it was necessary for the government to develop a more effective mechanism by which creditors and debtors could reschedule debts, debtors could be reorganised, and creditors could seize control over debtors' assets. The closure of forty-six finance companies in late 1997 alone left an estimated US$18 billion worth of corporate assets up for grabs. The crisis also dramatically strengthened the position of the IMF which made it clear that it expected significant reform in this area in return for its financial assistance. With the IMF effectively drawing a line in the sand, the Thai government had little choice but to agree to a wide variety of insolvency law reform measures as part of the various Letters of Intent it negotiated with that organisation (*FEER* 1998; *Nation* 1998a). In any case, although there was significant opposition to insolvency law reform from some members of the Thai Senate who had financial interests in heavily indebted local companies, the dominant reformist elements within the Democrat-led coalition government appeared genuinely to support insolvency reform and, given their numerical superiority within parliament, were in a position to push reform bills through.

The result was the introduction of an extensive range of reforms in the insolvency area. In June 1998, the Thai Central Bank established the Corporate Debt Restructuring Advisory Committee (CDRAC) to promote and administer negotiation of debt-restructuring between debtors and creditors. This was followed in early 1998 and early 1999 by amendments to the country's bankruptcy laws that made it possible for insolvent companies to be reorganised and provided for the establishment of a special bankruptcy court. In early 1999, the parliament also passed a new foreclosure law that was intended to speed up the receivership process. So extensive were the reforms that the usually critical World Bank, although still concerned about the possibility for delays in the receivership process, declared that the Thai bankruptcy court was 'clearly off to an excellent start' (World Bank 2000:19).

It has become clear, however, that there are significant problems with the implementation of the new laws and the operation of the new court. Possibly because of concerns about judicial corruption and the workability of the new insolvency system, few local companies and their creditors have sought to use the new system. As the World Bank (2000:19) explains:

> Given that the level of non-performing loans in Thailand is still extraordinarily high (38%), the number of companies covered under the bankruptcy and CDRAC frameworks is relatively insignificant. There are said to be many cases where private negotiations outside these legal frameworks have taken place between corporate debtors and their creditors. Even taking into account the restructuring covered by the CDRAC framework and voluntary, out-of-court arrangements, a legitimate issue for inquiry is why the number of corporate insolvencies filed with the Bankruptcy Court and covered by the CDRAC framework is low.

Indonesia

Indonesia fits the profile of model 3(a) in table 8.1 (page 238). In contrast to Thailand, the dominant economic ideas in Indonesia have been nationalist rather than internationalist. Ever since Indonesia achieved independence in 1949, important sections of the country's political and bureaucratic elite have argued that extensive state intervention in the economy is necessary to promote national economic development and, in particular, to develop an autonomous industrial sector capable of producing not only low value-added products, but also complex capital and intermediate goods. They have also argued that state intervention is necessary to overcome foreign economic domination and to promote the development of indigenous business enterprise. At the same time, the indigenous petty bourgeoisie and other marginalised elements within society have supported radical populist agenda that have had strong parallels with nationalist economic ideas. Liberal economic ideas, by contrast, have had relatively little influence in the country. It has been only when the dominant anti-reform groups have been weakened at times of economic crisis—such as the mid 1960s, the mid 1980s, and the period since the onset of the Asian economic crisis in 1997—that these ideas have had more than a minimal impact on policy (Chalmers and Hadiz 1997; Robison 1997:29–31; Rosser 1999a).

Also as in model 3(a) (table 8.1, page 238), the state's institutional capacity has been low. Like the Thai government, the Indonesian government has been characterised by high levels of inefficiency and corruption—indeed, if the regular transparency and corruption ratings from organisations such as Transparency International are to be believed, Indonesia has been even more corrupt and inefficient than Thailand. Senior political and bureaucratic figures have sold access to state facilities—such as export and import licences, forestry concessions, and state bank loans—in exchange for material rewards. They have also used state enterprises to provide business opportunities for well-connected business groups and to generate extra-budgetary revenues for organisations such as the military (Crouch 1988; Robison 1986; Robison 1997). Regulatory agencies such as Bank Indonesia (the central bank) and Bapepam (the Capital Market Supervisory Agency), have been staffed by poorly qualified personnel (except at the most senior levels) and have had insufficient resources at their disposal to be adequate watchdogs (Rosser 1999a:81–200). As in Thailand, the judiciary has been inefficient and corrupt, meaning that Indonesia has also lacked a proper enforcement mechanism for economic rules (World Bank 1993; Thoolen 1987).

The coalitional consequences of the Asian economic crisis for Indonesia have also been consistent with model 3(a) (table 8.1, page 238). As in the Thai case, the crisis severely weakened anti-reform elements within the country, most notably the politico-bureaucrats who controlled access to state facilities and the major domestic conglomerates, most of which had benefited considerably from privileged access to these facilities. The collapse of the rupiah multiplied the domestic currency cost of the conglomerates' (generally substantial) foreign debt obligations, forcing most of them to default on their loans and making it almost impossible for them to raise new credit. In addition, the political instability produced by the crisis—and, in particular, the growing violence towards ethnic Chinese business people—forced many conglomerate owners to flee the country. The crisis also provided an opportunity for opposition figures, such as

Amien Rais, Megawati Sukarnoputri, Abdurrahman Wahid, and various student groups, to challenge the authority of the New Order regime that had sustained and rewarded the conglomerates and their politico-bureaucratic patrons. Massive student demonstrations occurred, culminating in the capture of the Indonesian parliament and the forced resignation of President Soeharto in late May 1998.

However, reform-oriented coalitions were too weak to take full advantage of this situation. The crisis increased the structural leverage of mobile capitalists and, most notably, their representative organisations, the IMF and the World Bank. At several key points during the crisis, the IMF and the World Bank withheld their financial support in an attempt to force the government to move ahead with the various IMF reform agreements it had signed—in each case with significant effect. But mobile capitalists could not translate their structural power into direct political power because most of them were foreign and therefore unable to hold government office. The country's liberal technocrats were too weak to assume direct political power because of their lack of a strong domestic power base. Although their policies had the support of mobile capitalists, their domestic support base did not extend beyond some local economists and media commentators, and some downstream producers (Robison 1988:69; Rosser 1999a:62). They were consequently to remain important (but not dominant) players in the policy-making process. During the Habibie interregnum, the technocrats had a continued presence in the cabinet and the main economic policy-making bodies, but not a dominant one. Indeed, for the entire Habibie period, it seemed that the most influential members of Habibie's economic team were not the technocrats but figures associated with the previous government, such as Chief Economics Minister Ginandjar Kartasasmita and the populist forces aligned with Minister for Cooperatives Adi Sasono. The fall of Habibie and the formation of a new government under Abdurrahman Wahid have done little to improve the technocrats' position. If anything, these events have made it worse. Although some technocrats have been appointed to Wahid's economic advisory council, none has been given a cabinet posting. With the shift to a political system in which power is spread among a variety of political parties, Wahid has been forced (to ensure continued sufficient support for his presidency) to allocate ministerial positions on the basis of party affiliation rather than on the basis of qualifications and expertise. To be sure, some of Wahid's ministers, such as Kwik Kian Gie and Laksamana Sukardi, are known for having liberal economic views. But, as Sukardi's shock dismissal as minister for State-Owned Enterprises in early 2000 demonstrated, their position within cabinet is far from dominant.

In accordance with model 3(a) (table 8.1, page 238), Indonesia appears, in the wake of the crisis, to be undergoing a partial program of neo-liberal reform in which there are serious problems of implementation. The case of accounting policy illustrates this well.

Like Thailand's insolvency system, Indonesia's regulatory and institutional framework for accounting was relatively weak before the crisis. The collapse of international oil prices in the mid 1980s had made it necessary for the government to improve the quality of financial reporting within the country to promote the development of the capital market as a mechanism for attracting new sources of investment funds. But resistance to accounting reform on the part of the conglomerates and the politico-bureaucrats, both of whom were concerned that it would force them to be more transparent and accountable, made it difficult for the technocrats, the World Bank, and other groups that supported reform to make much progress. In the wake of a series of highly publicised financial reporting scandals (Rosser 1999a:162–9), the technocrats were able to push through the introduction of a new set of accounting standards that was based largely on International Accountancy Standards (IAS), and were able to ensure the inclusion of provisions in the new Companies Code and Capital Markets Law that gave this set of standards legal backing. The technocrats were also able to ensure the inclusion of provisions that made company directors and commissioners personally liable for any losses incurred by investors as a result of untrue or misleading information in company reports, that specified the general format of financial reports, and that imposed fines on company directors, commissioners, and major shareholders who did not report material events to the public (Cole and Slade 1999; IF 1995; JP 1996).

But the technocrats were to make very little progress in the area of enforcement. In the mid 1980s, the government had officially prohibited foreign accountants from practising in the country, forcing international auditing firms to operate through domestic affiliates rather than set up their own offices. This situation suited the conglomerates because it meant that they could have their books audited by firms that, although they operated under the names of major international firms, were not (in most cases) directly controlled by these international firms, and consequently did not always apply the same standards. In early 1997, following calls from the World Bank for Indonesian auditors to be more independent, the technocrats were able to push through regulations permitting foreign accountants to practise within the country on an individual basis. They were not, however, able to push through regulations giving foreign accountants permission to set up their own firms (MA 1998). Nor were the technocrats able to promote reform of the country's court system, the institution that was ultimately responsible for enforcing accounting regulations. Indonesia's judiciary was widely regarded as inefficient, poorly trained, and corrupt; it was widely known that court decisions, in many cases, were for sale. But despite the problems cased by the collapse of oil prices, the politico-bureaucrats and the conglomerates remained strong enough to stave off attempts for judicial reform.

The collapse of the rupiah in 1997–98 was to provide an opportunity for the technocrats and the World Bank to push the process of accounting reform a step further. Much public analysis of the crisis argued that poor accounting practices, although not solely responsible for the crisis, had contributed to its severity (*AWSJ* 1998; Rahman 1998). Some commentators, such as the head of the US Federal Reserve, Alan Greenspan, argued that recovery would not occur until countries within the region adopted better and clearer accounting rules (*AWSJ* 1999). In addition, as noted earlier, the crisis strengthened the position of elements that supported accounting reform, most notably the controllers of mobile capital and their representative organisations, the IMF and World Bank. In this context, the government was to push ahead with the process of accounting reform, introducing a requirement for all limited companies above a certain size to publish audited financial reports and (through the Jakarta Stock Exchange) a set of corporate governance regulations for publicly listed companies (*JP* 1998; Rosser 1999b:15).

Importantly, for our purposes however, it did not go any further than this. In particular, it did nothing to try to improve the quality of auditing within the country or to reform the judiciary. In this connection, a useful comparison can be drawn with Thailand where, as have seen, the political and social preconditions for reform have been much stronger. In that country, the government responded to criticisms concerning the quality of financial reporting by local companies by not only improving its accounting regulations (World Bank 2000:21–2), but also by launching an assault on several international auditing firms. In August 1998, for instance, the Securities and Exchange Commission suspended two auditors, one at SGV-Na Thalang and Co. Ltd and the other at Deloitte Touche Tohmatsu Jaiyos Ltd, for failing to comply with standards when auditing the financial reports of finance companies that subsequently failed (*Nation* 1998b). Around the same time, the commission also launched an investigation into the local affiliate of Peat Marwick over accounting irregularities at Alphatec Electronics that were reported to amount to more than AUS$40 billion (*Australian* 1998; see also MacDonald 1998). The Thai government also pressed ahead with judicial reform, and the national parliament approved a bill to give judges greater independence from the Justice

Ministry (*Nation* 1999). In short, then, the different political and social environments within the two countries produced different reform outcomes: whereas the Indonesian government's program of accounting reform was only partial in nature—being focused on the production of new regulations, but not on their implementation and enforcement—the Thai government's program was much more comprehensive.

Singapore

Singapore's political economy has two distinct elements: first, a tradeable sector largely controlled by foreign capital and, second, a powerful domestic sector composed of government-led companies (GLCs) that effectively dominate the domestic economy and are strongly linked to the ruling People's Action Party (PAP). The effective political and policy segmentation of the economy between the external and the domestic sectors reduces (although it does not eliminate) potential conflicts between the two sectors. However, the powerful domestic enterprises are the core component of Singapore's dominant coalition. Therefore any analysis of the policy reform in Singapore over the past decade or so needs to take into account the pivotal economic and political role of GLCs in Singapore's dominant coalitions. Indeed, even as privatisation and deregulation have proceeded apace, the government used key holding companies—Temasek, Singapore Technology, and Health Corporation holdings—to retain control over some of the biggest corporate entities in Singapore (Rodan 1997; see also Vennewald 1994).

A significant facet of Singapore's liberalisation over the past decade has been its ability to separate ownership and control. Even as state enterprises were privatised, those controlling this powerful sector of the economy have had close links with the PAP. In this context, Rodan points out that 'this virtual "class" of public entrepreneurs is closely connected to the ruling political party, the upper echelons of the civil service having been the main recruiting for the PAP for some time' (Rodan 1997:160). Indeed, in this respect, Singapore's political economy differs significantly from that of other Tigers (South Korea, Taiwan, and Hong Kong) in relying on state-led companies rather than predominantly on private capital.

In fact, one of the distinctive features of the Singaporean political economy over the past fifteen years has been the gradual movement of state enterprises into the private sector without a concomitant shift in control of these enterprises. Singapore has, in effect, created a powerful group of what could be termed 'nomenklatura capitalists' who exercise immense control over the enterprises they manage but are yet dependent on the PAP for their position. From our perspective, this close linkage between the GLCs and the ruling party accounts for the failure of an alternative reform coalition to emerge. Even if there were powerful economic interests pushing for reform, such interests would have to operate outside the politically entrenched PAP—a difficult task in Singapore. Of course, it is quite possible that, in future, these nomenklatura capitalists will move towards establishing more direct ownership of the enterprises they now manage, but such a prospect is still in the distant future.

Three further factors condition the nature of policy reform. First, the Singaporean state has exceptional fiscal resources that not only moderated structural pressure from the global economy, but also allowed the state to intervene to prop up ailing economic sectors (Velloor 1998). Second, the Singaporean state has considerable institutional capacity. In fact, as much of the developmental state literature suggests (see Weiss and Hobson 1995), its economic development has relied on the coordination capacity of the state. Finally, the Singaporean technocracy is strongly internationalist in orientation. In fact, of all the economies in South-East Asia, the Singaporean state is the most deeply permeated by an internationalist ethos.

This unique combination of an entrenched status quo coalition with a high degree of institutional capacity and internationalist orientation in the bureaucracy produces limited reform with good implementation (see model 2b, table 8.1, page 238). Alternatively, this type of reform can be conceived of as 'offensive adjustment to structural pressure'. The essence of offensive adjustment is the protection of companies within the dominant coalition by a process of gradual and selective liberalisation. It seeks to make GLCs and other parts of the dominant coalition more competitive by subjecting them to more international competition, but this is done in a manner that will not threaten the economic and political position of the dominant coalition. Rather, it seeks to use this gradual liberalisation to further entrench its dominance within the Singaporean political economy. A good example of this process is economic policy-making in Singapore's telecommunications industry.

Singapore has made significant moves to liberalise and deregulate its telecommunications market. In part, this is due to the dramatic global technical change that transformed telecommunications markets. In parallel with these global changes there has been significant international pressure on the Singaporean government to liberalise its telecommunications market. The impetus for these changes can also be located in the continuing effort by the Singaporean government to develop its information technology industries through the vehicle of its own GLCs. Given these potentially contradictory imperatives, the telecommunications reform provides an important window into the management of policy reform.

Three distinctive features of reform stand out.

First, there has been a policy of gradual liberalisation in segmented markets—such as mobile telephones—within the telecommunications sector. In 1995, the government issued a licence for a second mobile provider to commence services from 1997. In 1998, the market was further liberalised in a range of areas (Singh 1999) and, in January 2000, the government brought forward its liberalisation program and lifted limits on foreign equity. However, a significant aspect of these reforms is the fact that most new licences are in partnership and alliance with government-led companies (Singh 1999). Therefore, although the market has been liberalised, the government has ensured that strategic domestic corporate entities have become players within the newly liberalised market. As Singh (1999:23) points out:

> Competition among government linked firms is potentially as effective as among profit-oriented firms, suggesting that under appropriate conditions it is possible for the government to introduce competition into markets without necessarily allowing unlimited competition.

One of the key advantages of the strategy of guided liberalisation is that it allows the state to focus on competition (rather than on ownership) in the deregulated market, and this dovetails with the Singaporean government's privatisation strategy which separates the marketisation of government-owned assets from their ownership and control. It is a strategy that provides a significant advantage to powerful GLCs that benefit from liberalisation without ceding managerial control over their corporations.

Second, the size and financial strength of SingTel—a GLC—gives it a significant competitive advantage over the rest of the market. However, the gradual liberalisation of the market exposes SingTel to the international market forces without threatening its fundamental economic strength. Hence, the policy of guided liberalisation in a range of markets from telecommunication to finance dovetails with the corporate and strategic interest of SingTel (Singh 1999). However, as Rodan points out (chapter 5, this volume), these strategies might well be increasingly problematic when government-led corporations attempt to compete in international markets.

Finally, the telecommunication regulator, the Information Development Authority (IDA), is not independent of the executive. Given SingTel's influence and power within the government, the IDA's limited regulatory autonomy casts doubt on its ability to reign in entrenched dominant market players. Moreover, the IDA's mandate is not only to develop competition, but also to develop strategic industry policies for the Singapore information industry. It is clear that the government's liberalisation policies will be limited by this mandate to develop industry policies. Again, given the critical role of GLCs in the implementation of these policies, it can safely be assumed that policy reform will not adversely affect the strategic capacity of these firms.

To summarise, the distinctive feature of the program of economic liberalisation pursued by the Singapore government is the introduction of guided or limited liberalisation that does not threaten key links between the GLCs and the state. One of the lessons of the Singapore liberalisation experience is that we need to focus not only on the structure of the playing field, but also on the players themselves; markets are embedded in systems of power and interests. In short, the dominant coalition places limits on the extent to which liberalisation can challenge patterns of ownership and control of key domestic companies. However, the financial and policy capacity of the government enables it to use competition as a means of enhancing the global competitiveness of its companies. It is a policy of offensive adjustment to changing global markets.

Malaysia

In Malaysia, as with Singapore, the economy is divided into two sectors: a tradeable sector largely owned by foreign capital, and a domestic sector composed of enterprises with strong links to a ruling party. Central to the Malaysian political economy was the adoption (beginning in 1971) of the New Economic Policy (NEP) designed to promote greater Malay entrepreneurship in the domestic economy, which was previously largely in the hands of Chinese capital. It is beyond the brief of this chapter to document the working of the NEP (see Khoo, chapter 6, this volume), but two significant effects need to be noted.

First, the NEP created strong incentives for powerful Chinese capitalists to enter into alliances and relationships with Malay politicians. This nexus, which became increasingly important during the 1990s, blurred the distinction between Chinese and Malay capital and formed the basis for a broadly based dominant coalition (Gomez and Jomo 1997).

Second, the NEP initially rested on an ambitious state-driven industrialisation policy led by large state enterprises. These enterprises were controlled by powerful bureaucrats with close ties to the dominant political apparatus. However, after the economic recession of the late 1980s, Malaysia embarked on a program of quite extensive privatisation and deregulation. As with Singapore, this privatisation resulted in a shift of ownership from the public to the private sector, but control over the newly privatised assets was still dependent on links to the dominant political party—in Singapore, the PAP; in Malaysia, the United Malays National Organization (UMNO). However in Malaysia, this was achieved through the creation of private companies that were controlled by UMNO. In short, in Malaysia, ownership of key strategic enterprises shifted from state to party. As Bowie points out, these developments have led to the 'erection of corporate empires blessed with unrestricted access to state-issued licences and Malay preferences that is under the direct control of the governing party, UMNO, and is used to raise funds for constituent and electoral purposes' (Bowie 1994:182). As with Singapore, Malaysia created its own brand of nomenklatura capitalists that are a key component of the dominant coalition.

Although the crisis has severely undermined the viability of these enterprises, it is clear that the links between UMNO and key sectors of the domestic economy are so strong that any attempt to introduce market-oriented reform will be strongly resisted. The brutal treatment of Anwar Ibrahim is ample testimony to the strength of this domestic coalition. As with Singapore, the creation of a kind of nomenklatura capitalism allows very little political space for the emergence of an alternative reform-oriented coalition. However, unlike in Singapore, there are significant pockets of domestic capital that might form the basis of a future reform coalition. The recent electoral setbacks for the ruling party suggest that this might well be a plausible scenario.

In terms of institutional capacity, the Malaysian state is fiscally highly constrained; there are significant limits to the extent to which it can bail out strategically connected enterprises. Nevertheless, the state does have a relatively greater capacity to implement economic programs than is the case in either Indonesia or Thailand. More strikingly, Malaysian economic policies have a strongly nationalist orientation. As Khoo (1995:329) has pointed out:

> But it aspires to find its fulfilment in an equally committed Malaysian nationalist goal of competing equally with the advanced nations of the world. Mahathir himself has alluded to all this before.

The strength of the dominant coalition and the weakness of any putative reform coalition, combined with the strongly nationalistic orientation of Malaysian economic policy-making, suggest that the prospects for neo-liberal reform programs are weak. But, unlike in Singapore, the Asian economic crisis greatly weakened the economic viability of key enterprises that would preclude the kind of offensive adjustment to the crisis that was evident in Singapore. Malaysia's response to the crisis was much more defensive and led to a temporary withdrawal from the international financial system (Nesadurai 2000).

Malaysia's response to the Asian crisis was dramatic. It imposed capital controls and turned its back on the kind of reforms being pursued in countries such as Thailand and Indonesia. Apart from the imposition of capital controls by Bank Negara, the Malaysian government instituted a range of policies in both the financial and corporate sectors to protect politically linked firms and banks. It established an Asset Managing company to purchase non-performing loans from the financial sector to protect the banks from unmanageable debts, and also established a special-purpose vehicle to recapitalise banks (Nesadurai 2000). Given the fact that these agencies lack any real independence, it is clear that the underlying imperative for these moves has been to salvage the politically connected financial institutions and conglomerates.

It is clear that these reforms in the financial sector imposed by the Malaysian government represent a defensive adjustment to the structural pressures imposed by the global economy. It is defensive in the sense that the Malaysian response to the crisis exemplifies a series of moves to protect the economic and political interests of an entrenched dominant coalition that had become significantly vulnerable (see model 1b, table 8.1, page 238). Indeed, it is instructive to compare the Malaysian strategy with the Singaporean policies that have moved to gradually liberalise Singapore's financial sector—for example, by lifting restriction of foreign entry to its banking sector (Rodan, chapter 5, this volume). Although both states have dominant coalitions that are deeply entrenched, the difference in the two strategies lies in the degree to which these coalitions have been exposed to the structural pressures of the global market.

The key, then, to understanding the Malaysian defensive reform strategy is the extent to which it has reflected the close connections among the dominant political apparatus and key financial and corporate entities. As Nesadurai (2000:106) argues:

> . . . adjustment has not altered the essential structures of Malaysia's patronage based economic system, which remain in place. Although the course of adjustment in Malaysia bears the stamp of the present Prime Minister, any other leader, irrespective of any neo-liberal leanings, would have to work within the constraints imposed by both the ethnic based distributive policy and the politics of patronage that have become entrenched in the Malaysian economy.

In essence, the policy response to the crisis has been dictated by the fact that the privatisation of state enterprises that took place in the 1990s created a new group of nomenklatura—Malay capitalists who, acting in alliance with significant sections of non-Malay capital, controlled the commanding heights of the Malaysian economy. The crisis was particularly severe on these new capitalist groupings concentrated in sectors such as finance, infrastructure, and real estate. Indeed, as Khoo (2000:222) notes:

> . . . as corporate figures and their political allies joined to secure privatised projects, they intensified the politicisation of commerce and commercialisation of politics (locally derided as 'money politics').

Given the absence of an alternative reform coalition the populist response to the crisis was all but inevitable.

Conclusion

The overriding issue to emerge from this analysis is the extent to which the enacting of liberal economic reform is enmeshed in the political process. Liberalisation strikes at the heart of deeply entrenched political and economic interests. To be successful, therefore, an economic liberalisation program must galvanise its own political support. From this perspective, economic liberalisation is not merely a technical exercise to implement the 'right' policies, but a political project undertaken by the putative winners of liberalisation. For this reason, economic liberalisation is likely to be a deeply contested and a prolonged process. Our analysis of liberalisation serves to underscore the fact that markets are not neutral abstract entities; they are deeply embedded in a constellation of power and interests.

In this respect, our analysis differs from orthodox accounts that regard reform as a mere exercise in getting the policies right. Of course, many studies of economic reform, in explaining the widespread inability of governments to pursue active programs of economic reform in post-crisis Asia, have given great emphasis to issues of institutional failure. However, in these accounts, politics is conceived as external to the market, and the failure to get the policies right is often attributed to rent-seeking or irrational politics. Our understanding of politics is that it is not extrinsic to, but constitutive of, markets. A constitutive theory of markets being advocated in this chapter suggests a different understanding of politics from that which informs neo-classical political economy (see chapter 1, this volume).

The overview of economic reform in South-East Asia also suggests that the post-crisis period is marked by a significant diversity of reform trajectories. In the 'boom' years of growth in the 1990s, there was remarkable similarity of economic strategies and policies. However, after the crisis, there has been considerable divergence—some states, such as Thailand, have embarked on reform; others, such as Indonesia, are in prolonged crisis; Malaysia has seen the emergence of a nationalist backlash; and, Singapore has pursued a policy of offensive adjustment to the global market. In short, economic policies in South-East Asia are characterised by diversity, rather than by uniformity. This has major implications for regional organisations such as APEC, AFTA, and ASEAN, because consensus over issues such as trade liberalisation will be much more difficult to achieve.

In this context, it seems far too early to declare the victory of liberal markets in South-East Asia. Although the crisis has almost certainly brought an end to oligarchic–crony capitalism in Indonesia—or at least that brand of oligarchic–crony capitalism centred around the interests of the Soeharto family—and has given great impetus to economic liberalisation in Thailand, it does not appear to have had similar effects in Singapore and Malaysia. Indeed, the political and economic systems that existed in those countries before the crisis appear to have survived more or less intact. And it is by no means clear that the reforms currently under way in Thailand and Indonesia will produce properly functioning liberal market systems. In the absence of new regulatory frameworks, and proper implementation and effective enforcement of such frameworks, new forms of oligarchic capitalism might emerge in these countries. In short, the crisis might, in the end, lead simply to a reconstitution of the Asian economic model, rather than its demise and replacement with liberal market systems.

References

AB, see *Asian Business (AB)*.

Asian Business (AB) (1997), September 1997.

Asian Wall Street Journal (AWSJ) (1997), 13 November 1997.

Asian Wall Street Journal (AWSJ) (1998), 20 October 1998.

Asian Wall Street Journal (AWSJ) (1999), 3 May 1999.

ASWJ, see *Asian Wall Street Journal (AWSJ)*.

Australian (1998), 15 September 1998.

Beeson, Mark (1998) 'Globalisation, the East Asian Crisis and Indonesia', paper presented to the ICSSR–IIAS Conference on *Identity, Locality and Globalisation*, New Delhi–Sariska, February.

Bowie, Alasdair (1994) 'The Dynamics of Business–Government Relations in Industrialising Malaysia', in A. Macintyre (ed.) *Business and Government in Industrialising Asia*, Sydney: Allen and Unwin, pp 167–94.

Buchanan, J. (1980) 'Reform in the Rent-Seeking Society', in J. Buchanan, R. Tollison and G. Tullock (eds) *Toward a Theory of the Rent-seeking Society*, College Station: Texas A&M University Press, pp 359–67.

Cathie, J. (1997) 'Financial Contagion in East Asia and the Origins of the Economic and Financial Crisis in Korea', *Asia Pacific Business Review*, Winter 1997/Spring 1998, 4(2/3):18–28.

Chalmers I. and V. Hadiz (eds) (1997) *The Politics of Economic Development in Indonesia: Contending Perspectives*, London: Routledge.

Chaudhry, K. (1993) 'The Myths of the Market and the Common History of Late Developers', *Politics and Society*, 21(3):245–74.

Chaudhry, K. (1994) 'Economic Liberalization and the Lineages of the Rentier State', *Comparative Politics*, 27 (October):1–25.

Cole D. and B. Slade (1999) 'The Crisis and Financial Sector Reform', in H. Arndt and H. Hill (eds) *Southeast Asia's Economic Crisis: Origins, Lessons and the Way Forward*, pp 107–18, St Leonards: Allen and Unwin.

Crouch, H. (1988) *The Army and Politics in Indonesia*, Ithaca: Cornell University Press.

EAER, see *East Asian Executive Reports (EAER)*

East Asian Executive Reports (1977), 15 November 1997.

Evans P. (1992) 'The State as Problem and Solution: Predation, Embedded Autonomy, and Structural Change', in S. Haggard and R. Kaufman (eds) *The Politics of Economic Adjustment*, Princeton: Princeton University Press, pp 139–81.

Evans, P. (1995) *Embedded Autonomy: States and Industrial Transformation*, Princeton: Princeton University Press.

Far Eastern Economic Review (FEER) (1998), 5 March 1998.

FEER, see *Far Eastern Economic Review (FEER)*.

Frankel, J. (1998) 'The Asian Model, the Miracle, the Crisis', paper delivered at US International Trade Commission, April, <www.stern.nyu.edu/~nroubini/asia/AsiaHomepage.html>.

Fukuyama, F. (1999) 'Asian Values and the Current Crisis', <http://wbln0018.worldbank.org/eap/eap.nsf/6ab4a4/3f71de9e0d22cc 42852568110078670>.

Gibbons, D. (1996) 'Bankruptcy in Thailand', *Commercial Law Bulletin*, 11(4):50–4.

Girling, J. (1981) *The Bureaucratic Polity in Modernizing Societies: Similarities, Differences and Prospects in the ASEAN Region*, Singapore: Institute of Southeast Asian Studies.

Gomez, E.T. and K. S. Jomo (1997) *Malaysia's Political Economy: Politics, Patronage and Profits*. Cambridge: Cambridge University Press.

Haggard, S. and R. Kaufman (1992) 'Institutions and Economic Adjustment', in S. Haggard and R. Kaufman (eds) *The Politics of Economic Adjustment*, Princeton: Princeton University Press, pp 3–37.

Harberger A. (1993) 'Secrets of Success: A Handful of Heroes', *American Economic Review*, AEA Papers and Proceedings, May 1993, pp 343–50.

Hewison, K. (1997) 'Thailand: Capitalist Development and the State', in G. Rodan et al. (eds) *The Political Economy of South-East Asia: An Introduction*, Melbourne: Oxford University Press, pp 93–120.

IF, see *Info Finansial (IF)*.

Info Finansial (IF) (1995), October 1995.

Jakarta Post (JP) (1996), 18 January 1996.

Jakarta Post (JP) (1998), 23 February 1998.

Jomo, K.S. (ed.) (1998) *Tigers in Trouble: Financial Governance, Liberalisation and Crises in East Asia*, London: Zed Books.

JP, see *Jakarta Post (JP)*.

Khoo, Boo Teik (1995) *Paradoxes of Mahathirism*, Oxford: Oxford University Press.

Khoo, Boo Teik (2000) 'Economic Nationalism and its Discontents: Malaysian Political Economy after July 1997', in R. Robison, M. Beeson, K. Jayasuriya and Hyuk-Rae Kim (eds) *Politics and Markets in the Wake of the Asian Crisis*, London: Routledge, pp 212–38.

Krueger, A. (1993) *Political Economy of Policy Reform in Developing Countries*, Cambridge, Mass.: MIT Press.

MA, see *Media Akuntansi (MA)*.

MacDonald, S. (1998) 'Transparency Transparency in Thailand's 1997 Economic Crisis: the Significance of Disclosure', *Asian Survey*, 38(7):688–703.

MacIntyre, A. (1994) 'Business, Government and Development: Northeast and Southeast Asian Comparisons', in A. MacIntyre (ed.) *Business and Government in Industrialising Asia*, Sydney: Allen and Unwin, pp 1–28.

MacIntyre, A. (1999) 'Political Institutions and the Economic Crisis in Thailand and Indonesia', in H. Arndt and H. Hill (eds) *Southeast Asia's Economic Crisis: Origins, Lessons, and the Way Forward*, Singapore: Institute of Southeast Asian Studies, pp 142–57.

Media Akuntansi (MA) (1998), June 1998.

Nation (1998a), 25 February 1998.

Nation (1998b), 13 August 1998.

Nation (1999), 7 April 1999.

Nelson, J. (1990) 'Introduction: The Politics of Economic Adjustment in Developing Nations', in J. Nelson (ed.) *Economic Crisis and Policy Choice: The*

Politics of Adjustment in the Third World, Princeton: Princeton University Press, pp 3–32.

Nesadurai, Helen E.S. (2000) 'In Defence of National Autonomy? Malaysia's Response to the Financial Crisis', *Pacific Review*, 13(1):73–113.

Pasuk Phongpaichit and C. Baker (1997) 'Power in Transition: Thailand in the 1990s', in K. Hewison (ed.) *Political Change in Thailand: Democracy and Participation*, London: Routledge, pp 21–41.

Pasuk Phongpaichit and C. Baker (1998) *Thailand's Boom and Bust*, Chiang Mai: Silkworm Books.

Pempel T.J. (1998) *Regime Shift: Comparative Dynamics of the Japanese Political Economy*, Ithaca and Lonson: Cornell University Press.

Polanyi, K. (1944) *The Great Transformation*, New York: Octagon Books.

Rahman, M. (1998) *The Role of Accounting Disclosure in the East Asian Financial Crisis: Lessons Learned?*, UNCTAD.

Riggs, F. (1966) *Thailand: The Modernization of a Bureaucratic Polity*, Honolulu: East–West Center Press.

Robison, R. (1986) *Indonesia: The Rise of Capital*, Sydney: Allen and Unwin.

Robison, R. (1988) 'Authoritarian States, Capital-Owning Classes and the Politics of Newly Industrializing Countries', *World Politics*, 41(1):52–74.

Robison, R. (1997) 'Politics and Markets in Indonesia's Post-oil Era', in G. Rodan, K. Hewison and R. Robison (eds) *The Political Economy of South-East Asia: An Introduction*, Melbourne: Oxford University Press, pp 29–63.

Robison, R. and A. Rosser (1999) 'Surviving the Meltdown: Liberal Reform and Political Oligarchy in Indonesia', in R. Robison et al. (eds) *Politics and Markets in the Wake of the Asian Crisis*, London: Routledge, pp 171–91.

Rodan, Garry (1997) 'Singapore: Economic Diversification and Social Divisions', in Garry Rodan et al. (eds) *The Political Economy of Southeast Asia*, Sydney: Oxford University Press, pp 148–78.

Rosser, A. (1999a) 'Creating Markets: The Politics of Economic Liberalisation in Indonesia Since the Mid-1980s', unpublished PhD dissertation, Murdoch University.

Rosser, A. (1999b) 'The Political Economy of Accounting Reform in Developing Countries: The Case of Indonesia', Asia Research Centre Working Paper No. 93, July.

Schamis, H. (1999) 'Distributional Coalitions and the Politics of Economic Reform in Latin America', *World Politics*, 51:236–68.

Singh, Kulwant (1999) 'Guided Competition in Singapore's Telecommunications Industry', *Industrial and Corporate Change*, 7(4):585–99.

Thoolen, H. (1987) *Indonesia: The Rule of Law*, International Commission of Jurists.

Velloor, Ravi (1998) '$2b Boost for Economy', *Straits Times* 30 June.

Vennewald, W. (1994) 'Technocrats in the State Enterprise System in Singapore', *Working Paper No. 32*, Murdoch University: Asia Research Centre.

Weiss, L. and J. Hobson (1995) *States and Economic Development: A Comparative Historical Analysis*, Oxford: Polity Press.

Williamson, J. (1994) 'In Search of a Manual for Technopols', in J. Williamson (ed.) *The Political Economy of Policy Reform*, Washington, D.C.: Institute for International Economists.

Williamson, J. and S. Haggard (1994) 'The Political Conditions for Economic Reform', in J. Williamson (ed.) *The Political Economy of Policy Reform*, Institute for International Economics, Washington, D.C., pp 527–96.

Winters, J. (1999) 'The Financial Crisis in Southeast Asia', in R. Robison et al. (eds) *Politics and Markets in the Wake of the Asian Crisis*, London: Routledge, pp 34–52.

World Bank (1993) *Indonesia: Sustaining Development*, Washington, D.C.: World Bank.

World Bank (1997) *World Development Report 1997: The State in a Changing World*, Oxford: Oxford University Press.

World Bank (2000) *Thailand Economic Monitor*, Washington, D.C.: World Bank.

9

The Social Construction of Developmental Labour Systems: South-East Asian Industrial Restructuring

Frederic C. Deyo

Economic development involves a broadly based transformation of economic and social institutions, one outcome of which is sustained economic growth. The sociopolitical process through which this transformation occurs normally produces winners and losers as it alters patterns of economic claims and income flows. For this reason, economic development is typically a contested process, one in which shifting and emergent groups and coalitions contend for favourable economic positions in a changing and uncertain social order and in which the very nature and extent of development is an outcome of social and class contention.

Such a political–economic view of economic development can usefully be applied to an understanding of the role of organised labour in the rapid industrialisation of South-East Asia during recent years. Of particular importance are changes in the 'labour systems' through which labour is socially reproduced, mobilised for economic ends, utilised in production, and controlled and motivated in support of economic goals. These changes are joint products of the economically driven labour strategies of government and business elites, of global political and economic pressures and constraints, of the process of industrialisation itself and, in some cases, of the individual and collective responses of workers to elite strategies and industrial pressures.

This chapter explores the labour implications of recent economic development in the capitalist countries of South-East Asia, a region where rapid industrial development is being powerfully shaped and conditioned by two global transformations in economic ideology and policy. The first of these is the growing world influence of neo-liberalism, a broad economic approach emphasising increased reliance on market forces to direct international and national economic processes. The second involves adoption of more flexible post-Fordist production systems as a condition for success under intensified global economic competition. Neo-liberalism and the need for increased production flexibility have powerfully influenced the nature of industrial change in the region and, consequently, the emergent characteristics of labour systems as well. Thus, the global context in which industrialisation is occurring during the process of economic development is closely related to the issues of contestation between workers and trade unions on the one hand, and between government and business elites on the other.

The chapter begins with a brief overview of labour and development in capitalist South-East Asia during past years. It explores the way in which changing economic strategies of governments and firms over recent years have been reflected in corresponding labour policies, and the response of workers to those policies. It is seen that, with some exceptions, labour has been unable effectively to challenge elite strategies, and that labour's weakness derives in large measure from political constraint, rooted initially in the imperatives of regime survival itself, and subsequently in the perceived requirements of the economic strategies of both firms and governments. Equally important, however, has been the labour impact of economic structural change itself, the temporal sequencing of political and economic change, the world system timing of industrial deepening in a volatile post-Fordist global economy and, most recently, the economic crisis of the late 1990s.

Labour and development in South-East Asia

Until relatively recently, the economies of South-East Asia were based largely on agriculture and service industries. As late as 1970, services alone accounted for two-thirds of GDP in Singapore, and 46 per cent in Malaysia. Services and agriculture together accounted for 75 per cent of GDP in Thailand and Malaysia, 67 per cent in Indonesia, and 69 per cent in the Philippines. These two sectors together accounted for even larger shares of the workforce, ranging from 73 per cent in Singapore to 95 per cent in Thailand (World Bank 1995).

Much of the large service sector consisted at that time of small commercial establishments, government services, and a heterogeneous grouping of informal-sector jobs, self-employment, and unpaid family labour. In agriculture, the overwhelming majority of the workforce owned or worked on small family farms, the remainder serving as plantation workers.

Trade unions and other types of labour organisations in these countries were confined largely to plantation workers (especially in Malaysia,

Indonesia, and the Philippines), dockworkers, miners, workers in large manufacturing companies, transportation workers, mill workers and, where legal, state enterprise employees (especially public-utility workers), and civil servants. Despite low levels of unionisation and confinement of unionism to these few occupational sectors, organised labour played a significant role in national politics through to the mid twentieth century. In Malaysia and the Philippines, labour militancy during the 1930s economic crisis strengthened calls for a realignment of development policy away from reliance on exports of primary products and towards protection and encouragement of domestic industry. In Indonesia, the Philippines, and Malaysia, labour participated actively in anti-colonial independence struggles, especially after World War II (Ingelson 1981; Arudsothy and Littler 1993; Wurfel 1959). During the 1950s, militant labour groups in the Philippines pushed successfully for enactment of what was, by regional standards, highly progressive labour legislation (Ofreneo 1995). And, in Singapore, leftist labour mobilisation came close to creating a socialist government in the early 1960s, and clearly shaped the social agenda of the government that was established after the defeat of the Left (Deyo 1981).

By the late 1960s, however, restrictive state controls over trade unionism and labour activism had substantially tamed and depoliticised organised labour. In Malaysia, ethnic and communal conflict that threatened both state structures and conservative ruling groups was met by tight controls over organised labour. More generally across the region, a political assault on the independence and power of organised labour, associated with Western-supported efforts to contain communism, initiated a downward spiral of union influence (c.f. Hewison and Rodan 1994). In Singapore, Chinese communalism precipitated a violent confrontation with anglicised moderates in the ruling People's Action Party (PAP) leading to decimation of the Chinese Left, consolidation of moderate PAP leadership, and the institution of tight pre-emptive controls over organised labour through a government-dominated National Trades Union Congress (NTUC). Although labour organisation and agitation in the Philippines initially elicited a response of political accommodation and the establishment of a liberal, US-modelled labour-relations system, it was met in later years by ever harsher restrictions, culminating in 1972 in martial law repression justified in part by the need to contain Left radicalism and popular sector insurgency (Hutchison 1993).

Similarly, organised labour in Thailand was effectively suppressed under intermittent anti-communist military rule over much of the 1940s–1960s period, especially after the 1957 coup (Hewison and Brown 1994). In Indonesia, following the 1965 military coup that sought to eliminate growing Leftist influence in national politics, the powerful, communist-aligned, national labour federation (Sentral Organisasi Buruh Seluruh Indonesia, SOBSI) was banned and later replaced by a government-sponsored federation.

But this was not to be the end of labour influence in the region. Even under tight political controls, labour continued in some countries to wield moderate influence in policy-making and implementation, in many cases through community-based political mobilisation linked only loosely to trade unionism. Labour's oppositional potential became especially evident during interludes of political crisis and government transition. Following the collapse of military rule in Thailand in 1973, for example, labour militancy frequently paralysed business in Bangkok and elsewhere. During the subsequent three years of open politics, labour pressed successfully for enactment of new legislation that provided for union recognition and collective bargaining rights, established a minimum wage, and required employers to provide a number of new benefits, including workers' compensation. These labour victories were to provide a foundation for re-establishment of worker rights under subsequent democratic governments in the late 1980s and in the 1990s. Similarly, it will be seen below that during the economic crisis in the Philippines in the 1980s, a seemingly moribund labour movement mounted strong opposition to structural reforms, as well as to the Marcos regime itself, in the context of a growing debt and economic crisis. In Singapore and Malaysia, a greater degree of political continuity precluded such periods of dramatic labour mobilisation. But even here, workers and unions continued to press employers and government for improved wages and benefits during the 1960s and into the 1970s.

If, by the late 1960s, South-East Asian labour movements had already been partially tamed under restrictive political regimes, subsequent decades were to see a further diminution in labour influence at enterprise and national levels. This continuing decline can be documented by reference to changes in union density, collective bargaining, and the political role of trade unions. By the mid 1990s, regional union densities were quite low. As a percentage of the employed labour force, Malaysia and Singapore registered quite modest 15 per cent and 14 per cent unionisation levels respectively. This compared with 12 per cent in the Philippines, and 1.6 per cent in Thailand (ILO 1996:184).

In Malaysia (as in Thailand), private-sector unionisation rates are substantially lower, at roughly 7 per cent (Arudsothy and Littler 1993). More importantly, over the previous ten years, these union densities had, in some cases, noticeably declined despite continuing industrial development: by

20.4 per cent in Singapore, 13.4 per cent in Malaysia, and 7.4 per cent in Thailand (for earlier figures, see Kuruvilla 1995). Only the Philippines showed an increase in union density over this period. It will be noted below that the decline in Thailand is partly explained by the forced dissolution of unions in the highly organised state-enterprise sector following the 1991 military coup.

The weakness of organised labour in the region is further reflected in the restriction of collective bargaining agreements to a very small percentage of employed workers (roughly 5 per cent in Thailand, the Philippines, and Malaysia) (Arudsothy and Littler 1993; Brown and Frenkel 1993; Kuruvilla 1995).

At national levels, the weak political position of organised labour is similarly evident across the region. In Singapore and Indonesia, the dominant national trade union federations, the NTUC and Serikat Pekerja Seluruh Indonesia (SPSI) respectively, were so tightly integrated into ruling party structures in the mid 1990s that they could not provide an independent channel of representation for workers (Deyo 1989; MacIntyre 1994). In Malaysia, the largest national federation (the Malaysian Trades Union Congress) was losing ground to a more conservative federation (the Malaysian Labour Organisation) promoted by, and closely aligned with, government. Although Thai state enterprise workers achieved some limited political goals in the 1980s including, most notably, passage of the comprehensive *Social Security Act* of 1990, the trade union movement has more generally been marked by divisiveness and factionalism, seen most dramatically in the existence of five competing major union federations, each supported by high-level military and/or bureaucratic elites. Labour movements in the Philippines and Malaysia suffer from similar problems of disunity and internal competition (Hutchison 1993; Crouch 1993; Arudsothy and Littler 1993).

The weak political position of labour is perhaps most dramatically seen in the relative inability of workers to seize new opportunities flowing from democratic reforms in Thailand and the Philippines. In both cases, workers joined with middle-class groups in opposing military rule and in instituting more open electoral regimes. But in neither case has the organisational strength or collective bargaining position of trade unions been subsequently enhanced. To the contrary, labour movements under the new democratic regimes have remained divided and stagnant.

In this context, it is not surprising that elite developmental and labour policies were rarely significantly challenged by organised labour. And to the limited extent that labour opposition was politically consequential, it took other forms, typically involving spontaneous action on the part of small groups of workers or, alternatively, community groups protesting against government policies or inaction in matters of local concern.

It is noteworthy that stagnation in South-East Asian labour movements has occurred in the context of social transformations that, elsewhere, have been historically associated with the empowerment of labour and other popular sector groups. At the base of these transformations is the continuing course of industrial development itself. Singapore, Malaysia, the Philippines, and Thailand all have substantial manufacturing sectors and provide industrial employment for a sizeable portion of their workforces.

Table 9.1 Industrial and social indicators

Manufacturing as percentage of GDP, 1999

Singapore	Malaysia	Thailand	Philippines	Indonesia
26%	35%	32%	21%	25%

Source: World Bank (2001:296–7, table 12)

Manufacturing as percentage of total employment, 1997

Singapore	Malaysia	Thailand	Philippines	Indonesia
23%	28%	13%	10%	13%

Source: United Nations (1998)

Percentage of industrial employment, 1997

Singapore	Malaysia	Thailand	Philippines	Indonesia
30%	38%	20%	17%	19%

Source: United Nations (1998)

Percentage male/female industry labour force,* 1992–97

Singapore	Malaysia	Thailand	Philippines	Indonesia
39% male	36% male	22% male	19% male	21% male
25% female	30% female	17% female	13% female	16% female

*Industry includes mining and quarrying (including oil production), manufacturing, electricity, gas and water, and construction.

Source: World Bank (2001:50–3, table 2.4)

Percentage urban population, 1999

Singapore	Malaysia	Thailand	Philippines	Indonesia
100%	57%	21%	58%	40%

Source: World Bank (2001:276–7, table 2)

Adult illiteracy rate (% of people 15 years and above), 1998

Singapore	Malaysia	Thailand	Philippines	Indonesia
4% male	9% male	3% male	5% male	9% male
12% female	18% female	7% female	5% female	20% female

Source: World Bank (2001:276–7, table 2)

In addition, these countries boast high levels of literacy and education, usually considered useful predictors of social awareness and political participation. Industrial development in Singapore, Malaysia, and Thailand has been associated with industrial deepening into more sophisticated, technology-intensive and capital-intensive production. Important too is the emergence across the region of an ever more settled and thus organisable urban proletariat (see Hadiz 1994), an important basis for early unionisation in Western countries.

But despite these seemingly propitious socioeconomic changes, rapid industrialisation has nowhere spawned effective trade unionism or enhanced worker participation in political or economic arenas. In part, the weak collective bargaining and political role of South-East Asian labour during recent years derives from a continuation of earlier forms of political constraint. But, unlike the experience in earlier periods, these controls have been oriented less to the political imperatives of regime stability than to the requirements of economic strategies and initiatives. Because of this increasingly close relationship between labour regimes and developmental initiatives (see Deyo 1989; Kuruvilla 1994), we consider these factors together in the discussion that follows, emphasising throughout the ways in which the successful implementation of each of these strategies has been rooted in, while subsequently reinforcing, the weakness of South-East Asian labour movements. The strategies of particular regional interest during recent years include the shift to light export-oriented industrialisation (EOI), economic liberalisation and structural adjustment, industrial deepening under 'second-stage' EOI, and, most recently, adoption of post-Fordist flexible production systems in manufacturing. Although light EOI and neoliberal economic reforms are common to all the capitalist countries in the region, the implications of industrial deepening and post-Fordist flexibility are greatest in the industrially most advanced countries (Singapore, Malaysia, Thailand, and, arguably, the Philippines). For this reason, much of the remaining discussion centres on these countries.

Labour under early export-oriented industrialisation

Light industry-based EOI in Singapore and the Philippines in the 1970s, and in Malaysia, Thailand, and Indonesia in the 1980s, was premised on the successful mobilisation of low-cost semi-skilled labour for the assembly and manufacture of products for world markets. In Singapore, Thailand,

and Malaysia, and in the export-processing zones of the Philippines and Indonesia, light EOI relied heavily on direct foreign investment.

The twin pressures of cost-containment on the one hand, and multi-national locational requirements for both political stability and low labour costs on the other, encouraged governments to impose or enhance stringent constraints on labour. In Singapore, these pressures elicited new labour legislation in 1968 that reduced permissible retrenchment benefits, overtime work, bonuses, maternity leave, and fringe benefits. Thenceforth, unions could not demand, nor could managers offer, benefits greater than those stipulated under law. In addition, the National Wages Council, a tripartite body, established wage guidelines that held industrial wages down through the 1970s. And a second statute gave management full discretionary power in matters of promotion, transfer, recruitment, dismissal, reinstatement, assignment or allocation of duties, and termination. These topics were now removed by law from the range of legally negotiable issues. This array of legislation, along with a parallel set of new investment incentives, was followed by a wave of foreign investment that continued until the mid 1970s recession (Deyo 1989; Begin 1995).

In Malaysia, where legislation similar to that in Singapore also removed from collective bargaining a broad range of personnel matters, union organisation and collective bargaining were banned throughout the early 1980s in electronics, the single most important manufacturing export industry. Union militancy was repressed in the export-processing zones of the Philippines also.

In the wake of declining oil prices in the early 1980s, the Indonesian government intensified labour controls under a more centralised national labour federation, and gave special encouragement to light, export-oriented manufacturing to replace diminished oil export earnings (Hadiz 1994:195). In Thailand, even under democratisation, exclusion of state enterprise workers from union coverage continues to undermine the national labour movement insofar as the state-enterprise unions have traditionally played the lead union role in that country. And in the Philippines, the new Aquino regime took a hardline stance on strikes defined as illegal under existing Marcos-era labour legislation (Ofreneo 1994).

The association between early EOI and cost-containment labour regimes has been noted frequently in the literature on East Asian industrialisation (Kuruvilla 1994). A recent International Labour Office (ILO) study of world employment trends explicitly links the globalisation of capital, production, and markets with reduced labour protection in developing countries, arguing that global integration has adversely affected the ability of governments to enact and enforce labour legislation. Globalisation, notes the ILO, gives 'governments an incentive to dilute, or fail to enact, measures intended to protect the welfare of workers, or to turn a blind eye to infringements of legislation with this in mind' (ILO 1995:72–3). This same report also notes an increasing erosion of the quality of formal-sector employment through reduced job security, the diminished significance of local or national-level collective bargaining, new policies of 'firm-centric cooperation,' union-avoidance strategies, promotion of company unions, reduced access to information, and diminished bargaining leverage on the part of local unions.

Less well-documented has been the extent of labour opposition to such labour practices and the cost-focused labour systems they have created. Throughout the region, groups of young women newly hired in export-manufacturing industries have protested against low wages and benefits, harsh working conditions, and lack of enforcement of labour standards legislation. Such protest was especially pronounced in the export-processing zones of the Philippines and Indonesia (Lambert 1993).

But, having said this, it remains the case that such protests have rarely brought enduring gains for workers. This follows, in part, from the characteristics of employment in light export sectors, with their relatively transitory labour force comprised of large numbers of young women in unstable low-skill jobs with little career opportunity. The difficulties of organising such a workforce into effective unions, along with the associated difficulty of mounting well-organised pressure on employers, continue to undercut labour movements among workers in the large export-manufacturing sectors of South-East Asia (Deyo 1989).

Economic liberalisation and structural adjustment

Compounding this EOI-linked structural demobilisation of labour are continuing international pressures, often associated with ongoing regional and global trade agreements, to open domestic markets further to imports. Trade liberalisation has, in turn, subjected firms to intensified competition in both domestic and international markets. In developing countries, with their relatively labour-intensive, export-oriented industrial structures, managers have sought to meet these new competitive pressures through cost-cutting measures directed in large part at reducing labour costs. Such measures have both reflected and reinforced labour's already weakened bargaining position. Competitive pressures have created a credible threat of shutdowns, retrenchments, and relocation of production to cheaper labour sites in the absence of effective labour-cost containment. In addition, some cost-cutting measures, including the increased use of temporary and contract labour and greater out-sourcing of production, have directly undercut organised labour while at the same time addressing a second set of competitive requirements, discussed below, stemming from the globalisation of post-Fordist production systems.

In response to high levels of indebtedness among some countries in the region, a broader set of structural adjustments—including privatisation of state enterprises, reduced state regulation of the economy, and reduced public expenditures—has been urged by international agencies and lenders, including, most prominently, the World Bank, the Asian Development Bank, and the International Monetary Fund (Hutchison 1993). Privatisation, most prevalent in Thailand, Malaysia, and the Philippines, in turn subjects large firms in public transport, communications, and other sectors to heightened competition, and thus to the possibility of workforce retrenchment, and of wage and benefit reduction.

These and other neo-liberal economic reforms were often met by labour opposition and public demonstrations. In Malaysia, Thailand, and the Philippines, trade unions fought vigorously for legislation to restrict the use of temporary workers. In Thailand, public-sector unions successfully slowed privatisation during the late 1980s through mass demonstrations in central Bangkok. And in the Philippines, a wave of strikes and public demonstrations opposing structural adjustment measures during the early 1980s contributed to the political crisis that ultimately brought down the Marcos regime.

These labour campaigns against economic liberalisation slowed, but did not stop, ongoing economic reforms. In Thailand, the use of temporary workers continued to expand despite legislation restricting the practice. Efforts to stop privatisation met with somewhat greater success, particularly in Thailand. There, as elsewhere, effective opposition drew strength from a cross-class defensive coalition of labour and bureaucratic/military elites whose economic interests and power base were threatened by privatisation of the enterprises they controlled. In addition, state-enterprise workers were politically insulated from many of the competitive pressures that progressively undercut organised labour in the private sector. Thus, they continued to struggle from a position of relative strength. But, in the end, larger state interests dictated a silencing of opposition from this 'unrestructured' Thai labour sector through a banning of all state-enterprise unions following the 1991 military coup.

The more general undermining of labour movements under these various economic reforms has been furthered by a third strategic initiative, this time at the enterprise level, involving the incremental introduction of flexible production systems in manufacturing sectors during the 1990s. The following discussion assesses the labour impact of this most recent industrial transition in the context of industrial deepening.

Labour under recent industrial restructuring

In response to heightened economic competition and uncertainty, firms in South-East Asia, as elsewhere, are seeking to enhance manufacturing flexibility and adaptability. Flexibility here refers to the ability to introduce changes in product and process quickly, efficiently, and continuously. Such flexibility yields a superior capacity to respond to the intensified pressures of liberalised trade, world market volatility, market fragmentation, heightened demand for just-in-time production and continuous improvements in productivity and quality, and rapid technological change.

A useful distinction is often made between 'static' and 'dynamic' forms of flexibility. Static flexibility, which focuses on short-term adaptability and cost-cutting, is the predominant managerial approach in the labour-intensive export sectors that have figured so prominently in many of Asia's developing economies. The reasons for this strategic choice are clear. Intensified global competition under trade liberalisation places firms under extreme pressure to cut costs in the short term. Risky long-term investments in training, research, and organisational development might be eschewed where they seem to place a firm at a short-term disadvantage *vis-à-vis* other firms that do not make these investments. In some countries, lack of adequate public investment in collective goods (for example training, research and development, and physical infrastructure) further discourages such long-term investments, whereas lack of effective government support for minimal labour standards, adequate wages and benefits, and fair employment practices encourages firms to compete through union avoidance and reduction in labour costs.

It is clear that such static flexibility, with its negative consequences for labour, predominates in many countries and industrial sectors in the region. There is evidence of increased use of subcontracting, casualisation, and contract labour ('numerical flexibility') in the large export sectors of the Philippines (Ofreneo 1994) and Thailand (Deyo 1995). Guy Standing (1989) similarly documents increasing numerical flexibility and casualisation in electronics and other export sectors in Malaysia. Indeed, even in industrially advanced Singapore, James Begin (1995) reports continued reliance on static numerical flexibility. In many cases, employers adopt such labour strategies in part explicitly to undercut unions or unionisation drives. These strategies have the known effects of creating an insecure, floating workforce and of encouraging a further dispersal of production to small, contracted firms and households. As a result, unions throughout the region have fought strenuously to institute legislative restrictions on the employment of temporary workers and similar practices (Charoenloet 1993; Ofreneo 1994).

Dynamic flexibility strategies, although less prevalent, are pursued in product niches requiring high levels of quality, batch vs mass-production, and continuing innovations and improvements in process and product technologies. Such strategies are encouraged where states underwrite a supportive social infrastructure of training, education, and R&D, where they enforce adequate labour standards, and where they provide incentives to firms to invest in training and organisational development. Finally, such strategies are most likely to be undertaken by large, resourceful firms that are able, in part, to create their own support infrastructure, and that operate in relatively protected or oligopolistic markets characterised by moderate, rather than extreme, competitive pressure. For these various reasons, dynamic flexibility strategies tend to occur in the upper-tier NICs with developmentally active states (for example in Singapore, South Korea, and Taiwan) and among dominant firms in semi-protected industrial sectors across the region.

Most research on dynamic flexibility has focused on the experience of innovative industrial firms in the developed countries of Japan, Europe, and North America. In these settings, dynamic flexibility has generally been associated with enhanced worker welfare and security, as well as with increased worker participation in organisational decision-making as firms have sought both to increase worker commitment and loyalty, and to encourage workers to assume increased responsibility for enterprise success. A distinction has been drawn in this regard between 'bargained' forms of flexibility (which are associated with strong, independent unions and high levels of participation in instituting and operating new production systems) and 'participative' flexibility (characterised by captive enterprise unions and more circumscribed forms of worker participation confined largely to shop-floor problem-solving)—see Turner and Aur, Herzenberg, and other chapters in Deyo (1996). This body of research seems generally to suggest that the instituting of dynamic flexibility, whether of bargained or participative forms, should have a similarly salutary effect for workers and perhaps unions in developing Asia. In fact, it has not.

In the higher value-added market niches where technological and product quality requirements preclude continued reliance on low-skill temporary workers and static flexibility, Asian firms are pressed to make long-term investments in worker training, product development, organisational restructuring, and other programs supportive of enhanced dynamic flexibility. In addition, such firms sometimes institute suggestion systems, modified quality circles, labour-management councils, and other means of mobilising worker involvement in quality and productivity improvements (on Malaysia, see Rasiah 1994). But even such instances of dynamic flexibility, typically accompanied by improved wages and benefits and other measures to enhance the stability and commitment of workers, rarely permit the level of worker decision-making found even under participative flexibility. Indeed, improvements in compensation levels and working conditions are as often introduced to avoid unions as to foster long-term organisational improvements (see, for example, Deyo 1995). In general, flexibility-enhancing organisational reforms are overwhelmingly attentive to managerial agenda driven by competitive economic pressures, to the exclusion of the social agenda of workers and unions. And, in many cases, such strategies, along with their relatively benign labour-welfare policies, are confined to a few critical production processes, thus fostering internal labour-market dualism between core, stable workers on the one hand, and casual or contract workers on the other (Deyo 1995).

The reasons for the more autocratic forms of dynamic flexibility found across the region are not hard to discern.

First is the vicious circle defined by initially weak labour movements, the subsequent reorganisation of industry exclusively around managerial goals, and the resultant institutionalisation of autocratic forms of industrial flexibility. Here we see most clearly the way in which the political resources and effectiveness of labour determine institutional outcomes that reinforce existing power inequalities. And in the cases of Singapore and Malaysia, as noted earlier, state labour regimes have further encouraged the institution of autocratic flexibility by excluding from collective bargaining such matters as job assignment and work transfers, that are important elements of 'labour flexibility'. Correspondingly, multinational corporations often insist on operating in a union-free environment (Rasiah 1994; Kuruvilla 1994).

Second, it might be that worker participation and empowerment is less critical to the success of programs of dynamic flexibility in developing Asian countries than in industrially mature economies. Following Amsden (1989), we can distinguish between innovative and learning-based industrialisation. Innovative industrialisation relies on development of a stream of new products and technologies for changing markets. Learning-based industrialisation, by contrast, relies on local adoption of technologies and products developed elsewhere. Insofar as newly developing countries pursue technology-dependent, learning-based industrialisation, employers might seek to institute forms of flexibility that minimise worker participation in favour of unchallenged managerial control over production. This is so because learning-based industrialisation depends mainly on local adaptation and implementation of already debugged production processes and products, thus minimising the need for an extensive involvement of workers in dealing with shop-floor production problems. In such a context, engineers and production managers assume the primary role in reorganising production around imported technologies. Thus, more autocratic forms of flexibility are adequate to the demands of industrialisation. Given that multinational firms, whose investments provide a major conduit for technology transfer and diffusion to Asian firms, are reluctant to relocate major R&D functions to foreign subsidiaries in developing countries, the perpetuation of learning-based industrialisation into future years might imply a long-term stability of such autocratic forms of flexibility and a corresponding discouragement of union or worker empowerment at the workplace level. In such a context, human-resource mobilisation efforts will continue to confine collective forms of shop-floor participation to co-optive, officially sanctioned, and closely circumscribed deliberative forums (such as quality circles and labour-management councils) and, more generally, to eschew collective participation in favour of suggestion systems, informal consultation, merit-based incentives, job ladders, and other individualised modalities of worker participation and involvement in organisational development.

In this context, state labour regimes have been substantially transformed. As employers have increasingly gained the upper hand in their dealings with workers, labour-market 'deregulation,'—the counterpart of economic liberalisation and marketisation—has proven a more effective policy than has continued repression. Such deregulation has not typically been accompanied by proactive labour-protection measures that might provide a level playing field for unions in their bilateral dealings with employees. The Malaysian and Thai governments have ratified only eleven of the ILO's labour conventions, and only minimally enforce existing labour standards legislation—thus effectively subjecting workers to capricious managerial domination, attacks on unions, and non-compliance with minimum wage, health, and safety legislation (Brown and Frenkel 1993). In Thailand, union organisers receive no legal protection during organisational drives up until the actual date of official union registration, thus impeding organisation drives. In both Thailand and the Philippines, labour-market deregulation under democratic reforms, unaccompanied by corresponding measures to strengthen and institutionalise trade unionism, has thus resulted in increased employer domination at the enterprise-level along with heightened union factionalism and conflict (Brown and Frenkel 1993).

Industrial deepening: the impact of developmental sequencing

It has been noted that, despite the political and economic constraints facing organised Asian labour, there have been recent cases of dramatic labour activation. In the 1980s, resistance to structural reforms in the Philippines provides the most striking exception to the broader pattern of decline among organised labour. To understand this exception, as well as the more general context of union weakness and decline, it is necessary to consider the temporal context of the economic structural changes discussed earlier. In particular, how have the domestic developmental sequencing of political and industrial change, and the historical timing of regional industrialisation, influenced the consequences of development for labour? In this section, we explore the impact of developmental sequencing. Later discussion examines the effects of historical timing across the region more generally.

The Philippines differs from the other countries in this discussion in its continuing economic and industrial stagnation and relatively higher levels of unemployment, which are powerful impediments to strong labour movements. In such an inhospitable setting, it is not surprising to find low and declining overall union densities, negligible unionism in many industries, and collective agreement coverage for only a small proportion of wage workers. It is important to recognise, however, that the growing economic crisis of the 1980s precipitated a 'rise in militant unionism whose depth and breadth has no parallels in the country's history' (Ofreneo 1995:3; see also Hutchison 1993). In part, this militancy, which preceded the 'democratic coup' of 1986, can be attributed to a sustained and successful process of industrialisation oriented to the domestic market, that sets the Philippines off from other countries in the region and that parallels more closely the experience of several Latin American countries that pursued similar development strategies during the 1950s and 1960s. The Philippine 'exception' underscores the importance for labour movements of differences in developmental sequencing.

It is often noted that early Latin American industrialisation in the 1940s and 1950s was based on import substitution, whereas that occurring during subsequent decades in Asia was more strongly rooted in export manufacturing. Latin American import-substituting industrialisation (ISI) sought initially to defuse a growing political crisis (occasioned by the collapse of primary export-based development) by fostering industrial growth, employment, and labour peace under policies of economic nationalism and the building of corporate–political coalitions that encompassed strong, if dependent, trade union federations. Protection of local companies from foreign competition permitted sustained industrial development along with ever higher wages and social benefits for politically supported trade unions in key economic sectors. Indeed, rising industrial wages were seen as supportive of continued industrial growth by increasing consumer demand for local products.

The Philippines, like these ISI-based Latin American countries, entered a sustained ISI phase during the 1940s and 1950s in which successful import substitution was combined with labour regimes (in this case, more liberal than corporatist) that encouraged unionisation and collective bargaining. In response to a balance-of-payments crisis associated with the collapse of the primary-commodity export strategy of early decades of the twentieth century, protective tariffs and foreign exchange controls marked a shift towards ISI-led development. This shift was, in turn, associated with enactment of new labour legislation that greatly enhanced worker welfare and union security in the formal sector of manufacturing. Especially important was new minimum wage legislation in 1951 and the *Industrial Peace Act* of 1953, subsequently dubbed the 'Magna Carta of Labour,' which was patterned after the US *National Labour Relations Act* of 1935 in providing protection for trade unions and encouraging effective collective bargaining at the enterprise level (Ofreneo 1995). This 'misplaced' Latin American experience, stemming in part from US political influence, led to the emergence of strong local unions that, under subsequent years of martial law and state repression (1972–86), sustained a latent, community-based opposition movement. This movement provided the essential foundation for labour mobilisation and militancy during the economic and political crisis of the mid 1980s.

The Philippines' case contrasts strongly with the developmental sequencing of political and economic change elsewhere in the region. Early industrialisation in most countries of the region was accompanied by authoritarian state controls that sought either to repress or to co-opt organised labour. It was noted that these political controls, encouraged and supported by Western governments, comprised part of a larger global strategy of communist containment. Pre-emptively demobilised or co-opted at the outset of sustained industrialisation, most Asian labour movements lacked the political capacity to shape new labour relations institutions in the early years of industrial development. The developmental labour systems subsequently created were to ensure continued labour subordination during later years of industrial deepening.

The crisis of the late 1990s: the Thai case

In view of these various political, structural, and temporal impediments to the collective mobilisation and representation of South-East Asian labour, it appears that the sharp economic crisis of the late 1990s might present something of a *coup de grâce* to organised labour in much of the region. Although it is too early to assess the enduring labour impact of the crisis, a few preliminary observations can be offered. In recognition of the divergent outcomes of the crisis across the region, the discussion here is confined largely to Thailand, a country for which substantial material is available on the labour politics of the 1997–2000 crisis (Deyo 2000).

A common view of the impact of the crisis for labour emphasises the disempowering consequences of high levels of unemployment, increased threat of layoffs, heightened cost pressures on employers, intensified efforts by employers to contain and demobilise labour unions, and relaxed government surveillance of the labour practices of hard-hit firms. But these suggestions of a further demobilisation and weakening of labour under the hardships and dislocations of the crisis must be balanced by an understanding of some broader political outcomes. Indeed, even as the crisis has effectively undercut the structural position of workers in their dealings with employers, national-level labour politics has assumed an increasingly important role in evolving government policies of crisis management. This enhanced political role might be understood, in part, by reference to continuing democratic institutional reforms. But more important have been processes of politicisation and social mobilisation among workers themselves.

Economic crisis was widely accepted as an important factor underlying passage of a new constitution in October 1997. The new constitution establishes a broad spectrum of human rights for civil society groups, creates a fully popularly elected Senate, and permits citizens (including popular sector groups such as farmers associations and trade unions) the right to introduce parliamentary bills upon securing 50 000 signatures on a petition. Although Thai farmers and urban workers have periodically availed themselves of this constitutional provision (farmers organisations pressed successfully for parliamentary establishment of a system of local, provincial, and national farmer councils for the debate of agricultural policy), it is generally the case that the newly institutionalised avenues of representation have led to few substantial policy outcomes. In part, this minimal result is linked to other offsetting political factors associated with the crisis, including especially a heightened exclusion of parliament from critical economic policy matters relating to trade and economic reforms under negotiation with the World Bank and the International Monetary Fund, as well as a shift of influence from the ministries of Labour and Social Welfare, Industry, Agriculture and Co-operatives (and other functional ministries accessible to lobbying and political representation by popular sector groups), to Finance, Commerce, and other less-accessible, reform-directed ministries (Deyo 2000). For this reason, the roots of popular sector collective action are less readily found in changing political institutions than in processes of social mobilisation more directly associated with the economic and policy outcomes of the crisis.

The financial crisis linked to the July 1997 collapse of the Thai Baht was followed by a stream of multilateral assistance programs organised with the IMF, the World Bank, and the Asian Development Bank. Under the terms of assistance, the Thai government was committed to accelerating its own structural-adjustment programs while adopting IMF-negotiated austerity budget guidelines including reduced government deficits, high interest-rate policies, and reduced public-service subsidies. These and other externally negotiated policy prescriptions dramatically heightened the privations and dislocations of the crisis in ways that both politicised and focused popular sector groups, including peasants, rural and urban workers (such as unemployed persons), self-employed and micro-enterprise workers, and the urban poor. Protest and collective action among these groups sometimes followed traditional patterns, as when state-enterprise workers fought to slow or reverse programs of accelerated privatisation and corporatisation built into multilateral assistance programs. A case in point is the success of employees of the Electricity Generating Authority of Thailand in stalling and partially reversing the privatisation of Thailand's largest power plant at Rachaburi based on the terms of agreement of the World Bank assistance program.

More often, new patterns of labour protest emerged from the structural dislocations of the crisis. Particularly important was a new tendency towards convergence and mutuality among the various popular sector groups as they defined common grievances and demands, and as they sought to support one another in the context of crisis-induced structural disempowerment. Such mutuality flowed from: growing levels of unemployment; a growing perception of shared hardship under government austerity budgets; a corresponding unity of focus on government agencies and policies rather than employers; an increased consensus that the IMF and other multilateral institutions had imposed policies that only exacerbated the economic crisis; a shared antipathy to a perceived growing dominance of foreign corporations in the Thai economy; and the growing influence of national and international non-governmental organisations that reinforced the emergent bases for cooperation. From the standpoint of organised labour, it might not be too great a distortion to point to a shift from a traditional politics of production to an emergent politics of collective consumption as various groups of workers converged on demands for expanded social and developmental provision by government.

Paradoxically, even as workers (broadly defined) found themselves economically disempowered and strategically marginalised by the force of the crisis, they found new collective *political* sources of strength to challenge national economic policies more successfully than before. Perhaps their greatest successes have included: a slowing and political renegotiation of privatisation programs; official rethinking of ongoing trade-liberalisation policies; continuance of sectoral (especially farm) subsidy programs for small farmers; dramatic new support programs for small businesses (Deyo 1999); and major, externally supported, social assistance, and social safety-net programs. Whether these various policy responses to the popular sector politics of crisis will be sustained into the post-crisis period is uncertain, although it is likely that the new modes of political mobilisation and collective action, and the emergent political institutions they have defined at local, national, and international levels, will have enduring consequences for state–society relations over future years, whatever the fate of Thailand's new democratic constitution.

The impact of historical timing

The historical *timing* of industrial change was as important as developmental sequencing for Asian labour movements. It was noted that labour-intensive EOI under post-Fordist production regimes differs from earlier standardised-production EOI in shifting the locus of labour control from state to enterprise and in fragmenting and dispersing the workforce to a greater extent than in the earlier period. More generally, the global–temporal context of industrial deepening into more capital-intensive and technology-intensive production has shifted appreciably. Despite unfavourable developmental sequencing, earlier Fordist industrial deepening gave somewhat greater encouragement and scope to emergent labour movements in South Korea, Taiwan, and elsewhere. Under flexible production regimes, by contrast, incipient deepening into high value-added industrial production in Thailand and Malaysia has encouraged pre-emptive enterprise participative structures that often displace or co-opt unions. In Thailand, such resourceful and market-dominating firms as Toyota, Siam Cement, and Yamaha, although discouraging independent or oppositional collective action, have instituted skill-based job ladders, suggestion systems, enterprise unions, carefully circumscribed quality circles, dualistic internal labour markets, and other measures that mobilise worker ideas and involvement. In Malaysia, state encouragement for Japanese-style enterprise unionism contributes further to such an effect. More advanced technology-deepening in Singapore has been associated with even greater official sponsorship and encouragement of labour management councils, sponsored enterprise unions, and other pre-emptive participatory forums.

Conclusion

To return to the central question guiding this chapter, it is clear that organised labour has not played a forceful role in the sociopolitical construction of the developmental labour systems through which enterprise and state elites have sought to further their economic strategies. In addition, organised labour's role has largely diminished over recent decades in response not only to political constraint, but also to economic structural changes associated with liberalising economic reforms and the introduction of new, more flexible production systems in manufacturing. Finally, the developmental sequencing and world-system timing of development have further contributed to labour's continuing decline. Whether the politicisation of workers during Thailand's recent economic crisis will durably enhance labour's political role is still uncertain, although the likely scenario of heightened social mobilisation amid continued political exclusion foreshadows higher levels of class conflict than during pre-crisis years, regardless of a gradual return to rapid economic growth.

Setting aside the new issues raised by the crisis, a number of political and developmental ramifications flows from the generally diminished role of South-East Asian labour. First, economic liberal reforms and recent post-Fordist industrial restructuring have been associated with a growing irrelevance and anachronism of state labour controls, increasingly supplanted by enterprise controls rooted in market discipline or co-optive participation, except in a few 'unrestructured' sectors (for example Thai state enterprises) where repressive controls remain in place (c.f. Hutchison 1993:208). Second, the growing power of employers over workers at enterprise levels provides an opportunity for national governments to respond more fully to international demands for improved recognition of labour and human rights without threatening economic growth or political stability. Third, it also provides a solution to the problem posed by the internal instability of authoritarian regimes under sustained economic development and the rapid expansion of a new middle class, in part by enhancing the prospects for democracy by reducing the likelihood that labour can exploit new political opportunities offered by parliamentary reforms. Alternatively stated, the structurally rooted exclusion of labour from democratic politics under regimes of 'exclusionary democracy' has enhanced the usefulness to business of parliamentary institutions, thus creating a critical political base for those institutions.

But what are the implications of a labour-exclusionary path of development for the economic future of the region? In the short term, a relatively weak popular sector role in economic policy processes (increasingly dominated by private firms) speeds development inasmuch as private firms and government agencies need attend but minimally to the social implications of their strategies. The longer term is less certain, however. Developmental sustainability requires, *inter alia*, a political base. Popular sector exclusion fosters inequities and alienation among large segments of the population, thus eroding this essential base and, in the long term, bringing increased resistance even to the democratic institutions increasingly favoured by elites.

Similar considerations apply to the sustainability of firm-level economic strategies as well. The degree of strong, politically protected unions, along with human-resource policies that are oriented mainly towards cost-cutting and static flexibility, have encouraged short-term opportunism at the expense of long-run organisational development. Where training and human-resource investments have been undertaken, they have not been accompanied by increased worker participation in production decisions, so essential to higher levels of organisational adaptability and innovation. Nor have they generally been accompanied by the commitment-enhancing labour policies that provide a motivational foundation for the success of such participation.

States can play an essential role in this regard by providing the collective goods that individual firms are unlikely to produce, and by providing incentives and inducements for longer-term R&D, training, and organisational development on the part of firms. A good example of such an inducement is the use, in Singapore and Malaysia, of a skill development levy under which employers contribute to a general training fund, receiving back portions of that fund to be used only for approved employee training programs. Without such external pressures and support from unions (even if co-opted, as in Singapore) and governments, short-term cost-cutting and static flexibility will characterise firm level strategies in much of the region, while consigning even the more advanced industrial sectors of these countries to learning-based, rather than innovative, global production and market niches.

References

Amsden, Alice (1989) *Asia's New Giant: South Korea and Late Industrialisation*, New York: Oxford University Press.

Arudsothy, Ponniah and Craig R. Littler, (1993) 'State Regulation and Union Fragmentation in Malaysia', in Stephen Frenkel (ed.) *Organised Labour in the Asia–Pacific Region*, Ithaca, New York: ILR Press, pp 107–32.

Begin, James P. (1995) 'Singapore's Industrial Relations System: Is It Congruent with Its Second Phase of Industrialisation?', in Stephen Frenkel and Jeffrey Harrod (eds) *Industrialisation and Labour Relations*, Ithaca, New York: ILR Press, pp 64–87.

Brown, Andrew and Stephen Frenkel (1993) 'Union Unevenness and Insecurity in Thailand', in Stephen Frenkel (ed.) *Organised Labour in the Asia–Pacific Region*, Ithaca, New York: ILR Press, pp 82–106.

Charoenloet, Voravidh (1993) 'Export-Oriented Industry in Thailand—Implications for Employment and Labour', in Arnold Wehmhoerner (ed.) *NIC's in Asia: A Challenge to Trade Unions*, Singapore: Friedrich-Ebert Stiftung Foundation, pp 7–14.

Crouch, Harold (1993) 'Malaysia: Neither Authoritarian nor Democratic', in Kevin Hewison, Richard Robison and Garry Rodan (eds) *Southeast Asia in the 1990s*, Sydney: Allen and Unwin, pp 133–58.

Deyo, Frederic (1981) *Dependent Development and Industrial Order*, New York: Praeger.

Deyo, Frederic (1989) *Beneath the Miracle: Labour Subordination in the New Asian Industrialism*, Berkeley: University of California Press.

Deyo, Frederic (1995) 'Human Resource Strategies and Industrial Restructuring in Thailand', in Stephen Frenkel and Jeffrey Harrod (eds) *Industrialisation and Labour Relations*, Ithaca, New York: ILR Press, pp 23–36.

Deyo, Frederic (ed.) (1996) *Social Reconstructions of the World Automobile Industry*, Baskingstoke: Macmillan.

Deyo, Frederic (1999) 'The Politics of Crisis Management: Thailand's SME Sector', *Auckland Working Papers in Development Studies*, No. 3, University of Auckland, Centre for Development Studies (September).

Deyo, Frederic (2000) 'Reform, Globalisation and Crisis: Reconstructuring Thai Labour', *Journal of Industrial Relations*, 42 (2):258–74.

Hadiz, Vedi R. (1994) 'Challenging State Corporatism on the Labour Front: Working Class Politics in the 1990s', in David Bourchier and John Legge (eds) *Democracy in Indonesia, 1950s and 1990s*, Monash papers on Southeast Asia no. 31, CSEAS, Monash University, pp 190–203.

Hewison, Kevin and Andrew Brown (1994) 'Labour and Unions in an Industrialising Thailand: A Brief History', *Journal of Contemporary Asia*, (4):483–514.

Hewison, Kevin and Garry Rodan (1994) 'The Decline of the Left in Southeast Asia', in *The Socialist Register 1994*, London: Merlin Press, pp 235–62.

Hutchison, Jane (1993) 'Class and State Power in the Philippines', in Kevin Hewison, Richard Robison and Garry Rodan (eds) *Southeast Asia in the 1990s*, Sydney,: Allen and Unwin, pp 191–212.

ILO, see International Labour Office (ILO).

Ingleson, John (1981) 'Worker Consciousness and Labour Unions in Colonial Java', *Pacific Affairs*, 54(31):485–501.

International Labour Office (ILO) (1995) *World Employment 1995: An ILO Report*, Geneva: ILO Press.

International Labour Office (ILO) (1996) *World Employment 1996/97: National Policies in a Global Context*, Geneva: ILO Press.

Kuruvilla, Sarosh (1994) 'Industrialisation Strategy and Industrial Relations Policy in Malaysia and the Philippines', Proceedings of the Forty-Sixth Annual Meeting of the Industrial Relations Research Association, Boston, 3–5 January.

Kuruvilla, Sarosh (1995) 'Industrialisation Strategy and Industrial Relations Policy in Malaysia', in Stephen Frenkel and Jeffrey Harrod (eds) *Industrialisation and Labour Relations*, Ithaca, New York: ILR Press, pp 37–63.

Lambert, Rob (1993) *Authoritarian State Unionism in New Order Indonesia* Working Paper no. 25, Asia Research Centre, Murdoch University (October).

MacIntyre, Andrew (1994) *Organising Interests: Corporatism in Indonesian Politics* Working Paper no. 43, Asia Research Centre, Murdoch University (August).

Ofreneo, Rene E. (1994) 'The Labour Market, Protective Labour Institutions, and Economic Growth in the Philippines', in Gerry Rodgers (ed.) *Workers, Institutions, and Economic Growth in Asia*, Geneva: International Institute for Labour Studies, pp 255–301.

Ofreneo, Rene E. (1995) 'The Changing Terrains for Trade Union Organising', unpublished manuscript, School of Labour and Industrial Relations, University of the Philippines.

Rasiah, Raja (1994) 'Flexible Production Systems and Local Machine Tool Subcontracting: The Case of Electronics Components Transnationals in Malaysia' *Cambridge Journal of Economics*, 18(3):279–98.

Singapore Department of Statistics (1999) *Yearbook of Statistics 1998*, Singapore.

Standing, Guy (1989) 'The Growth of External Labour Flexibility in a Nascent NIC: Malaysian Labour Flexibility Survey (MLFS)', World Employment Programme, Research Working Paper No. 35 (November) Geneva: ILO.

United Nations (2000) *Statistical Yearbook 1997*, New York: United Nations.

World Bank (1995) *World Development Report 1995: Workers in an Integrating World*, Washington, D.C.: Oxford University Press.

World Bank (2001), *World Development Report 2000/2001: Attacking Poverty*, Oxford: Oxford University Press.

Wurfel, David (1959) 'Trade Union Development and Labour Relations Policy in the Philippines', *Industrial and Labour Relations Review*, 12 (4):582–608.

10

Japan and South-East Asia: The Lineaments of Quasi-Hegemony

Mark Beeson

Japan has had a profound influence on South-East Asia. Whether it is measured by Japan's often brutal, but ultimately liberating, wartime occupation of the region, or by the more recent economic interaction, Japan has played a major part in shaping South-East Asia's political and economic development. At one level this is hardly surprising. Japan, as Pempel (1999:27) reminds us, 'remains the Gulliver in a region of economic Lilliputs'. In an East Asian region in which it continues to account for approximately two-thirds of economic output, Japan towers over its neighbours and inevitably exercises a major influence through sheer economic weight. And yet the most striking quality of this undoubted economic power, is that it is not matched by an equivalent political influence—or certainly not at the conspicuous level of international diplomacy. This chapter will attempt to account for this paradox.

To try to make sense of Japan's complex and contradictory relations with South-East Asia, I shall adopt an approach that is situated squarely in the increasingly influential tradition of international political economy (IPE). Although there is a number of divergent positions subsumed under the IPE rubric, its central concerns involve the exploration of the relationship between power and wealth, and the extension of our understanding of the interaction between international relations and economics (see Higgott 1994). In terms of the models identified in chapter 1 of this volume, the approach taken here draws on both state-centred historical institutionalism and social conflict theory, although, in this chapter, much of this is implicit rather than explicit.[1] One of the main insights and motivating principles of the broadly conceived IPE approach is that the political and the economic are deeply interconnected and simply cannot be separated in the manner implied by specialist academic disciplines. IPE also generates distinctive and important analytical insights and questions. In the context of a discussion of Japan's regional role, key questions revolve around the relationship between economic and political power. Why has Japan failed to develop a political presence to match its economic might? What influence have wider geopolitical and strategic considerations had on regional relationships? What implications do the development and contemporary position of Japan's distinctive political-economy have for the region, and for relations with key actors such as the United States of America (USA)? Answers to such questions necessitate considering a much wider range of factors than conventional economic or political science perspectives allow.

If we want to understand why there has been such a noteworthy divergence between Japan's political and economic roles, we need to look beyond East Asia and consider the wider international order in which the region is embedded. One of the most profound influences on Japan's distinctive developmental trajectory over the past fifty years or so has been Japan's wartime experience. World War II, and Japan's relationship with the USA in particular, have shaped and moulded Japan's subsequent approaches to economic and foreign policy, with long-term implications both for Japan's own place in the world, and for the course of regional development more generally. Consequently, despite Japan's phenomenal rise as an economic power, it has not enjoyed a concomitant political influence; unlike earlier rising powers, economic might has not translated into wider systemic or 'hegemonic' influence. Japan, in short, has remained a 'quasi-hegemon'.

The first part of this chapter traces the origins and evolution of Japan's quasi-hegemony. I argue that Japan's preoccupation with economic reconstruction and expansion, its reliance on the USA for security, and its general reluctance to adopt an active and independent foreign policy position, have lent a distinctively mercantilist cast to its external policies, which systematically privileges the economic over the political. The second section of the chapter looks at the impact of this stance on relations with South-East Asia. I suggest that, unless Japan develops a greater capacity and willingness to play a more prominent political role in keeping with its economic power, even this economic influence might be eroded. As Japan's domestic economy continues to languish, Japan's importance as a source of investment, as a market, and as a potential regional role model are inevitably diminished, with potentially significant consequences for Japan's international political position. The point to re-emphasise at the outset, therefore, is that only by considering the complex, interconnected continuum of Japan's political practices and economic structures can we hope to understand Japan's domestic position and the way that this has influenced its external relations.

Japan's quasi-hegemony

Japan's economic development in the postwar period has, until relatively recently at least, been routinely described as 'miraculous'. Indeed, it is true that Japan's rise from the ruin and defeat of World War II to its position as the second-largest economy in the world is an unparalleled and astonishing achievement. Whatever difficulties Japan might currently be facing, this experience remains a crucially important exemplar of a successful state-led form of economic development that not only contradicts much 'Western' economic thinking (Fallows 1993), but also has provided a role model for a number of other states in the East Asian region (Amsden 1995). And yet, despite Japan's rapid economic growth and confident assertions that it would rapidly overtake the USA (Fingleton 1995), Japan has not had anything like the same degree of 'hegemonic' influence that other rising powers before it have enjoyed. Although Japan might currently compare unfavourably with the USA, there is no doubt that it remains a major economic actor, and so this relative lack of political influence needs explaining.

If we step back for a moment and situate capitalist development and the concomitant rise and fall of 'great powers' in the sort of longer time-frame adopted by the French historian Fernand Braudel (1992), something is particularly striking: fortunate nations enjoy particular advantages at certain times that allow them to dominate an era economically (see also Kennedy 1988). This economic superiority provides the material basis with which a nation can attempt to establish a broader political order that reflects and furthers its own interests. In short, one nation can become the hegemonic power of a particular time. The two definitive examples of states that have enjoyed a dominant or hegemonic position are the United Kingdom in the nineteenth century and the USA in the second half of the twentieth century. Each of these nations was the dominant economic power of its day, but each of them also generated a concomitant legitimating ideology and the requisite institutional infrastructure for an international trade and investment regime that defined a specific world order (Cox 1987).

It is important to note that when we talk about 'hegemony' there is a number of distinctive uses of the term. These broadly reflect liberal and radical perspectives. Both liberal and radical paradigms make normative assumptions about the possible role that a hegemonic power can play— either in underwriting a stable international order or in exploiting the power's dominant position. Although a detailed examination of these differences is not possible here,[2] the key point to emphasise is that the historical record suggests that rising powers such as Japan can be expected to challenge the existent order and try to translate their own economic power into political influence (Chase-Dunn 1998:184). Yet, despite Japan's rise to economic prominence, it has made comparatively little effort to shape the international system of which it is a part, even at the regional level. To understand why, we need to look more closely at Japan's relationship with the USA, a country that remains at the apex of what is now described as a unipolar international order (Matsanundo 1997).

Japan and the USA

The defining influence on Japan's foreign policy and the nature of its economic interaction with South-East Asia occurred more than fifty years ago. Japan's defeat in World War II and its subsequent occupation by US forces under General Douglas MacArthur exerted a profound and lasting influence upon Japan (LaFeber 1997). Not only did the Americans give the Japanese a new constitution that enshrined the idea of Japan as a non-aggressive power, but also they effectively incorporated Japan into an emerging world order in which the USA was the strategic and economic linchpin of the capitalist economies.

This is not to suggest either that the USA effectively remade Japan in its own image or that Japan was the hapless victim of a preponderant USA. On the contrary, not only was the USA unable to eliminate the sort of distinctive Japanese corporate structures and bureaucratic practices of which the Americans disapproved (Johnson 1982), but also Japan was able to exploit and benefit from the emerging Cold War order. The outbreak of the Korean War in 1950 provided a crucial catalyst for the reconstruction of Japan's industrial base. Yet, despite the clear benefits that infusions of US capital and the demands of the Korean conflict provided for Japan, this period helped consolidate a bilateral relationship marked by a good deal of dependence and subordination on the Japanese side (Cumings 1997).

It is important to emphasise, however, that the self-effacing and subordinate character of Japan's postwar foreign policy has been intentional and self-consciously pursued. As Pyle (1988:452) observed:

> Japan's political passivity in the postwar era has ordinarily been understood as a product of wartime trauma, the unconditional surrender, popular pacifism, nuclear allergy, the restraints of a 'peace constitution', and sometimes bureaucratic immobilism. All of these factors are without question ingredients in forming Japan's postwar international role; they have established the parameters within which political leadership has operated. Nevertheless, we would miss the essence of postwar Japanese leadership if we overlooked the fact that *the fundamental orientation toward economic growth and political passivity was also the product of a carefully constructed and brilliantly implemented foreign policy.* [Emphasis added.]

This preoccupation with economic development at all costs, while simultaneously keeping a low diplomatic profile, came to be known as the

'Yoshida doctrine', after Prime Minister Shigeru Yoshida, who established many of Japan's policy priorities in the immediate postwar period. Japan was able to take advantage of the overarching Cold War strategic preoccupations of the USA, thus allowing Japan to concentrate its national resources on economic development and spend comparatively little on its own defence. Significantly, even when Japan can afford to provide for its own defence and the USA has actively encouraged it to do more 'burden-sharing', Japan's relatively modest military spending and posture lends a highly distinctive trait to its overall external orientation (Pyle 1998).

Japan's dependence on the USA extends across a number of areas and has important effects—some beneficial, some not. Japan is reliant on the USA not only strategically but also economically as Japan's economic development has been dependent on maintaining access to lucrative US markets. One of the most striking aspects of the US–Japan bilateral trade relationship is that the seemingly inexorable increase in Japan's trade surpluses that underpinned Japanese economic development has been mirrored by a similar increase in US trade deficits (Bergsten and Noland 1993). This has led to a seemingly interminable series of trade disputes between Japan and the USA and concerted pressure by the latter to force Japan to open up domestic markets and liberalise its financial sector. Although the continuation of these disputes suggests that American pressure has had only limited success in forcing change and liberalisation in Japan, it is important to recognise that such pressure *has* had an impact, especially where domestic forces in Japan are sympathetic to the liberalisation agenda (Schoppa 1997). In other words, although Japan has clearly benefited from its relationship with the USA, the latter does have a good deal of potential leverage that, at the very least, constrains Japan, and that might gradually be eroding the close relationship that has existed between Japan's industrial and financial sectors (Leyshon 1994). The possible implications of such structural changes within Japan's distinctive political economy will be considered in greater detail later. The point to emphasise at this stage is that the perceived need to accommodate the USA has constrained Japanese policy options and placed limits on its own hegemonic ambitions and potential.

One of the most tangible manifestations of the potential influence of the USA on Japanese policy was the so-called 'Plaza Accord', under which Japan agreed to encourage the yen's appreciation against the dollar (Funabashi 1988). This ultimately led to a major restructuring of Japanese industry and a dramatic increase in Japanese investment, particularly in the rest of Asia. Before we consider this development and its effects in any detail, however, it is necessary to situate this process in the wider context of Japan's attitude to economic security more generally. For if there is one factor that distinguishes Japanese policy in both its proactive and reactive modes, it is the overwhelming desire to maintain economic independence and enhance economic security wherever possible.

Economic security

At the heart of Japan's trade and industry policies has been a determination to overcome perceived insecurity (Samuels 1994). The very process of modernisation from its earliest days during the Meiji Restoration period was given urgency and legitimacy by the perceived need to 'catch-up' with the industrialised West, or risk being left behind and at the mercy of more-powerful external forces. The neomercantalist trade and industry policies that have attracted both condemnation and admiration were intended to develop systematically an independent wealth-generating capacity that would make Japan more autonomous and less vulnerable to forces beyond its control. But for a country lacking in many of the basic resources necessary for successful industrialisation, Japan has, of necessity, been forced to rely on external supplies of key economic inputs. The 'oil shocks' of the 1970s, which saw dramatic increases in the cost of one of Japan's most crucial sources of energy, dramatically brought home to Japanese planners just how potentially vulnerable the country was to events over which it had little control.

In 1980 this perceived vulnerability culminated in the doctrine of 'comprehensive security'. Simply put, the policy of comprehensive security 'views diplomatic, economic and cultural initiatives to be as important as military means in guaranteeing Japan's security' (Nester 1990:70). In many ways this more-encompassing conception of security, which embraces non-military factors as a major component of, and means to, ensuring national security, reflects a more widespread East Asian perception—one that Japan's success has been instrumental in consolidating (Beeson 1999a). Indeed, the Japanese approach to security can be understood as reflecting a long-term historical shift in which military power and security generally have come to occupy a less prominent position than does economic development in the priorities of many policy-makers (Luttwak 1990). In an era when military force—at least among the established major powers—has become a less effective or utilisable expression of national power (Mueller 1989), *economic* power has become increasingly important. Japan, therefore, is the quintessential example of a modern 'trading state' that makes its way in the world by economic rather than military expansion (Rosecrance 1986).

Japan is not, however, the only contemporary state that might be thought of as a successful trading state. A number of Western European countries, particularly Germany, might be considered in the same way. What distinguishes Japan is the nature of its domestic political economy and the way in which this is linked with the outside world. The close relationships between, on the one hand, key officials in prominent bureaucratic departments such as the Ministry of International Trade and Industry (MITI) and the Ministry of Finance (MoF) and, on the other hand, members of Japan's corporate sector, have meant that economic policy has been coordinated with the intention of systematically developing Japan's industrial structure and technological capacity. The efficacy of such collaborative efforts, especially in the 'high growth period' of Japan's early postwar recovery, has been widely documented and is generally well understood (see, for example, Freeman 1987; Weiss and Hobson 1995). What is generally less well recognised is the way that Japanese public officials and business leaders have utilised and built upon such institutionalised relationships and practices to manage even the internationalisation of 'Japanese' industry.[3]

It is at this point, where Japan's highly developed capacity for coordinated public policy intersects with the pursuit of *international* economic goals, that Japan's distinctive quasi-hegemony is most apparent and important. In the wake of the economic traumas of the 1970s, Japanese policy-makers embarked upon a very deliberate policy of resource and supplier diversification that minimised Japanese dependence on external suppliers. A central element of this strategy was the development of coordinated public-sector and private-sector activities designed to secure Japan's resource supplies, while simultaneously furthering the interests of Japanese business (Bobrow and Kurdle 1987). Significantly, the pattern of coordinated public-sector and private-sector activities that had characterised Japan's domestic development was extended to the international sphere. This style of collaboration reached its most sophisticated form in Japan's official development assistance (ODA). Ostensibly intended to provide developmental assistance to poorer countries, Japan has utilised its ODA to promote a number of strategic objectives that reflects Japan's national interest and assists the international expansion of Japanese corporations. Although this is not a uniquely Japanese phenomenon, what distinguishes the Japanese approach to ODA is the 'structural inclusion' of Japanese business in the construction and implementation of policy. The key objective of ODA is the promotion of Japanese trade and investment, and the coordination of 'the commercial agendas of private sector actors . . . with the strategic and economic agendas of the economic ministries' (Arase 1994:172).

This pattern of close collaboration is coming under sustained pressure from a complex array of domestic and external forces, as well as from more general structural pressures that are being generated by the evolving international political economy. Before speculating on what implications such changes might have for Japan and for the region of which it is a part, we need to examine the historical record of Japan's involvement in the region generally and with South-East Asia in particular.

Japan and South-East Asia

Japan's relationship with South-East Asia, like its external relationships and international position more generally, has been powerfully shaped by events that occurred before and during World War II. Consequently, before looking in any detail at recent developments and the specifics of Japan's political and economic involvement in the region, it is important to remind ourselves briefly of the region's history because it continues to cast a long shadow over contemporary intra-regional relations.

The wartime legacy

Japan's occupation of South-East Asia before World War II is not simply an important historical episode that continues to colour contemporary relations; it also provides an important illustration of the changing nature and application of power among nations.

As the first nation successfully to industrialise in Asia, Japan borrowed much from the West. However, in addition to embarking on a Western-inspired modernisation of domestic political, bureaucratic, and economic institutions, the Japanese embarked on the sort of imperial expansion that had characterised competition among the major European powers towards the end of the nineteenth century (Hobsbawm 1987). Japan's expansion into weak China and Korea, particularly in the face of Russia's imperial ambitions, was the almost inevitable consequence of its successful industrialisation and growing militarism (Beasley 1990). Indeed, the occupation of Manchuria, its exploitation as an economic resource, and its usefulness to Japan's authoritarian leaders as a source of mass mobilisation, imparted a certain logic to subsequent events (Young 1998). Imperial expansion, especially into the 'inner-ring' of North-East Asia made sense in the context of an era in which the occupation and colonisation of foreign lands not only provided potential economic benefits, but also was an established, if not legitimate, form of international behaviour.

Japan's expansion into South-East Asia, however, although superficially driven by similar imperatives, had distinctive qualities that made it an altogether more uncertain enterprise. The underlying logic of Japan's move into South-East Asia was the same as it had been in North-East Asia—to secure natural resources to fuel further economic development and, eventually, to develop export markets to buy Japanese products (Beasley 1987). Two factors lent a particular danger and urgency to this project in South-East Asia. First, the region was largely under the control of the European colonial powers and, second, the USA was becoming increasingly concerned about Japan's imperial ambitions, especially when combined with rising militarism and nationalism. Any move into South-East Asia, therefore, inevitably risked a clash with the European powers and, more significantly in the long run, with the increasingly powerful USA. Significantly, it was the US economic embargo of Japan introduced in 1940—and its explicit threat to Japan's autonomy and economic security—that provided the trigger for conflict. Japan's dependency on South-East Asia for crucial supplies of natural resources, such as oil and rubber, left it with few options if it wanted to maintain economic independence (Willmott 1982).

Japan's goal of establishing a so-called 'Greater East Asian Co-Prosperity Sphere' in the region as a response to perceived threats to its economic security is, therefore, important for a number of reasons. When seen from the longer term perspective of regional development the significance of the putative 'co-prosperity sphere' is that, Japan's self-serving imperial interests notwithstanding, it represented the first exclusively *Asian* regional entity, and was an entity that self-consciously repudiated the style and legitimacy of Western European colonisation. Japan was bent on the self-appointed task of liberating Asia from the yoke of Western imperial rule—a task that could be achieved only by substituting Japanese regional hegemony for Western hegemony (Beasley 1987:243). Seen in this context, Japanese occupation was a crucial watershed in South-East Asia's political development, and effectively marked the end of European control, signalling the emergence of the independence and nationalist movements that would prove so influential in countries such as Indonesia and Vietnam (Yahuda 1996). But Japan's occupation also revealed the difficulties of sustaining long-term economic control of occupied territories in the face of internal and, especially, external opposition. It was a lesson that was profoundly to influence postwar Japanese policy.

Thus, Japan's wartime colonisation of South-East Asia had ambiguous but deep-seated effects. On the one hand it played a crucial role in freeing the region from European imperial control. On the other hand, it engendered lingering nervousness and suspicion regarding Japan's hegemonic ambitions—suspicion that has continued to influence intra-regional relations to the present day. This wartime legacy helps to explain the style and content of Japan's more recent interaction within the region.

Japan's postwar involvement in South-East Asia

The key point to make about Japan's postwar external relations generally, and its involvement with South-East Asia in particular, is that it is over-whelmingly *economic*, and currently spearheaded by business rather than by battalions. The repudiation of militarism in Japan has become a deeply entrenched and institutionalised part of Japanese social life and normative values (Katzenstein 1996). Although the Japanese government continues to enjoy a good deal of support for policies that privilege Japan's economic interests, there is simply no foreseeable likelihood of this translating into the sort of military aggression that characterised its earlier foray into the region. In other words, Japan represents a new and distinctive approach to national development that sees security as flowing from the enhancement of its overall 'technoeconomic' position. Significantly, this increased material capacity has not been correlated with, or translated into, military advantage—in the way that conventional theory of international relations might lead us to expect (see Heginbotham and Samuels 1998). Japanese hege-mony, in short, is truncated, selective, and very different from other historical exemplars.

The most tangible aspects of Japan's engagement with the region have been through trade and investment. It is possible to identify a number of distinct phases in Japan's postwar economic relations with South-East Asia. In the first period, from 1950 to 1965, Japan occupied what Morris-Suzuki (1991:38) has described as an 'intermediate' position in a triangular Asia–Pacific relationship, in which Japan imported industrial goods from the USA and exported simple manufactures to South-East Asia.[4] At this time, before Japan had completed its own industrial transformation, it actu-ally ran trade deficits with the USA. The next phase of Japan's economic engagement with the region, from 1965 until 1975, saw the maturing of Japan's own economic position and the beginning of Japan's large-scale investment in the region. As the economies of South-East Asia began to develop, they employed a combination of tariffs and inducements to pro-mote domestic industrialisation. Japan responded to this by massively increasing investment to protect markets and take advantage of cheaper production costs in South-East Asia. During this decade Asia became the biggest recipient of Japanese manufacturing investment, especially in areas such as textiles, which Japanese planners encouraged to move offshore in a continuing and systematic attempt to upgrade Japan's domestic industrial structure.

It should be noted that precisely the same logic that encouraged Japanese investment in this second phase—protecting markets and overcoming tariff barriers—was also driving investment in other parts of the world. The USA has been the biggest single recipient of Japanese investment, largely as a consequence of protectionist pressures. What is significant about Japan's investment in Asia is the large number of Japanese companies involved (Machado 1995:46), and the impact that even a portion of Japan's outward investment flows can have on the comparatively small economies of South-East Asia in particular.[5] Indeed, it is important to recognise that one of the major attractions from a Japanese perspective of further investment in the region after 1975 has been as a continuation of the triangular relationship with the USA. However, the structure of this triangular relationship has changed profoundly. More recently, as Japanese industry has continued to develop and consequently capture increased shares of the US market in particular, investment in South-East Asia has provided a method of deflecting or circumventing protectionism in the USA by establishing export platforms in the region (Petri 1992).

The Plaza Accord (see page 287) provided an additional impetus for a fresh wave of Japanese foreign investment that gained momentum during the 1980s. This episode illustrates how important developments in the wider international system generally, and with the USA in particular, can be in shaping what appear, at first glance, to be strictly regional outcomes. The dramatic appreciation of the yen encouraged by the US-inspired Plaza Accord, combined with the abundance of capital available at the height of the 'bubble economy' in Japan in the late 1980s, lent additional momentum to Japan's increased foreign investment. It is worth emphasising that so great was the outflow of capital during the second half of the 1980s, that it exceeded Japan's total accumulated capital exports up until 1980 (Stevens 1996:72). The economies of Asia proved to be major beneficiaries—not only of this general outflow, but also of the reduced flows that resulted in the wake of the collapse of the bubble economy.[6]

In the 1990s, an emphasis on cost-cutting and a need to increase competitiveness made production in low-cost Asia increasingly attractive. Asia's share of Japan's total foreign investment flows doubled from 11.8 per cent in 1985 to 23.7 per cent in 1994. Of this, the so-called 'first-tier' economies (Singapore, Taiwan, Hong Kong, and South Korea) saw their share decline from 54 to 41.3 per cent between 1985 and 1994, and the 'second-tier' industrialising economies of South-East Asia (Indonesia, Malaysia, the

Philippines, and Thailand) saw their share expand from 45 to 56 per cent (Thompson and Poon 1998:18). Between 1980 and 1992, Japan overtook the USA to become the largest investor in each of the first-tier and second-tier nations, with the exception of the Philippines—a former US colony (Dobson 1997:8).[7]

The precise contemporary significance of Japan to the region can be seen more clearly in table 10.1 (below). Not only is Japan a major trade and investment partner for all of the South-East Asian economies, but also it is an important source of tourist income, especially for Thailand. The other important point that emerges from these figures is that a significant proportion of the debt owed by the countries of the region is denominated in yen—making these countries vulnerable to fluctuations in currency values that have more to do with the state of the Japanese economy than with their own. Interestingly, however, there appears to have been little attempt by the Japanese government to translate this latent power into political influence through the formation of a 'yen bloc' (Frankel 1993). Moon and Rhee (1999) account for this inaction by arguing that Japan's domestic capital markets are underdeveloped, and that 'Japan wants to take the benefit but not the burden and responsibility of the internationalization of the yen'. In other words, not only is Japan unwilling to play an overt political leadership role in this context, but also financial authorities might be concerned about a possible erosion of Japanese autonomy as a consequence of the yen's greater internationalisation. Again, the limits to Japanese hegemony are apparent, and are confirmed by its inability to play a more decisive role in managing the recent crisis.

Table 10.1 Significance of Japan and the yen to South-East Asia, 1997

	Proportion (%) of debt denominated in yen	Proportion (%) of exports destined for Japan	Proportion (%) of imports sourced from Japan	Proportion (%) of incoming tourists from Japan	Proportion (%) of FDI from Japan
Indonesia	39.5	21.0	18.0	16.6	6.8
Korea	54.0	15.0	25.6	13.4	23.1
Thailand	23.0	10.8	19.2	42.9	7.9
Malaysia	15.0	12.6	21.9	5.0	9.9
Philippines	25.0	16.2	20.6	7.1	36.8
China	32.0	17.4	20.3	23.0	19.0
Average	31.4	15.5	20.9	18.0	17.3

Source: Bhaskaran (1998)

Although the extent of Japanese investment in the region has clearly been a major factor in accelerating the industrialisation process in South-East Asia in particular, the way in which this has occurred has influenced the course of development and the role that the economies of the region have played in an emerging regional division of labour. In short, Japan's distinctive quasi-hegemony has powerfully shaped the political economy of South-East Asia in ways that merit closer scrutiny.

Japanese hegemony in practice

One of the more noteworthy transformations in public policy over the course of the past several decades, especially in the developing world, has been a change in the way that foreign investment is regarded. Whereas it was formerly viewed with suspicion and caution, it is now the subject of intense international competition as governments throughout the world actively court footloose multinational corporations. Despite this enthusiasm, the activities of Japanese corporations serve to remind us of several facts. First, all foreign investment and multinational behaviour is *not* identical (Encarnation 1994); second, even multinationals retain distinctive 'national' characteristics (Pauly and Reich 1997); and, finally, there might still be costs as well as benefits from foreign investment.

Revealingly, Japanese corporations were initially 'reluctant multinationals' (Doner 1991:83). Because Japanese large-scale corporations, or *keiretsu* groups, benefit from their distinctive structure of closely interlinked companies, established networks of suppliers, and privileged access to capital,[8] they were concerned about the possible impact of breaking up such institutionalised patterns of relationships if forced to move offshore into alien environments. The corporations solved this problem by reproducing the *keiretsu* structures throughout the rest of Asia (Dobson 1993). The hierarchically organised corporate structures that had developed in Japan, and that seemed to have given Japanese corporations clear competitive advantages for many years, were transferred overseas as smaller supplier companies followed their *keiretsu* group leaders offshore. Even where Japanese corporations used local suppliers, this was not necessarily an unqualified boon for the local economy. As Hatch and Yamamura's (1996) detailed analysis of the economic and political relationship between Japan and Asia demonstrates, local suppliers were also integrated into a complex, hierarchically organised, regional division of labour, centered on Japan. This Japan-centric production structure had a potentially negative impact on indigenous development: Japan controlled 'subordinate' firms in Asia by strictly controlling access to technology and knowhow, effectively determining the pace and quality of local industrialisation (Hatch and Yamamura 1996:60).[9]

Japan's possible role in either promoting or hindering economic development is an important determinant of its capacity to play a wider, more orthodox hegemonic role at the regional level. The conventional wisdom in Japan itself, assiduously promoted by influential Japanese economists, is that Japan would spearhead a 'flying geese' model of regionwide develop-ment.[10] Japan, as 'leading goose', would pull other countries along in its wake, allowing the rest of the region to replicate its own developmental experience. However, critics argue that Japan has neither passed on tech-nology to the rest of the region, nor acted as a market to allow neighbours to pursue the sort of export-led industrialisation that has characterised Japan's own development (Bernard and Ravenhill 1995). Indeed, one of the most striking aspects of Japan's trade relationship with the region has been that Japan has also amassed major trade surpluses with Asia, predicated on the latter's continuing dependence on exports of Japanese capital goods (Hatch and Yamamura 1996:8–9; Gangopadhyay 1998).

In some ways this asymmetrical relationship might be explained as the inevitable consequence of the interaction of economies at different stages of development. What distinguishes Japan, however, is its highly atypical pat-tern of low inter-industry trade (Lincoln 1990), and the coordinated, state-assisted approach to regional integration. Not only have Japan's pro-tectionist policies made it unable to play the sort of market-of-last-resort role that the USA has in the wider international system, but also policy-makers and business-leaders have cooperatively exploited Japan's position to secure the privileges that accrue to economic power. This is not to sug-gest that the USA has not utilised its 'structural power' to derive benefits from its dominance of the international system; on the contrary, it has (Strange 1994). The significance of Japan's quasi-hegemony is that, especi-ally in the Asian region, this hegemony has emerged from the consciously planned, strategically oriented interaction of Japan's private and public sectors.[11] By using a complex array of low-interest loans, technical assist-ance, administrative guidance, labour-training programs, and, especially, integrated ODA packages, Japanese planners and corporations have attempted to bind the political and economic elites of South-East Asia to them in an intricate web of dependence. As Hatch and Yamamura (1996:131) have observed:

> . . . it would be incorrect to conclude Japan has merely 'purchased' influence in Asia. It has done much more. In large part, Japanese business and political elites have 'schmoozed' their way to power. They have, in other words, mastered the fine art of networking in Asia, a region in which most countries do not have a modern legal framework for commerce. They have used social bonds to overcome what is, for most Western business people, a source of confusion, uncertainty, and thus risk.

Despite the apparent obstacles to the development of a more expansive form of Japanese hegemony that encompasses a political or ideational dimension to match its apparent economic influence, Japan has, nevertheless, exerted a wider influence on South-East Asia in particular. Unsurprisingly, perhaps, it has been ambiguous and contradictory. A closer look at this more overtly political aspect of Japan's influence highlights its limits, and hints at its possible future course.

The strengths and weaknesses of Japanese hegemony

Japan's economic power, as we have seen, has established a regional division of labour with its apex in Japan that effectively locks neighbouring countries into subordinate positions. This is most dramatically illustrated in the structure of regional car production, where major Japanese corporations have taken advantage of improvements in transportation and communication, and of the possibilities opened up by increasing disaggregation of production processes, to organise manufacture on a transregional basis. Toyota, for example, uses Thailand to supply diesel engines and electronics, the Philippines for transmissions, Malaysia for steering components, and Indonesia for petrol engines. Given the important role played by Japanese multinationals in local economies, this has led directly to *political* initiatives by these South-East Asian nations designed to encourage further investment and to distinguish South-East Asia in the international competition for mobile investment. Thailand, Malaysia, the Philippines, and Indonesia have, for example, inaugurated a brand-to-brand 'complementation pact' that halves tariffs on imports from member countries and thus makes the region more attractive to Japanese multinationals that operate according to a transnational logic (Machado 1995).

At the material level, then, there is a clear correlation between sheer economic might and a concomitant political influence. But Japan also has a more subtle ideational influence that, somewhat paradoxically, also highlights the limits of Japanese hegemony. The success of the Japanese model has clearly had a major impact on the region. Malaysia's attempted emulation of the Japanese model in its 'Look East' policy is perhaps the clearest example of this ideational influence (Jomo 1994:3–10). However, the continuing difficulties experienced by the Japan's domestic economy throughout the 1990s must cast doubt on the continuance of this dimension of its regional influence. Powerful and persuasive criticisms have been made of Japan's domestic political economy, making it a less attractive role model (Katz 1998). Likewise, the continuing difficulties experienced by Japan's heavily indebted banking sector in particular, mean that Japan has become a less important source of external capital (*Economist* 1999) and, therefore, a potentially less influential regional power.

And yet Japan has had opportunities to play a political role in the region in keeping with its economic status. In the aftermath of the recent economic crisis in Asia, when Japan suggested that it might establish an Asian Monetary Fund to help neighbouring economies weather the crisis, it appeared that Japan might finally play a decisive and unambiguous leadership role. Such a possibility was rapidly quashed by the USA, however, in an episode that revealed much about both the continuing regional influence of the USA and Japan's continuing subordination (Higgott 2000). In sharp contrast to Japan, the USA was able to exploit its pre-eminent position in, and influence over, a number of key intergovernmental organisations, such as the International Monetary Fund (IMF), in a concerted attempt to impose its preferred model of economic organisation on the East Asian region (Beeson 1999b). US hegemony is bolstered by an uncomplicated and uncritical certitude about its 'manifest destiny' and perceived obligation to act as a world leader (Nye 1990). Revealingly, despite the relative economic decline of the USA in the postwar period, it has been able to maintain its dominant position in part by the aggressive promotion of ideational agenda that reflect its own interests and normative values. Despite Japan's increasing economic presence in key international institutions such as the World Bank and the IMF, it has been unable to articulate, let alone realise, its own distinctive vision for an international political and economic order.

Similar inhibitions and uncertainties have prevented Japan from either endorsing or playing a leading role in an exclusively regional economic grouping, such as the East Asian Economic Caucus (EAEC) proposed by Malaysia's premier, Mahathir Mohamad. Although the possibility remains alive that an exclusively Asian regionwide grouping will develop, particularly because of the prominent role played by the Association of South-East Asian Nations (ASEAN),[12] Japan's role in it remains uncertain. Japanese policy-makers still seem reluctant to confront or antagonise the USA, upon which Japan remains strategically and economically dependent,[13] and Japanese people more generally have had a long-standing ambivalence towards 'Asia' and Japan's place in it (Funabashi 1995:231). As a consequence of these contradictory influences and pressures, Japan has found it difficult to present agenda of its own that extend beyond narrow national self-interest.

A number of major criticisms has been made of Japan in this regard. First, critics argue that Japanese foreign policy has been too 'reactive', unduly influenced by external pressures, and hamstrung by bureaucratic infighting (Calder 1998). Second, and more fundamentally, it is argued that because

Japan does not possess the sort of universalisable principles that have been such a prominent part of the liberal world order constructed by US hegemony, it cannot hope to play a similar international role (Rapkin 1990). In other words, Japan does not possesses a vision or cluster of values that might provide agenda for the future or a salve for the past. Indeed, Japan's continuing inability to come to terms with and acknowledge the often brutal role it played during World War II remains a major obstacle to its assuming a more prominent regional role. Many of Japan's neighbours are actually happy to see Japan's continuing strategic dependence on the USA precisely because of the doubts engendered by this lingering wartime legacy. Paradoxically enough, therefore, despite the declining importance of military as opposed to economic power, the overall hegemonic position of the USA continues to be bolstered by its dominant strategic position. In East Asia's complex intra-regional relations, the USA might continue to play an important, and generally welcome, 'balancing' role (Ross 1999), underwriting regional stability, but effectively placing limits on Japan's own regional ambitions.

Despite Japan's overwhelming economic presence, which leads some commentators to claim that Japan has already become a 'regional political superpower' (Drifte 1996:164), there are plainly several constraints that continue to circumscribe Japan's role and delimit the nature of its hegemonic influence or capacity. Even though Japan's economic power gives it the chance to play a more prominent role in a number of increasingly influential transnational agencies (Yasutomo 1993), the comparatively lacklustre recent performance of its own economy is making it more difficult to translate economic power into political influence—at least at the formal level of interstate relations. Compounding this problem—and giving the lie to simplistic notions of 'Japan Inc.' or a seamless and unproblematic 'national interest'—has been domestic policy contestation between the manufacturing and financial sectors, which have very different opinions about the appropriate value of the yen (Wade 1998:702). Ironically, what had been Japan's most unambiguous asset—the strength and performance of its economy—has now become a source of concern and criticism, both internationally and domestically.

Conclusion

If we take the notion of hegemony to mean the capacity to exert a political and economic influence beyond domestic borders with the intention of furthering perceived national interests, then Japan clearly has claims to such status, albeit at a predominantly regional level and with a number of important caveats. The most important constraint on Japanese hegemony flows from its relationship with the USA. The USA is a *global* hegemon, and thus inevitably able to shape the wider international system in a manner that Japan cannot, and Japan remains dependent on the USA to underwrite its own security in ways that reinforce Japan's subordinate position. Yet Japan has systematically and self-consciously eschewed militarism in favour of a single-minded neo-mercantilism that has defined and delimited its own potential influence. As a consequence, Japanese hegemony, although novel and—within specific limits—highly effective, is also constrained and somewhat subterranean.

Through a complex array of ODA packages, investment strategies, and trade linkages, the collaborative efforts of Japanese political and business elites have clearly exerted a major influence on the much smaller economies of East Asia generally and South-East Asia in particular. Governments and policy-makers across the region have attempted to accommodate, or self-consciously to emulate, the style and content of Japan's public policy initiatives. This is plainly evidence of Japanese hegemony at both the overt material level of investment flows and production strategies, and at the more subtle ideational level as a role model. Yet given that Japan's ideational influence has largely been a consequence of its success as the original East Asian development state, and given that that model is now subject to widespread criticism and scrutiny both outside and inside Japan, there are grounds for questioning whether even this limited influence will continue to be as significant as it was. Indeed, seasoned observers suggest that Japan itself is being subjected to a fundamental 'regime shift', which is transforming many of the established relationships and practices that were associated with the Japanese developmental state (Pempel 1998).

Thus, to understand the transformations that are under way in Japan, and the possible impact they might have on its external relations, we need to consider the politics and economics of Japan, and the complex inter-relationships that bind them together. Indeed, seen from a political-economy perspective it becomes clear that 'Japan' is a far more complex, less unified entity than such a label implies. While an overwhelming imperative for reconstruction and catching-up existed, and where policy generated unambiguous gains, such differences were repressed in the 'national interest'. But Japan's distinctive model of state-led development has now accomplished its task, and is actually perceived to be an impediment to necessary reform, causing possible conflicts of interest to become apparent. Japan's apparent inability to resolve its own domestic problems, and its failure to act decisively or effectively during the Asian economic crisis, have seriously undermined its leadership credentials.

Yet whatever outcomes are generated by Japan's domestic economic and political difficulties, one thing is certain: Japan will continue to exert a major influence over the countries of South-East Asia. The sheer size of the Japanese economy, and the existing network of relationships and production networks throughout the region, mean that Japan will continue to benefit from an embedded structure of influence for the foreseeable future. Whether Japan can translate this into a more overt political leadership in the region—leadership that is capable of transcending its problematic historical relationships with the countries of the region and with the USA—is another question. Unless it can, Japan will remain a somewhat contradictory, paradoxical, and quasi-hegemonic presence in the region.

Notes

1 For a more extensive discussion of these theoretical issues, especially within the institutional literature, see Beeson (forthcoming a).

2 For a more detailed examination of theories of hegemony, see Beeson (forthcoming b).

3 Although Japanese industry remains more characteristically 'Japanese' than some of its competitors, the whole question of the internationalisation of industry raises a number of complex questions about what constitutes a 'national' company in an era of increased international integration where both the ownership structure and spatial configuration of an individual company make the question of national identity increasingly problematic. For a discussion of these issues see Beeson (2000).

4 This discussion draws heavily on Morris-Suzuki (1991).

5 Richard Stubbs (1999:239) makes the interesting point that the flood of Japanese investment into the small economies of South-East Asia might actually have contributed to their problems, by fuelling unrealistic expectations and unsustainable investment 'bubbles'.

6 See Katz (1998) for a useful discussion on the rise and fall of the bubble economy.

7 It should also be noted that a new and major source of investment has been intra-Asian investment, primarily from the established first-tier nations—something that looks set to increase in the future and possibly undermine the economic importance of Japan.

8 For an extremely useful discussion of the *keiretsu*, see Gerlach (1992).

9 It should be noted that there is evidence to suggest the ability of Japanese firms to control structures of production within the region is limited. A number of companies in the electronics sector has developed more 'open' coordination mechanisms that give a greater, more autonomous role to affiliates. See Ernst (1997).

10 For a discussion of the flying-geese model in particular, and Japanese perspectives on regional development more generally, see Korhonen (1994).

11 This planned approach to regional economic expansion was most apparent in a number of proposals put forward by key agencies such as MITI (see Unger 1993 for a discussion of these schemes). Critics claim that Japanese planners have been intent on recreating the Greater East Asian Co-prosperity Sphere by more peaceful means. See Johnson (1993).

12 The ASEAN summit meeting of late 1999 was most noteworthy for the inclusion of Japan, China, and South Korea, representing a de facto EAEC grouping.

13 The link between the USA and Japan is not simply the largest bilateral economic relationship in the world, but it highlights the contradictory nature of interdependence. Although Japan clearly wishes to maintain access to the crucial and lucrative markets of the USA, the USA is also deeply dependent on Japanese savings to underwrite its ever-expanding trade deficits. In many ways, Japan appears to have greater latent structural power than the USA. However, it is significant that Japan has shown little preparedness to utilise it. See Yoshikazu (1997).

References

Amsden, Alice (1995) 'Like the rest: South-East Asia's "late" industrialization', *Journal of International Development*, 7(5):791–9.

Arase, David (1994) 'Public–private sector interest coordination in Japan's ODA', *Pacific Affairs*, 67(2):171–99.

Beasley, W.G. (1987) *Japanese Imperialism, 1894–1945*, Oxford: Clarendon Press.

Beasley, W.G. (1990) *The Rise of Modern Japan: Political, Economic, and Social Change Since 1850*, London: Weidenfeld and Nicolson.

Beeson, Mark (1999a) 'States, markets, and economic security in post-crisis East Asia', *Asian Perspective*, 23(3):33–52.

Beeson, Mark (1999b) 'Reshaping regional institutions: APEC and the IMF in East Asia', *Pacific Review*, 12(1):1–24.

Beeson, Mark (2000) 'Globalisation and international trade: international economic policies and "the national interest"', in P. Boreham, G. Stokes and R. Hall (eds) *The Politics of Australian Society: Political Issues for the New Century*, Frenchs Forest: Longman, pp 213–31.

Beeson, Mark (forthcoming a) 'Theorising institutional change in East Asia', in M. Beeson (ed.) *Reconfiguring East Asia: Regional Institutions and Organizations After the Crisis*, London: Curzon Press.

Beeson, Mark (forthcoming b) 'The construction of international regimes in post-crisis Asia: Coercion, consensus and collective goods', in S. Sargeson (ed.) *Shaping*

Common Futures: Case Studies of Collective Goods, Collective Actions in East and Southeast Asia, London: Routledge.

Bergsten, Fred C. and Marcus Noland (1993) *Reconcilable Differences? United States–Japan Economic Conflict*, Washington: Institute for International Economics.

Bernard, M. and J. Ravenhill (1995) 'Beyond product cycles and flying geese: Regionalization, hierarchy, and the industrialization of East Asia', *World Politics*, 47(2), pp 171–209.

Bhaskaran, M. (1998) *The Asian Crisis—Impact and Outlook*, paper to the Asia–Europe Foundation/CEPII's conference on the Asia Crisis, Paris 11–12 May.

Bobrow, Davis B. and Robert T. Kurdle (1987) 'How middle powers can manage resource weakness: Japan and energy', *World Politics*, 39(4):536–65.

Braudel, Fernand (1992; 1979) *The Perspective of the World*, Berkeley: University of California Press.

Calder, Kent E. (1998) 'Japanese foreign economic policy formation: explaining the reactive state', *World Politics*, 40(4):25–54.

Chase-Dunn, Christopher (1998) *Global Formation: Structures of the World Economy*, Lanham: Rowan and Littlefield.

Cox, Robert W. (1987) *Production, Power, and World Order: Social Forces in the Making of History*, New York: Columbia University Press.

Cumings, Bruce (1997) 'Japan and Northeast Asia into the twenty-first century', in Peter J. Katzenstein and Takashi Shiraishi (eds) *Network Power: Japan and Asia*, Ithaca: Cornell University Press, pp 136–68.

Dobson, Wendy (1993) *Japan in East Asia: Trading and Investment Strategies*, Singapore: Institute of Southeast Asian Studies.

Dobson, Wendy (1997) 'East Asian integration: Synergies between firm strategies and government policies', in W. Dobson and Yue Chia Siow (eds) *Multinationals and East Asian Integration*, Singapore: Institute of Southeast Asian Studies, pp 3–27.

Doner, Richard F. (1991) *Driving a Bargain: Automobile Industrialization and Japanese Firms in Southeast Asia*, Berkeley: University of California Press.

Drifte, Reinhard (1996) *Japan's Foreign Policy in the 1990s: From Economic Superpower to What Power?*, London: Macmillan.

Economist (1999) 'Softly, softly', November 27:84.

Encarnation, D. (1994) 'Investment and trade by American, European, and Japanese multinationals across the Triad', in M. Mason and D. Encarnation (eds) *Does Ownership Matter? Japanese Multinationals in Europe*, Oxford: Clarendon Press, pp 205–27.

Ernst, Dieter (1997) 'Partners for the China Circle? The Asian production networks of Japanese electronic firms', *BRIE Working Paper 91*, Berkeley: Berkeley Roundtable on the International Economy.

Fallows, James (1993) *Looking at the Sun: The Rise of the New East Asian Economic and Political Systems*, New York: Pantheon Books.

Fingleton, E. (1995) *Blindside: Why Japan is Still on Track to Overtake the US by the Year 2000*, Boston: Houghton Mifflin.

Freeman, C. (1987) *Technology and Economic Performance: Lessons from Japan*, London: Pinter.

Frankel, Jeffrey A. (1993) 'Is Japan creating a yen bloc in East Asia and the Pacific?', in J.A. Frankel and M. Kahler (eds) *Regionalism and Rivalry: Japan and the United States in Pacific Asia*, Chicago: University of Chicago Press, pp 53–85.

Funabashi, Yoichi (1988) *Managing the Dollar: From the Plaza to the Louvre*, Washington: Institute for International Economics.

Funabashi, Yoichi (1995) *Asia Pacific Fusion: Japan's Role in APEC*, Washington: Institute for International Economics.

Gangopadhyay, Partha (1998) 'Patterns of trade, investment and migration in the Asia–Pacific region', in G. Thompson (ed.) *Economic Dynamism in the Asia–Pacific*, London: Routledge, pp 20–54.

Gerlach, Michael (1992) *Alliance Capitalism: The Social Organization of Japanese Business*, Berkeley: University of California Press.

Hatch, Walter and Kozo Yamamura (1996) *Asia in Japan's Embrace: Building a Regional Production Alliance*, Cambridge: Cambridge University Press.

Heginbotham, Eric and Richard J. Samuels (1998) 'Mercantile realism and Japanese foreign policy', *International Security*, 22(4):171–203.

Higgott, Richard (1994) 'International political economy', in A.J.R. Groom and M. Light (eds) *Contemporary International Relations: A Guide to Theory*, London: Pinter, pp 156–69.

Higgott, Richard (2000) 'The international relations of the Asian economic crisis: A study in the politics of resentment', in R. Robison et al. (eds) *Politics and Markets in the Wake of the Asian Crisis*, London, Routledge, pp 261–82.

Hobsbawm, E. (1987) *The Age of Empire*, London: Weidenfeld and Nicolson.

Johnson, Chalmers (1982) *MITI and the Japanese Miracle: The Growth of Industry Policy 1925-1975*, Stanford: Stanford University Press.

Johnson, Chalmers (1993) 'History restarted: Japanese–American relations at the end of the century', in R. Higgott et al. (eds) *Pacific Economic Relations in the 1990s: Cooperation or Conflict?*, St Leonards: Allen and Unwin, pp 39–61.

Jomo, K.S. (1994) 'Introduction', in K.S. Jomo (ed.) *Japan and Malaysian Development: In the Shadow of the Rising Sun*, London: Routledge, pp 1–17.

Katz, Richard (1998) *Japan: The System That Soured*, Armonk: M.E. Sharpe.

Katzenstein, Peter J. (1996) *Cultural Norms and National Security: Police and Military in Postwar Japan*, Ithaca: Cornell University Press.

Korhonen, P. (1994) *Japan and the Pacific Free Trade Area*, London: Routledge.

Kennedy. Paul (1988) *The Rise and Fall of Great Powers: Economic Change and Military Conflict from 1500 to 2000*, London: Fontana.

LaFeber, Walter (1997) *The Clash: US–Japanese Relations throughout History*, New York: W.W. Norton.

Leyshon, Andrew (1994) 'Under pressure: finance, geo-economic competition and the rise and fall of Japan's postwar growth economy', in S. Corbridge et al. *Money, Power and Space*, Oxford: Blackwell, pp 116–45.

Lincoln, Edward J. (1990) *Japan's Unequal Trade*, Washington: The Brookings Institute.

Luttwak, Edward (1990) 'From geopolitics to geo-economics', *The National Interest*, Summer:17–23.

Machado, Kit G. (1995) 'Japanese foreign direct investment in East Asia: The expanding division of labor and the future of regionalism', in S. Chan (ed.) *Foreign Direct Investment in a Changing Global Political Economy*, London: Macmillan, pp 39–66.

Matsanundo, Michael (1997) 'Preserving the unipolar moment: Realist theories and US grand strategy after the Cold War', *International Security*, 21(4):49–88.

Moon, Woosik and Yeongseop Rhee (1999) 'Asian monetary cooperation: Lessons from the European Monetary integration', *Journal of International and Area Studies*, 6(1):33–49.

Morris-Suzuki, Tessa (1991) 'Reshaping the international division of labour', in J. Morris (ed.) *Japan and the Global Economy*, London: Routledge, pp 135–53.

Mueller, John (1989) *Retreat from Doomsday*, New York: Basic Books.

Nester, William R. (1990) *Japan's Growing Power over East Asia and the World Economy: Ends and Means*, London: Macmillan.

Nye, J. (1990) *Bound to Lead: The Changing Nature of American Power*, New York: Basic Books.

Pauly, Louis W. and Simon Reich (1997) 'National structures and multinational corporate behaviour: enduring differences in the age of globalization', *International Organization*, 51(1):1–30.

Pempel, T.J. (1998) *Regime Shift: Comparative Dynamics of the Japanese Political Economy*, Ithaca: Cornell University Press.

Pempel, T.J. (1999) *Triangle of Troubles: Japanese Foreign Policy at Century's End*, paper for a conference on 'Japan and Its Neighbours in the Global Village', Nanzan University, Nagoya, 16–17 October.

Petri, Peter A. (1992) 'Platforms in the Pacific: Trade effects of direct investment in Thailand', *Journal of Asian Economics*, 3(2):173–96.

Pyle, Kenneth B. (1988) 'Japan, the world, and the twenty-first century', in T. Inoguchi and D. Okimoto (eds) *The Political Economy of Japan: Volume 2, The Changing International Context*, Stanford: Stanford University Press, pp 446–86.

Pyle, Kenneth B. (1998) 'Restructuring foreign policy and defence policy: Japan', in A. McGrew and C. Brook (eds) *Asia–Pacific in the New World Order*, London: Routledge pp 121–36.

Rapkin, David P. (1990) 'Japan and world leadership?', in D.P. Rapkin (ed.) *World Leadership and Hegemony*, Boulder: Lynne Rienner, pp 191–212.

Rosecrance, Richard (1986) *The Rise of the Trading State: Commerce and Conquest in the Modern World*, New York: Basic Books.

Ross, Robert S. (1999) 'The geography of peace: East Asia in the twenty-first century', *International Security*, 23(4):81–118.

Samuels, Richard J. (1994) *"Rich Nation, Strong Army": National Security and the Technological Transformation of Japan*, Ithaca: Cornell University Press.

Schoppa, L.J. (1997) *Bargaining with Japan: What American Pressure Can and Cannot Do*, New York: Columbia University Press.

Stevens, Rob (1996) *Japan and the New World Order*, London: Macmillan.

Strange, Susan (1994) *States and Markets*, London: Pinter Publishers.

Stubbs, Richard (1999) 'States, sovereignty and the response of Southeast Asia's "miracle" economies to globalization', in D.A. Smith, D.J. Solinger and S.C. Topik (eds) *States and Sovereignty in the Global Economy*, London: Routledge, pp 229–45.

Thompson, Edmund R. and Jessie P.H. Poon, (1998) 'Determinants of Japanese, US and UK foreign direct investment in East and Southeast Asia, 1985–1994', *Journal of Asian Business*, 14(3):15–39.

Unger, Daniel (1993) 'Big little Japan', in R.O. Slater et al. (eds) *Global Transformation and the Third World*, Boulder: Lynne Rienner, pp 283–308.

Wade, R (1998) 'From "miracle" to "cronyism": explaining the Great Asian Slump', *Cambridge Journal of Economics*, 22:693–706.

Weiss, Linda and John M. Hobson (1995) *States and Economic Development: A Comparative Historical Analysis*, Cambridge: Polity Press.

Willmott, H.P. (1982) *Empires in the Balance*, Maryland: Naval Institute Press.

Yahuda, Michael (1996) *The International Politics of the Asia Pacific*, London: Routledge.

Yasutomo, D.T. (1993) 'The politicization of Japan's "post-Cold War" multilateral diplomacy', in G.L. Curtis (ed.) *Japan's Foreign Policy After the Cold War: Coping with Change*, Armonk: M.E. Sharpe, pp 323–45.

Yoshikazu, Yakao (1997) 'Behind Hashimoto's remark on dumping US Treasuries', *Japan Echo*, 24(5):15–19.

Young, Louise (1998) *Japan's Total Empire: Manchuria and the Culture of Wartime Imperialism*, Berkeley: University of California Press.

Index

Notes
1 In this index: 'Asian boom' refers to period mid 1980s–mid 1990s; 'Asian crisis' refers to period 1997–98.
2 Abbreviations used in this index: ASEAN (Association of South-East Asian Nations); GDP (gross domestic product); GLCs (government-linked companies); EOI (export-oriented industrialisation); ILO (International Labour Office); IMF (International Monetary Fund); ISI (import-substitution industrialisation); NGO (non-government organisation); NIC (newly industrialised country); PAP (People's Action Party); UMNO (United Malays National Organization).